Should the public policy exception be statutorily defined? The example of Indian arbitration law

Europäische Hochschulschriften Recht

European University Studies in Law

Publications Universitaires Européennes de Droit

Band/Volume 6761

Nihal Bernard Dsouza

Should the public policy exception be statutorily defined? The example of Indian arbitration law

PETER LANG

Lausanne - Berlin - Bruxelles - Chennai - New York - Oxford

Bibliografische Information der Deutschen Nationalbibliothek
Die Deutsche Nationalbibliothek verzeichnet diese Publikation
in der Deutschen
Nationalbibliografie; detaillierte bibliografische Daten sind im
Internet über http://dnb.d-nb.de abrufbar.

Zugl.:Bonn, Univ., Diss., 2023

D 38
ISSN 0531-7312
ISBN 978-3-631-90877-8
E-ISBN 978-3-631-90882-2
E-ISBN 978-3-631-90883-9
DOI 10.3726/b21193

Verlegt durch: Peter Lang GmbH, Berlin, Deutschland

info@peterlang.com http://www.peterlang.com/

Diese Publikation wurde begutachtet.

Dedication

This book is dedicated to my family to whom I owe eternal gratitude for teaching me everything good I know, for being my inspiration, pillars of strength and being the guiding compass throughout my life.

Acknowledgment

I am deeply grateful to Prof. Dr. Matthias Lehmann, and Prof. Dr. Dr. h.c. Thomas Pfeiffer for their steadfast support and guidance, without which this thesis would not have been possible.

This project would not have been possible if not for the opportunity and support provided by the Law Faculty of the University of Bonn and the IMPRS for Successful Dispute Resolution in International Law, for which I am extremely grateful.

Table of contents

List of abbreviations

AALCC	Afro-Asian Legal Consultative Committee
Art.	Article
BGB	Bürgerliche Gesetzbuch (German Civil Code)
BGH	Bundesgerichthof (German Federal Court of Justice)
CPC	Code of Civil Procedure, 1908
DDA	Delhi Development Authority
EC Treaty	Treaty establishing the European Community
ECJ	European Court of Justice
e.g.	Example
EGBGB	Einführungsgesetz zum Bürgerlichen Gesetzbuche (Introductory Act to the German Civil Code)
EU	European Union
FARE Act	Foreign Awards Recognition and Enforcement 1961
FCPA	The Foreign Corrupt Practices Act 1977
FERA	Foreign Exchange Regulation Act 1973
GATT Agreement	General Agreement on Tariffs and Trade 1994
GDP	Gross domestic product
Geneva Convention	Geneva Convention on the Execution of Foreign Arbitral Awards 1927
Geneva Protocol	Geneva Protocol on Arbitration Clauses 1924
Hague Judgments Convention	Convention on the Recognition and Enforcement of Foreign Judgments in Civil or Commercial Matters 2019
IAA	The Arbitration and Conciliation Act (including all amendments to date)
IAA 1996	The Arbitration and Conciliation Act, 1996 (India), without amendments
IAA(Am.) 2015	The Arbitration and Conciliation (Amendment) Act, 2015 (India)
IAO 2020	The Arbitration and Conciliation (Amendment) Ordinance, 2020
IBA	International Bar Association
ICC	International Chamber of Commerce

ICC Arbitration Rules 2021	Rules of Arbitration of the International Chamber of Commerce. In force as from 1 January 2021
ILA	International Law Association
ITO	International Trade Organization
LCIA Rules 2020	The London Court of International Arbitration, Arbitration Rules. In force as from 1 October 2020
NCDRC	National Consumer Disputes Redressal Commission
New York Convention	The Convention on the Recognition and Enforcement of Foreign Arbitral Awards 1958
NIP	New Industrial Policy
No.	Number
OHADA	Organisation for the Harmonization of Business Law in Africa
ONGC	Oil & Natural Gas Corporation Ltd
PCA	Prevention of Corruption Act (India) 1988 (as amended in 2018)
Sec.	Section
TFEU	Treaty on the Functioning of the European Union
TRIPS Agreement	Agreement on Trade-Related Aspects of Intellectual Property Rights 1994
UAE	United Arab Emirates
UDHR	Universal Declaration of Human Rights 1948
UK	United Kingdom of Great Britain and Northern Ireland
UK Arbitration Act (1996)	Arbitration Law of the United Kingdom (excluding Scotland)
UN	United Nations
UNCITRAL Model Law/Model Law	UNCITRAL Model Law on International Commercial Arbitration, 1985
UNCTAD	United Nations Conference on Trade and Development
United States (U.S.)	The United States of America
WTO law	Law of the World Trade Organisation
ZPO	Zivilprozessordnung (German Code of Civil Procedure)

Abstract

The Indian Arbitration and Conciliation Act in its current form (IAA) largely incorporates[1] the UNCITRAL Model Law on International Commercial Arbitration.[2] India is also party to the New York Convention on the Recognition and Enforcement of Foreign Arbitral Awards.[3] Given its roots, it is clear that the IAA was meant to be an arbitration-friendly legislation. This means that under Indian law there should, at least in theory, be a general leaning towards the enforcement of arbitral awards. The public policy exception is a notable exception to the general rule that foreign awards should be enforced. Just like the international framework on which it is based, the IAA in section 48 also provides for the public policy exception as a ground for refusing to enforce foreign arbitral awards. This exception is, however, meant to be construed narrowly.

The narrow interpretation of the exception has sometimes been disregarded in the Indian context. In the past, there have been situations where Indian courts have struggled to find the right balance between respect for party autonomy and their desire to ensure the necessary safeguards which guarantee a fair trial. In some early rulings, Indian courts interpreted the law to increase their powers of intervention and to refuse enforcement of awards. In deciding to intervene the courts largely relied on the public policy exception. The approach of the Indian judiciary towards the public policy exception has not always been consistent or coherent. In the span of a decade, Indian courts have sought to reverse their approach with regards to the public policy exception, significantly and sometimes overly restricting its scope. As will be shown in this thesis, while there is a general need for restricting the use of public policy, overly doing so could have the untoward consequence of undermining the use of the exception itself.

The Law Commission, which the government tasked with solving the problems caused by judicial intervention, suggested that the scope of the public policy exception needed to be statutorily defined. Based on its recommendations, the government defined the scope of public policy in the IAA. Such an approach was

1 Fali S. Nariman, 'India and International Arbitration' (2009) 41 George Washington International Law Review 367, 371.

2 Vereinte Nationen (ed), UNCITRAL Model Law on International Commercial Arbitration: 1985 ; with Amendments as Adopted in 2006 (United Nations 2008).

3 UN Convention on the Recognition and Enforcement of Foreign Arbitral Awards 1958 (330 UNTS 38).

novel, as few other countries, notably UAE, Sweden, New Zealand and Australia, have defined the scope of public policy in their arbitration statutes. This thesis will evaluate the wisdom of statutorily defining public policy. Although it has been argued that defining the exception helps restrict the courts from giving it a broad meaning, the definition itself consists of such broad terms that it risks failing its purpose.

This research traces the evolution of arbitration law in India by analyzing how the courts and legislature treated the public policy exception. The thesis seeks to compare how the Indian approach differs from that of select common and civil law jurisdictions. The aim of this thesis is to answer the broader question as to whether the public policy exception needs to be defined. In case an affirmative answer can be given to the need for a definition, the thesis addresses two other questions: which authority, i.e., the legislature or judiciary, is competent for determining the scope of the public policy exception? And what are the ingredients of any such statutory definition?

Delimiting the public policy exception – an introductory note

The finality of awards is one of the key benefits of arbitration.[4] By doing away with the appeal procedure that is inherent to the court system, arbitration ensures that disputes are resolved expeditiously and helps reduce expenses and uncertainty for the parties involved. A keystone to the edifice of finality is the prohibition of excessive judicial intervention, especially by review of the arbitral awards on merits.[5] However, there are sometimes situations where this finality must be sacrificed to protect the most basic principles of a national legal system. The public policy exception has been formulated for this purpose.

The discourse about the use of the public policy exception gives rise to some interesting conflicts and difficulties. The need for protecting the parties right to choose a private settlement of their disputes is enshrined in the principle of party autonomy.[6] According to this principle, parties are free to choose the forum in which they wish to settle their disputes.[7] It enables parties to choose arbitration by 'opting out national courts systems'.[8] Arbitration itself is derived from the Latin term *arbitrium*, which means *'free will'*.[9] By extension, courts are generally required to respect parties desire to choose arbitration and abstain from unnecessarily intervening in the arbitral process. Moreover, Article III of the New

---

4 See, Clive M. Schmitthoff, 'Finality of Arbitral Awards and Judicial Review', in Julian D. M. Lew (ed), *Contemporary Problems in International Arbitration* (M Nijhoff ; Distributors for the US and Canada, Kluwer Academic Publishers 1987) 230.

5 Pramod Nair, 'Surveying a Decade of the "New" Law of Arbitration In India' (2007) 23 Arbitration International 699, 729.

6 Donald Francis Donovan, 'International Commercial Arbitration and Public Policy' (1995) 27 NYU Journal of International Law and Politics 645, 647.

7 Charles Chatterjee, 'The Reality of the Party Autonomy Rule in International Arbitration' (2003) 20 Journal of International Arbitration 539, 541; See also, David A. R. Williams and Anna Kirk, 'Balancing Party Autonomy, Jurisdiction and the Integrity of Arbitration: Where to Draw the Line', in Neil Kaplan and Michael J Moser (eds), *Jurisdiction, Admissibility and Choice of Law in International Arbitration: Liber Amicorum Michael Pryles* (Wolters Kluwer 2018).

8 See, Alexis Mourre, 'Arbitrability of Antitrust Law from the European and US Perspectives' in Gordon Blanke and Phillip Louis Landolt (eds), *EU and US Antitrust Arbitration: A Handbook for Practitioners* (Kluwer Law International 2011) 6.

9 Jan Paulsson, *The Idea of Arbitration* (1st edn, Oxford University Press 2013) 1.

York Convention, to which India and most major jurisdictions are signatories, requires courts to recognise and enforce arbitral awards regardless of where they are made.

Even party autonomy has its limitations.[10] As astutely pointed out by Jan Paulsson, although parties to a contract desire to have freedom – they also want to be protected by law.[11] The public policy exception, which embodies the fundamental requirements of justice and the legal system, acts as a constraint to unrestrained freedom. Through the use of the exception, the desire of the parties to privately resolve their disputes comes in direct conflict with the court's duty of ensuring fair and equitable dispute resolution.[12]

National courts need to find a balance between the need for finality of arbitral awards and for a fair trial that respects essential procedural safeguards. While reducing judicial oversight on awards encourages finality, judicial supervision in limited measure can help ensure fairness[13] and protection of essential public interest, such as free competition. This is especially true in cases where courts are dissatisfied and feel an arbitral award breaches the fundamental principles of the legal system. In such circumstances, the public policy exception enables domestic courts to intervene in foreign arbitral awards and consequently endanger its finality. As observed by Paulsson, as a general rule, parties can go about contracting as they please, so long as they do not violate public policy or mandatory law.[14]

In India and elsewhere, the public policy exception has been the subject of immense controversy because of the way it has been relied upon to resist the enforcement of arbitral awards. Public policy is unpredictable, and some authors have argued that it contrasts with the 'logic' and 'structure of legal reasoning'.[15] Because of the discretion it gives domestic courts to disregard foreign arbitral awards, the exception has been considered as the single biggest threat to

10 Michael Pryles, 'Limits to Party Autonomy in Arbitral Procedure' (2007) 24 Journal of International Arbitration 327.

11 Paulsson (n 9) 1.

12 Amelia Rendeiro, 'Indian Arbitration and "Public Policy"' (2010) 89 Tex. L. Rev. 699.

13 William W. Park, Arbitration of International Business Disputes: Studies in Law and Practice (2nd edn, Oxford University Press 2012) 316.

14 Paulsson (n 9) 2.

15 Farshad Ghodoosi, International Dispute Resolution and the Public Policy Exception (Routledge 2016) 8.

arbitration as a means of dispute settlement.[16] Such descriptions, however, do not take into consideration the essential purposes that the exception serves.

The public policy exception enables domestic courts to set aside or refuse enforcement of arbitral awards in certain special but limited circumstances. Judicial intervention should only be on narrow grounds, and judges are obliged to exercise restraint when it comes to reviewing the arbitrators' decisions substantively.[17] The public policy exception is of utmost importance insofar as it acts as one of the only checks to absolute party autonomy in choosing to resolve disputes before a private forum and in ensuring fairness in the arbitration process. However, its scope had never been concretized. This is because public policy *per se* has long been thought of as a concept which is 'vague' and of 'uncertain import'.[18] Indian lawmakers have, however, decided to diverge from this view.

Although this thesis will primarily focus on the public policy exception in the context of India, the use of the exception for refusing the enforcement of arbitral awards is not unique to India.[19] Indeed, public policy is provided for as an exception to enforcement of arbitral awards in most international arbitration law instruments and national arbitration statutes.[20] It is referred to as *'ordre public'* in civil law countries, where it is given a wider scope.[21]

India is one of the few countries to have statutorily set out a definition for the scope of the public policy exception. In setting out the scope of the definition, it could be argued that the Indian legislature has attempted to succeed where most other jurisdictions have failed.[22] The rationale behind this move can be deciphered from the parliamentary debates.[23] Previously the inconsistent use of this exception by courts meant that parties would avoid seating their arbitrations in India and would be wary of enforcing awards in India. It was thought that

---

16 Joel Junker, 'The Public Policy Exception to Recognition and Enforcement of Foreign Arbitral Awards' (1977) 7 California Western International Law Journal 228.

17 Donovan (n 6) 648.

18 *Mukesh H Mehta v Harindra H Mehta* (1995) 3 BomCR 686 (Bombay High Court) [25].

19 As will be shown in Chapter 3, courts in both civil and common law jurisdictions have not hesitated to rely on the exception.

20 See *infra* Chapter 3.

21 A. J. van den Berg, The New York Arbitration Convention of 1958: Towards a Uniform Judicial Interpretation (Kluwer Law and Taxation 1981) 359.

22 The statutory definition of public policy has been enshrined in Section 48(2)b of the IAA and will be elaborated on in Chapter 4(III).

23 'Lok Sabha Debates (Lower House-Indian Parliament), Sixteenth Series, Vol.XIV, Sixth Session, 2015/1937 (Saka), No. 16'.

defining the public policy exception would change the approach of the courts and any associated negative perceptions in the business community. This approach, however, needs to be looked at with a fair bit of caution. There must, after all, be valid reasons why even the most 'arbitration friendly' countries do not statutorily define the scope of public policy.

The decision to define the scope of the public policy exception was taken based on anxiety about a broad judicial interpretation. In the past, Indian courts have inconsistently and sometimes expansively interpreted the public policy exception causing much uncertainty to parties as to whether they would be able to enforce their awards.[24] Such anxiety dissuaded foreign parties from choosing India as a seat of arbitration.[25] It also meant that foreign parties were hesitant to engage in business transactions with Indian enterprises, as there would be no adequate forum for resolving any future disputes.[26]

The Indian legislature sought to allay the fear of investors by seeking recommendations from the executive body responsible for legal reform, i.e., the Law Commission of India, as to what changes could be made to reduce judicial intervention. The Law Commission, in its 246th report, concluded that statutorily restricting the scope of the public policy exception would remove the flexibility which had enabled inconsistent judicial interpretations in the past.[27] These recommendations set the foundation for the legislature to define the scope of the exception in the Arbitration and Conciliation Amendment Act 2015 (IAA(Am.) 2015).

The current statutory definition of the public policy exception under Indian law gives rise to certain difficulties. It involves the use of broad and relatively vague terms such as 'morality and justice' and 'fundamental policy of Indian law', which have been left to the courts to interpret.[28] While this may in some ways be advantageous insofar as the courts are able to apply the public policy exception

---

24 See Chapter 2 for an elaboration on the treatment of public policy exception by Indian courts.

25 Justice B. N. Srikrishna, 'Report of the High Level Committee to Review the Institutionalisation of Arbitration Mechanism in India' (2017) 19 <http://legalaffairs.gov.in/sites/default/files/Report-HLC.pdf> accessed 15 August 2020.

26 See ibid 8. The report recognised the problem and discusses the need to reform arbitration framework in order to improve the ease of doing buisiness in India.

27 Justice A. P. Shah, 'Amendments to the Arbitration and Conciliation Act 1996' (Government of India, Law Commission of India 2014) 246.

28 See explanatory notes to Sec. 48(2)b of The Arbitration and Conciliation (Amendment) Act 2015 (No 3 of 2016).

based on evolving legal standards, it also gives rise to certain challenges. The vague definition could enable judges to stretch public policy according to their wishes, defeating the very purpose of the statutory definition. The intended limitation of the exception could become elusive.

In the past, the courts have endeavored to define terms such as 'morality and justice' and 'fundamental policy of Indian law' with limited success.[29] In their attempt to turn India into an arbitration-friendly jurisdiction, the courts have sometimes defined the terms very restrictively, potentially exceeding the intention of the legislature. On the other hand, the courts have sometimes taken the opposite approach by giving the exception a more open-ended interpretation. This lack of coherence by the judiciary causes uncertainty to parties and raises doubts as to whether the statutory definition of public policy is the right approach.

I. Research question

This thesis will evaluate whether the uncertainty in India regarding the scope of the public policy exception should be attributed to the legislator or to the judiciary. If uncertainty is due to the courts, can the lack of coherence in the approach of judges be set right by more legislation? In this context, doubts arise as to whether the Indian legislature is in effect trying to solve a problem that needs to be solved by the courts in the first place. In other words, the thesis will primarily look at whether it is the task of the legislature to define public policy – or would this fall under the prerogatives of the judiciary.

The problem of interpreting the statutory definition of public policy under the IAA(Am.) 2015 is compounded by the fact that it does not address the distinction between international and national public policy, neither does it elaborate on specific procedural and substantive aspects of public policy. Under the IAA, vague and broad terms such as the fundamental policy of Indian law, morality and justice have been used. These terms can be used to include certain important grounds of procedural conditions, such as lack of due process, the impartiality of arbitrators and *res judicata*. The same is true also for substantive public policy, where it could be interpreted to cover principles of anti-trust law, consumer protection, foreign exchange rules, IP rights, insolvency principles, certain banking and finance matters. The problem is that there is no limit to what could be meant

29 See infra, Chapter 4 for a further elaboration on how these terms have been elucidated in the Indian context.

by terms such as 'fundamental policy'. Furthermore, there is also the question to be addressed under what circumstances the IAA would include *transnational public policy* or *international public policy.*

In order to understand how the treatment of the public policy exception has evolved under Indian law, this thesis will analyze the approach of Indian courts. As a common-law country with a great focus on 'judicial activism' or judge-made law, courts in India have often demonstrated their willingness to exercise not just interpretation but sometimes also law-making powers. The study of court decisions is particularly important because of the high value given to precedence and *stare decisis* under Indian law.

This thesis will also look at the external factors influencing the decisions of Indian courts, including foreign jurisprudence and literature. A comparative study of the approaches of courts in other jurisdictions towards the public policy exception at different stages of the arbitral process, *vis-à-vis* the Indian approach, will be made.

Furthermore, this thesis will also look at how successful the Indian legislature and judiciary have been in limiting the scope of the public policy exception as a means of upholding party autonomy. It will evaluate whether their approach is justified by examining how other arbitration-friendly jurisdictions have approached this problem. This will be aimed at answering the broader question of whether it is possible and worth codifying the public policy exception at all.

This thesis will have the following structure:

The *first chapter* will provide an introductory and explanatory background and foundation on which the other chapters will be built. It will do so by explaining the origins and usage of public policy in civil law and common law systems both inside and outside the context of international arbitration.

The *second chapter* of this thesis will look at the conditions that necessitated the intervention of the legislature in amending the Indian Arbitration Act 1996[30] (IAA 1996). In doing so, it will examine the legislative backdrop and the inefficiencies in the IAA 1996 in fulfilling the goals of the New York Convention. This chapter will then evaluate how the Indian Supreme Court and various high courts have interpreted the scope of the exception in the past and examine if the criticisms raised regarding excessive and unwarranted intervention by Indian courts are justified. Emphasis will be placed on evaluating the uncertainty caused by the lack of uniformity in the courts' decisions.

30 The Arbitration and Conciliation Act 1996 (No26 of 1996).

The *third chapter* will make a comparative study of how courts in other jurisdictions have approached the problem of delimiting the scope of the exception at different stages of arbitration, i.e., in the underlying contract, during the arbitration, and at the time of enforcement. It will then compare the Indian approach with that of courts in other major common law and civil law jurisdictions.

In the *fourth chapter*, we will analyze how public policy is defined under the IAA(Am.) 2015 and how Indian courts have interpreted this new definition. This chapter will look at the treatment of the exception both from the standpoint of substantive public policy and procedural policy. A closer look will be taken into the individual components of the statutory definition of public policy, i.e., 'fundamental policy of Indian law' and 'morality and justice', in order to find what the public policy exception actually encompasses. In doing so, the rationale used by the Indian Supreme Court in dealing with the exception in its previous decisions will be looked into.

The *fifth chapter* will weigh whether statutorily codifying the scope of the public policy exception is in itself a good idea. In doing so, the chapter will analyze whether the task of interpreting or defining a vague conception such as public policy falls on the shoulders of the legislature or the judiciary. This will be done by taking guidance from the doctrine of separation of powers. The chapter will also try to take a rationalist approach and evaluate what has worked best in other countries that have a pro-arbitration leaning. Both the advantages and disadvantages will be looked at in order to form the basis for proposals as to how the exception needs to be interpreted and by whom.

The *sixth chapter* recognises that there are different considerations involved at different stages of the arbitral process. This chapter is aimed at determining the competent authority for deciding on public policy claims at each of these stages. The *seventh chapter*, will conclude the thesis with the help of observations from a comparative perspective.

II. Background to research

The Indian economy has long been held back by problems peculiar to most developing countries.[31] Domestic courts in India are extremely backlogged, and traditional means of dispute settlement are very slow.[32] This was reflected by the

31 For an overview of how the treatment of arbitration has evolved in developing countries see, Joseph T. McLaughlin, 'Arbitration and Developing Countries' (1979) 13 The International Lawyer 211, 215.

32 Rendeiro (n 12).

Indian Supreme Court in the *Guru Nanak* decision, where the court lamented on the '*interminable, time consuming, complex and expensive court procedures*.'[33] Furthermore, the overall rate of economic growth in India has far outpaced the rate of growth of dispute resolution mechanisms.[34] Rapid economic growth has naturally led to an increased burden on domestic courts. According to a recent estimate, Indian courts have a backlog of 33 million cases.[35] Also, India is in a precarious situation of having a ratio of 13 judges to a million people, the lowest in the world.[36] These are very strong motivations for India to encourage arbitration as an alternative to traditional modes of dispute resolution. Unfortunately, arbitration has quite often been held back by judicial intervention.

India can certainly stand to benefit from a more effective system of private dispute settlement.[37] It is therefore not surprising that Indian law has tried to encourage arbitration and reduce judicial intervention by basing its statute on the UNCITRAL Model Law.[38] Arbitration as a means of dispute settlement provides both the parties to the dispute as well as the legal system with numerous benefits. It is *conditio sine qua non* for providing effective remedies to businesses. Arbitration provides parties confidentiality, speed, flexibility, neutrality, universal enforceability and a degree of finality.[39] It also greatly reduces the caseload of state courts by acting as an effective alternative means for settling commercial

---

33 *Guru Nanak Foundation v Rattan Singh and Sons* 1981 4 SCC 634 (Supreme Court of India) [1].

34 Krishna Sarma, Momota Oinam and Kaushik Angshuman, 'Development and Practice of Arbitration in India –Has It Evolved as an Effective Legal Institution' Center on Democracy, Development and the Rule of Law (CDDRL) Stanford University, Working Paper 103 of 2009 <https://fsi.stanford.edu/sites/default/files/No_103_Sarma_India_Arbitration_India_509.pdf> accessed 23 July 2016.

35 Amy Kazmin, 'India's Court System Offers Little Hope of Justice' *Financial Times* (New Delhi, 3 June 2017).

36 Phillip D'Costa, 'Under analysis – changing dispute resolution trends in India' (2015) <http://www.penningtons.co.uk/news-publications/latest-news/under-analysis-changing-dispute-resolution-trends-in-india/> accessed 21 July 2016.

37 See statement of Chief Justice of India NV Ramana in, Shagun Suryam, 'Courts Should Be Last Resort, Only after Exploring Alternative Dispute Resolution: CJI NV Ramana' *Bar and Bench* (4 December 2021) <https://www.barandbench.com/news/courts-last-resort-after-alternate-dispute-resolution-cji-nv-ramana> accessed 22 January 2022.

38 Vereinte Nationen (n 2).

39 For further elaboration on the benefits of arbitration see, Funke Adekoya, 'The Public Policy Defence to Enforcement of Arbitral Awards: Rising Star or Setting Sun?' (2015) 2 BCDR International Arbitration Review 203, 203.

disputes. Effective laws and jurisprudence relating to international arbitration can, therefore, have a significant impact on India's ability to grow as a destination for foreign investment.[40]

Although more arbitration is needed in India, parties have been dissuaded from arbitration, fearing judicial intervention in arbitral awards on the grounds of public policy.[41] The legislature has tried to curb judicial impulses through statute, but this conflicts with the broad acceptance of judicial activism and supremacy *vis-à-vis* the legislature in Indian society. There is a void in the literature regarding who is the competent authority to decide on the bounds of the public policy exception in India and what these bounds should be. This thesis will seek to address this void.

40 Rendeiro (n 12).

41 Manu Thadikkaran, 'Judicial Intervention in International Commercial Arbitration: Implications and Recent Developments from the Indian Perspective' (2012) 29 Journal of International Arbitration 681.

Chapter 1: Public policy and its many contours

Before going into the core issues of this research and evaluating how public policy has been treated under the Indian arbitration regime, and before examining how the exception needs to be defined, it is important to briefly clarify some preliminary topics to contextualize this research. Firstly, this part will elucidate on how the public policy exception evolved both in the common law and civil law systems. Secondly, we will look at what role public policy plays in different legal systems both outside and within the context of international arbitration. This will help us then understand the arguments raised later regarding how it must be interpreted. Thirdly, we will look at public policy from a purely arbitration related standpoint and evaluate the limitations of judicial review at the enforcement stage of the arbitration process.

I. The origins of public policy in civil and common law systems

The use of the term 'public policy' permeates most legal systems, several international instruments and many fields of law, and it is vastly referred to in both arbitrations as well as court proceedings.[42] Dolinger has aptly described it as being 'among the oldest and most important principles of private international law'.[43] From time immemorial, states would determine their policy on a variety of social and legal issues. This policy, of course, would keep evolving with time. In early Rome, for instance, the law prohibited enforcement of winnings from gambling – while this policy was not rigorously enforced initially, it became a very important part of Emperor Justinian's imperial policy.[44] Public policy, according to its early understanding, was based on the principle of '*privatorum*

42 Farshad Ghodoosi, 'The Concept of Public Policy in Law: Revisiting the Role of the Public Policy Doctrine in the Enforcement of Private Legal Arrangements' (2015) 94 Nebraska Law Review 685, 687.

43 Jacob Dolinger, 'World Public Policy: Real International Public Policy in the Conflict of Laws' (1982) 17 Texas International Law Journal 167.

44 Suzanne B. Faris, 'Changing Public Policy and the Evolution of Roman Civil and Criminal Law on Gambling' (2012) 3 UNLV Gaming Law Journal 199.

conventio juri publico non derogat',[45] which was understood to mean agreements against the law would be without effect.[46]

The civil law concept of '*ordre public*' and the common law 'public policy' are often used synonymously.[47] This is especially true in the context of arbitration. This is demonstrated by the fact that the drafters of international instruments such as the New York Convention, with its official languages being, inter alia, French and English, did not provide any distinction in article V(2)b. There are, however, subtle differences in how these concepts evolved and are understood.

The modern notion of *ordre public* in the civil law tradition in the context of Private International Law is rooted in the works of Savigny, where he was critical of practices in certain legal systems such as polygamy and slavery, especially where local law considered excluding such practices to be *publica utiliata* (in public interest)[48] and was against applying foreign law that was contrary to 'fundamental legal/moral' principles of the forum.[49] It was Mancini from Italy who expounded on the mandatory nature of the doctrine.[50] France was the first civil law country to introduce the term in its statute book.[51] Article 6 of the *Code Civil*

---

45 Jacob Dolinger (n 43).

46 *A Treatise of the First Principles of Laws in General and of the Interpretation of Them* (Printed by WB for Richard Sare at Greys Inn Gate in Holborn 1705) 144 <https://books.google.de/books?id=ZjDk3MOFCaIC&printsec=frontcover#v=onepage&q&f=false> accessed 10 August 2018.

47 An example of this can be seen in 'Defining European Public Order: An Impossible Task', in Kanstantin Dzehtsiarou (ed), *Can the European Court of Human Rights Shape European Public Order?* (Cambridge University Press 2021) 62 et seq.

48 Friedrich Karl von Savigny, Private International Law. A Treatise on the Conflict of Laws: And the Limits of Their Operation in Respect of Place and Time (T & T Clark 1869) 36.

49 Jacob Dolinger (n 43) 168.

50 For a translation of Mancini's arguments for precluding the application of a foreign law that violates ordre public of the forum see Kurt H. Nadelmann, 'Mancini's Nationality Rule and Non-Unified Legal Systems: Nationality versus Domicile' (1969) 17 The American Journal of Comparative Law 418, 425; See also, María Elena Alvarez de Pfeifle, *Der Ordre Public-Vorbehalt Als Versagungsgrund Der Anerkennung Und Vollstreckbarerklärung Internationaler Schiedssprüche: Unter Berücksichtigung Des Deutschen, Schweizerischen, Französischen Und Englischen Rechts Sowie Des UNCITRAL-Modellgesetzes* (P Lang 2009) 129.

51 See Franz T. Schwarz and Helmut Ortner, 'The Arbitration Procedure – Procedural Ordre Public and the Internationalization of Public Policy in Arbitration', in Christian Klausegger and Peter Klein (eds), *Austrian Yearbook on International Arbitration 2008* (MANZ Verlag Wien 2008) 135.

1803 (French Civil Code) precludes parties from derogating from laws forming *l'ordre public et les bonnes moeurs* (public policy or good morals).[52]

In common law, the violation of public policy is rooted in the ancient concept, '*encounter common ley*', which means something going against the interests of the community or commonwealth, which was laid down in *Dyer's* case of 1413.[53] In this case, an agreement restraining an apprentice from carrying out his trade for six months was not enforceable because there was a lack of consideration, and it went against common law.[54] While some scholars have claimed that the unconscious use of public policy even predated equity,[55] the conscious use of the term public policy is of relatively recent vintage. In England, its use can first be seen in the mid-18th Century.[56] In the landmark *Egerton* ruling by the House of Lords, the court described public policy to be the foundation of law itself and based it on the *nihil quod est inconveniens est licitum* principle laid down by Lord Coke,[57] which means that it is better for an individual to suffer a mischief than for many to be inconvenienced.[58]

Despite their differing origins, there is a common underlying reasoning which can be seen in both the common law *public policy* and the civil law *ordre public.* Both of them seek to place restrictions on private behavior for the protection of the common good. For the purpose of this thesis, these concepts will henceforth be referred to interchangeably.

As seen above, public policy is a notion that has served different functions of both a substantive and procedural nature. In purely domestic situations such as the Dyers case, it was used to invalidate a contract, but in the international context, it can also be used by courts to safeguard essential public interests such as free and fair competition. Furthermore, in the context of arbitration, it can be used to ensure that essential procedural safeguards are met. These functions

52 Code Civil 1803 (Version en vigueur depuis le 15 mars 1803).

53 For a more detailed overview of the evolution of this doctrine see, Farshad Ghodoosi, 'The Concept of Public Policy in Law: Revisiting the Role of the Public Policy Doctrine in the Enforcement of Private Legal Arrangements' (n 42) 691.

54 Gary Minda, 'The Common Law, Labor and Antitrust' (1989) 11 Berkeley Journal of Employment and Labor Law 461, 475.

55 Percy H. Winfield, 'Public Policy in the English Common Law' (1928) 42 Harvard Law Review 77.

56 W. S. M. Knight, 'Public Policy in English Law' (1922) 38 Law Quarterly Review 207.

57 *Egerton v Brownlow* [1853] 10 ER 359 (House of Lords) 417.

58 W. S. M. Knight (n 56).

and their application in the Indian context will be further elaborated in Part D of this thesis.

II. The different shades of public policy

Public policy is an effective tool in the hands of the legislature and the courts. It has procedural and substantive dimensions, and it can encompass many things and serves multiple purposes.[59] The meaning of public policy needs to be understood based on the underlying context. It can be given a different understanding based on who applies it and for what reason it is being applied. Due to its extremely vast scope, public policy is to be given a different understanding in different circumstances, even in the same country or legal system.

Public policy may be applied by the legislator, the judge or the arbitrator. Each of them has different considerations in mind. The legislator may enact laws to protect the public interest and regulate private behavior. It may also provide public policy as a ground for judicial intervention.

The public policy of the legislator when drafting a law would be different from that of the judge when interpreting the law. The public policy considerations of the lawmaker when drafting statutes would be broader, as the legislature tries to provide clarity in the statute by covering all possible circumstances. This would differ from public policy that a court would use when deciding whether to enforce an arbitral award. Here the public policy interpretation would be by nature narrow, as the court has to follow the intention of the lawmaker embodied in a general rule to the specific facts and circumstances of the case before him.[60] The application of public policy by national courts again differs from that of the private arbitrator. The arbitrator's primary interest is fulfilling the will of private parties and rendering an enforceable award.[61] So public policy considerations

59 Piotr Wiliński, Excess of Powers in International Commercial Arbitration: Compliance with the Arbitral Tribunal's Mandate in a Comparative Perspective (Eleven International Publishing 2021) 27–28.

60 *Bharat Aluminium Company and Ors Vs Kaiser Aluminium Technical Service, Inc and Ors* 2012 9 SCC 552 (Supreme Court of India) [61]. In this decision, the Indian Supreme Court favourably considered the English case of Duport steel wherein it was held '...the role of the judiciary is confined to ascertaining from the words that Parliament has approved as expressing its intention what that intention was, and to giving effect to it'.

61 Martin Platte, 'Arbitrator's Duty to Render Enforceable Awards' (2003) 20 Journal of International Arbitration 307, 309.

will be in his mind only for helping achieve this purpose.[62] This is in stark contrast to the role of a public authority such as the judge. The judge acts as an instrument of the community and therefore needs to keep societal/public interest in mind when determining the scope of public policy.[63] This would, for instance, include the interest of the community in a free market.

Even judges interpret public policy differently in different situations. They would take differing approaches, for instance, based on the geographic location of the parties to a contract. The understanding of public policy in normal domestic contractual relations would differ from the understanding of public policy in the field of international commercial arbitration, where it is used with more restraint.

This part will give a broad overview of how public policy is to be given a different outlook based on different circumstances.

1. As an instrument of making and interpreting laws

In purely domestic cases, public policy can arise both in legislative action and in cases before courts. In drafting a statute, the law-maker articulates legislative policy and sometimes even public policy.[64] An anti-corruption statute or a statute countering money laundering, for instance, would seek to criminalize behavior that would go against public policy. One must not, however, conflate 'legislative policy' and public policy. As pointed out by the Indian Supreme Court, while 'policy of law' and public policy are sometimes used synonymously, they are actually two entirely different concepts.[65] While the former deals with a general policy of the government, the latter deals with fundamental provisions of the legal system.

---

62 Some arbitrators refuse jurisdiction where they feel that egregious violations of public policy have occurred. See for instance Judge Gunnar Lagergren in *ICC Award No 1110 of 1963*. This is however an exception, and there is a tendency of arbitrators to accept jurisdiction. This tendency has been further elaborated on in Chapter 6.

63 Richard Zitrin, 'The Judicial Function: Justice Between the Parties, or a Broader Public Interest?' (2004) 32 Hofstra Law Review 1565, 1568–1569.

64 See D. M. Olson and M. L. Mezey, 'Parliaments and Public Policy', in David M. Olson and Michael L. Mezey (eds), *Legislatures in the Policy Process: The Dilemmas of Economic Policy* (Cambridge University Press 1991) 1.

65 Murlidhar Aggarwal vs State of Uttar Pradesh and Ors [1974] 2 SCC 742 (Supreme Court of India) [28].

Public policy is deeply rooted in a state's constitution and the rights guaranteed therein.[66] Sometimes the legislature may make a law that contravenes constitutional law provisions or human rights. Controlling laws for compliance with constitutional mandate and human rights is then the job of the courts. The Indian Supreme Court in *Madras Bar Association* ruling pointed out that courts can strike down a statute goes against core human rights and thereby violates essential provisions (public policy) enshrined in the Constitution.[67] This could be used as a means of or restraining legislative or executive action. In such circumstances, purely domestic public policy would be taken into account. In the context of protecting fundamental rights, unlike in arbitration, public policy can be interpreted expansively.

2. To regulate private contractual behavior

Public policy is also used as an instrument to regulate private contractual relations.[68] For instance, in some countries, e.g., in Singapore, it is part of public policy not to enforce an agreement for recovering debts arising out of an illegal act or gambling.[69] It will not be far-fetched to imagine a similar public policy against private contracts for slave trade or child labour. Indeed, in India, such contracts are criminalized under the Child Labour (Prohibition & Regulation) Act of 1986 and there is a definitive Governmental policy in combatting this societal evil.[70]

While the above examples concern contracts that would be against public policy in most jurisdictions, normally, public policy is treated differently in purely domestic proceedings and in conflict-of-laws cases. In the former, it is given a more expansive understanding, and in the latter, it is to be understood

66 See generally, Peter B. Rutledge, *Arbitration and the Constitution* (Cambridge University Press 2012).

67 *Madras Bar Association v Union of India & Anr* [2021] Writ Petition Civ No502 (Supreme Court of India) [39].

68 Bram Akkermans, 'Public Policy (Orde Public)' (2019) 8 European Property Law Journal 260.

69 See, K. C. Lye and Chuan Tat Yeo, 'Singapore', in Carel J. H. Lynden (ed), *Enforcement of Judgments, Awards & Deeds in Commercial Matters: Jurisdictional Comparisons* (1st edn, Thomson Reuters 2013) 264.

70 'The Policy of the Government on the Issue of Child Labour' <https://labour.gov.in/sites/default/files/PolicyofGovernmenontheissueofChildLabour.pdf> accessed 4 February 2022.

more narrowly.[71] The French have articulated these distinctions by categorizing public policy into *ordre public interne* and *ordre public externe.*[72]

Ordre public interne is used in the domestic context. It concerns those legal provisions from which parties cannot derogate by private agreement.[73] A good example would be the French Civil Code, Article 1162 of which provides that 'a contract cannot derogate from public policy either by its stipulations or by its purpose'.[74] It also empowers courts to intervene in contractual relations between parties if there is an overwhelming public interest at stake.[75] *Ordre public externe* enables courts to reject foreign laws that go against fundamental principles of the states legal system.[76]

3. In applying foreign laws and recognising foreign judgments

Traditionally, at least in private international law, courts are obliged to apply foreign law and enforce foreign judgments. Here, public policy can be invoked in two circumstances.

Firstly, it can be used as an exception to the general conflicts of law rule of recognising applicable foreign law. The aim is to safeguard the fundamental principles of the legal system. Enonchong has described this as being similar to a judge using a 'Chinese wall' to keep away the effects of foreign law that contravene the forum's fundamental policy.[77] It acts as a defensive mechanism 'reservation/

---

71 Paul Torremans and JJ Fawcett (eds), *Cheshire, North & Fawcett: Private International Law* (15th edn, Oxford University Press 2017) 133.

72 For an elaboration on the meaning of these terms see Nigel Blackaby and others, *Redfern and Hunter on International Arbitration* (6th edn, Oxford University Press 2015) 600; George A. Bermann, 'Mandatory Rules of Law in International Arbitration' (2007) 18 American Review of International Arbitration 1, 3.

73 Martin Gebauer, 'Ordre Public (Public Policy)', in Rüdiger Wolfrum (ed), *Max Planck Encyclopedia of Public International Law [MPEPIL]* (Oxford University Press 2007) <opil.ouplaw.com/home/EPIL> accessed 18 August 2019, para 5.

74 The Law of Contract, the General Regime of Obligations, and Proof of Obligations 2016 (Ordonnance n° 2016-131), the new provisions of the Code civil, translated by John Cartwright<http://www.textes.justice.gouv.fr/art_pix/THE-LAW-OF-CONTRACT-2-5-16.pdf> accessed 15 August 2019.

75 Kent Murphy, 'The Traditional View of Public Policy and Ordre Public in Private International Law' (1981) 11 Georgia Journal of International & Comparative Law 596.

76 ibid 596–597.

77 Nelson Enonchong, 'Public Policy in the Conflict of Laws: A Chinese Wall around Little England?' (1996) 45 International & Comparative Law Quarterly 634.

Vorbehaltsklausel' and helps in preventing results that would be completely alien to or irreconcilable with the legal system of the forum.[78] For instance, if applying a foreign law would lead to recognising a polygamous marriage when it was against the basic principles of the court's domestic legal system, public policy would prevent such a result. The judge will reject such foreign law and instead choose to apply the law of the forum.[79] In Germany, a foreign legal rule will be not given effect where it goes against the fundamental principles of German (constitutional) law in a way that is manifest.[80]

Another situation where public policy could be invoked is in refusing enforcement of a foreign judgment to prevent the same consequences. An example would be a judgment providing exemplary damages, which would be against the public policy in some countries. The need for such a mechanism is reflected in Article 7 of the 2019 Hague Judgments Convention, which provides that recognition and enforcement of a foreign judgment may be refused if it would be 'manifestly incompatible' with the public policy of the country.[81] The Convention provides examples, including where, for instance, enforcement would lead to adversely affecting the security or sovereignty of the enforcing country.

The public policy exception in the context of refusing enforcement of foreign judgments could also be invoked if essential procedural safeguards and principles of natural justice are ignored by the court or tribunal in reaching its judgment.[82] This is also reflected in Article 7 of the Hague Judgments Convention, which provides for non-enforcement on public policy grounds where the judgment was reached by means that are incompatible with fundamental principles of procedural fairness of the country where enforcement is sought. The same applies under several other legal instruments such as Art 45(1) of the Brussels I bis Regulation.[83] A similar provision is Art 27 of the Brussels

---

78 See, Dieter Martiny, 'Public Policy', in Jürgen Basedow and others (eds), *The Max Planck Encyclopedia of European Private Law*, vol II (Oxford University Press 2012) 1396.

79 Tim Corthaut, *EU Ordre Public* (Wolters Kluwer Law & Business 2012) para 1.02.

80 See, Ioanna Thoma, 'Public Policy', in Jürgen Basedow and others (eds), *Encyclopedia of Private International Law* (Edward Elgar Publishing 2017) 1454. See also, Dieter Martiny, 'Public Policy', in Jürgen Basedow and others (eds), *The Max Planck Encyclopedia of European Private Law*, vol II (Oxford University Press 2012) 1397.

81 Convention on the Recognition and Enforcement of Foreign Judgments in Civil or Commercial Matters, 2019.

82 Lawrence Collins, Adrian Briggs, and Jonathan Hill (eds), *Dicey and Morris on the Conflict of Laws* (13th edn, Sweet & Maxwell 2000) paras 14R-141 et seq.

83 Regulation (EU) no. 1215/2012 on jurisdiction and the recognition and enforcement of judgments in civil and commercial matters (recast) 2012 (OJ L 351).

Convention.[84] This defence was made use of in the *Krombach* decision where a German court refused to recognise a French judgment on public policy grounds where the defendant was not given a fair hearing. This was ultimately condoned by the European Court of Justice.[85]

4. In the field of arbitration

Public policy is used in many circumstances other than the traditional conflict-of-laws problem of application of foreign law or recognition of judgments of foreign courts. It must be treated differently based on the context in which it is used. As will be dealt with in detail later in this thesis, in international arbitration, it can be used for setting aside or refusing enforcement of arbitral awards that violate the fundamental legal principles of the forum. There is a general consensus in the literature that public policy, when applied to arbitration agreements, is to be given a narrow construction in order to safeguard party autonomy.[86] Here also, concepts of public policy vary from state to state based on differing socio-economic, religious and political considerations.[87] Wolff has astutely observed that what some states consider to be refusing enforcement to protect their fundamental moral or legal precepts could be considered as hostile anti-enforcement bias in other countries.[88]

Differences in treatment of the exception can be seen based on the type of arbitration. Public policy in investment arbitration would not necessarily have the same connotation as public policy relating to commercial arbitration.[89] An award against a sovereign state that violates investment treaty obligations by taking measures to protect the health and safety of its citizens through mandating

---

84 Brussels Convention on jurisdiction and the enforcement of judgments in civil and commercial matters, 1968 (OJ L 299).

85 Dieter Krombach v André Bamberski Case, C-7/98 [2000] ECR I, I–01935.

86 Blackaby and others (n 72).

87 See Penny Madden, Ceyda Knoebel and Besma Grifat-Spackman, 'Arbitrability and Public Policy Challenges', in J William Rowley and others (eds), *The Guide to Challenging and Enforcing Arbitration Awards* (2nd edn, Global Arbitration Review, Law Business Research Limited 2021) 38.

88 See, Reinmar Wolff, 'Article V (2)(b)', in Reinmar Wolff (ed), New York Convention: Convention on the Recognition and Enforcement of Foreign Arbitral Awards of 10 June 1958 ; Commentary (CH Beck ; Hart ; Nomos 2012) para 491.

89 Eric De Brabandere, 'The (Ir)Relevance of Transnational Public Policy in Investment Treaty Arbitration – A Reply to Jean-Michel Marcoux' (2020) 21 The Journal of World Investment & Trade 847, 854.

labeling on cigarette packets cannot be compared to an award against a private company that has breached its contractual obligations. There would be a different threshold for enforcing awards in each of these cases.

5. In trade law

The use of public policy is also seen in trade law but in a completely different context.[90] Here it is mostly used for ensuring that the goods or services entering a country do not go against domestic standards. This could, for instance, include measures restricting the free movement of contraband drugs, prevention of child labour, animal welfare, controlling the sale of arms or pornographic material. Such provisions can be seen both under WTO and EU law.

Article 36 of the Treaty on the Functioning of the EU (TFEU),[91] for instance, acts as an exception to the fundamental freedoms enshrined under EU law and allows Member states to impose '*prohibitions or restrictions on imports, exports or goods in transit justified on grounds of public morality, public policy or public security*'.

Similar provisions can be found under WTO law which takes into consideration the need of governments to safeguard public health, environment and local industries to determine a countries decision to use tariffs to encourage or constrain cross-border trade in goods and services.[92] Article XX of the General Agreement on Tariffs and Trade (GATT) specifically permits states to adopt measures for protecting 'public morals', 'human, plant and animal life' etc.[93] A similar provision is seen in Article 27.2 of the TRIPS Agreement,[94] which provides states with the freedom to exclude granting patents 'to protect *ordre public* or morality, including to protect human, animal or plant life or health or to avoid serious prejudice to the environment'.

---

90 See more generally, Dominic Coppens and Bart De Meester, Public Policy and WTO Law: Regulating Globalization, International Law FORUM du droit international (BRILL 2005) 138.

91 Consolidated version of the Treaty on the Functioning of the European Union [2012] OJ C 326.

92 Diane A. Desierto, 'Balancing National Public Policy and Free Trade' (2015) 27 Pace International Law Review 554.

93 General Agreement on Tariffs and Trade 1994, Apr. 15, 1994, Marrakesh Agreement Establishing the World Trade Organization 1994 (1867 UNTS 187).

94 Agreement on Trade-Related Aspects of Intellectual Property Rights, Apr. 15, 1994, Marrakesh Agreement Establishing the World Trade Organization 1994 (1869 UNTS 299).

6. Common values underlying public policy

Despite the apparent differences, there is significant overlap in policy considerations, even in different areas of law. For instance, protecting morals is considered an essential part of public policy both in arbitration and in WTO law. Similarly, while an arbitral award that is immoral because it was illegally obtained through fraud or corruption can be refused enforcement on public policy grounds, the same public policy considerations may give rise to criminal sanctions in some national legal systems.

In this case, however, there is an important distinction in the use of public policy. When it comes to enforcing a foreign award, due to the pro-enforcement bias, courts would sometimes be willing to enforce an arbitral award if the breach of public policy is insignificant. For example, the Singapore High Court held that for the public policy exception to be violated, mere fraud was insufficient. Rather, such fraud must have caused 'substantial injustice' or have a 'substantial impact on the making of the award'.[95] While this may be true in arbitration, the criminal courts will not ignore a violation because it is not of significant magnitude. Fraud will give rise to criminal sanctions regardless of the sum involved. Therefore, the scope for judicial action is higher in criminal cases than in commercial law, even for violation of the same public policy.

While differing policy considerations means that the threshold for invoking the exception may have different shades, i.e., may be lower in WTO law or criminal law than for commercial arbitration, the underlying reasoning behind the use of public policy remains the same, i.e., ensuring sovereign control of private behavior to safeguard national interest. This means that despite the numerous criticisms, the exception serves an important role. As will be demonstrated below, this is especially true in international commercial arbitration.

III. The role of public policy in international commercial arbitration

Parties choose arbitration in order to be able to resolve their disputes away from the public sphere. Arbitration gives them a degree of confidentiality and efficiency that cannot be found in traditional court proceedings.[96] Ideally, there

95 Swiss Singapore Overseas Enterprises Pte Ltd v Exim Rajathi India Pvt Ltd [2009] SGHC 231 (High Court of Singapore) [29].

96 Hans Bagner, 'Confidentiality – A Fundamental Principle in International Commercial Arbitration?' (2001) 18 Journal of International Arbitration 243.

should be no need whatsoever for parties to approach courts, given that they have freely chosen arbitration and given the need for maintaining future business relations, comply with arbitral awards voluntarily. However, as pointed out by Lew, arbitration cannot be effective in a vacuum without any legal system or the assistance of the courts.[97] Ultimately, the same parties who run away from litigation and their arbitrators rely on national law and the court system to legitimize and give effect to the arbitration process. Public policy in arbitration, as will be shown, is one element of judicial control.

Despite the need to respect the aforementioned intention of parties to settle their disputes privately, there are certain limitations that every legal system puts into place to regulate private behavior. The public policy exception acts as such a limitation. It acts as an interface between private arbitration and the outside world by balancing party autonomy with national and transnational interests and state sovereignty.[98] The need for public control stems from a desire to ensure an overarching need for justice. Paulsson has articulated this in his statement that 'public justice is more valuable than safeguarding private arrangements'.[99] The idea behind the exception is that as public policy is fundamental and pervasive, parties should not be able to derogate from it by way of private arbitration.

Public policy plays a very important role in international commercial arbitration. Wolff has gone so far as to observe that the New York Convention would not have been such a success if it did not provide countries with the option of providing for the exception.[100] With increased globalization, the use of arbitration has grown exponentially in the past decades, and there are very few legal mechanisms in place to exercise some degree of control over it. Public policy is one such instrument used by courts for this purpose. The following reasons justify the use of the public policy exception:

Firstly, the exception acts as a deterrent. Parties who are aware that courts will refuse enforcement of awards where the underlying contract is illegal/breaches public policy may avoid undertaking such illegal contracts. Similarly, it will deter

97 Julian D. M. Lew, 'Does National Court Involvement Undermine the International Arbitration Processes?' (2009) 24 American University International Law Review 489, 492.

98 Christopher S. Gibson, 'Penn State Law Review Symposium: Building the Civilization of Arbitration: Arbitration, Civilization and Public Policy: Seeking Counterpoise between Arbitral Autonomy and the Public Policy Defense in View of Foreign Mandatory Public Law' (2009) 113 Penn State Law Review 1227, 1237–1239.

99 Paulsson (n 9) 24.

100 See, Reinmar Wolff, Article V (2)(b), in Wolff (n 88) para 490.

parties from engaging in corruption/fraud during the arbitration if they know that awards so obtained will be denied enforcement. In effect, as explained by Ghodoosi, it dissuades parties from using arbitration to escape from the fundamental norms of the state.[101] Furthermore, the exception also acts as a penalty, i.e., it penalizes illegal behavior by preventing parties from benefitting from awards so obtained.

Secondly, public policy helps ensure arbitral tribunals conduct their proceedings in a way that is fair and in consonance with the fundamental procedural requirements of the legal system of the enforcing state. Arbitrators have a duty to render an enforceable award and are therefore obliged to take into consideration mandatory norms and public policy of the enforcing state both during the proceedings and in reaching the award.[102] They will not breach public policy or procedural norms if they know that such awards could later be refused enforcement on public policy grounds.

An additional factor is that unlike judges in court proceedings, arbitrators are not always trained legal professionals, and in the case of ad-hoc proceedings, there is a chance of violating essential procedural or legal requirements. This is where the public policy exception comes into play. It helps essential legal norms and moral beliefs of the enforcing state in what is otherwise a predominantly private process.

Despite the advantages pointed out above, public policy must be used rarely for refusing the enforcement of arbitral awards. The use of public policy by courts is justified in normal litigation, as parties use the public courts to resolve their dispute at public expense, and it would be difficult for courts to ignore the breach of public policy in such situations.[103] Arbitration, on the other hand, is predominantly a private process chosen by parties to escape from the inflexible court system. Parties bear the complete cost of the proceedings, and they voluntarily give up recourse to courts. Party autonomy, therefore, demands that courts should intervene only exceptionally. The exception should be invoked to protect the public good and not to help parties who have entered into foolish contracts escape their obligations.[104] Furthermore, the use of public policy must

101 Ghodoosi (n 15) 54.

102 Günther J. Horvath, 'The Duty of the Tribunal to Render an Enforceable Award' (2001) 18 Journal of International Arbitration 135, 147.

103 Ghodoosi (n 15) 10.

104 Paulsson (n 9) 2.

be restricted in order to avoid the danger, pointed out by Chng, that the invoking of public policy does not become the norm but remains an exception.[105]

IV. The importance and limitations of judicial review of arbitral awards

A core element of this thesis is how much judicial review is actually necessary when it comes to arbitration. While judicial review draws its roots from the need of courts to supervise administrative or legislative action, and it has been considered acceptable or even essential in this context, its need in the field of arbitration is much more contested.[106] For arbitration to work effectively, judges and arbitrators do not need to compete for jurisdiction and power. Rather their role, as described by Professor Goldman, is to be 'complementary and collaborative'.[107] A direct consequence is reduced judicial intervention.

Scholars have argued that judicial review, especially on public policy grounds, can undermine the benefits of arbitration by delaying 'justice' and 'eroding confidence' in arbitration.[108] Furthermore, judicial review erodes the finality of awards. According to Born, the principle of judicial non-intervention forms the 'central pillar of international arbitration'.[109] National courts, furthermore, may have a tendency to be biased in favor of local parties.[110] Arbitration is primarily meant to be a private means of dispute settlement. This explains why almost every international instrument and national law on arbitration stress on the general rule of enforcing awards and thereby respecting party autonomy.

---

105 Kenny Chng, 'A Theoretical Perspective of the Public Policy Doctrine in the Conflict of Laws' (2018) 14 Journal of Private International Law 130, 132.

106 Frances T. Freeman Jalet, 'Judicial Review of Arbitration the Judicial Attitude' (1960) 45 Cornell Law Review 519, 520.

107 See, Berthold Goldman, 'The Complementary Roles of Judges and Arbitrators in Ensuring that International Commercial Arbitration is Effective', in *60 Years of ICC Arbitration, A Look at the Future: Programme of the 60th Anniversary of the Court of Arbitration of the ICC* (International Chamber of Commerce 1984) 257.

108 Jessica L. Gelander, 'Judicial Review of International Arbitral Awards: Preserving Independence in International Commercial Arbitrations' (1997) 80 Marquette Law Review 625, 626.

109 Gary B. Born, 'Principle of Judicial Non-interference in International Arbitral Proceedings, The Anniversary Contributions – International Litigation & Arbitration' (2009) 30 University of Pennsylvania Journal of International Law 999, 1033.

110 Won Kidane, *The Culture of International Arbitration* (Oxford University Press 2017) 100.

Despite these arguments, limited judicial review can be of utmost importance. It supports the arbitration process and gives it legitimacy in the eyes of the parties and society. While priority must be given to enforcing awards, every country needs to protect the fundamental policies of its legal system. In this regard, the insertion and continued use of the public policy exception give testimony to the need for limited judicial review. As will be shown later on in this thesis, a careful balance is necessary. Judges should protect public policy while refraining from stepping into the shoes of the arbitrator. A possible way to find a balance, as suggested by Otto and Elwan, is for judges to not look at whether the award itself contravenes public policy but rather only to evaluate if its enforcement would have such an effect.[111]

There is another intrinsic benefit of judicial review. Judicial discourse helps in shaping future legislations and can provide valuable guidance to the lawmaker. In India, the definition of public policy under the IAA(Am.) 2015 directly copies the definition provided by the Indian Supreme court in the *Renusagar* case. Similarly, in France, the decree amending the arbitration law codified the rulings of the *Cour de cassation.*[112]

For jurisdictions that are not in favor of external judicial interference, there is, however, an alternative suggested by scholars such as Zamir and Segal, which could work as a possible middle ground, i.e., providing an appeal mechanism within the arbitration process.[113] Such a mechanism can also be seen in arbitral institutions such as JAMS,[114] which provides the possibility of an appeal with the agreement of the parties, and the ECA, which in Art 28 of its rules mandates such an appeal procedure.[115] Even in India, the Supreme Court in its *Centrotrade* ruling, held that an appeal mechanism within arbitration (two-tier arbitration)

111 See Dirk Otto and Omaia Elwan, 'Article V(2)' in Herbert Kronke and Patricia Nacimiento (eds), *Recognition and Enforcement of Foreign Arbitral Awards: A Global Commentary on the New York Convention* (Kluwer Law International; Wolters Kluwer Law & Business 2010) 366.

112 Guido Carducci, 'The Arbitration Reform in France: Domestic and International Arbitration Law' (2012) 28 Arbitration International 125, 128.

113 Noam Zamir and Peretz Segal, 'Appeal in International Arbitration – an Efficient and Affordable Arbitral Appeal Mechanism' (2019) 35 Arbitration International 79.

114 'JAMS Optional Arbitration Appeal Procedure' <https://www.jamsadr.com/files/Uploads/Documents/JAMS-Rules/JAMS_Optional_Appeal_Procedures-2003.pdf> accessed 11 June 2019.

115 'Arbitration Rules of the European Court of Arbitration' <https://cour-europe-arbitrage.org/arbitration-rules/> accessed 11 June 2019.

would be completely in line with the IAA, and would not violate Indian public policy.[116]

There are several reasons for having such a mechanism. If a party has been adversely affected by an (alleged) breach of public policy, and this can be set right by an arbitral appeal mechanism, there is then no need to approach courts. This could be either before an entirely new tribunal empanelled by the same arbitral institution (in the case of institutional arbitration) or chosen by the parties. Furthermore, courts will be more hesitant to intervene when the parties have already had the right to appeal and the tribunal has addressed the parties' grievances.

The appeal process is considered important by parties to normal court proceedings, as grave injustice will be done if a judge makes a mistake in fact or law, either advertently or inadvertently, and there is no remedy for the parties.[117] Usually, parties give up this right when choosing arbitration so as to benefit from finality and speedy procedures. Furthermore, unlike in state courts, parties to an arbitration choose their own arbitrator and therefore have more trust in this process. While providing for appeal may cost extra time and expense, the efficiency and speedy procedure may be in vain if courts would have to step in at a later point. One can argue that an appeal procedure within arbitration itself may therefore hold the key to resolving excess judicial intervention on public policy grounds.

Such an approach may, however, not necessarily be the right solution. By its very nomenclature, the term 'public policy' lends itself more to public control than private control. It is not possible to delegate the duty of controlling for public policy to private bodies rather than courts. Judicial review, although exercised in a very narrow and limited manner, cannot be completely replaced by arbitral review. There is no guarantee that the second privately constituted arbitral tribunal will get public policy right the second time when the first tribunal has failed in this regard. Limited judicial review on the grounds of public policy, as a measure of last resort, is, therefore, a necessary 'evil', which cannot and should not be done away in the context of international commercial arbitration.

---

116 Centrotrade Minerals & Metal Inc v Hindustan Copper Ltd (2017) 2 SCC 228 (Supreme Court of India) [46].

117 For an elaboration on whether and how appeal could play a role in correcting judicial errors see, Harlon Dalton, 'Taking the Right to Appeal (More or Less) Seriously' (1985) 95 Yale Law Journal 62, 73.

Chapter 2: Use and abuse of the public policy exception under the Indian arbitration law

I. Introduction

The treatment of the public policy exception has played a key role in the shaping of arbitration law in India. In the past, the exception has often been used as an excuse for approaching courts seeking refusal of enforcement of arbitral awards on frivolous grounds.[118] In many countries, including India, judges have not shied away from using the exception. One of the drawbacks of the exception is that, even when a losing party may not be successful in its attempt to escape from the arbitral award, it often uses a public policy challenge as a delaying tactic to frustrate the party seeking enforcement.[119] The abuse of the exception by parties has led to both the courts and the legislature restricting its scope.

Despite the drawback referred to above, the public policy exception acts as a 'necessary evil' when it comes to arbitration. It was incorporated in order to serve the essential purpose of ensuring that national sovereignty is given due regard and to give national courts 'ultimate control over the outcomes of arbitration'.[120] Understandably, states would want to retain some degree of sovereignty even if entering into international instruments such as the New York Convention would be beneficial.[121] The exception itself in the IAA is therefore not the subject of criticism in this chapter, but rather its use (or abuse), the background to which will be looked at below.

The IAA 1996 was drafted by taking into account the UNCITRAL Model Law. India was also one of the first countries to sign and give effect to the New York Convention.[122] Both the New York Convention in Article V (2)(b), as well as the

118 Fort further elaboration, see Part B(III).

119 Nariman (n 1) 372.

120 Helena Hsi-Chia Chen, Predictability of 'public Policy' in Article V of the New York Convention under Mainland China's Judicial Practice (Kluwer Law International BV 2017) 2.

121 Marike Paulsson, *The 1958 New York Convention in Action* (Kluwer Law International BV 2016) 217.

122 Gary B. Born and Suzanne Spears, 'International Arbitration and India: "A Truly Excellent Judgment!"' (2012) 1 Indian Journal of Arbitration Law 1, 4.

Model Law in Article 36(b), provide that recognition of an award may be refused if the award is in contravention of a state's 'public policy'. These provisions have been incorporated in section 48(2) b of the IAA, which states that 'enforcement of an award may be refused if a court finds that enforcement [...] would be contrary to Indian public policy.'

In the *Konkan Railway* case, the Indian Supreme Court held that it would not be bound to take into account the Model Law for interpreting the IAA.[123] As these proceedings were purely domestic, this logic cannot be applied to the context of international arbitration. Rather one must take into account the subsequent *Chloro Controls* ruling where the same Court acknowledged that the legislature intended to *'bring international commercial arbitration in consonance with UNCITRAL Model (law), New York Convention and the Geneva Convention'*.[124]

By virtue of its ratification, the drafting history of the New York Convention also influences the interpretation by Indian courts. The Working Party involved in drafting the New York Convention felt that public policy for refusing enforcement of arbitral awards should be given a narrow construction.[125] This would mean that the IAA must also be interpreted so as to provide for the pro-enforcement perspective of these instruments towards international commercial arbitration.

Despite the widespread adoption of the public policy exception by numerous countries in their arbitration laws, neither the New York Convention nor the Model Law gives any definite guidance as to what public policy entails. This is probably because there was no consensus as to a uniform definition even among all countries involved in the drafting of the Convention.[126] Until recently, Indian law was also silent on the scope of the public policy exception.

In 2015, the Indian Parliament decided to amend the IAA 1996, and in doing so, it chose, unlike most other countries, to statutorily define the exception. Its decision was a reaction to several decisions of the Indian Supreme Court, which had given the public policy exception an inconsistent and sometimes a broad

---

123 Konkan Railway Corporation Ltd vs Rani Construction Pvt Ltd (2002) 1 SCR 728 (Supreme Court of India) [16].

124 Chloro Controls (India) Pvt Ltd Vs Severn Trent Water Purification Inc (2012) 13 SCR 402 (Supreme Court of India) [88].

125 'United Nations Conference on International Commercial Arbitration: Summary Record of the Seventeenth Meeting,12 September 1958, UN Economic and Social Council, E/CONF. 26/ SR.17' 3.

126 Chen (n 120) 15.

definition. This chapter will look at these court decisions as well as the other factors that influenced the Indian parliament in coming to its decision. It will also look at how the special circumstances influencing the evolution of arbitration in India have influenced the legislature and courts in their treatment of the public policy exception. This will build the foundation for the coming chapter, which will seek to analyze the definition of public policy under Indian law.

II. Contextualizing the research with a historical background

Arbitration in some (rudimentary) form or the other was a preferred mode of resolving dispute settlement commercial disputes across jurisdictions. In early Rome, arbitration pre-dated and was considered preferable to courts.[127] It was also found in ancient Greece, China, Mesopotamia and Islamic cultures.[128] In this part, we will see that arbitration was not an alien concept also in ancient India.

It is important to briefly look at the historical background of how arbitration has evolved as a dispute settlement mechanism in India in order to better understand the current treatment of arbitration in the Indian context, and indeed to get an insight into what drives the legislature and the judiciary in their formulation and interpretation of the public policy exception,

1. Historical reasons why India should be a pro-enforcement regime

Given its historical background, India should be a hotspot for arbitration. As astutely described by its former President K. R. Narayanan and before him by the former Chief Justice of the Bombay High Court, Sir Amberson Marten, arbitration is a '*striking feature of ordinary Indian life*'.[129] Even Mahatma Gandhi's first success as a barrister was an arbitration case.[130]

127 Earl S. Wolaver, 'The Historical Background of Commercial Arbitration' (1934) 83 University of Pennsylvania Law Review 132.

128 Paulsson (n 9) 10.

129 'NOTES AND CURRENT DEVELOPMENTS Speech by the President of India at the Inauguration of the International Council for Commercial Arbitration Conference 2000' (2000) 17 Journal of International Arbitration 154–155.

130 'NOTES AND CURRENT DEVELOPMENTS Speech by the President of India at the Inauguration of the International Council for Commercial Arbitration Conference 2000' (n 129).

Although Indian arbitration law and practice, as it stands today, is based on a predominantly western conception of arbitration, dispute settlement outside the confines of the judicial setup is not a completely alien concept to Indian legal thinking. In the past, the Indian approach has not been one of hostility to arbitration. Indian culture itself has been open to alternative ways of settling disputes. A study of ancient Hindu law shows that a prototype system of dispute settlement did exist through informal bodies such as *Kulani* (village council), *Sreni* (corporation) and *Puga* (assembly).[131] Similarly for commercial dispute resolution forums such as *Mahajans* and *Chambers* existed.[132] Also, at the village level, an informal prototype of the modern-day concept of arbitration did exist, wherein customarily, people used to and even still prefer going to local dispute settlement bodies consisting of village elders called *Panchayats* to help them resolve disputes.[133] The Panchayat system has now been formalized and given legal mandate under Indian law through the Panchayat Raj Act 1994 and Art. 243 of the Indian Constitution. While this serves to demonstrate that any hostility by the judiciary towards arbitration cannot be attributed to arbitration being a completely foreign concept, it must be remembered that arbitration in its modern understanding was previously not commonly used in commercial practice.

Reflective of the colonial period, the Indian law governing commercial arbitrations took its roots both from English law as well as from the commercial influences of the East India Company. Even during this time, public policy could be invoked, albeit rarely, as grounds for challenging an arbitral award. This can be seen in the Bengal Regulation of 1772, which was in the Indian context the first recorded attempt encouraging arbitration in its modern form.[134] It provided that no arbitral award could be set aside, except until fully proven with witnesses that the arbitrators were guilty of gross partiality or corruption in making the award.[135] Given that the East India Company had a strong interest in encouraging commerce, it is not surprising that the very first arbitration law had a marked pro-enforcement leaning. Despite these developments, it was only much later that a specialized arbitration statute was adopted, i.e., the Indian

131 Bharat Aluminium Company and Ors. Vs. Kaiser Aluminium Technical Service, Inc. and Ors. (n 60) para 32.

132 Bharat Aluminium Company and Ors. Vs. Kaiser Aluminium Technical Service, Inc. and Ors. (n 60).

133 Sarma, Oinam and Angshuman (n 34).

134 Justice H. R. Khanna, '76th Report on the Arbitration Act 1940' (Law Commission of India, Government of India-Ministry of Law & Justice 1978) para 1.14.

135 ibid.

Arbitration Act of 1899, which was based on the UK Arbitration Act 1889.[136] This statute also took public policy considerations into account by providing for judicial intervention by way of setting aside of arbitral awards that were procured by the misconduct of arbitrators, or by 'improper' means (Sec. 14), or remitting such awards where there is fresh evidence not considered by the arbitrators (Sec. 13).[137]

2. Background to the current treatment of public policy under Indian law

Since the beginning of the 20th century, changes in Indian arbitration law have been largely reflective of international developments. Under British rule, India became a party to the Geneva Protocol[138] and the subsequent Geneva Convention.[139] Subsequently, the Arbitration (Protocol and Convention) Act 1937 dealt with Convention and Protocol awards, i.e., foreign awards, and the Indian Arbitration Act 1940 was enacted to encompass domestic awards. Section 7 of the 1937 Act explicitly provided that awards would not be enforced if their subject matter was not arbitrable under Indian law or violated Indian public policy.

Post-independence, India ratified the New York Convention in 1958, and in line with this development, the government enacted the Foreign Awards Recognition and Enforcement (FARE) Act 1961, which updated the enforcement mechanism of foreign awards. Both the Geneva Convention and the New York Convention provided public policy as grounds for refusing the enforcement of awards. In line with the New York Convention, the FARE Act in section 7(1)(b) provided that the award will not be enforced by the court if 'the enforcement will be contrary to public policy.'[140]

---

136 *Bharat Aluminium Company and Ors. Vs. Kaiser Aluminium Technical Service, Inc. and Ors.* (n 60), Para 34 of the judgment provides a detailed account of the origins of Arbitration law in India; see also, Sarah E. Hilmer, 'Did Arbitration Fail India or Did India Fail Arbitration?' (2007) 10 International Arbitration Law Review 33.

137 H. N. Morison, Esq., *The Indian Arbitration Act, Act XI of 1899* (2nd edn, Thacker, Spink & Co 1914) <http://jkarchives.nic.in/Record_Holdings_PDF/Acc.%20No.%201149.pdf> accessed 3 June 2021.

138 Protocol on Arbitration Clauses 1924 (League of Nations, Treaty Series, vol 27) 157.

139 Geneva Convention on the Execution of Foreign Arbitral Awards 1927 (League of Nations, Treaty Series, vol 92) 301.

140 The Foreign Awards (Recognition and Enforcement) Act, Act No. 45 of 1961 1961 (Act No 45 of 1961).

In the decades following the enactment of the FARE Act, despite the pro-arbitration legislative framework, Indian courts were largely mistrustful of arbitration.[141] The arbitration law was thought to be inadequate to meet the needs of the arbitration community. The FARE Act had a major drawback – a prerequisite for the enforcement of a foreign award under this legislation was a decree from an Indian court. Obtaining this was often time-consuming and difficult for foreign parties who were not familiar with the Indian legal system.[142] Furthermore, foreign awards were treated in a similar manner as domestic awards, leading to what has been described as 'slow-track' arbitration.[143] The dissatisfaction with excessive scope for judicial intervention under the aforementioned statutory regimes led to delays and uncertainty,[144] to such an extent that in the *Guru Nanak* case before the Indian Supreme Court, Justice Desai famously said, *'the way in which the proceedings under the Act are conducted … has made lawyers laugh and legal philosophers weep'*.[145] It was only in the 1980s that there was a pro-arbitration shift by the courts,[146] as can be seen in the Renusagar case, which will be discussed in more detail later in this thesis.

The reasons for the slow take-off of international arbitration in India had to do with primarily the fact that Indian parties were not economically strong enough to defend claims before overseas tribunals, and besides this, Indian courts treated arbitration in a somewhat paternalistic fashion.[147] In fact, courts were not keen on facilitating international arbitration even when a valid agreement to arbitrate existed.[148] One reason for this could be that courts in India strongly feel the need to regulate conduct and exercise control in order to protect the rights of citizens when they believe that the legislature has not performed its function effectively.

The conservative approach towards arbitration must be looked at from a macro-economic perspective. India pre-1990s was a closed economy and followed the Soviet model, which, while aiming for self-sufficiency, shunned

141 Gary B. Born and Suzanne Spears (n 122) 5.

142 Tracy S. Work, 'India Satisfies Its Jones for Arbitration: New Arbitration Law in India' (1997) 10 Transnational Lawyer 227.

143 A. K. Bansal, 'Towards a New Law on International Arbitration in India' (1995) 12 Journal of International Arbitration 67, 67–68.

144 Rendeiro (n 12).

145 Guru Nanak Foundation v. Rattan Singh and Sons (n 33).

146 F. S. Nariman, 'Foreign Arbitral Awards in India: Problems, Pitfalls, and Progress' (1989) 6 Journal of International Arbitration 25, 30.

147 Nariman (n 1).

148 Gary B. Born and Suzanne Spears (n 122) 5.

foreign investment.[149] During this period, there was a deep scepticism in developing countries regarding arbitration.[150] It was believed that arbitration in its modern form was a predominantly western concept, and arbitrators were biased and always favored companies from developed economies.[151] These apprehensions, while occasionally justified, were often exaggerated due to a lack of familiarity with how international arbitration works.[152]

The economic crisis in 1991 saw an opening up of the Indian economy to investment with the governments New Industrial Policy (NIP).[153] This meant that foreign investment from a meagre $100 million in 1991[154] soared to $63 billion in 2015[155] and to $76.3 billion in 2021.[156] The reason for the enactment of the IAA 1996 was to keep up with India's liberalization and economic reform of the 1990s.[157] The increased inflow of investment urgently necessitated effective dispute resolution mechanisms like arbitration. India, like other developing countries, warmed to the idea that arbitration was a way of attracting further investment. It was also considered as a 'technically superior' way of settling disputes than local courts.[158]

The emergence of the UNCITRAL Model Law in 1985 gave impetus to the Indian Parliament to reform the Indian legal regime to meet international standards. The UNCITRAL Model Law itself was drafted because of proposals by

---

149 Tracy S. Work (n 142) 220.

150 Hernando Díaz-Candia, 'Non-Recognition of Kompetenz-Kompetenz in Developing Countries – The Venezuelan Example' (2007) 24 Journal of International Arbitration 25, 26.

151 Amr A. Shalakany, 'Arbitration and the Third World: A Plea for Reassessing Bias under the Specter of Neoliberalism' (2000) 41 Harvard International Law Journal 419, 423.

152 Nicholas Peacock, 'Arbitrating in "Developing" Arbitral Jurisdictions: A Discussion of Common Themes and Challenges Based on Experiences in India and Indonesia' (2010) 13 International Arbitration Law Review 227–228.

153 Tracy S. Work (n 142) 222.

154 Rendeiro (n 12).

155 Courtney Fingar, 'India knocks China from top of FDI league table' Financial Times (20 April 2016) <https://next.ft.com/content/94351bda-0620-11e6-a70d-4e39ac32c284> accessed 22 July 2016.

156 'Foreign Direct Investment Policy of India' <https://www.investindia.gov.in/foreign-direct-investment> accessed 11 July 2021.

157 Dhruv Garg and Utkarsh Srivastava, 'The Unruly Horse Goes Further Astray: Defining "Fundamental Policy of Indian Law" in Arbitral Jurisprudence' [2016] Statute Law Review 1.

158 Amr A. Shalakany (n 151) 427.

the Afro-Asian Legal Consultative Committee (AALCC) to ensure that arbitration was more suited to the needs of developing countries.[159] The Model Law was welcomed as it served as an instrument for harmonization. It was accepted by developing countries as it was a mechanism that could be adopted by states without compromising on their 'public policy' or 'national interest'.[160] It would also greatly facilitate international commerce, as parties did not have to know the arbitration laws of every country before entering into an agreement.[161] It is clear that such a harmonized framework would be attractive for companies planning to invest and would therefore be beneficial to developing countries. This is because, as has been rightly pointed out, developing countries need arbitration even more than developed countries in order to overcome the mistrust in their domestic court system.[162]

The preamble to the IAA mirrors the goal of the UNCITRAL Model Law of having a uniform legal framework for settling disputes arising out of international commercial relations.[163] By enacting the IAA 1996, the Indian legislators sought to unify the pre-existing laws into a single framework and bring the Indian law up to international standards. In fact, the goal of the IAA 1996 was to 'inspire confidence…attract foreign investments and reassure international investors as to the reliability of the Indian legal system to provide an expeditious dispute resolution mechanism'.[164] The pro-arbitration nature of the IAA can be derived from the 1950 Indian Constitution itself. Article 51(c) of the Constitution of India obliges the State to 'foster respect for international law and treaty obligations…and encourage settlement of international disputes by arbitration.'

Despite these legislative moves, Indian courts still used to define the public policy exception in an arbitrary and somewhat broad fashion, which was widely criticized.[165] There was a race between common law countries in Asia to reform

159 M. Sornarajah, 'The UNCITRAL Model Law: A Third World Viewpoint' (1989) 6 Journal of International Arbitration 8.

160 Andrew I. Okekeifere, 'Public Policy and Arbitrability under the UNCITRAL Model Law' (1999) 2 International Arbitration Law Review 70, 70–71.

161 ibid 76–77.

162 Mauro Rubino-Sammartano, 'Developing Countries Vis a Vis International Arbitration' (1996) 13 Journal of International Arbitration 21.

163 See the preamble to the Arbitration and Conciliation Act, 1996, Act No. 26 of 1996.

164 Sarma, Oinam and Angshuman (n 34).

165 Justice A. P. Shah (n 27).

and build confidence in their arbitration laws and thereby attract investment.[166] Indian lawmakers were keen to join this trend and transform the country into a pro-arbitration jurisdiction. With this goal in mind, the legislature decided to statutorily define public policy exception in the IAA(Am.) 2015.[167]

III. The interpretation of the public policy exception by the Indian judiciary

The treatment of the public policy exception under Indian law must be read within the broader context of how Indian courts have looked at arbitration as a whole. This is extremely important as Indian courts bind themselves to the principle of *stare decisis,* i.e., they will only depart from precedent in extraordinary circumstances.[168] Therefore, a decision defining public policy by the Supreme Court usually has long-term implications with regard to the use of the exception in India.

Although Indian courts were initially unfamiliar with arbitration, they have, in time, taken a strong pro-arbitration stance and recognised the importance of arbitration as a means of helping reduce their caseload. The public policy exception has, however, created controversy, as it is one of the only means by which parties have (albeit rarely) been able to successfully convince courts to intervene in arbitral awards.

In the view of the Indian Supreme Court, public policy, although impossible to precisely define, is synonymous with the public interest, and public interest varies from time to time. The Court explained that in the Indian context

> As new concepts take the place of old, transactions which were once considered against public policy are now being upheld by the courts and similarly, where there has been a well-recognized head of public policy, the courts have not shirked from extending it to new transactions and changed circumstances and have at times not even flinched from inventing a new head of public policy.[169]

---

166 Choong Yeow Choy and Warren P. Ganesh, 'Public Policy Considerations in Arbitral Proceedings in Selected Common Law Jurisdictions' (2014) 44 Hong Kong Law Journal 179, 180–182.

167 See, statement of Law Minister of India, D. V. Sadananda Gowda in 'Lok Sabha Debates (Lower House-Indian Parliament), Sixteenth Series, vol. XIV, Sixth Session, 2015/1937 (Saka), No. 16' (n 23).

168 *Shanker Raju vs Union Of India* [2011] Writ Petition Civ No 311 2010 (Supreme Court of India).

169 Central Inland Water Transport Corporation Limited and Anr v Brojo Nath Ganguly and Anr 1986 3 SCC 156 (Supreme Court of India) [95].

This judgment is demonstrative of the changing nature of the exception, and the discretion that courts have used, in the absence of legislative guidance, to determine the scope of the public policy exception. A very arbitration-friendly approach was taken by the court in *PASL,* where it held that courts can no longer create new heads of public policy and must be bound by judicial precedent.[170] While this is an excellent decision and certainly a step in the right direction, it is also demonstrative of the ever-changing approach of Indian courts towards the public policy exception and the recognition of the need for more stability in its application.

In the Indian context, although there has been confusion as to the exact bounds of public policy, it is clear from the Supreme Court that public policy refers solely to the law in force in India, i.e., both federal and state law.[171] The exact bounds of Indian public policy were elaborated by the Supreme Court in the *Renusagar* case and subsequent decisions, which will be looked at below.

1. Interpretation of public policy before the enactment of Indian Arbitration Act 1996

The move by the Indian legislature to restrict the scope of the public policy exception was prompted by decisions of the courts where they demonstrated inconsistency regarding the use of the exception. It cannot be said that Indian courts have always been overly reliant on the public policy exception. There has been much contradiction in the courts' approach over the years. As can be seen, they, at best, have taken a mixed approach with regard to the exception, sometimes broadening and sometimes restricting its scope.

As will be shown below, Indian courts initially started with a pro-enforcement approach. This is in stark contrast to other arbitration-friendly countries where there was an early trend for courts to review awards both on merits and on the law.[172]

170 *PASL Wind Solutions v GE Power Conversion India* [2021] Civ Appeal No 1647 (Supreme Court of India) [80].

171 Lion Engineering Consultants Vs State of Madhya Pradesh & Ors [2018] MANU/SC/0313 (Supreme Court of India) [9].

172 Roman Mikhailovich Khodykin, 'National Court Review of Arbitration Awards: Where Do We Go From Here?', in Stavros L. Brekoulakis, Julian D. M. Lew and Loukas A. Mistelis (eds), *The Evolution and Future of International Arbitration* (Kluwer Law International 2016) para 16.5.

The Indian Supreme Court had early on realized the perils of relying too much on public policy exception and took a strict stance on its use. This can be seen in its *Gherulal* decision in 1959, where the court elaborately reasoned why the exception should rarely be used.[173] In this case, the court held that wagering contracts were not contrary to Indian public policy and must be upheld. It also acknowledged that it is for the legislature to make laws prohibiting illegal contracts and not for courts to engage in 'judicial legislation'.[174] Also, the Supreme Court's ruling in the *Misra* case (1978) is a good example for judicial restraint – here, the court, when relying on common law reasoning, held that public policy is '*a very unsafe, questionable and unreliable ground for judicial decision and courts cannot, but be very cautious to mount this treacherous horse even if they must.*'[175]

The approach of the Court changed in later decisions where it interpreted the exception broadly. For this reason, the legislature had a genuine apprehension that the judiciary would excessively intervene and refuse to enforce awards by giving the public policy exception a broader construction. One such case was the *Brojo Nath* ruling in 1986, where the court held that the general rule of freedom to contract is subject to limitations of public policy and that 'the principles governing public policy must be and are capable, of… expansion'.[176]

The contradictory approaches meant that when it came to unwarranted interference in arbitral awards, Indian courts have sometimes had difficulty in 'striking the right balance between party autonomy and a fair trial'.[177] Parties who are dissatisfied with their foreign arbitral awards have quite often approached Indian courts to resist enforcement on the grounds of the public policy exception.

The first landmark decision of the Indian Supreme Court with regard to the public policy exception in the context of enforcing an arbitral award was the *Rensusagar* case of 1994.[178] The case arose out of an agreement between *Renusagar*, an Indian company and General Electric (GE), a US-based company, for setting up a thermal power plant. The agreement provided New York law as the

---

173 *Gherulal Parekh v Mahadeo Dass Maiya* 1959 Supp 2 SCR 406 (Supreme Court of India).

174 ibid 64.

175 Union Of India v Shri Gopal Chandra Misra And Ors [1978]3SCR12 (Supreme Court of India).

176 Central Inland Water Transport Corporation Limited and Anr v. Brojo Nath Ganguly and Anr. (n 169) para 79.

177 Nair (n 5) 699.

178 Renusagar Power Co Ltd Vs General Electric Company and Anr 1994 Supp1 SCC 644 (Supreme Court of India).

governing law, and the arbitration clause provided Paris as the seat with ICC rules applicable.

A dispute arose, and the arbitral tribunal in its award held that Renusagar must pay compensatory damages in the form of compound interest. Renusagar brought an appeal before the Indian Supreme Court based on the then valid Foreign Awards Act 1961.[179] It claimed that an award for payment of compensatory damages in the form of compound interest amounted to 'damages on damages' and that such an award would enable the unjust enrichment of GE and was therefore contrary to both the public policy both of India and New York.

The Supreme Court laid down a three-pronged test to determine if an award would violate Indian public policy. It ruled that enforcement should be refused on the grounds of the award being contrary to the public policy if such enforcement would be against (i) fundamental policy of Indian law; or (ii) the interests of India; or (iii) justice or morality. In the courts reasoning, a mere violation of legal provisions would not in itself constitute a breach of public policy.[180]

In this case, the Court, in upholding a narrow construction of public policy, relied heavily on European as well as American jurisprudence.[181] It approvingly quoted the US Supreme Court's reasoning in the *Parsons* decision that '*the general pro-enforcement bias informing the Convention...points toward a narrow reading of the public policy defence. An expansive construction of this defence would vitiate the convention's basic effort to remove pre-existing obstacles to enforcement*'.[182]

The *Renusagar* case set the benchmark as to what would constitute sufficient grounds for refusing enforcement of an award on public policy grounds in India. This was a watershed moment, as there was previously no standard for determining what the scope of the exception would be in the Indian context; rather, subordinate courts were free to use their discretion to intervene in foreign awards. However, as India is a common law country, precedence meant that the Supreme Court's decision instantly became binding law. By restricting the scope of public policy exception, the Court laid down a test that would be followed by

179 The Foreign Awards (Recognition and Enforcement) Act, Act No. 45 of 1961.

180 For an analysis of the Supreme Courts reasoning in this case see Aravapalli Krishna Thej, 'An Adieu to the Doctrine of Patent Illegality: A Comment on the Indian Supreme Court's Decision in Shri Lal Mahal Ltd v Progetto Grano' [2014] International Arbitration Law Review 37, 39.

181 Lawrence F. Ebb, 'Reflections on the Indian Enforcement of the GE/Renusagar Award' (1994) 10 Arbitration International 143.

182 Renusagar Power Co. Ltd. Vs. General Electric Company and Anr. (n 178) para 57.

subordinate courts in future decisions[183] and by the legislature when drafting the IAA(Am.) 2015.

2. Subsequent scepticism of the courts towards arbitration

Although the pro-arbitration leaning of the Supreme Court in the *Renusagar* decision was very much appreciated, it did not take much time for the Court to change its approach. In a series of decisions, which can be justifiably described as the dark ages for arbitration in India, the Supreme Court took an approach which Born has been described as being 'contrary to the structure of the New York Convention' and against 'international authority'.[184]

The first of these cases, which is reflective of the negative outlook which the Supreme Court had towards arbitration, is the *Bhatia* decision in 2002.[185] The case arose out of a challenge to an award rendered under ICC rules by a tribunal seated in Paris. In deciding on a challenge, the Court ruled that Part I of the IAA 1996, which had a lower threshold for judicial intervention and normally applied only to domestic arbitration, would also apply to foreign-seated international arbitrations.

The Bhatia decision may have been well-intentioned. It has been suggested that the court only sought to ensure a 'comprehensive arbitration statute' and 'provide a remedy for all arbitrations'.[186] However, it has been widely criticized for setting a precedent encouraging excessive judicial intervention in foreign arbitral awards.[187]

Another decision where the Supreme Court further expanded upon the *Renusagar* benchmark was the *Saw Pipes* case in 2003.[188] The dispute arose out of a contract wherein SAW Pipes Ltd. entered into an agreement to supply pipes to ONGC, an Indian public sector company. ONGC made a reduced payment

183 Lawrence F. Ebb (n 181) 161.

184 Gary B. Born and Suzanne Spears (n 122) 5.

185 Bhatia International v Bulk Trading SA and Anr 2002 4 SCC 105 (Supreme Court of India).

186 Amit M. Sachdeva, 'Unlimited Jurisdiction of the Indian Courts (to Intervene) in International Arbitrations: An Analysis of the Bhatia International Case' (2010) 13 International Arbitration Law Review 73.

187 Anjali Anchayil, 'Bhatia International to Videocon Industries and Tograj Infrastructure: Recasting the Foundations of Arbitration Law in India' (2013) 29 Arbitration International 105.

188 Oil & Natural Gas Corporation Ltd v SAW Pipes Ltd 2003 3 SCR 691 (Supreme Court of India).

to the respondent, citing a delay in supply. This gave rise to a dispute, and arbitration proceedings were subsequently commenced. The subsequent award was challenged by ONGC on the grounds of being contrary to Indian law.

In this case, the Court set aside the arbitral award for being erroneous, contrary to the contract and against Indian law, i.e., an award could be set aside if it was 'patently illegal'.[189] The Supreme Court, however, qualified its decision by saying that for the public policy exception to be invoked, the illegality must go to the 'root of the matter' and not be 'trivial'.[190] It also held that an award could be set aside on public policy grounds if it is 'so unfair and unreasonable that it shocks the conscience of the court.'[191]

The *Saw pipes* case created much uncertainty, as it contradicted the narrow interpretation of public policy given by the court in the *Renusagar* case. Controversially, the Supreme Court reasoned that because the term public policy was vague, it could be construed broadly or narrowly based on the particular circumstances of the case.[192] The decision has been strongly criticized by scholars who argue that it opened the floodgates for awards to be challenged before courts based on the merits.[193] It must be kept in mind, however, that the negative fallout of this decision is limited, as it was given when interpreting Part I of the IAA dealing with domestic awards. The biggest drawback of the decision was that it influenced the Court to broaden the public policy exception. This would mean that in future decisions, the court took a similar hostile approach to arbitration, even in the case of foreign arbitral awards.

The jurisprudence of the Supreme Court in the *Saw Pipes case* was controversially extended to foreign awards in the 2011 *Phulchand* decision.[194] The contract involved the sale of rice grain between an Indian seller and a Russian buyer. As the goods were not delivered on time despite payment, the arbitral tribunal required the seller to pay certain dues back to the buyer. Although the court dismissed sellers challenge to the arbitral award, it observed that public policy in foreign awards should also be given a 'wider meaning' for refusing enforcement of foreign awards and that foreign awards could be refused enforcement if they were patently illegal.[195] Such an approach of having the same threshold for

189 ibid 34.
190 ibid 30.
191 ibid.
192 ibid 15.
193 Aravapalli Krishna Thej (n 180) 40.
194 *Phulchand Exports Ltd v OOO Patriot* 2011 10 SCC 300 (Supreme Court of India).
195 ibid 13.

refusing enforcement of foreign and domestic awards set an unwanted precedent. It empowered courts to engage in expansive judicial intervention and thus came in the way of the emerging arbitration scene in India. The ruling was criticized in the literature. Notably, Kumar, Upadhyay and others characterized the outcome of the decision as being the 'antithesis' of the New York Convention.[196]

The *Venture Global* ruling (2008) was another decision in which the court chose to expand its powers of intervention.[197] The dispute arose out of a shareholders agreement between an American company (Venture Global) and an Indian Company (Satyam). Satyam sought arbitration before an LCIA arbitrator, and an award was made in its favor. Venture Global approached Indian courts to set aside the award on the grounds of the underlying agreement being contrary to Indian law. The Supreme Court ruled that it had the power to set aside foreign awards which are contrary to Indian statute, as they would be against Indian public policy.

The expansive interpretation and inclusion of 'patent illegality' by the court in these judgments came under severe criticism.[198] The decisions cumulatively empowered Indian courts to expand their supervisory role and led to the excessive intervention of the Indian judiciary in foreign seated awards.[199] Furthermore, in these decisions, the court showed its willingness to look into the merits of a foreign arbitral award to see if the award was patently illegal. Such an approach would be similar to the *révision au fond* approach of French courts, where they were able to evaluate if the foreign court properly assessed the law and facts in the case at hand.[200] This approach has long been abandoned in France.[201] These early decisions of the Indian Supreme Court in effect negated the purpose

196 See Ashutosh Kumar, Raina Upadhyay, Anusha Jegadeesh and Yakshay Chheda, 'Interpretation and application of the New York Convention in India', in George A. Bermann (ed), *Recognition and Enforcement of Foreign Arbitral Awards: The Interpretation and Application of the New York Convention by National Courts* (Springer: Berlin, Heidelberg 2017) 473 et seq.

197 Venture Global Engineering v Satyam Computer Services Ltd and Anr 2008 4 SCC 190 (Supreme Court of India).

198 Tushar Kumar Biswas, Introduction to Arbitration in India: The Role of the Judiciary (Kluwer Law International 2014) 117.

199 Jory Canfield, 'Growing Pains and Coming-of-Age: The State of International Arbitration in India' (2014) 14 Pepperdine Dispute Resolution Law Journal 335, 342.

200 Gilles Cuniberti, *Conflict of Laws: A Comparative Approach: Text and Cases* (Edward Elgar Publishing 2017) 308.

201 ibid.

of the IAA 1996, which was to provide for 'speed, cost-effectiveness and certainty' in the resolution of commercial disputes.[202]

3. Recent shift towards a more pro-arbitration approach

Although it is true that Indian courts have in the past harbored scepticism towards arbitration, that scepticism has since given way to a more benign approach. In recent decisions, the Supreme Court has recognised the importance of arbitration in settling international commercial disputes.[203] In a series of rulings, the Court has narrowed the scope of the public policy exception and has consciously moved towards reducing judicial intervention.[204] The *favor arbitrandum* (pro-enforcement) doctrine of the New York Convention can be seen in the recent decisions of the Indian Supreme Court.

The Court took the opportunity to relook its approach towards international arbitration in the year 2012 in its landmark *BALCO* ruling.[205] The dispute arose out of an agreement between an American company, Kaiser Aluminium, and an Indian company, *BALCO*, for the supply of computer-based systems. The agreement contained an arbitration clause, which provided that the seat would be London and disputes would be settled by arbitration pursuant to English law.

A dispute arose regarding the performance of the agreement, and the arbitral tribunal made an award in favor of Kaiser Aluminium. The application by BALCO to set aside the award was rejected. The Supreme Court held that Part I of the IAA 1996 would not have an extraterritorial effect and therefore no longer apply to foreign-seated awards, which would rather exclusively be governed by Part II of the Act. Effectively, the court clarified that a higher threshold would apply for refusing enforcement of foreign awards *vis-à-vis* setting aside domestic awards. The objective of this decision was to shield foreign arbitral awards from excessive interference by domestic courts.[206] Importantly, it set a precedent overruling the controversial *Bhatia* and *Venture Global* decisions.

202 Canfield (n 199) 342.

203 Renusagar Power Co. Ltd. Vs. General Electric Company and Anr. (n 178) para 22.

204 Kartikey Mahajan, 'Reversing the Clock on "Public Policy" for Foreign Awards' (2013) 16(6) International Arbitration Law Review N-43.

205 Bharat Aluminium Company and Ors. Vs. Kaiser Aluminium Technical Service, Inc. and Ors. (n 60).

206 Delphine Constantin, 'India's Amended Arbitration Law: What's New for Foreign Investors?' (2016) 1 International Business Law Journal 41, 43.

This decision heralded a marked shift in the Supreme Court's outlook towards international arbitration and was effectively a step away from the interventionist approach taken by the Court in the past. This ruling meant that in the future, parties would no longer be able to unnecessarily delay enforcement as foreign arbitral awards would be significantly harder to challenge than domestic awards. The ruling was thus welcomed by arbitration practitioners globally. Canfield considered it to signal that India is an arbitration-friendly jurisdiction whose courts are less likely to intervene in foreign awards.[207] According to Born, it was '*a historic event…which marks a turning point in the development of international arbitration*' itself.[208] This decision meant that finally, under Indian law, the 'territoriality' principle would apply, i.e., the law regulating arbitration proceedings would be that of the seat and not Indian law.[209] In effect, the ruling precluded Indian courts from annulling awards in arbitrations having a foreign seat.[210]

The *Lal Mahal* case of 2014 is one more decision where the Supreme Court revaluated its approach towards public policy.[211] The case concerned a dispute arising from a contract between an Indian wheat supplier and an Italian buyer. The claim was regarding allegedly substandard wheat that was supplied. The GAFTA Tribunal seated in London ordered the seller to pay damages. The seller resisted enforcement of the award on the grounds that it violated Indian public policy as it was patently illegal, and the tribunal had gone beyond the terms of the contract agreed by the parties.

The Supreme Court overruled the Phulchand decision and held that refusal of enforcement can only be under the narrow conditions stipulated in the *Renusagar* case. In this decision, the Court differentiated how public policy exception is to be treated in setting aside proceedings under section 34 of the IAA 1996 from how it is to be treated in proceedings for refusing enforcement under section 48 of the Act. It ruled that in case of setting aside proceedings of a domestic award, a wider interpretation can be given, but in case of proceedings to refuse enforcement of a foreign award, the exception must be construed narrowly.[212]

207 Canfield (n 199) 337.
208 Gary B. Born and Suzanne Spears (n 122) 4.
209 K. S. Harisankar, 'Supervisory Jurisdiction of Indian Courts in Foreign Seated Arbitration: The Beginning of a New Era or the End of Bhatia Doctrine' (2013) 3 The Arbitration Brief 56, 61.
210 Gary B. Born and Suzanne Spears (n 122) 4.
211 *Shri Lal Mahal Ltd v Progetto Grano Spa* 2014 2 SCC 433 (Supreme Court of India).
212 ibid 25.

In another recent decision, the *LIC* ruling, the Supreme Court showed its unwillingness to use the exception in contractual matters because public policy is '*always imprecise, difficult to define, and akin to an unruly horse.*'[213] The Court, in this case, borrowed from the famous English decision *Richardson v. Mellish,* where Burrough J described public policy to be akin to a '*very unruly horse... once you get astride it, you never know where it will carry you. It may lead you from the sound law.*'[214]

While the current approach of Indian courts towards arbitration is largely pro-enforcement, the Supreme Court has in the past shown its willingness to suddenly change its approach, from pro-enforcement in Renusagar to expansive intervention in Bhatia and again pro-enforcement in BALCO. The next part will evaluate the factors influencing the approach of Indian courts in their outlook towards international arbitration.

IV. Understanding the outlook of Indian courts

In civil law countries, the law is usually codified, whereas, in common law systems, the decisions of courts play a major role in lawmaking.[215] Traditionally in common law countries, judges are vested with a lot of discretion regarding how they interpret the law. Judicial review also plays an extremely important role in the common law system. Justice Kerr has described it as 'a bulwark against corruption, arbitrariness, bias, improper conduct and...incompetence'.[216]

Although India is a common law country, its courts have gone even further in their 'judicial activism' than English courts. The Indian legal system provides an exceedingly important role to judges. Through precedent, not only do they exercise expansive powers of interpretation, but they also effectively make binding law. Through its activism, the Indian Supreme Court has acquired powers that would otherwise rightfully fall within the domain of the legislature or the executive.[217]

---

213 LIC of India v Insure Policy Plus Services Pvt Ltd and Ors AIR 2016 SC 182 (Supreme Court of India) [15].

214 *Richardson v Mellish* (1824) 2 Bingham 229 (Court of Common Pleas) 252.

215 J. G. Sauveplanne, Codified and Judge Made Law: The Role of Courts and Legislators in Civil and Common Law Systems (North-Holland 1982) 95.

216 Michael Kerr, 'Arbitration and the Courts: The Uncitral Model Law' (1985) 34 The International and Comparative Law Quarterly 1, 15.

217 T. R. Andhyarujina, 'The Unique Judicial Activism of the Supreme Court of India' (2014) 130 Law Quarterly Review 53, 54.

It is possible that the prior decisions of Indian courts that expansively interpreted the public policy exception are reflective of the hesitation of judges to give up their power of oversight and control that they were used to exercising. Due to the important role of judges in the Indian legal system, any study of arbitration law in India will be incomplete without looking at the background underlying the courts' decisions.

1. The traditional role of the courts in the Indian legal system

The approach of Indian courts to the arbitration process can be better understood if it is looked at from the prism of how Indian courts generally look at their role. In most countries, the role of the judges is to adjudicate disputes and apply the law as it stands. The role of the judiciary in the Indian legal system is more expansive than in other countries. Not only does the Indian judge adjudicate, but she also plays the role of an activist.[218] In justifying a broader role for judges than merely applying the law, former Chief Justice of the Indian Supreme Court P. N. Bhagwati has argued that judicial activism in interpreting the law is 'imperative' to 'strengthen democracy' and protect 'basic human rights'.[219]

The Indian judiciary has historically seen itself as a check to legislative excess and apathy. The former, because the duty of courts was to safeguard the fundamental rights from being breached by the legislature or other institutions of the state, the latter because it saw itself as filling in the role when the legislature was too slow in taking action. Because of these reasons, the Indian Supreme Court, unlike courts in other western countries, is vested with enormous power. The Supreme Court has itself acknowledged in its *Raghubir Singh* ruling that its power far exceeds those exercised by English courts and that judicial review exercised by the Indian judiciary is 'the widest and most extensive known to the world of law'.[220]

While judicial activism of courts is mainly aimed at the state, it is natural for the use of such power to trickle into and influence judicial attitudes towards other institutions and areas of law that have a bearing on deciding on the rights

---

218 Shubhankar Dam, 'Lawmaking Beyond Lawmakers: Understanding the Little Right and the Great Wrong (Analyzing the Legitimacy of the Nature of Judicial Lawmaking in India's Constitutional Dynamic)' (2005) 13 Tulane Journal of International and Comparative Law 109.

219 P. N. Bhagwati, 'The Role of the Judiciary in the Democractic Process: Balancing Activism and Judicial Restraint' (1992) 18 Commonwealth Law Bulletin 1262.

220 *Union Of India & Ors vs Raghubir Singh* (1989) 3 SCR 316 (Supreme Court of India).

of parties. The activist role of the Indian judge can also explain why the Indian court would have a leaning towards policy making in defining what constitutes the public policy exception.

2. Legislative contribution to initial judicial hostility towards arbitration

The Indian legislature has a role to play in contributing to increased judicial scepticism. This has to do both with the procedure by which the arbitration law was enacted but also by the way in which the Indian legislature and judiciary interact.

The IAA 1996 was meant to be a pro-arbitration legislation. It brought drastic changes to the arbitration scene in India. So drastic was the statutory shift that it left ineffective decades of past jurisprudence of domestic courts, which were sceptical of arbitration. While the change of law was in and of itself a positive development, the way it was brought about was controversial.[221] Before enacting the law through parliament, the government initially pushed through the law thrice by re-promulgating ordinances rather than the regular legislative route.[222]

The ordinance mechanism is a means provided by Article 123 of the Indian Constitution, empowering the President of India to quickly pass a law where urgent action is required, and Parliament is in recess. This means that there is a lack of necessary parliamentary debates and checks and balances. It is an exception to the usual rule that the legislature and not the executive branch will enact laws. While ordinances have the advantage that they immediately address a pressing need, without the delays of normal parliamentary procedure, they have the downside that the law is not properly debated and scrutinized and is therefore looked at with caution by the courts. The Supreme Court has been disapproving of repeated use of Ordinances rather than the normal legislative route. In the *Krishna Kumar Singh* case, it went so far as to hold that repeat re-promulgation of ordinances amounted to a 'fraud on the constitution'.[223]

Scholars have argued that the lack of debate and engagement, whether with the public or by involving the judiciary in the consultative process, was one of the key reasons for the judiciaries refusal to acknowledge the limits imposed

221 See Harisankar K. Sathyapalan and Aakanksha Kumar, 'India', in Gary F. Bell (ed), *The UNCITRAL Model Law and Asian Arbitration Laws: Implementation and Comparisons* (Cambridge University Press 2018) 30.

222 ibid.

223 Krishna Kumar Singh & Anr vs State Of Bihar & Ors (2017) 2 SCJ 136 (Supreme Court of India).

upon their power by the IAA 1996.[224] This meant that the statute lacked what could have been an effective source of legitimacy. This was also raised during the parliamentary debate preceding the passing of the law by Justice Lodha M. P., who decried the misuse of the ordinance power to pass the law as being 'illegal, insufficient' and a 'misuse of legislative power'.[225]

While there was a reasonable justification for the legislature to act quickly in reforming the arbitration law, more transparency in the process, engagement of the judiciary and following the normal route of lawmaking would have provided more legitimacy to the statute and thereby increased understanding by the courts.

Another reason why Indian courts did not see themselves as bound by legislative approaches to public policy is the traditional power struggle between the Indian legislature and the judiciary. While the Indian parliament has often tried to limit the judiciary's role through statute, the Supreme Court, which considers itself as the guardian of individual rights, has tried to place limits on the ability of the legislative branch to take such measures.[226] It has therefore looked upon any law that restricts its power of intervention with a degree of suspicion. The Indian courts' approach contrasts with the U. S. Supreme Court's approach, which can be seen in the *Missouri K. and T.R. Co.* decision where Justice Holmes also considered the legislature to be 'the ultimate guardian of the liberties of the people'.[227]

Even if Indian courts were to give due consideration to the will of Indian Parliament regarding the public policy exception, this will was not clear when it came to the IAA 1996. If we look at the drafting history of the IAA 1996, while legislators mostly agreed on the need to promote arbitration, some parliamentarians were adamant that this should not come at the cost of protecting public policy. Justice Lodha M. P., for instance, during the debates, cautioned about the need to prevent an arbitrator sitting in another country violating the interest of India, or Indian public policy as enshrined in the provisions of the Indian

224 Sarma, Oinam and Angshuman (n 34).
225 See, Justice Guman Mal Lodha, in 'XI Lok Sabha Debates, Session II, Budget Thursday, August 1, 1996 / Sravana 10, 1918 (Saka)'.
226 Maureen Callahan Vander May, 'The Role of the Judiciary in India's Constitutional Democracy' (1996) 20 Hastings International and Comparative Law Review 104 et seq.
227 *Missouri, K & T Ry Co of Texas v May* (1904) 194 SCt 267 (Supreme Court of the United States) 270.

Constitution.[228] Such discourses in Parliament may have, of course, had an impact on the approach of Indian courts as well.

3. Conflicting approach to judicial powers under Indian civil law

One could also explain the approach of Indian courts towards arbitration proceedings by looking at their normal practice when enforcing foreign judgments under the Indian Code of Civil Procedure (CPC), i.e., the Indian law dealing with civil procedure.[229] India is not a signatory to the 2019 Hague Judgments Convention. Therefore, a more roundabout method applies to the recognition and enforcement of foreign judgments. Section 44A of the CPC provides that an Indian court will execute a decree of a superior court from a reciprocating state like it is a domestic decree. While this may seem like a very straightforward process, very similar to the procedure for enforcement of foreign arbitral awards. The procedure for recognising and enforcing a foreign decree under the CPC is much more cumbersome.

Two important points need to be considered. Firstly, there are only a handful of states considered to be reciprocating territories under the CPC. Secondly, and more importantly, the execution of decrees under the CPC is subject to section 13, which gives vast discretion to courts to refuse recognition or enforcement of foreign judgments in situations such as '*where it has not been given on the merits of the case; where (the judgment is) founded on an incorrect view of international law or a refusal to recognise the law of India; where the proceedings in which judgment was obtained are opposed to natural justice (or) fraud; where (the judgment) sustains a claim founded on a breach of any law in force in India.*'[230]

Although the CPC does not apply to arbitration, it can have a strong effect on the mindset of the judiciary. This is because the same judges have to switch between relying on the CPC when enforcing foreign judgments and the IAA when enforcing arbitral awards. While the use of CPC is an everyday task for a judge, challenges to arbitral awards before courts are relatively rare. For these reasons, it is not unthinkable that Indian judges are influenced by the rationale of the CPC when dealing with arbitral awards. This risk may be even greater given the importance given to the CPC under the Indian legal system.

---

228 See, Justice Guman Mal Lodha, in 'XI Lok Sabha Debates, Session II, Budget Thursday, August 1, 1996 / Sravana 10, 1918 (Saka)' (n 225).

229 The Code Of Civil Procedure (Act No 5 of 1908).

230 See Section 13, ibid.

4. Foreign influences on the judicial interpretation of public policy

The approach of Indian courts to public policy did not develop in a vacuum and therefore cannot be looked at in isolation. Indian jurisprudence has long been influenced both by the decisions of foreign courts, as well as the works of foreign scholars. The willingness of Indian courts to rely on foreign material is in contrast to that of the United States, where it is controversial, i.e., welcomed by liberal justices such as Ginsburg but repelled by conservative judges such as Scalia.[231]

This dialogue between legal systems is especially important in an area such as arbitration, which has developed at the international level and that is so dependent on the cooperation of courts in different countries. The ILA, in its report, strongly recommended that in determining the scope of public policy, judges need to take account of decisions of courts in other jurisdictions.[232] The reliance of courts on foreign sources is justifiable because underpinning values such as respect for human dignity and fundamental rights are common to most legal systems.[233] A study of the interpretation of public policy by Indian courts will be incomplete without studying how the court has been influenced by foreign decisions.

This approach of the Indian judiciary is especially noticeable in the *Ayyasamy* decision of the Indian Supreme Court, where it ruled that Indian courts must interpret the IAA in a way that is 'consistent with prevailing approaches in the common law world'.[234] Similarly, in its *Enercon* ruling, the Supreme Court based its pro-arbitration approach on the two 'principles recognised in most (especially Model Law) jurisdictions', i.e., *principle of least intervention* and the principle of maximum judicial *support of arbitration*.[235]

---

231 Stephen Yeazell, 'When and How US Courts Should Cite Foreign Law' (2009) 26 Constitutional Commentary 59.

232 See Recommendation 1(g), in Pierre Mayer and Audley Sheppard, 'Final ILA Report on Public Policy as a Bar to Enforcement of International Arbitral Awards' (2003) 19 Arbitration International 249, 257.

233 Michel Bastarache, 'How Internationalization of the Law Has Materialized in Canada' (2009) 59 University of New Brunswick Law Journal 190.

234 *A Ayyasamy v A Paramasivam & Ors* 2016 10 SCC 386 (Supreme Court of India) [43].

235 *Enercon (India) Ltd and Ors Vs Enercon GMBH and Anr* [2014] Civ Appeal No 2086 (Supreme Court of India) [84].

Indian courts enjoy a broad leeway in using foreign authorities, especially from common law countries, to support their decisions. However, although these foreign sources are *de jure* not considered to be binding by Indian courts and are given persuasive or aspirational value,[236] they are in practice very important and form the basis for many decisions of the Supreme Court in relation to the public policy exception.

(a) Influence of foreign courts

Courts in common law countries are quite willing to use comparative jurisprudence when it comes to arbitration law.[237] This is also true with regard to the Indian Supreme Court. With over 300 years of British rule, Indian law in many areas takes its roots from English law. Therefore, it is not surprising that Indian courts, when coming to their decisions, carefully examine how English courts deal with the particular legal issue. This approach can be seen right from the first major decisions.

In *Gherulal Parekh,* for instance, the Indian Supreme Court based its narrow reading of the public policy exception on the reasoning provided for in English case *Egerton v. Brownlow,* where the House of Lords argued that the public good was for the legislature to determine, and cautioned about the dangers of excessive use of the public policy exception by courts.[238] The court, in this case, placed much weight on the common law of England and the decisions of Lord Atkins and other law Lords in giving public policy a narrow construction. It found such a delimitation of public policy to be reflective of the modern understanding fit for the needs of current times.[239] It upheld an award arising out of a wagering contract because such contracts would not contravene public policy under 'the common law of England and that of India.'[240]

---

236 Adam M. Smith, 'Making Itself a Home – Understanding Foreign Law in Domestic Jurisprudence: The Indian Case' (2006) 24 Berkeley Journal of International Law 218, 265.

237 Stacie I. Strong, 'Legal Authorities and Comparative Law in International Commercial Arbitration: Best Practices versus Empirically Determined Actual Practices' 19 <https://papers.ssrn.com/sol3/papers.cfm?abstract_id=3452332> accessed 5 January 2019.

238 Gherulal Parekh v. Mahadeo Dass Maiya (n 173) para 48.

239 ibid 55.

240 ibid 64.

Indian courts, in reaching their decisions, also rely heavily on American jurisprudence and authorities.[241] The borrowing of concepts such as 'fundamental rights' and 'judicial review' under Indian law has 'Americanized' the Indian legal system.[242] In the landmark *Renusagar* case, the Indian Supreme Court, in deciding to give the public policy a narrow construction, relied on the narrow interpretation given by the New York Court of Appeals in *Loucks v. Standard Oil.*[243] In this case Cardozo, J had strongly argued against judges whimsically refusing enforcement based on 'individual notions of expediency and fairness'.[244]

The Supreme Court has also occasionally relied on jurisprudence from other common law countries.[245] For instance, in the Renusagar decision, the court held that 'interest on interest' or 'compound interest' awarded by the arbitral tribunal would not breach Indian public policy. It supported its ruling by referring to a similar approach taken by the Canadian Federal Court in *Algonquin v. Dart Industries (1987).*[246]

It is notable that the Supreme Court relied upon foreign decisions only when it sought to give public policy a narrow construction. In decisions where the Indian Supreme Court increased its use of the exception or gave the public policy a broad construction, it has usually not made reference to foreign case law. In most such decisions, the court looked inwards and based its expansive approach to public policy either on binding precedent or on the facts and circumstances of the case. This can be seen in the *Saw Pipes* case, where the court relied on its own reasoning in the *Brojo Nath* ruling, where public policy was broadly construed.[247] A similar approach was also taken in the *Venture Global* ruling, as well as the *Phulchand* decision. There are, however, exceptions, notably the *Brojo Nath* decision, where the Supreme Court justified the reliance on public policy

---

241 K. G. Balakrishnan, 'The Role of Foreign Precedents in a Country's Legal System' (2010) 22 National Law School of India Review 1, 7.

242 Adam M. Smith (n 236) 233.

243 Renusagar Power Co. Ltd. Vs. General Electric Company and Anr. (n 178) para 51.

244 *Loucks v Standard Oil Co of New York* (1918) 224 NY 99 (Court of Appeals of New York) 111.

245 Krishan S. Nehra, 'The Impact of Foreign Law on Domestic Judgments (Country Note-India)' (The Law Library of Congress, Global Legal Research Center 2010) 47 <https://www.loc.gov/law/help/domestic-judgment/impact-of-foreign-law.pdf> accessed 5 November 2017.

246 Renusagar Power Co. Ltd. Vs. General Electric Company and Anr. (n 178) para 85.

247 Oil & Natural Gas Corporation Ltd v. SAW Pipes Ltd (n 188) para 16.

by citing Lord Denning in the *Enderby* ruling,[248] where it was held that 'with a good man on the saddle' the unruly horse (public policy) 'can be controlled and jump obstacles'.[249]

Indian courts have preferred to base their understanding of public policy on a combination of domestic case law and Anglo-American jurisprudence. In contrast, the rulings of judges in civil law jurisdictions have not had a similar impact on their Indian counterparts. There are two possible reasons for this. First, judges generally tend to rely on sources from countries with similar legal systems due to what Professor Strong has described as an unconscious bias.[250] Second, Indian judges can find more comfort in the extensive explanations to the reasoning behind decisions that are provided in common law decisions. Courts in civil law countries such as France prefer to give basic reasoning and find detailed explanations in judgments counterproductive.[251] This makes it more difficult to justify to the Indian reader the reliance placed on such decisions.

(b) *Influence of foreign literature*

The Indian Supreme Court's elaboration of public policy is often based not only on binding precedent and the specific facts and circumstances of the case at hand but also increasingly on scholarly literature. While Indian literature has an important place in shaping the Court's understanding, Indian judges are not averse to relying on foreign literature as well. This is especially true in the field of international arbitration. Due to the fact that Indian law is shaped so extensively by English law, the Supreme Court has predominantly relied on the works of English scholars in coming to its understanding of public policy.

The use of literature in judicial reasoning is a useful development. Bell has argued that the use of comparative literature by judges is more effective than relying on foreign judgments, as it provides a more balanced and objective analysis of foreign law.[252] Furthermore, there is more scope for providing detailed consideration of the issues in scholarly literature, as authors are not bound by the

248 Central Inland Water Transport Corporation Limited and Anr v. Brojo Nath Ganguly and Anr. (n 169) para 95.

249 Enderby Town Football Club Ltd v The Football Association Ltd (1971) 1 Ch 591 (Court of Appeal).

250 Stacie I. Strong (n 237) 34.

251 John Bell, 'Researching Globalisation: Lessons from Judicial Citations' (2014) 3 Cambridge Journal of International and Comparative Law 961, 968–969.

252 ibid 972.

same constraints and time considerations as judges in court, who would rather quickly get to the point. In fact, the civil law approach is to not rely on foreign judgments directly unless they have already been extensively discussed in scholarly literature.[253]

The Indian Supreme Court has relied on foreign literature mainly in three instances. Firstly, the use of literature specific to the foreign country has helped the court in better understanding the treatment of public policy, the limits of judicial intervention or other aspects of the foreign legal system. This can be seen in the Supreme Court's early elaboration of the public policy exception in the *Gherulal Parekh* ruling where the court approvingly cited *Cheshire and Fifoot, Ansons Law of Contract* and *Halsbury's laws of England* to reach its conclusion that public policy varies from time to time, but must be used sparingly.[254]

Secondly, the study of foreign literature helps the court in understanding specific issues in arbitration law. For instance, in the *Renusagar* decision, the court ruled that the IAA does not allow a party to impeach an award on merits. It based its findings on the interpretation of the New York convention in important authorities such as *van den Berg* and *Redfern & Hunter*.[255] Similarly, in its *BALCO* ruling, the court mainly relied on the works of practitioners such as *Born* to help its understanding of how the New York Convention delineates the powers of annulment of awards to courts at the seat.[256]

Thirdly, to help understand the conflicts of law approach to 'public policy'. In *Renusagar*, when justifying its position not to intervene, the court relied on scholarly literature such as *Dicey and Morison on Conflict of laws*.[257] The court also came to its conclusion that public policy would only mean 'public policy of India', by referring to the interpretation of the UK Arbitration Act in what it referred to as 'authoritative textbooks' such as *Russel on Arbitration* and *Dicey and Morris*, where it was held that public policy would only refer to 'English' public policy.[258]

253 ibid.
254 Gherulal Parekh v. Mahadeo Dass Maiya (n 173) paras 44–46.
255 Renusagar Power Co. Ltd. Vs. General Electric Company and Anr. (n 178) para 35.
256 Bharat Aluminium Company and Ors. Vs. Kaiser Aluminium Technical Service, Inc. and Ors. (n 60) para 149.
257 Renusagar Power Co. Ltd. Vs. General Electric Company and Anr. (n 178) para 32.
258 Renusagar Power Co. Ltd. Vs. General Electric Company and Anr. (n 178).

(c) Analysis

As the notion of public policy under the IAA refers to 'Indian public policy' rather than foreign public policy, one can question the appropriateness of Indian judges relying on foreign authorities. After all, the understanding of public policy in a foreign country would be based on the particularities of its own legal system, which includes socio-cultural and economic developments. It is uncertain if the judge when relying on the foreign understanding of public policy is aware of the context underlying its elaboration in the foreign legal system. Justice Thomas mirrored these concerns in *Foster v Florida* where he argued that it is not for US courts to impose *'foreign moods, fads, or fashions on Americans'*.[259]

The above argument, however, does not take into consideration the international nature of commercial arbitration. The principles underlying international arbitration are today more or less 'globalized'. As the IAA is largely based on the UNCITRAL Model law and India is a party to the New York Convention, it is obvious that Indian courts would give effect to the 'narrow' view of public policy envisioned by the drafters of these instruments. This viewpoint is supported by Bachand, who argues that when a jurisdiction is prepared to promote arbitration by signing the abovementioned instruments, then it is, of course, justifiable for courts in this country to take recourse to international solutions when there is a void in local law.[260]

Justice Ginsburg has spoken of the need for 'comparative dialogue – on sharing and learning' from the experiences of different jurisdictions.[261] Such dialogue can help in finding a common solution to the shared problem of narrowing down the exception. Even Justice Alito, generally a conservative judge of the U. S. Supreme Court, found that using foreign law justifiable in certain situations. Although he held that reliance on foreign law would be unconstitutional, 'undermining democracy' and 'impractical' when used to interpret constitutional provisions, he acknowledged that it could be useful and legitimate in interpreting an international treaty signed by many states.[262] Similarly, Justice Scalia acknowledged that

---

259 *Foster v Florida* (2002) 537 US 990 (Supreme Court of the United States).

260 Frederic Bachand, 'Court Intervention in International Arbitration: The Case for Compulsory Judicial Internationalism Symposium' (2012) 2012 Journal of Dispute Resolution 83, 84.

261 Ruth Bader Ginsburg, '"A Decent Respect to the Opinions of [Human]Kind": The Value of a Comparative Perspective in Constitutional Adjudication' (2005) 64 Cambridge Law Journal 578.

262 'Confirmation Hearing on the Nomination of Samuel A. Alito, Jr. to Be an Associate Justice of the Supreme Court of the United States: Hearing before the Committee on

if the foreign judgment helps in interpreting a US statute that is in furtherance of an international treaty, it would be relevant.[263] This is true regarding the New York Convention. Indian judges have mostly placed reliance on decisions of English and American courts. Despite both these countries not adopting the Model Law, such reliance is justifiable as both these jurisdictions have predominantly given effect to the objectives of the New York Convention.

Furthermore, one needs to look at how foreign sources are used by Indian judges. There are different ways in which the decisions of foreign courts can influence a judge.[264] The first approach is for the judge to use a foreign decision as a binding/authoritative reason for reaching his conclusion. Such an approach would be ill-advised, given the varying nature of public policy across jurisdictions. Justice Scalia has urged that courts should stop using 'foreigners' views as…basis of its decisions'.[265] Indian courts certainly do not take such an approach.

Under the second approach, the judge may not feel bound by the foreign judgment but would consider it when making a decision. Such an approach where foreign sources play only an advisory role would help in dispelling arguments grounded in sovereignty.[266] Indian courts predominantly take this approach when dealing with how foreign sources approach the public policy exception. There is much to be learned from the use of foreign sources. Justice Ginsburg has pointed out that by using foreign sources without relying on them as binding precedence, it is possible to *'learn from the experience and good thinking'* of foreign jurists.[267] In her view, although one must keep in mind the different contexts, foreign sources would provide a 'store of knowledge' that could be used to find solutions to difficult problems.[268] In practice, by using foreign sources, but not blindly, the Indian judge is able to tailor a solution that has been successfully

---

the Judiciary, United States Senate' 370 <https://www.govinfo.gov/content/pkg/GPO-CHRG-ALITO/pdf/GPO-CHRG-ALITO.pdf> accessed 12 September 2019.

263 Antonin Scalia, 'Keynote Address: Foreign Legal Authority in the Federal Courts' (2004) 98 American Society of International Law Proceedings 305.

264 For a detailed elaboration on how foreign decisions can influence national courts see, John Bell (n 251) 967 et seq.

265 *Roper v Simmons* (2005) 543 US 551 (US Supreme Court).

266 Jeremy Waldron, 'The Experience and Good Thinking Foreign Sources May Convey: Justice Ginsburg and the Use of Foreign Law' (2011) 63 Hastings Law Journal 1243, 1247.

267 Ruth Bader Ginsburg (n 261) 580.

268 ibid.

used in a foreign country to the Indian context. It may also reduce the likelihood of the incorrect application of a foreign concept.

There is, however, an inherent danger to the use of foreign sources. A judge may only use foreign authorities that support a decision he has already reached while ignoring other jurisprudence. For instance, if the court would like to interpret public policy broadly, the judge will only rely on literature that furthers such an approach. This may lead to skewed or harmful results.

Surprisingly, much emphasis is given to British and American sources, and sources closer to home are often ignored. This 'cherry-picking' may seem rather unusual as Indian law can gain valuable insights from authorities from other Asian countries such as Singapore and Hong Kong, which have been successful in developing their arbitration regimes. Such an approach is also questionable because, unlike the IAA, neither the United States FAA nor the UK Arbitration Act are adaptions of the Model Law. In any case, to get a better understanding of what drives Indian courts to act the way in which it does, it is important to look at the approach of courts in different jurisdictions. This will be the focus of the next chapter.

Chapter 3: An overview of how the Indian approach to public policy compares with other jurisdictions

I. The rationale for a comparative approach

Every country with an arbitration regime that is a party to the New York Convention is obliged to facilitate enforcement of foreign arbitral awards. The same legal problem, therefore, arises across states as to when enforcement is to be limited. Given that most legal systems provide the public policy exception as a ground for resisting enforcement of arbitral awards, but approaches vary considerably across jurisdictions, a comparative analysis can prove valuable. Such a comparative approach is important as it helps in learning lessons from the success or shortcomings in the way different jurisdictions address the same problem of defining public policy. It can help throw light on possible solutions to a given legal problem where national law fails to do so.[269] Although, as seen in the previous chapter, the Indian approach has been influenced by that of other jurisdictions, there has sometimes been a divergence. This chapter will look at where the Indian approach converges and where it differs from that of other jurisdictions.

This chapter will compare how the legislative framework and judicial attitudes towards arbitration and public policy evolved in India *vis-à-vis* other major common law and civil law jurisdictions. This evolution of legal practice is important, as pointed out by Justice Oliver Wendell Holmes Jr. of the U. S. Supreme Court in his seminal work in 1881, 'to know what the law is, one must know what the law has been'.[270] Both approaches of common law regimes such as the United States, England and practices in major civil law regimes such as France and Germany will be evaluated. Finally, this part will provide an analysis of lessons to be learnt from the comparison.

---

269 Frederic Bachand (n 260) 83.

270 Oliver Wendell Holmes, Jr., *The Common Law* (Paulo J. S. Pereira and Diego M. Beltran eds, University of Toronto Law School Typographical Society 2011) 37.

II. Comparison with specific common law jurisdictions

The Indian approach to public policy has been heavily influenced by legal developments in other common law countries. The approach of courts in common law jurisdictions, as described by the U. S. Supreme Court in *Kulukundis*, was initially characterized by significant jealousy (of the powers of arbitral tribunals) and the need for preserving their jurisdiction.[271] As will be seen, this approach subsequently gave way to a much more liberal pro-arbitration approach. Such a pendulum-like approach towards arbitration can also be reflected in the development of arbitration in India.

1. The English approach to public policy

(a) Evolution of doctrine

Arbitration evolved early, both in the east and the west. We have previously seen how an early form of arbitration evolved to settle commercial disputes in ancient India;[272] similarly, arbitration in the British Isles dates back to when it was a part of the Roman Empire, where it was used to resolve conflicts arising between international traders conducting business between different states.[273] A notable dispute in Roman Britain was between members of the early Church, where Constantine himself is said to have arbitrated.[274] Just like Britain was later to gift its arbitration culture and laws to India, the United States, and other colonies, Britain itself was a beneficiary of Roman arbitration culture as a colony of the Roman Empire.[275] Despite this early head start, the move towards arbitration

---

271 Kulukundis Shipping Co v Amtorg Trading Corp 126 F2d 978 985.

272 For an elaboration on the historic evolution of arbitration in the Indian context see Chapter 2(II)i

273 J. Martin Hunter, 'Arbitration Procedure in England: Past, Present and Future' (1985) 1 Arbitration International 82.

274 B. G. Abrahams, 'The Origins of Arbitration in Britain' (1988) 54 Arbitration 263; For an interesting elaboration of the time of Emperor Constantine in Roman Britain especially York see also, John B. Firth, *Constantine the Great, The Reorganisation of the Empire and the Triumph of the Church* (H. W. Charless Davis ed, G P Putnam's Sons 1905) 258 <https://tile.loc.gov/storage-services/public/gdcmassbookdig/constantinegreat01firt/constantinegreat01firt.pdf> accessed 28 January 2023.

275 Derek Roebuck, 'Bricks Without Straw: Arbitration in Roman Britain' (2007) 23 Arbitration International 143, 149.

in England came to a grinding halt during the dark ages when trade declined[276] and was only revived during the middle ages.[277]

The doctrine of public policy in commercial arbitration has also been long in use in English law – its evolution has been extensively dealt with in Chapter 1.[278] Despite its common law heritage, it is natural for differences to exist in the approach of Indian and English courts toward public policy. This could be attributed to differences in how the law evolved. While the Indian approach to arbitration and the public policy exception has been heavily influenced by other legal systems,[279] the English approach, in contrast, apart from early Roman culture, has evolved largely independently from foreign influences. This aversion to foreign influence characteristic to both the English and the American legal systems is demonstrable in how both states were initially reluctant to join the New York Convention 1958 and did not model their arbitration statutes on the UNCITRAL model law. Steyn argues that the reason for the English reluctance was a strong 'antipathy' towards multilateral instruments and a firm belief that 'purity of common law' is more important than promoting international commerce.[280] In a more recent context, this antipathy was clearly visible in the context of Brexit, where one of the key arguments made by Brexiteers was that the UK would no longer be bound by EU law but rather could take "control" of its law.[281] Such antipathy to foreign influences was absent in the Indian context. In fact, the opposite situation prevailed.

(b) *Legislative framework*

Both India and the UK are composed of a union of different states/territories. While the IAA applies to the whole of India, arbitration law in the UK is more fragmented, with the UK Arbitration Act applying to England, Wales and Northern Ireland, with Scotland having its own separate arbitration law.

---

276 J. Martin Hunter (n 273) 82.

277 Edward Powell, 'Settlement of Disputes by Arbitration in Fifteenth-Century England' (1984) 2 Law and History Review 21, 25.

278 See supra Chapter 1(III)1.

279 See Chapter 2(4).

280 Johan Steyn, 'England's Response to the UNCITRAL Model Law of Arbitration' (1994) 10 Arbitration International 1, 2.

281 For an elaboration of the narrative leading to Brexit see, Tim Oliver, 'The World after Brexit: From British Referendum to Global Adventure' [2016] International Politics 689.

Despite its early existence, arbitration was only formalized in English statute with the enactment of the 1698 Arbitration Act. This early enactment also kept in mind public policy considerations by providing that if the arbitration is found to be tainted by 'corruption or by undue means', it shall be void and would be set aside by a court.[282] In Scotland, too, the 1695 Articles of Regulation provided for appeals to courts if the tribunal engaged in corruption, bribery falsehood.[283]

Eventually, at the onset of the 19th century, due to increased competition and conflict between courts and arbitration, the interpretation of the public policy exception by English courts expanded, and parties to a dispute were not precluded from approaching courts despite the existence of an agreement to arbitrate.[284]

The legislative move towards encouraging arbitration only started with the enactment of the Common Law Procedure Act of 1854.[285] Almost every arbitration statute that came after was a step closer towards facilitating arbitration. In fact, the 1889 Arbitration Act did not make mention of the public policy exception. Rather, it provided a more general test in section 11 for setting aside an award in case of misconduct by the arbitrator or irregularities in the arbitration proceedings or in obtaining the award. It was only the Arbitration (Foreign Awards) Act of 1930, which provided under section 3 for refusing enforcement in case of contravention of English public policy. Subsequent laws have carried forward the same approach. This is in contrast to the Indian statute, where the public policy exception was not provided for in early legislation such as the Indian Arbitration (Central Government) Act of 1940 but only introduced later on.

Although the public policy exception has been provided for under English law, the scope of the exception has never been a definite concept. It has been asserted that the notion of public policy under English law covers a 'multitude of sins, varying in their degree of turpitude'.[286] The judicial interpretation was

282 See 'William III, 1697-8: An Act for determining Differences by Arbitration. [Chapter XV. Rot.Parl. 9 Gul. III.p.3. n.5]', in John Raithby (ed), *Statutes of the Realm: 1695–1701*, vol 7 (1820) 369–370 <http://www.british-history.ac.uk/statutes-realm/vol7/pp369-370> accessed 13 January 2021.

283 Hew R. Dundas, 'The Arbitration (Scotland) Act 2010: Converting Vision into Reality' (2010) 76 Arbitration: The International Journal of Arbitration, Mediation and Dispute Management (Chartered Institute of Arbitrators, Sweet & Maxwell) 2, 4.

284 J. Martin Hunter (n 273) 84.

285 ibid.

286 Torremans and Fawcett (n 71) 133.

succinctly elucidated by Lord Truro when he interpreted public policy to be the principle that no person can do something 'injurious to the public.'[287]

The United Kingdom acceded to the New York Convention only in 1975, much later than India. While both the current Indian and the English arbitration laws' were drafted in the same year, 1996, they are some notable differences. India bases its law on the UNCITRAL Model law, whereas England does not. The equivalent to section 48 of the IAA can be found in section 103(3) of the UK Arbitration Act[288] and section 20(4) of the Arbitration (Scotland) Act 2010. According to this provision, '*recognition or enforcement of the award may also be refused ... if it would be contrary to public policy to recognise or enforce the award.*' Unlike the IAA, the scope of the public policy exception has not been defined under the UK Act or the Scotland Act. The English approach is seen in the *Deutsche Schachtbau* decision of the House of Lords, where it was held that it is not possible to define public policy exhaustively.[289] Instead, in line with common law practice, its interpretation has been left to the courts.

The reason for the different approach taken in the UK could be that the circumstances that existed in India, which gave rise to the need for a statutory definition, were not prevalent in the UK. In recent times, there have not been grounds to fear excessive judicial intervention or judges creatively interpreting and expanding on the scope of the public policy exception. It has been argued that English judges are unable to create new categories of public policy because their hands are tied by the need to strictly follow judicial precedent.[290] In contrast, although Indian courts follow judicial precedent and the common law system, judicial activism is not uncommon.

(c) *Judicial attitudes*

It is possible that the initial scepticism of the Indian judiciary towards the arbitral process was rooted in the early scepticism of foreign courts such as in England towards arbitration. Just like in India, English courts were also initially sceptical of giving layman arbitrators too much power. English jurists questioned how a

287 Egerton v. Brownlow (n 57) 437.

288 Arbitration Act 1996 (Chapter 23).

289 Deutsche Schachtbau-und Tiefbohr-Gesellschaft MBH v Shell International Petroleum Co Ltd [1990] 1 AC 295 (House of Lords) 316.

290 For an elaboration on this school of thought see, Stavros Brekoulakis, 'The Evolution of Public Policy and Judicial Function in English Law' (2019) 10 Journal of International Dispute Settlement 475 et seq.

'layman can be expected to act as a judge' and considered such notions to be 'absurd'.[291] Even at the time of the drafting of the UNCITRAL Model Law, the delegation of the United Kingdom was worried that a narrow construction of public policy would lead to a party being unable to safeguard itself in the face of 'serious procedural injustice'.[292] In fact until the second half of the 19th-century arbitration agreements were considered incapable of enforcement, as they were thought to oust the jurisdiction of the courts.[293] This was a consequence of the doctrine of revocability, laid down in the early decision *Kill v. Hollister*,[294] whereby parties could always revoke consent to arbitration and instead approach local courts.

There has, however, been a sea change in the approach of English courts. In recent times they have demonstrated their lack of willingness to rely on the public policy exception to refuse enforcement of arbitral awards,[295] so much so that it was said that 'there is no case in which this exception has been applied by an English court'.[296] This is despite the fact that the UK Arbitration Act was not based on the UNCITRAL Model Law but only cognizant of it.[297] In fact, in England, applying a 'pro-enforcement bias' is itself considered to be an essential part of public policy.[298]

The finality of arbitral awards forms an essential public policy under English law.[299] This principle applies not only in arbitration and is based on the belief that no one should have to litigate the same cause of action twice.[300] The

291 F. A. Mann, 'Private Arbitration and Public Policy' (1985) 10 Holdsworth L. Rev. 11.

292 'UNCITRAL, 18th Session, Analytical Compilation of Comments by Governments and International Organizations on the Draft Text of a Model Law on International Commercial Arbitration – Report of the Secretary General (Addendum 2)' (1985) A/CN.9/263/Add.2 10.

293 Adam Samuel, 'Separability of Arbitration Clauses – Some Awkward Questions about the Law on Contracts, Conflict of Laws and the Administration of Justice' (2009) 9 Arbitration and Dispute Resolution Law Journal 36 et seq.

294 *Kill v Hollister* (1746) 95 ER 532 (Court of King's Bench).

295 Blackaby and others (n 72) para 11.106.

296 Michael Kerr, 'Concord and Conflict in International Arbitration' 13 Arbitration International 121.

297 See Louis Flannery, 'The English Statutory Framework', in Julian D. M. Lew and others (eds), *Arbitration in England: With Chapters on Scotland and Ireland* (Kluwer Law International 2013) para 11-2.

298 Blackaby and others (n 72) para 11.107.

299 Jacob B. van de Velden, Finality in Litigation: The Law and Practice of Preclusion: Res Judicata (Merger and Estoppel), Abuse of Process and Recognition of Foreign Judgments (Kluwer Law International 2017) 26.

300 ibid.

importance of finality automatically means that courts are less willing to refuse enforcement of awards and that public policy under English law should be narrowly construed.

In England, courts are precluded from going into the merits of the case on the grounds of mistake of law or fact by the arbitrator.[301] This approach has been echoed by the Indian legislature in section 48 of the IAA(Am.) 2015. The approach of the English courts has been elucidated by Justice Moore-Bick in the High Court decision of *Tongyuan* where he held that *'there is a very strong public policy consideration in favour of enforcing awards, ... it would require a very strong and unusual case'* to treat the enforcement of award as being *'contrary to public policy.'*[302]

As in the Indian context, English courts have refrained from using international/transnational public policy. They have interpreted the applicable public policy to be that of England.[303] However, the public policy exception would also be applicable if the enforcement of the award leads to a breach of the UK's international obligations, which previously included EU Law.[304] While it is unlikely that English courts will give weight to European public policy post-Brexit, enforcement under English law may nevertheless be denied on public policy grounds if the contract seeks to violate the law of a 'friendly foreign state'.[305]

English courts have been consistent in giving the public policy a restrictive interpretation. The threshold which they have laid down for refusing enforcement of an award based on the public policy exception is very high.[306] This has been elaborated on by Gross J in the *IPCO* case, where he held that public policy, in resisting enforcement, must *'be approached with extreme caution'*. The court also held that the exception must not be construed as an open-ended escape route

301 Lord Collins and others (eds), *Dicey, Morris and Collins on the Conflict of Laws*, vol 1 (15th edn, Sweet & Maxwell/Thomson Reuters 2012) paras 16–137.

302 See, 'UK No. 58, Tongyuan (USA) International Trading Group v. Uni-Clan Limited, High Court of Justice, Queen's Bench Division (Commercial Court), 19 January 2001', in Albert Jan van den Berg (ed), *Yearbook Commercial Arbitration*, vol 26 (Kluwer Law International 2001) 886–892.

303 Craig Tevendale and Andrew Cannon, 'Enforcement of Awards' in Lew and others (n 297) para 26–70.

304 Ibid.

305 Lord Collins and others (n 301) 16–150.

306 Maxi Scherer, 'IBA Subcommittee on Recognition and Enforcement of Arbitral Awards, the Public Policy Exception under Article V(2)(b) – Methodological Approaches Country Report England' (2014).

for refusing New York Convention awards. [307] According to this approach, English courts would not go into the merits, and they have applied the public policy exception only rarely and on a case-by-case basis.[308] The exception would come into play when there is 'unconscionable or reprehensible conduct'.[309]

Different approaches have been taken in India and in England with regard to what is considered to be a violation of public policy. A good example would be whether illegality would be a ground for refusing the enforcement of an award. In the past, Indian courts were not averse to refusing enforcement of a foreign arbitral award in case of patent illegality.[310] This was heavily criticized as it was thought that such an approach led to judicial overreach in the arbitral process.[311] The legislature, when drafting the IAA(Am.) 2015, therefore, excluded 'patent illegality' from the scope of the public policy exception. This means that Indian courts are precluded from refusing enforcement of foreign awards on this ground. According to the Act, the public policy exception is not usually breached if the underlying contract violates public policy unless enforcing an award based on the contract would go against the fundamental policy of Indian law.

The position of law in India is surprisingly more restrictive than that of other civil and common law countries where illegality would be a ground for refusing enforcement. In fact, the breach of public policy due to the illegality of contract is among the most commonly used grounds for English courts to refuse enforcement of arbitral awards.[312] This is notably seen in the *Soleimany* decision, where the Court of Appeal ruled that it would be against public policy to enforce an award based on an illegal contract to smuggle carpets out of Iran.[313]

Under English law, however, it is important to consider which jurisdiction's laws have been violated. Where the underlying contract is illegal under the law of the place of performance, an award based on such a contract can still be enforced in England so long as it is legal according to the applicable law and the law of the

307 *IPCO (Nigeria) Ltd v Nigerian National Petroleum Corp* 2005 EWHC 726 Comm (High Court Of Justice, Queens Bench Division, Commercial Court) para 13.

308 Scherer (n 306) 5.

309 *Protech Projects Construction (Pty) Ltd v Mohammed Abdulmohsin Al-Kharafi* [2005] APPLR 1014 (High Court of Justice (Queens Bench Division)) [29].

310 Phulchand Exports Ltd v. OOO Patriot (n 194).

311 For a more detailed elaboration see Chapter 2(III)2.

312 Craig Tevendale and Andrew Cannon, 'Enforcement of Awards' in Lew and others (n 297) para 26–72.

313 *Soleimany v Soleimany* 1999 QB 785 (Queens Bench).

seat.[314] Before refusing enforcement, English courts are required to evaluate the nature and extent of the illegality of the contract, and how it was dealt with by the tribunal and then balance the need for ensuring finality of awards, with the need for making sure that the enforcing powers of English courts are not abused.[315] In the *Soleimany* case, the Court of Appeals, in reaching its decision, took into account the fact that the arbitral tribunal had itself held that there was illegality.[316]

As seen above, despite the strong pro-enforcement bias, even English courts have seen the need to occasionally refuse enforcement of an award on public policy grounds. Just like in India, ensuring that proceedings before an arbitral tribunal comply with the principles of natural justice is extremely important in English law. Challenges based on lack of a fair hearing, where for instance, a party is unable to properly present his case, or parties not being given equal treatment, would leave the arbitral award on shaky ground, and there is the possibility that such awards would violate public policy.[317] There is, however, an important rider in the English approach, which can be helpful if emulated in the Indian context – a party is precluded from challenging enforcement of an arbitral award if the party itself does not make use of the opportunity provided to it during the arbitral proceedings.[318] Such an approach prevents abuse of process by precluding parties from strategically using litigation as a means of delaying enforcement of awards when their grievance could have easily been remedied by the arbitral tribunal itself.

2. The American approach to the public policy exception

(a) Evolution of doctrine

The United States shares with the Indian legal system a common law heritage, respect for judicial precedent and a colonial legacy. Just like in India, modern notions of arbitration were brought to the United States as a result of British colonialism.[319] Records show that arbitration as a means of dispute settlement was provided for in early colonial statutes in Connecticut, Pennsylvania, South

314 Lord Collins and others (n 301) paras 16–150.
315 ibid para 16–150.
316 *Soleimany v. Soleimany* (n 313) 794 et seq.
317 Lord Collins and others (n 301) paras 16–140.
318 ibid.
319 Derek Roebuck, 'The English Inheritance – What the First American Colonists Knew of Mediation and Arbitration' (2016) 2016 Journal of Dispute Resolution 325, 347.

Carolina and Massachusetts.[320] Just like in India, even in the United States early arbitration was more of a 'community' matter,[321] in contrast to the formalized institutional setup common today.

Given the early distrust of English courts towards arbitration, it is unsurprising that the early American approach to public policy was also peppered with judicial scepticism. While arbitration was prevalent even in colonial New York in the 17th century, the judiciary exercised considerable control and arbitrators discretion was quite limited.[322] Arbitration in the United States till the early 20th century was subject to the common law doctrine of revocability (of arbitration agreements).[323] This doctrine was also present in early English law. While English law saw a pro-arbitration reform in 1854, it was only with the enactment of the 1926 Arbitration Act that the doctrine of revocability was made redundant in the United States.[324]

The commonalities due to the English influence must not, however, be overstated. Both India and the United States have charted their own unique paths in the evolution of their respective arbitration statutes and in dealing with the recognition and enforcement of foreign arbitral awards. As will be demonstrated, while on the surface, significant differences exist between the American and the Indian approaches towards public policy, at least on paper, both jurisdictions seek the same outcome, i.e., to further arbitration by ensuring recognition and enforcement.

(b) Legislative framework

The reason for the contrast between the United States and Indian approaches towards commercial arbitration should be looked at from the prism of the drafting history. Before World War II, India, as a British colony, acceded to international agreements promoting arbitration and was bound by the pro-arbitration approach of the British Empire. Imperial Britain had a strong interest in promoting arbitration both at home and in the colonies to protect its global

320 Sabra A. Jones, 'Historical Development of Commercial Arbitration in the United States' (1928) 12 Minnesota Law Review 240, 246.

321 James Oldham and Su Jin Kim, 'Arbitration in America: The Early History' (2013) 31 Law and History Review, American Society for Legal History 241, 245.

322 Eben Moglen, 'Commercial Arbitration in the Eighteenth Century: Searching for the Transformation of American Law' (1983) 93 Yale Law Journal 135, 138.

323 Wharton Poor, 'Arbitration under the Federal Statute' (1926) 36 Yale Law Journal 667.

324 ibid.

commercial interests.[325] The United States, in contrast, was already free to chart its own course as it was no longer a colony.

There was an early aversion of United States law-makers to actively engage in international instruments (a notable example being the ITO). The US did not ratify the 1927 Geneva Convention on Execution of Foreign Arbitral Awards. Furthermore, unlike India, the US did not base its arbitration law on the UNCITRAL Model Law. The United States became a party to the New York Convention nearly a decade after India. Unlike Indian law, the current US arbitration law, i.e., the Federal Arbitration Act 1925 (FAA), was already in place before the 1958 Convention came into force, and so the legislature could not take into consideration the goals of the drafters of the New York Convention when enacting the law. In fact, even after the coming into force of the Convention, there was a reluctance by the US delegation to become a party to the Convention as it was believed that this would necessitate substantial changes to US federal and state law.[326] It was only subsequently, when the costs of litigation and transnational commerce increased, that the anomaly was remedied.[327] This was done by the addition of Chapter 2 of the FAA to ensure conformity with the New York Convention.[328] The United States rather showed a preference for regional instruments; it is a signatory to the Inter-American Convention of International Commercial Arbitration, i.e., the Panama Convention, which would take precedence over the New York Convention when parties to the dispute come from one signatory state.

Prior to the enactment of the FAA, US law and courts did not always look kindly on private commercial agreements to oust their jurisdiction.[329] This bias was mostly due to concerns regarding the capacity of arbitrators to adequately address complex issues given the expedited process and also due to an

---

325 Christian R. Burset, 'Merchant Courts, Arbitration, and the Politics of Commercial Litigation in the Eighteenth-Century British Empire' (2016) 34 Law and History Review 615, 623.

326 Louis Del Duca and Nancy A. Welsh, 'Enforcement of Foreign Arbitration Agreements and Awards: Application of the New York Convention in the United States' (2014) 62 The American Journal of Comparative Law 69, 70.

327 ibid.

328 Alper Tosun, 'Public Policy Concepts in International Arbitration' (UC Berkeley 2019) 24 <https://escholarship.org/uc/item/4xj024n0> accessed 8 September 2020.

329 Pedro J. Martínez-Fraga, The American Influence on International Commercial Arbitration: Doctrinal Developments and Discovery Methods (Cambridge University Press 2009) 6 et seq.

unwillingness to permit disputes to be decided privately where there is public interest involved.[330] This approach changed drastically after the enactment of the FAA. This change in attitude was reflective of the goal of the FAA to reduce the hesitancy of courts to give effect to arbitration agreements.[331] It was also reflective of societal changes – from the 18th century when agriculture was a mainstay of the economy to the rapid commercialization and industrialization that happened subsequently, which required new and speedy means of resolving commercial disputes.[332]

A key similarity of the FAA with the IAA is that both laws are structured so that domestic arbitration and international commercial arbitration are covered in different parts of the same legislation. This means that Chapter I of the FAA, just like Part I of the IAA, deal with domestic awards, whereas Chapter II of the FAA, similar to Part II of the IAA, deal with foreign awards. In both laws, there exists a difference in treatment when it comes to foreign and domestic awards. A higher threshold exists for the challenge of foreign awards in both jurisdictions.

The FAA differs from the IAA insofar as it does not expressly provide for the public policy exception as a ground for refusing enforcement nor define its scope. Instead, § 207 of the Federal Arbitration Act takes an indirect approach by obliging courts to recognise an award unless they fall under the exceptions provided for in the New York Convention.[333] This is similar to the approach taken under German law. In interpreting this provision, both American scholars[334] and courts have called for a more restricted application of the public policy exception. As with the UK, in the US, there exists a public policy of enforcing arbitral awards.[335]

Although the exception has not been defined under the FAA, according to the U. S. Supreme Court, the public policy exception should be *'well defined and dominant, and is to be ascertained by reference to the laws and legal precedents and*

---

330 ibid 9.

331 Alper Tosun (n 328) 24.

332 Charlene Sun and James E. Berger, 'The Evolution of Judicial Review Under the Federal Arbitration Act' (2009) 5 New York University Journal of Law & Business 745, 748.

333 The Federal Arbitration Act 1925 (9 USC Sect 1 et seq).

334 James Moran, 'Public Policy Exception in Judicial Review of Arbitration Awards' (1989) 15 William Mitchell Law Review 767, 791.

335 Mélida Hodgson and Anna Toubiana, 'IBA Public Policy Project – Country Report, USA (1)' (IBA Sub-Committee on Recognition and Enforcement of Awards 2015) 1.

not from general considerations of supposed public interests'.[336] This means that, while the IAA provides for a definition within the statute, in the US courts are free to instead look at other US laws and related judicial precedent to see if there has been a violation of public policy. For instance, in *Delta Airlines*, the U.S. Eleventh Circuit spoke about the danger of enforcing an arbitral award which would undermine the clear public policy that condemns the operation of a passenger airplane by a pilot who is inebriated.[337] In this case, the court held that an agreement between the airline and the employee union requiring arbitration to deal with such conduct by a pilot would violate public policy and not be enforced. In reaching the conclusion that this was a violation of public policy, the courts looked at numerous state and federal laws, including the Federal Aviation Administration regulations that prohibited intoxicated pilots from flying passenger airlines.[338] Such an approach by US courts of adapting the scope of public policy and evaluating different statutes to evaluate if there has been a violation, would no longer be possible under in India under the IAA, considering the courts are restricted to the legislatively defined scope of public policy.

Not taking the Indian approach (of binding courts to look at the narrow definition provided only in the IAA) may, however, seem to give courts a lot of leeway to interfere. But this is not the case – instead, it allows courts to tailor the exception to the circumstances and particularities of the case at hand. As will be shown below, US courts have exercised utmost restraint in their reading of the exception. Even in the aforementioned case, it was held that courts could not interfere even if the arbitrators ruling is *'wrong…unsupported…poorly reasoned… (or) foolish'* rather, courts will only intervene if the violation is *'so offensive that one is to be seen only rarely.'*[339]

Both the United States and India follow federalist forms of government. Both countries consist of a union of states and have federal laws and state laws. Arbitration in both jurisdictions is governed by federal law. For the purpose of enforcement, in India, the scope of the public policy exception is laid out at the federal level, and public policy of individual states is irrelevant. At first glance,

---

336 W R Grace & Company v Local Union 759, International Union of Rubber, Cork, Linoleum & Plastic Workers of America [1983] 103 Ct 2177 (Supreme Court of the United States).

337 *Delta Air Lines, Inc v Air Line Pilots Association, International* (1988) 861 F2d 665 (United States Court of Appeals, Eleventh Circuit).

338 ibid.

339 ibid.

it appears that this is not necessarily the case in the United States. As the exception has not been defined under the FAA, public policy in the US could be interpreted to encompasses both federal and state public policy.[340] The Supreme Court of Appeals of West Virginia in *Clayton Brown* decision,[341] for instance, as a matter of West Virginian public policy, refused to enforce an arbitration clause in a nursing home admission agreement where there was medical negligence. The matter now seems to have been settled by the U. S. Supreme Court, which held that the Virginia court had erred in its decision and that if there is conflict, state law should give way to federal law.[342]

(c) *Judicial attitudes*

Courts in the United States, similar to their Indian counterparts, have quite often been faced with challenges to awards on the grounds of violation of public policy. In fact, a study by Ghodoosi has shown that US courts faced such challenges more than any other jurisdiction.[343] The reaction of US courts to such challenges has varied with time. Just as modern notions of institutionalized commercial arbitration, with limited judicial control, was initially met with a hint of scepticism in India, courts in the United States were also hostile to arbitration prior to the FAA.[344] As shown above, this was a remnant of early English approaches towards arbitration. This approach was reversed after the enactment of the FAA. This can be seen in the *Moses H. Cone* ruling, where the U. S. Supreme Court held that in case of doubt regarding arbitrability, courts must favor arbitration.[345] The court opined that there existed a strong bias favoring arbitration in the FAA, '*notwithstanding any state substantive or procedural policies to the contrary.*'[346]

---

340 Louis Del Duca and Nancy A. Welsh (n 326) 89. See also, L. Del Duca and N. A. Welsh, 'Interpretation and Application of the New York Convention in the United States' in A. Bermann (n 196) 1036.

341 *Clayton Brown v Genesis Healthcare Corp, et al* [2011] Supreme Court of Appeals West Virginia Case No. 35494.

342 *Marmet Health Care Center, Inc v Clayton Brown* (2012) 565 US 530 (Supreme Court of the United States).

343 Farshad Ghodoosi, 'Fall of Last Safeguard in Global Dejudicialization: Protecting Public Interest in Business Disputes' (2020) 98 Oregon Law Review 101, 124.

344 Charlene Sun and James E. Berger (n 332) 746.

345 Moses H Cone Memorial Hospital v Mercury Construction Corp 460 US 1 (Supreme Court of the United States) 25–26.

346 ibid.

The differences in the Indian and US approach towards arbitration can be attributed to differing political and economic systems in both countries. As the preamble to the Indian Constitution reaffirms India to be a 'socialist…democratic republic', there is naturally a higher degree of state intervention in private affairs, unlike the United States, which has for centuries followed a model of capitalism and a free-market economy.[347]

Despite some early hiccups described above, the reluctance of American courts to intervene is not a recent trend. In the United States, the move from initial scepticism to a 'federal policy' promoting arbitration is attributable more to court decisions rather than the legislature.[348] This is in contrast to the situation in India, where the legislature adapted the statute in order to constrain the courts and promote arbitration. The approach of the U. S. Supreme Court to limit judicial intervention can even be seen in some early decisions such as *Hilton v. Guyot,* where the Court refused to look into the merits of the case, even where there were allegations of serious procedural irregularities, fraud and breach of principles of natural justice in proceedings before a court and arbitrator in France.[349] The Court, in effect, held that provided a competent foreign court which has jurisdiction renders a judgment, and the issues have been addressed by this foreign court, the foreign judgment 'would be conclusive as to the merits' and it could not again be challenged before the US court.[350]

The non-interventionist approach has been carried forward by the U. S. Supreme Court also in arbitration proceedings. American courts have been vocal about their dislike for interfering with arbitral awards. In the *Scherk v. Alberto-Culver,* the Court, when warning about the dangers of excessive judicial intervention, ruled that *'parochial refusal by the courts* to enforce arbitral awards *'would invite …mutually destructive jockeying by the parties to secure tactical litigation advantages'* it would *'damage the fabric of international commerce and trade, and imperil the willingness and ability of businessmen to enter into international commercial agreements.'*[351]

347 Jonathan Levy, 'Ages of American Capitalism: A History of the United States.' (2021) 126 The American Historical Review 1608.

348 Farshad Ghodoosi, 'Fall of Last Safeguard in Global Dejudicialization: Protecting Public Interest in Business Disputes' (n 343) 130–131.

349 *Hilton v Guyot* [1895] 159 US 113 (Supreme Court of the United States).

350 ibid 123.

351 *Scherk v Alberto-Culver Co* [1974] 94 SCt 2449 (United States Supreme Court), 2457.

This approach was reiterated in the *Kulukundis Shipping* decision, where the Court urged the necessity to 'shake off the old judicial hostility to arbitration.'[352] In the landmark U. S. Supreme Court ruling in *Mitsubishi,*[353] the court, in justifying the need for giving public policy a narrow interpretation, placed emphasis on international comity and '*respect for ... foreign and transnational tribunals, and sensitivity to the need for predictability in the resolution of disputes.*'[354] More recently, in the *Epic Sys Corp.* decision, Justice Gorsuch cautioned against '*judicial antagonism*' against arbitration.[355]

Unlike Indian courts, the American courts do not take upon themselves the role of defining the scope of public policy. In *United Mine Workers,* the US Supreme Court was hesitant to give public policy an understanding '*beyond the careful and detailed scheme*' created by the legislative branch.[356] American judges have limited their discretion with regard to the use of the exception.[357] In *North West Airlines,* the US Court of Appeals for Columbia observed that judges could not impose '*their own brand of justice in determining applicable public policy*'; the exception can only be derived from statute or case-law and not from their conceptions of public interest.[358] The pro-enforcement leaning of US courts can also be seen in the Second Circuit in *Parsons & Whittemore,* where the Court held that the meaning of public policy under Article V(2)(b) of the New York Convention is not the same as national governmental policy, but rather to enduring fundamental social norms.[359]

---

352 Kulukundis Shipping Co. v. Amtorg Trading Corp. (n 271).

353 *Mitsubishi v Soler Chrysler-Plymouth* US 614 1985 105 SCt 3346 (US Supreme Court).

354 ibid 473 U. S. 628–640.

355 *Epic Systems Corp v Lewis* (2018) 138 Ct 1612 (Supreme Court of the United States) 1623.

356 Eastern Associated Coal Corp v United Mine Workers of America (2000) 531 U S 57 (US Supreme Court) 67.

357 See, Catherine M. Amirfar, Natalie L. Reid and Ina C. Popova, 'National Report for the United States of America (2018 through 2019)', in Lise Bosman (ed), *International Handbook on Commercial Arbitration (Supplement 106)* (Kluwer Law International 2019) 89.

358 *Northwest Airlines, Inc v Air Line Pilots Association, International, Appellant* 808 F2d 76 DC Cir 1987 (US Court of Appeals for the District of Columbia Circuit).

359 Parsons & Whittemore Overseas Co, Inc v Societe Generale De L'industrie Du Papier (rakta), and Bank of America, Defendants-appellees, Societe Generalede L'industrie Du Papier (rakta) 508 F.2d 969 (2d Cir. 1974).

In the 21st century, the approach of Indian courts towards the enforcement of arbitral awards and the use of the public policy exception has not differed significantly from the American approach. This may at first seem surprising because of the starkly contrasting legal traditions. American judges take a very different approach from their Indian counterparts in reaching their decisions. They usually rely almost exclusively on US jurisprudence and law in making their decisions, without much comparative analysis and reliance on foreign practices. This is not the case in India, where judges rely heavily on international arbitration practice and jurisprudence. The similarity may be attributed to the fact that many of the major decisions of the Indian Supreme Court have relied on American and English jurisprudence. This can be seen, for instance, in the landmark *Renusagar* ruling, where the Indian Supreme Court approvingly cited and relied on decisions of the U. S. Supreme Court such as *Scherk v. Alberto-Culver Co.* and the *Mitsubishi Motor Corp* ruling in finding that public policy must be narrowly interpreted.[360]

Certain dissimilarities between Indian and US legal systems persist regarding the scope of arbitrability. The US courts take a more liberal approach and are willing to allow parties to freely arbitrate disputes even in areas such as consumer disputes, labour disputes, anti-trust matters. The US understanding of public policy does not preclude this. The view on this is different in India and many other jurisdictions. In India, these matters are either not arbitrable, highly contested, or arbitration is not preferred in practice. One reason being that their adjudication as a matter of public policy lies solely with national courts or specialized tribunals.[361] This could be attributed to different perceptions regarding the boundaries of party autonomy. These differences have led to different understandings of what constitutes public policy. As labour arbitration is common in the United States, in case of a challenge to an arbitral award, courts will take into consideration claims of violation of public policies involving drugs, alcohol, sexual harassment, nuclear safety etc.[362] For instance, in *Delta Airlines*, the 11th Circuit relied on public policy to interfere in an arbitral award that reinstated an airline pilot who was fired for consuming alcohol before flying a passenger aircraft.[363] The need for reviewing arbitral awards on public policy grounds in

360 Renusagar Power Co. Ltd. Vs. General Electric Company and Anr. (n 178), para 58.
361 See infra, Chapter 6(I)2a.
362 Ann C. Hodges, 'Judicial Review of Arbitration Awards on Public Policy Grounds: Lessons from the Case Law' (2000) 16 Ohio State Journal on Dispute Resolution 91, 115.
363 Delta Air Lines, Inc. v. Air Line Pilots Association, International (n 337).

case of labour disputes hardly arises in India, as arbitration of such disputes, although in theory possible under section 10a of the Industrial Disputes Act, is very unpopular and hardly used.[364] Furthermore, in contrast to their American counterparts, the Indian judge is required to limit his understanding of public policy to the bounds strictly provided for under statute, i.e., the IAA.

III. Comparison with specific civil law jurisdictions

As seen above, Indian law has significant similarities to other common law countries in its approach to recognition and enforcement of foreign arbitral awards. In contrast, one cannot expect a similar degree of comparability to civil law jurisdictions, given the vastly differing roots and approaches, especially regarding the powers and discretion given to judges and the role of judicial precedent. Similar to common law countries, some early resistance towards arbitration was also seen in civil law jurisdictions.[365] There has since been a marked shift towards welcoming arbitration. An overview of the similarities and differences in approaches will be given below.

1. The German approach to public policy

(a) Evolution of doctrine

It must be noted at the onset that public policy under German law can be categorized quite broadly into *kollisionsrechtlicher ordre public* (in the context of private international law) and *verfahrensrechtlicher ordre public* (in the context of the German Code of Civil Procedure).[366]

While the Indian approach to public policy has its origins in common law, in Germany, the principle has its roots in the works of Savigny.[367] In the context of private international law espoused by Savigny, if conflict of laws were to point to the application of a foreign substantive law, German law is 'tolerant' and would

364 See O. P. Malhotra, 'Arbitration of Labour Disputes', in Shahid Z. M. Siddiqi and M. Afzal Wani (eds), *Labour Adjudication in India* (Indian Law Institute: New Delhi 2001) 37.

365 Kidane (n 110) 37.

366 Dieter Martini, 'Ordre Public', in *Handwörterbuch des Europäischen Privatrechts* (Max-Planck-Institut für ausländisches und internationales Privatrecht, Verlag Mohr Siebeck 2009) <http://hwb-eup2009.mpipriv.de/index.php/Ordre_public> accessed 29 September 2020.

367 Jacob Dolinger (n 43) 168. For a detailed elaboration see infra Chapter 1(III)1.

usually give this law the same effect as domestic law.[368] This would, however, not be the case if the application of the foreign law would go against the fundamental principles of the German legal system. In such a case, Savigny considered *ordre public* to work as an exception.[369] In consonance with this principle, the public policy exception provides an *Überdruckventil* (room for manoeuvre) or *Notbremse* (emergency break) for the judge to deny the application of such foreign law.[370] The exception is, in this context, used more as a shield than a sword – i.e., it is to have a negative rather than a positive function. The purpose of the exception here is to preclude the application of such foreign law. While this is relevant in the context of conflict of laws, its role in arbitration is limited. More important here is *verfahrensrechtlicher ordre public.*

Courts are more reluctant to use the exception in the case of *verfahrensrechtlicher ordre public*. The name *verfahrensrechtlicher ordre public* can be deceptive, while a literal translation would indicate that it refers to merely procedural public policy – it can be invoked both in case of violation of procedural public policy, e.g., the right to be heard or in case there is a violation of substantive public policy, e.g., if enforcing the arbitral award violates sanctions regime.

(b) Legislative framework

The development of German civil law was strongly influenced by Roman law.[371] It is unsurprising, therefore, that arbitration as a means of dispute settlement was accepted in Germany very early on. It was commonly used in treaties between German noblemen or principalities during the middle ages.[372] While jealousy of courts did come in the way of its development in the mid-17th century, these

368 See, v. Hein, EGBGB Art 6, in Münchener Kommentar Zum Bürgerlichen Gesetzbuch Bd. 12: Internationales Privatrecht I (8. Auflage, CHBeck 2020) Rn 1.

369 María Elena Alvarez de Pfeifle (n 50) 129.

370 See, v. Hein, EGBGB Art 6, in Münchener Kommentar Zum Bürgerlichen Gesetzbuch Bd. 12: Internationales Privatrecht I (n 368) Rn. 1.

371 Reinhard Zimmermann, 'The German Civil Code and the Development of Private Law in Germany' (*Oxford University Comparative Law Forum 1*, 2006) <https://ouclf.law.ox.ac.uk/the-german-civil-code-and-the-development-of-private-law-in-germany/> accessed 29 January 2020.

372 Henry S. Fraser, 'Sketch of the History of International Arbitration' (1926) 11 Cornell Law Review 179, 192.

problems were put to rest with the enactment of the Code of Civil Procedure in 1877.[373]

At least in the way the laws evolved, the German and Indian arbitration laws have some commonalities, not least of which is that both laws were introduced within a similar time period. Just like India, Germany too is a party to the New York Convention 1958, and Germany redrafted its arbitration law in 1998 largely in consonance with the UNCITRAL Model Law – the same model on which IAA 1996 was based. There is a difference in drafting history. At the time of drafting the new German arbitration law, arbitration was already widely used in commercial contracts in Germany – the law reform only served to provide an internationalized and modern legislative framework.[374] The IAA 1996, however, sought to give impetus to arbitration in a country where the courts were formerly deeply suspicious towards international arbitration.[375]

Unlike India, the German lawmaker did not decide to have a separate tailor-made arbitration statute. Instead, Book 10, Chapter 8 of the Code of Civil Procedure (ZPO) comprehensively provides mechanisms for (refusing) enforcement of both domestic and foreign awards. There is a presumption under this code that awards in international arbitrations will generally be enforced.[376]

Insofar as the public policy or *öffentliche Ordnung* with respect to arbitration is concerned, German law differs from Indian law, as it does not follow the UNCITRAL Model Law approach of specifically providing for public policy as grounds for refusing enforcement of foreign awards. This is in contrast to the IAA, which provides for and defines the scope of public policy exception both for domestic awards and foreign awards. Under German arbitration law, the public policy exception is only mentioned in section 1059 of the ZPO, which deals with domestic awards, and not in section 1061, which deals with foreign awards. With regard to foreign awards, the ZPO is more akin to the American FAA, which places general reliance on the provisions of the New York Convention. The reason for such an approach is because the German legislator wanted to distinguish between public policy in dealing with foreign awards and in the case

373 Allen Sultan, 'The United Nations Arbitration Convention and United States Policy' (1959) 53 The American Journal of International Law 807, 808.

374 Karl-Heinz Böckstiegel, 'An Introduction to the New German Arbitration Act Based on the UNCITRAL Model Law' (1998) 14 Arbitration International 19.

375 See *supra* Chapter 2.

376 Stefan M. Kroll, 'Recognition and Enforcement of Foreign Arbitral Awards in Germany' (2002) 5 International Arbitration Law Review 165.

of purely domestic awards- a distinction which has not been very clearly made in the UNCITRAL Model Law.[377]

While Indian law has moved towards statutorily defining public policy, German law has moved away from such an approach. The older version of the ZPO (before 1998) provided that the exception could be invoked where there was a 'violation of basic principles of German law' or 'constitutional rights'- this provision is now omitted.[378] Such an understanding is similar to the definition of public policy under the IAA(Am.) 2015, which includes the 'fundamental policy of Indian law'.

Although the Code of Civil Procedure does not provide guidance regarding the scope of the public policy exception under German arbitration law, it is possible to understand how the exception is treated by looking at Art 6 of the Einführungsgesetzes zum Bürgerlichen Gesetzbuche (German Civil Code). Here in the context of conflict of laws, courts can refuse to apply a foreign law, where its application would lead to a result that is manifestly contrary to the *wesentlichen Grundsätzen des deutschen Rechts* (basic principles of German law), particularly the *Grundrechte* (fundamental rights). This would include not only provisions of the German Federal Constitution but also Constitutions of the individual states and the basic principles of EU law.[379] The violation of EU public policy would also be a ground for refusing enforcement under the German *ordre public*. An example would be if the enforcement of the arbitral award would lead to a violation of EU competition law. This differs significantly from Indian law, where the public policy of individual states or any international union would be irrelevant.

(c) Judicial attitudes

While the definition of public policy in Indian law was provided to restrict the scope of the exception, the absence of a definition or express reference to the exception in the German ZPO does not make German law less arbitration-friendly. Quite to the contrary, in practice, German courts are much more restrictive in their use of the exception than most other jurisdictions. They guide themselves in their interpretation by looking at the New York Convention 1958.[380]

---

377 ibid 160.

378 See Stefan Kröll and Peter Kraft, 'Recourse against the Award', in Karl-Heinz Böckstiegel, Stefan Kröll and Patricia Nacimiento (eds), *Arbitration in Germany: The Model Law in Practice* (2nd edn, Kluwer Law International 2015) 411.

379 María Elena Alvarez de Pfeifle (n 50) 131.

380 See, § 1061, Volkert Vorwerk and Christian Wolf (eds), *Beck'scher Online-Kommentar ZPO*, vol 10 (37th edn, Beck-Online 2020) Rn 48.

As a ground rule, when it comes to enforcement, German courts will not discriminate so as to treat foreign awards worse off than purely domestic awards.[381] A distinction must be made here with regard to the use of public policy. Unlike Indian courts, which look at Indian public policy,[382] German courts, just like their French counterparts, will refuse enforcement of a foreign award if it violates *international* public policy.[383] This standard is considered to be more pro-recognition than public policy in a purely domestic context (*ordre public interne).*[384]

A mere violation of German domestic mandatory norms or German public policy will not necessarily meet the threshold for refusing enforcement of a foreign award.[385] Such intervention is only warranted if the mandatory principle violated is 'fundamental' in nature and to safeguard 'basic fairness'.[386] Furthermore, German courts will not always see it fit to refuse enforcement even if there has been a violation of public policy, but rather they will interfere where the enforcement of the award would violate public policy.[387] This is similar to the position under section 48(2)b of the IAA. To prevent a purely formalistic approach by courts in case of procedural public policy violations, a precondition for refusing enforcement by German courts is that the violation should have influenced the reaching of the award.[388]

As a general rule, the Bundesgerichthof (German Federal Court of Justice) has held that a foreign award will only be refused enforcement if the consequence would be a violation of the basic principles of German law and economic well-being.[389] Furthermore, the BGH has held that in the interest of international trade, a stricter standard will be applied for refusing enforcement of foreign

381 *BGH, Beschluss vom 30. September 2010 – III ZB 69/09* (German Federal Court of Justice (Bundesgerichtshof)).

382 Renusagar Power Co. Ltd. Vs. General Electric Company and Anr. (n 178).

383 Stefan M. Kroll (n 376) 172.

384 Volkert Vorwerk and Christian Wolf (n 380) Rn 48.

385 Friedrich Stein and others (eds), *Kommentar zur Zivilprozessordnung. Bd. 10: §§ 1025 – 1066* (23. Aufl, Mohr Siebeck 2014), para 317.

386 See, Stefan Kröll, Foreign Awards, in Böckstiegel, Kröll and Nacimiento (n 378) 487.

387 See, Stefan Kröll, Foreign Awards, in ibid.

388 OLG Frankfurt am Main, Beschluss vom 16 Januar 2014 – 26 Sch 2/13 (Higher Regional Court – Frankfurt).

389 *BGH Beschluss Vom 02. März 2017 – ZB 4216 – Juris* (German Federal Court of Justice (Bundesgerichtshof)).

awards on the grounds of international public policy.[390] This distinction can also be seen in Indian law, where it is more difficult to refuse enforcement of foreign awards. In practice, however, the standard for refusing enforcement of domestic awards in Germany is already quite high, so there is not much difference in treatment between domestic and foreign awards.[391]

While no fixed definition of public policy exists under the ZPO, the enforcement of awards can be denied in Germany both in case of a violation of procedural grounds such as violation of the right to be heard *'Verletzung des rechtlichen Gehörs'* and bias by the arbitrator, as well as substantive public policy including fraud or corruption.[392] While procedural grounds could also include abuse of legal process, substantive grounds could encompass prevention of slave labour, people smuggling and severe crimes including fraud, blackmail and robbery.[393] The scope of public policy of any legal system also depends on the importance placed on certain values. In Germany, for instance, confidentiality is of fundamental importance. It is for this reason that the OLG Frankfurt (Court of Appeal) observed that dissenting opinions in an award would violate German public policy and would be sufficient grounds to set aside an award, as it violates the confidential nature of the discussions between arbitrators.[394] This differs considerably from the common law approach, where dissenting opinions are very common.

Whereas Indian courts only apply Indian public policy based on the principle of supremacy of EU law, German courts are also obliged to apply EU public policy when deciding to enforce arbitral awards. This can be seen in the aftermath of the *Achmea* ruling of the European Court of Justice (ECJ). Here, an arbitral tribunal had ruled in favor of Achmea BV, a Dutch company that had brought an action against Slovakia based on a Netherlands Slovakia BIT. In this case, the ECJ effectively ruled against the validity of arbitration clauses in

---

390 *BGH Beschluss Vom 06. Oktober 2016 – ZB 1315 – Juris* (German Federal Court of Justice (Bundesgerichtshof)).

391 See, Adolphsen, UNÜ Art 5 in Wolfgang Krüger and Thomas Rauscher (eds), *Münchener Kommentar zur Zivilprozessordnung – Band 3* (5. Aufl, Beck, C H 2017), Rn. 69.

392 See, Adolphsen, UNÜ Art 5 in ibid, Rn. 72–82.

393 See Raeschke-Kessler, '§ 1061 ZPO', in Hanns Prütting and Markus Gehrlein (eds), *ZPO Kommentar* (12th edn, Hermann-Luchterhand-Verlag, Kluwer Law Online 2020) Rn 41.

394 OLG Frankfurt am Main, Beschluss vom 16 Januar 2020 – 26 Sch 14/18 (Higher Regional Court – Frankfurt).

intra-EU BIT's as they would contravene Art 267 and 344 of the TFEU that gives exclusive jurisdiction on questions of EU law to the ECJ.[395] The BGH, based on this decision, decided to annul the arbitral award as its enforcement would be a violation of EU law.[396] While this case does relate to investment treaty arbitration, it is still a good example of how national courts in some jurisdictions, such as EU member states, do not bind themselves solely to national perceptions of public policy.

The absence of a definition in the statute means that the grounds for refusing enforcement in Germany could theoretically be more wide-ranging than the understanding of public policy under Indian law. This is, however, not reflected in practice. Even in the case of domestic awards, German courts are willing to rely on the public policy to refuse enforcement only in extreme and exceptional situations.[397] This is even more the case when it comes to foreign awards. A further comparison of each of these individual categories will be made in Chapter 4.

2. *Ordre public* under French law

(a) Evolution of doctrine

The pro-arbitration bias is a characteristic feature of French arbitration law. While a formalized system of arbitration is a development of the 20th century in most States, arbitration was encouraged from early on in France. King Francis II, as early as 1560, required merchants to resort to arbitration in his *Edit de Fontainebleau.*[398] Today arbitration is widely used and encouraged. Paris is a favored seat of arbitration, and France is home to renowned arbitration institutions such as the International Chamber of Commerce Court of Arbitration. The Indian

---

395 *Slovak Republic v Achmea BV* [2018] Court of Justice of the European Union (Grand Chamber) C 284/2016.

396 *BGH Beschluss vom 31. Oktober 2018 – I ZB 2/15* (German Federal Court of Justice (Bundesgerichtshof)).

397 *BGH, Beschluss vom 28. Januar 2014 – III ZB 40/13 –, Juris* (German Federal Court of Justice (Bundesgerichtshof)).

398 'Edit de Fontainebleau (August 1560)' <https://www.trans-lex.org/601210/_/edit-de%C2%A0fontainebleau-august-1560/#:~:text=Edit%20de%20Fontainebleau%2C%20August%201560.,-Additional%20Information&text=N%C2%B0%2039.,%C3%A0%20des%20arbitres%20(1%20).> accessed 8 September 2020.

government policy think tank, Niti-Aayog, has looked at this as an example when trying to make India a hub of international arbitration.[399]

One of the main reasons for the growth of arbitration in France is the importance given to arbitration as a means of resolving disputes under French law and the pro-enforcement bias of French courts.[400] A key hallmark of the French approach is building an arbitral system without state interference.[401] The legislative framework and judicial attitude that made this possible will be looked at below.

(b) *Legislative framework*

The French *Code Civil* (civil code) or *Code Napoléon* of 1804, already set a framework of when agreements would not be enforced. Article 6 provides that parties cannot derogate from laws concerning public order or *bonnes moeurs* (good morals) by way of private agreement. While this could give guidance as to the scope of substantive public policy – for understanding public policy in the context of international arbitration, one needs to look at the French Code of Civil Procedure. While France is also party to the New York Convention, unlike India, and more akin to Germany, France does not have a dedicated statute dealing with arbitration law. The provisions are instead found in the French Code of Civil Procedure and are not based on the UNCITRAL Model Law.

The French approach to the public policy exception differs from both the Indian and the German approaches. As seen above, where the IAA makes reference to the public policy of India, the German ZPO merely refers to the New York Convention. In contrast, in the part dealing with foreign awards, Article 1514 of the French Code of Civil Procedure provides that awards are to be enforced unless such enforcement would manifestly violate *international public policy.* Similarly, 1520(5) provides that annulment of an arbitral award would only be possible if there is a violation of *international public policy.* In this regard, the

399 Bibek Debroy and Suparna Jain, 'Strengthening Arbitration and Its Enforcement in India – Resolve in India' <https://niti.gov.in/writereaddata/files/document_publication/Arbitration.pdf> accessed 21 October 2020.

400 See, Emmanuel Gaillard, Coralie Darrigade, 'Country Reports – France', in Frank-Bernd Weigand and Antje Baumann (eds), *Practitioner's Handbook on International Commercial Arbitration* (3rd edn, Oxford University Press 2019) para 8.01.

401 See Carmen Núñez-Lagos, 'The Principles of International Arbitration Practice in France', in Bernardo María Cremades, Miguel Angel Fernández-Ballesteros and David Arias (eds), *Liber Amicorum: Bernardo Cremades* (1st edn, La Ley 2010) 915.

French Code supersedes even the New York Convention as it goes even further than the Convention in enforcing foreign awards.[402]

International public policy is different from public policy, which would apply in purely domestic cases. As will be explained in more detail in Part D of this thesis, the French interpretation of international public policy is much narrower than public policy used in merely domestic cases. Unlike the Indian approach, the French Code does not, however, provide any guidance or definition of what would constitute international public policy. Interpreting the scope of the exception is therefore left to the courts.

Under French law, arbitral awards are given a presumption of validity.[403] Courts are precluded from going into the merits again or passing judgment on the arbitrator's decision. They are only permitted in exceptional circumstances to review the award itself.[404] Furthermore, according to Article 1466 of the French Code, parties are precluded from seeking judicial intervention if they have knowingly failed to seek the remedy before the arbitral tribunal.

(c) Judicial attitudes

Unlike India, French law does not provide a fixed statutory definition of public policy. For this reason, the role of defining the scope of public policy falls on the judges – who have the discretion to apply it as they see appropriate.[405] Similar to their German counterparts, French courts are generally reluctant to give public policy a broad interpretation. This has, however, not always been the case. Just as in India, French courts also initially supported a more expansive review of arbitral awards and only subsequently moved towards a narrow outlook. The expansive outlook can be seen in the *Plateau des pyramides* ruling of the *Cour de cassation,* where the court held that it could examine the underlying contract, and there was no limitation to its power to examine defects both in fact and law.[406]

---

402 Elie Kleiman, Shaparak Saleh, and Yann Dehaudt-Delville, 'Enforcement in France' [2017] *Global Arbitration Review* <https://globalarbitrationreview.com/jurisdiction/1004826/france> accessed 29 August 2019.

403 See, Dominique Hascher, 'France', in Emmanuel Gaillard (ed), *The Review of International Arbitral Awards IAI Forum, Dijon 12–14 September 2008* (Juris 2010) 98.

404 ibid.

405 María Elena Alvarez de Pfeifle (n 50) 137.

406 [1987] N° Pourvoi 84-17274 (Cour de Cassation, Chambre civile 1).

In the 1980s, the competition between lawmakers from different states to make their laws more in line with the needs of international commerce, which led to the reform of the IAA and adoption of the UNCITRAL Model Law, also had its impact on France. In effect, this competition led French legislators to make the law governing international arbitration more attractive and friendly.[407] French courts also constrained their use of the public policy exception. The restrictive approach by the *Cour de cassation* can be seen in *its Verhoeft v. Moreau* ruling. In this case, the court held that for international public policy to be invoked, the violation must be '*flagrante, effective et concrète*'.[408] This threshold was also followed in *SA Thalès Air Défense v. GIE* where the Paris Court of Appeal refused to annul an arbitral award on the grounds of violation of EU competition law, as the violation was not '*flagrante, effective et concrète*',[409] or as translated by Denis Bensaude, '*blatant, actual, and concrete.*'[410]

While French law does not specifically provide a distinction, in practice, enforcement of foreign arbitral awards can be refused both in case of violation of procedural public policy and substantive public policy concerning the merits of the case. Procedural grounds include – the tribunal must follow due process, the parties must be equally treated and given the right to be heard, parties must not make use of falsified evidence.[411] Substantive grounds, on the other hand, would be invoked when recognising or enforcing the arbitral award would lead to a result contrary to the 'fundamental convictions' of the French legal system.[412] This would be the case, for instance, when the award enforces a contract vitiated by corruption or an award that is based on discrimination.[413] Although not concretised in French statute, these grounds are similar to those provided for under the IAA.

---

407 Guido Carducci (n 112) 128.

408 'Verhoeft v. Moreau, Cour de Cassation (1re Ch. Civ.), 21 March 2000', Revue de l'Arbitrage; Comité Français de l'Arbitrage 2001 805.

409 *SA Thalès Air Defense v GIE Euromissile* [2004] Rev Arbitr 2005 751 (Cour d'appel Paris).

410 Denis Bensaude, 'Thalès Air Defence BV v. GIE Euromissile: Defining the Limits of Scrutiny of Awards Based on Alleged Violations of European Competition Law' (2005) 22 Journal of International Arbitration 239, 242.

411 See, French Law, in Philippe Fouchard, Emmanuel Gaillard, and Berthold Goldman, *Fouchard, Gaillard, Goldman on International Commercial Arbitration* (John Savage and Emmanuel Gaillard eds, Kluwer Law International 1999) 957 et seq.

412 See, French Law, in ibid 960 et seq.

413 ibid 961.

Although the global trend as seen in India and Germany has been towards narrowing down the scope of judicial review of arbitral awards, surprisingly, French courts have taken a different approach.[414] In recent decisions, where there were allegations of fraud or corruption, French courts have been more willing to undertake a more substantive and expansive review of arbitral awards even on the merits.

The decision *MK Group v. Onyx* is a case in point.[415] In this case, a Russian company MK group approached the Paris Court of Appeal *(Cour d'appel de Paris)*, seeking setting aside of an ICC arbitral award on the grounds of violating international public policy. It claimed, inter-alia, that the award was made based on forged documents submitted to the tribunal (i.e., two different versions of the same contract used to obtain government authorization for exploring gold mines) and that mandatory provisions of the law of the Lao People's Democratic Republic were violated. The *Cour d'appel de Paris* annulled the award. Although it found that foreign mandatory rules were not applicable, it found that fraudulently obtained government authorization violated international public policy in a way that was *blatant, actual and concrete*. In reaching its decision, the court held that there are no limits under French law on the courts' power to comprehensively re-look an arbitral award *'both in law and fact'*.[416]

French courts have demonstrated a willingness to undertake a similar expansive review where there are allegations of corruption. In *Alstom v Alexander*, the *Cour d'appel de Paris* had to decide whether to enforce an arbitral award that required Alstom to pay money in fulfillment of a consultancy contract.[417] Alstom

---

414 For a further elaboration on this trend see, Rory V. Wheeler, 'Recent Developments in the Paris Court of Appeal's Approach to Public Policy' (2019) XVI Revista Brasileira de Arbitragem, Kluwer Law International 107 et seq. See also, Caroline Duclercq and Talel Aronowicz, 'When French Judges Confirm the Expansion of Their Control over Arbitral Awards' [2018] *Young Arbitration Review* 72.

415 *Société MK Group vs SARL Onix Société Financial Initiative* [2018] N° 1521703 (Cour d'appel de Paris); for a translation and comment on this decision, see Nataliya Barysheva and Valentine Chessa, 'Société MK Group v. S.A.R.L. Onix and Société Financial Initiative, Court of Appeal of Paris, 16 January 2018' A contribution by the ITA Board of Reporters, Kluwer Law International.

416 Société MK Group vs. S.A.R.L. Onix Société Financial Initiative (n 415) 2.

417 *Société Alstom Transport SA et autre v Société Alexander Brothers Ltd* [2018] N° 1611182 (Cour d'appel de Paris); for a translation and comment on this decision, see Nataliya Barysheva and Valentine Chessa, 'Société Alstom Transport SA et Autre v. Société Alexander Brothers Ltd., Court of Appeal of Paris, 10 April 2018' [2018] A contribution by the ITA Board of Reporters, Kluwer Law International.

brought a challenge claiming that the tribunal wrongly decided that there was no corruption. The court held that enforcement could not be permitted if there was corruption. Furthermore, it observed that in determining if there was a violation of international public policy due to corruption, it would not be bound by the decision of the tribunal and that it had the power to make its own factual and legal examination. It finally required the parties to submit further evidence on the question of corruption.

The position taken by French courts in the above decisions is more expansive than under Indian law. While the IAA only envisions refusing enforcement if the award itself is affected by fraud or corruption, French courts have demonstrated a willingness to look at the merits of the dispute. This is not necessarily a negative development. Both approaches seek to combat the same menace of fraud and corruption. The French courts merely take a more thorough approach in this regard.

IV. Comparing approaches to procedural and substantive elements of public policy

In most legal systems, parties to an arbitration can approach national courts to seek refusal of enforcement of arbitral awards, either where their fundamental procedural rights have been violated or if they feel that there was serious illegality in the underlying contract or enforcement of the award would violate the fundamental policy of the given legal system. There is a lack of consensus in the literature regarding the role of national courts in each of these situations. While some scholars strongly opine that the public policy exception has both procedural and substantive dimensions,[418] others, notably Gary Born, have argued that the public policy exception under article V(2)(b) must be restricted to substantive public policy.[419]

In India, section 48 of the IAA does not distinguish between procedural public policy and substantive public policy as grounds for refusing the enforcement of awards. This is similar to the approach of the UNCITRAL Model Law and the New York Convention and is followed in most other jurisdictions as well. This

418 See Franz T. Schwarz and Helmut Ortner, 'Chapter III: The Arbitration Procedure – Procedural Ordre Public and the Internationalization of Public Policy in Arbitration', Christian Klausegger and Peter Klein (n 51) 133.

419 Gary Born, *International Commercial Arbitration* (2nd edn, Kluwer Law International 2014) 3687, 3688.

would mean that, at least in theory, courts, when deciding on whether to refuse an arbitral award, should be equally willing to take into consideration violations of both procedural public policy and substantive public policy. In practice, however, a study by Ghodoosi has shown that national courts are more likely to take into account procedural violations, whereas arbitral tribunals are more likely to take into account substantive violations of public policy.[420] The relative hesitancy of national courts to delve deep into substantive public policy can be attributable to a desire to abstain from going into the merits of the dispute- and leaving this to the arbitral tribunal.

A comparison of approaches of different jurisdictions will be provided below.

1. Where there is a violation of procedural public policy

Just like in litigation, although the need for ensuring procedural safeguards in international arbitration is universally accepted, there is variation in the level of procedural guarantees provided in different legal systems. There is a view in the literature that public policy must only guarantee a bare minimum of procedural safeguards in international arbitration.[421] This is grounded in the belief that parties have freely waived procedural safeguards ordinary available in court proceedings by freely choosing arbitration as a more speedy and efficient means of dispute settlements. Such a view, as will be shown below, is not shared by all countries. On the contrary, there is significant support for the position that certain procedural rights are so vital that they cannot be waived.[422] Such a view was taken by the Indian Supreme Court in its *BBNL* ruling where it held that party autonomy would not justify disregarding certain principles such as impartiality and independence of the tribunal.[423]

There are numerous instances where the behavior of the arbitrators or the parties during the arbitration proceedings could trigger invoking the public policy exception. The IBA Sub-Committee on Recognition and Enforcement of Arbitral Awards has, in its Report, provided some typical examples for such

420 Farshad Ghodoosi, 'Fall of Last Safeguard in Global Dejudicialization: Protecting Public Interest in Business Disputes' (n 343) 129.

421 See Stephen M. Schwebel and Susan G. Lahne, 'Public Policy and Arbitral Procedure' in Pieter Sanders (ed), *Comparative Arbitration Practice and Public Policy in Arbitration* (Kluwer Law and Taxation Publishers 1987) 209.

422 See *infra* Chapter 4(III)3a(iv).

423 Bharat Broadband Network Limited Vs United Telecoms Limited (2019) 5 SCC 755 (Supreme Court of India) [57].

violations of public policy, including 'violations of due process or right to be heard, lack of equal opportunity to present one's case, fraud, falsification of documents, lack of independence or impartiality of arbitrators, bribery or threats to arbitrators, violation of *res judicata*.'[424]

(a) The common law approach to protecting procedural public policy

The protection of procedural public policy has been given a great deal of importance by courts in common law countries. In India, as will be explained in detail later, the protection of these procedural rights are codified in the explanatory notes to section 48(2)b of the IAA(Am.) 2015. The importance of safeguarding procedural public policy in the Indian legal system can be seen, for instance, in the *Dalmia* judgment where the Delhi High Court held that even in case of foreign awards, it would be willing to refuse enforcement if the aggrieved party can prove infirmities in the arbitral proceedings such as lack of due process, violation of principles of natural justice, lack of fair hearing, including equal opportunity to present the case, and lack of proper notice.[425]

Even in the United States, the Second Circuit in *Europcar* held that 'a fraudulently obtained arbitration agreement or award' could preclude enforcement.[426] An early elaboration of this principle in the American context can be seen in the early *Underhill* decision, where a New York court ruled that judges need to '*be eagle-eyed in looking into the proceedings and conduct of the arbitrators, and the acts of the parties, to see that everything has been conducted fairly, impartially, and honestly*'.[427]

In England as well for an award to be enforceable, there should not be a breach of public policy during the arbitral proceedings. An important test laid down in the Minmetals case is certainly workable in the Indian context. According to this test, when deciding on whether to refuse enforcement on public policy grounds, courts must look at:

---

424 IBA Subcommittee On Recognition and Enforcement of Arbitral Awards, 'Report on the Public Policy Exception in the New York Convention' (2015) 14.

425 Glencore International Ag vs Dalmia Cement (Bharat) Limited [2017] EXP 752015 (High Court of Delhi) [25].

426 *Europcar Italia, S.pA v Maiellano Tours, Inc* [1998] 156 F3d 310 (United States Court of Appeals, Second Circuit) 315.

427 *Van Cortlandt v Underhill* (1819) 17 Johns 405 (Court for the Correction of Errors of New York) 421.

(1) the nature of the procedural injustice;
(2) whether the enforcee has invoked the supervisory jurisdiction of the seat of the arbitration;
(3) whether a remedy was available under that jurisdiction;
(4) whether the courts of that jurisdiction have conclusively determined the enforcee's complaint in favour of upholding the award;
(5) if the enforcee has failed to invoke that remedial jurisdiction, for what reason and in particular whether he was acting unreasonably in failing to do so.[428]

While the violation of public policy during the arbitral proceedings is sufficient grounds for courts to refuse enforcement of awards, courts will not always use this power. The use of the aforementioned test puts the onus on the aggrieved party to take all steps possible to seek remedy at the earliest time possible, preferably by approaching the arbitral tribunal itself, and only in case the tribunal does not provide a remedy then approach the courts at the arbitral seat rather than wait for the time of enforcement.

The requirement that parties first approach the tribunal is enshrined in the implied waiver doctrine. This doctrine is a general exception to the rule that violation of public policy during the arbitral process could justify refusing enforcement of the award at a later stage. It basically precludes parties from abusing the court system to delay enforcement when they had a remedy during the arbitration proceedings but did not avail of it.[429] In the UK, according to section 73 of the Arbitration Act, a party loses the right to object before a court on the grounds that the 'proceedings were improperly conducted' if it continues to take part in the arbitral proceedings without objecting. This doctrine is found in civil law jurisdictions such as Sweden as well.[430]

In the *Minmetals* case, the party resisting enforcement knew about the arbitrators' failure to comply with the rules but failed to bring their objections before the arbitral tribunal. Judge Collins, by rejecting the challenge to the award, held that a breach of the principles of natural justice would be grounds for refusing enforcement, provided that the lack of opportunity to present the case was not because the aggrieved party failed to make use of the opportunity available to

428 *Minmetals Germany GmbH v Ferco Steel Ltd* [1999] CLC 647 (Queen's Bench Division (Commercial Court)) 661.

429 Annette Magnusson, Jakob Ragnwaldh and Martin Wallin (eds), *International Arbitration in Sweden: A Practitioner's Guide* (2nd edn, Kluwer Law International 2021) 349.

430 Jennifer Lawler, 'Implied Waiver of Right to Challenge an Arbitral Award: An Analysis of the Swedish Approach in Comparison with the UNCITRAL Model Law' (Thesis in Procedural Law, Stockholm University 2014) 28.

it.[431] The position of law in India is very similar. Indian Supreme Court, in its *Quippo Construction* ruling, held that a party that fails to actively participate and raise jurisdictional concerns or concerns that the arbitrator has exceeded authority before the arbitral tribunal is deemed to have waived his right to challenge the award on these grounds at a later stage.[432]

(b) The civil law approach to protecting procedural public policy

Just like their common-law counterparts, courts in major civil law jurisdictions also believe that the need for enforcing arbitral awards must sometimes be tempered by the requirement of ensuring that the tribunal complies with procedural requirements. In Germany, *ordre public processualis* is given much importance and must be respected at every stage of the arbitral proceedings.[433] A recent example would be a BGH ruling in a dispute that involved examination of witnesses by the arbitrators in an online arbitration.[434] The court held that *prozessualer Waffengleichheit* (equality of arms) during the proceedings is a fundamental constitutional norm and forms an integral part of procedural public policy.[435]

German courts have shown restraint in refusing enforcement of foreign awards on the grounds of procedural public policy. In a case before the *Hanseatisches Oberlandesgericht,* enforcement of an award was resisted on the grounds that the arbitral tribunal did not fulfill due process requirements as it failed in its award to discuss the facts, the grounds for rejection of the parties objections and did not take into consideration expert opinions submitted by the defendant.[436] The court held that while such an award would violate German domestic public

431 Minmetals Germany GmbH v Ferco Steel Ltd (n 428) 657 et seq.

432 Quippo Construction Equipment Limited v Janardan Nirman Pvt Limited [2020] Civ Appeal No2378 (Supreme Court of India) [23].

433 See Franz T. Schwarz and Helmut Ortner, 'The Arbitration Procedure – Procedural Ordre Public and the Internationalization of Public Policy in Arbitration', in Christian Klausegger and Peter Klein (n 51) 148.

434 *BGH, Beschluss vom 23. Juli 2020 – I ZB 88/19* (German Federal Court of Justice (Bundesgerichtshof)).

435 ibid 19.

436 See, 'Germany No. 84, Not indicated v. Not indicated, Hanseatisches Oberlandesgericht [Hanseatic Court of Appeal], Bremen, 84, 30 September 1999', in Albert Jan van den Berg (ed), *ICCA Yearbook Commercial Arbitration 2006*, vol XXXI (Kluwer Law International 2006) 642.

policy, enforcement would not be denied unless the award breaches German international public policy.[437]

Just like in Germany, French courts have similarly occasionally intervened when necessary to protect the procedural rights of the parties to an arbitration. They have shown their willingness to interfere both in the pre-arbitration stage and set aside offending arbitral clauses to safeguard procedural public policy. In its recent PWC ruling,[438] the *Cour de cassation* sought to safeguard consumers from unfair arbitration clauses in B2C consumer contracts. The court, in effect, held that the arbitral tribunals right to rule on its own jurisdiction (*Kompetenz-Kompetenz)* would not override the protections provided to consumers under European law in this case the Art 3(1) of the Unfair Terms in Consumer Contracts Directive (1993/13), which provides that contractual terms that have not been individually negotiated are to be considered unfair. An arbitration clause that was violative of the requirements set out in the Directive would be liable to be set aside.[439]

In some jurisdictions, violation of procedural public policy is not acknowledged as separate grounds for refusing enforcement of arbitral awards. This is because these jurisdictions take the position that article V(1) of the New York Convention already provides extensive procedural safeguards, and there is, therefore, no need to again resort to using the public policy exception under article V(2)b.[440] The 2015 IBA subcommittee report gives an excellent illustration of the 'right to be heard', which is covered under Article V(1)b but is most definitely also an essential part of the public policy in most states.[441] In reality, it is immaterial if these procedural safeguards are guaranteed by relying on Article V(1) or by using the public policy exception under V(2)b. Both processes ensure the same result of protecting parties from awards tainted by fundamental procedural injustice.

---

437 See, 'Germany No. 84, Not indicated v. Not indicated, Hanseatisches Oberlandesgericht [Hanseatic Court of Appeal], Bremen, 84, 30 September 1999', in ibid 648 et seq.

438 a société PWC Landwell – PricewaterhouseCoopers Tax & Legal Services v Mme L. Y. ; et autres [2020] Arrêt N° 556 (Cour de cassation – Première chambre civile).

439 ibid 14.

440 IBA Subcommittee On Recognition and Enforcement of Arbitral Awards (n 424) 13.

441 IBA Subcommittee On Recognition and Enforcement of Arbitral Awards (n 424).

2. In case of violation of substantive public policy

In international arbitration, it is generally recognised that the notion of public policy, when viewed holistically, has both procedural and substantive dimensions.[442] Substantive public policy usually includes matters relating to 'public morals, health, safety and welfare' and focuses on 'the merits of the award.[443] The scope of what is included under substantive public policy differs based on the values and cultures of different legal systems. However, an award, which gives effect to something illegal, such as forced prostitution, drug trafficking etc., is almost universally a breach of substantive public policy.[444] In many jurisdictions, substantive public policy also includes 'competition law matters, *pacta sunt servanda*, equality of creditors in insolvency, state immunity, punitive damages, excessive interest rates.'[445]

National courts have usually been averse to going on a fishing expedition to find violations of substantive public policy. They have rather chosen to be very restrictive in deciding to relook the merits or second guess the arbitral tribunal on facts. This is usually to ensure their decisions are in line with the pro-enforcement bias of the New York Convention. In India, the IAA provides that courts can refuse enforcement if there is a breach of substantive requirements, such as when enforcement of the award would violate the fundamental policy of Indian law or the most basic notions of morality and justice.[446] Similarly, in Germany, the BGH ruled that enforcement of an arbitral award will be refused only when it goes against the fundamental principles of the German legal system.[447] According to the court, this could be the case when for instance, the arbitral award breaks a norm that is fundamental to the economic or social life or if it goes against the basic principles of justice.[448] In Switzerland, the Federal Supreme Court has ruled that substantive public policy would be breached in case there is

442 See, Franz T. Schwarz and Helmut Ortner, 'Chapter III: The Arbitration Procedure – Procedural Ordre Public and the Internationalization of Public Policy in Arbitration', in Christian Klausegger and Peter Klein (n 51) 133.
443 Fernando Mantilla-Serrano, 'Towards a Transnational Procedural Public Policy' (2004) 20 Arbitration International 333.
444 IBA Subcommittee On Recognition and Enforcement of Arbitral Awards (n 424) 16.
445 ibid 16 et seq.
446 A more detained elaboration can be found in Chapter IV(III) of this thesis.
447 BGH Urteil Vom 12. Juli 1990 – III ZR 17489 – Juris (German Federal Court of Justice (Bundesgerichtshof)) [8].
448 (n 447).

a violation of the basic principles of the Swiss legal system including, *pacta sunt servanda*, principles of good faith, and to ensure there is no discrimination.[449]

There is a tendency across jurisdictions, however, to move away from the aforementioned restrictive approach to substantive review when it comes to the violation of certain categories of substantive public policy. This is especially true where there are serious allegations of fraud or corruption in the underlying contract or where there is found to be an abuse of power by the arbitrators.[450] This tendency is even seen in arbitration-friendly jurisdictions in response to what Pizzuro, Gracia and Perla have described as an increasing 'suspicion' of arbitration.[451] Further analysis of the treatment by courts of the individual heads of substantive public policy will be looked at in the next chapter.

V. Analysis

While all the four aforementioned jurisdictions that have been compared to India are considered to be arbitration-friendly today, this has not always been the case. They rather mostly transitioned from judicial conservatism into a pro-arbitration framework. Even recently, there has been a surprising pushback against arbitration in some of these jurisdictions. A good example would be the EU Parliament and the Member States opposition to arbitration during the TTIP negotiations with the United States,[452] and the EU's initial preference during the Brexit negotiations, for giving jurisdiction in case of a potential dispute between the UK and the EU to the ECJ rather than an arbitral tribunal. Although this has more to do with arbitration in the context of trade and investment law – it still shows that reservations do exist in the minds of several jurisdictions of the efficacy of arbitration in some cases. It, therefore, cannot be expected that every country

449 Francelino da Silva Matuzalem v Fédération Internationale de Football Association (FIFA) [2012] BGE 138 III 322 327 (Swiss Federal Supreme Court).

450 See Joseph D. Pizzurro, Robert B. Garcia and Juan O. Perla, 'Substantive Grounds for Challenge', in J. William Rowley and others (n 87) 92 et seq.

451 See Joseph D. Pizzurro, Robert B. Garcia and Juan O. Perla, 'Substantive Grounds for Challenge', in ibid 97.

452 Bernd Lange (Rapporteur), 'Legislative Train Schedule – Reasonable and Balanced Trade Agreement with the United States, TTIP Negotiations on Investment Protection: Investor-State Dispute Settlement (ISDS)' <https://www.europarl.europa.eu/legislative-train/theme-reasonable-and-balanced-trade-agreement-with-the-united-states/file-ttip-investment-protection-investor-state-dispute-settlement-(isds)> accessed 6 February 2021.

immediately adopts a pro-arbitration approach. Such an approach should rather come naturally with the development of the legal system and society that accepts and has faith in arbitration. Courts will, of course, subsequently reflect such a change in thinking.

Another point to consider is that none of the jurisdictions that have been compared above to India has provided a statutory definition of public policy in their arbitration laws. Even courts in these jurisdictions do not attempt to provide an exhaustive definition as to the scope of the exception. This does not necessarily show that the Indian approach is the wrong one – in fact, every country needs to tailor their laws to meet local needs and circumstances. Indeed, the problem of excessive judicial intervention was much more troubling in India than in other jurisdictions in this comparison, and this could explain the different approaches. What one can, however, learn from this difference is that defining public policy is not necessarily the only way of promoting reduced judicial intervention. There are other factors that play a role. These factors will be looked at in Chapter 5.

A further notable factor in the comparison is the differing approach of states to international and transnational public policy. As demonstrated above, while civil law countries such as France and Germany provide for the use of international public policy for grounds for refusing enforcement of awards both in judicial decisions and even to some extent in statute, the same cannot be said for most common law jurisdictions. The Indian approach towards public policy has more in common with the US and English viewpoint, which has largely avoided the use of terms such as international public policy both in statute as well as jurisprudence. There is an even further aversion towards transnational notions of public policy. This could be because of a feeling that public policy constraints should be tailored to purely local circumstances.

Chapter 4: The innovative approach of Indian arbitration law in dealing with the public policy exception

In the previous chapter, we have seen how parties have time and again approached the Indian Supreme Court to resist the enforcement of arbitral awards. We have also seen how the Court has given the public policy exception varying and sometimes contradictory interpretations leading to a lack of certainty for parties regarding whether their arbitral awards would be enforced. Indian courts have in the past also chosen to interpret public policy under the IAA broadly so as to enable them to interfere in arbitral awards. All these problems arose because of the lack of clarity regarding what would fall under the public policy exception.

It was felt by the Indian legislature that the IAA 1996 did not go far enough in reducing the burden before domestic courts, this can be seen in the 2015 parliamentary debates, where the then law minister clarified that further amending of the IAA 1996 was among the government's main steps towards easing the caseload before courts.[453] The government also felt that work still needed to be done to reform the arbitration law to make India an arbitration-friendly country. This urge for legislative reform was accentuated by the fact that Indian courts had often intervened in foreign arbitral awards on public policy grounds. Legislators felt that judicial intervention by the Supreme Court in cases such as *Western Geco*[454] and *Associate Builders*[455] had led to a situation where the 'amorphous concept' of public policy was defined expansively. In arguing for bringing about an amendment, it was debated that the present situation gave rise to 'justifiable fears that every award could be set aside' for being contrary to public policy.[456]

---

453 See, statement of Law Minister of India, D. V. Sadananda Gowda in 'Lok Sabha Debates (Lower House-Indian Parliament), Sixteenth Series, vol. XIV, Sixth Session, 2015/1937 (Saka), No. 16' (n 23) 23.

454 Oil and Natural Gas Corporation Ltd Vs Western Geco international Ltd 2014 9 SCC 263 (Supreme Court of India).

455 Associate Builders v Delhi Development Authority 2015 3 SCC 49 (Supreme Court of India).

456 See, comments of Member of Parliament, B Senguttuvan in 'Lok Sabha Debates (Lower House-Indian Parliament), Sixteenth Series, vol. XIV, Sixth Session, 2015/1937 (Saka), No. 16' (n 23) 135–136.

In order to overcome the aforementioned difficulties and to provide increased clarity and certainty regarding the scope of the exception, the Indian parliament decided to take the unusual step of providing a statutory definition of the public policy exception in the IAA(Am.) 2015.[457] The goal of the legislation was to make India a preferred arbitration destination as competitive as London.[458]

The pro-arbitration stance of the drafters of the Indian statute was, however, not without criticism. During the parliamentary debates leading up to the amendment of the law, some legislators expressed apprehensions that the law was restricting the scope of public policy. It was argued that reducing the scope of the challenge of the awards on the grounds of public policy would be contrary to upholding the 'majesty of the law' of India.[459]

In this chapter, we will look at the reasoning behind the amendments to the statute and how the public policy exception is defined under the IAA(Am.) 2015. We will then look at how the Indian judiciary reacted to the new statutory definition. A comparative approach will be attempted in order to examine how the Indian approach fares *vis-à-vis* other jurisdictions.

I. Why the 2015 amendments to the IAA defined public policy

The scope of the public policy exception was previously not defined under the IAA but rather left to the interpretation of the courts. This was in consonance with international practice and following from the UNCITRAL Model Law. There is a good reason for this; Indian courts have accepted that public policy is a 'vague' notion of 'uncertain import',[460] and scholars have considered the exception to be 'impossible to define'.[461] Even under English law, which Indian law-makers so often replicate, no definition is provided for the public policy exception.

In the context of Indian law, some general clues exist regarding what public policy means. In its Glossary, the Indian Ministry of Law and Justice defines the term as 'principles in accordance to which actions of men need to be regulated to

457 Justice AP Shah (n 27).

458 Ibid 137.

459 See comments of Member of Parliament Joice George in 'Lok Sabha Debates (Lower House-Indian Parliament), Sixteenth Series, vol. XIV, Sixth Session, 2015/1937 (Saka), No. 16' (n 23) 160.

460 *Mukesh H Mehta v Harindra H Mehta* 1995 3 BomCR 686 (Bombay High Court) [25].

461 Nair (n 5) 729.

achieve the good of the entire community or public.'[462] This definition was generally used by courts as guidance in domestic cases and was not tailored to the needs of commercial entities. There was no specific guidance for courts as to how to interpret the public policy exception in the context of international arbitration. Furthermore, India has thousands of central laws, state laws, and delegated and subordinate legislation. It is clear that not every law, when violated, would result in a breach of public policy in the context of arbitration. Furthermore, many of these statutes, such as the Indian Contract Act 1872, Indian Trusts Act 1882, Special Marriage Act 1954, Indian Penal Code 1860, all make use of the term 'public policy'. But the meaning of public policy in these statutes must be seen in their specific contexts and cannot be the same in the context of international arbitration. There was, therefore, a lack of clarity for courts concerning the scope of public policy.

To solve the problems caused by excessive intervention due to broad judicial interpretation of the public policy exception, the 20th Law Commission, headed by former Chief Justice of the Delhi High Court, Justice AP Shah, was constituted by the Indian government. The Law Commission, in its Report, recommended wide-ranging amendments to the IAA,[463] including suggestions for defining the scope of the public policy exception.[464] The main objectives for defining the scope of the exception will be elaborated on below

1. To reduce the scope for judicial intervention and ensure arbitral awards are final and binding

From looking at the parliamentary debates before the enactment of IAA(Am.) 2015, it is clear that the Indian legislature decided to statutorily restrict the scope of public policy to undo the effect of Supreme Court decisions that had given the exception an extremely broad interpretation.[465] Such a broad interpretation by the courts put at risk the finality that is crucial for the success of arbitration as a means of dispute resolution. Before the amendment, public policy, as interpreted

462 Ministry of Law & Justice, Government of India, 'Legal Glossary' <http://lawmin.nic.in/Legis.htm> accessed 23 January 2017. Ministry of Law & Justice, Government of India, 'Legal Glossary' <http://lawmin.nic.in/Legis.htm> accessed 23 January 2017.

463 Justice A. P. Shah (n 27).

464 ibid 22.

465 'Lok Sabha Debates (Lower House-Indian Parliament), Sixteenth Series, vol. XIV, Sixth Session, 2015/1937 (Saka), No. 16' (n 23) 136.

by Indian courts, also included broad grounds such as 'interest of India' and 'patent illegality', which were done away with by the statutory definition.

There is a presumption in arbitration that awards will be final and binding.[466] This is one of the key contributions of the New York Convention and one of the reasons why the Convention did away with the process of 'double exequatur' in the enforcement of awards. It is this binding nature that makes arbitration attractive to the parties. The benefits of this finality, however, will not reach the parties if there is excessive intervention and review of decisions of the tribunal by national courts. As seen in the previous chapter, Indian courts were previously not averse to using their discretion to re-look the decisions of arbitral tribunals on merits. The legislature, therefore, decided that providing a definition of public policy would reduce unwarranted judicial intervention and thereby ensure the finality of arbitral awards.

2. To provide certainty to parties

The intention of the legislature in setting out to define the term public policy was to put to rest all controversies about its meaning, scope and ambit.[467] By providing a definition, the lawmaker would be able to provide certainty to the parties as to the scope of the exception. Certainty is vital for commercial parties who undertake business transactions internationally. An idea of what constitutes a country's public policy will allow businesses to tailor their contracts to avoid violating these provisions. Furthermore, parties would be able to avoid spending considerable resources in arbitration proceedings, where there is a manifest violation of the defined public policy, and it is clear that the chance of refusing enforcement of the award at a later stage is high.

Although the move by the Indian legislature to diverge from the UNCITRAL Model Law by defining the scope of the public policy exception was innovative, it was not surprising. Even if one were to look at the drafting history of the Model Law, in the eighteenth session, the Indian delegation raised concerns as to the inadequacy of the public policy exception under the Model Law. It urged that the term public policy in Article 36 para 1b(ii) was 'too vague and allowed

466 Brenda McGrath, 'Presumption of Finality in Arbitration' (1990) 5 Journal of International Banking Law N70–71.

467 Ministry of Law & Justice, Government of India, 'Proposed Amendments to the Arbitration & Conciliation Act, 1996' (2010) A Consultation Paper 128 <lawmin.nic.in/la/consultationpaper.pdf> accessed 26 July 2016.

conflicting interpretations'.[468] The move to define the public policy exception must be seen in the light of this drafting history. Furthermore, as emphasized by the Supreme Court in its *Konkan Railway* decision, the IAA is not meant to be a replica of the Model Law; rather, the Model Law was merely 'taken into account' by the drafters of the Act.[469] This could justify the legislatures decision to diverge from the Model Law approach and provide a definition of public policy.

India is not the only country to have decided on defining the public policy exception. A small but growing number of states across varied legal systems such as New Zealand, Malaysia, Australia, Sweden and the UAE have also chosen to provide some form of a statutory definition of public policy in their arbitration regimes. The approach of some of these states will be dealt with in more detail in Chapter 5.

II. The treatment of public policy under the Indian arbitration law

While the IAA does not replicate the UNCITRAL Model Law, it is still largely based on it.[470] However, a few important differences exist. Firstly, while the Model Law deals solely with international commercial arbitrations, and the New York Convention with foreign awards, the IAA is divided into two parts. Part I deals with domestic awards and Part II with foreign awards. This is different from some jurisdictions such as Australia and Singapore, where international arbitration and domestic arbitration are dealt with under separate statutes. The legislative choice of dealing with foreign and domestic awards under the same statute assumes significance insofar as it leads to there being two different versions/interpretations of public policy under the IAA.

Section 48 of the Act (in Part II), which provides grounds for refusing enforcement of a foreign award, places a higher threshold for intervention in foreign awards than in domestic awards on public policy grounds.[471] In contrast,

468 'UNCITRAL, 18th Session, Analytical Compilation of Comments by Governments and International Organizations on the Draft Text of a Model Law on International Commercial Arbitration – Report of the Secretary General' (1985) A/CN.9/263 54.

469 Konkan Railway Corporation Ltd. vs Rani Construction Pvt. Ltd. (n 123) para 16.

470 Pradeep Nayak, Sulabh Rewari, and Vikas Mahendra, 'Arbitration Procedures and Practice in India: Overview: A Q&A Guide to Arbitration Law and Practice in India' [2021] Practical Law Country Q&A, Thomson Reuters, Westlaw 3.

471 *Django Navigation Ltd vs Indo Ferro Metal Pvt Ltd* [2018] MANU/RH/0086 (Rajasthan High Court – Jaipur Bench).

section 34 (in Part I), which provides when domestic awards can be set aside, has a lower threshold for invoking the public policy exception. This means that under the Indian regime, it is significantly easier to invoke the public policy exception when dealing with domestic awards than when dealing with foreign awards. This is in line with the New York Convention, which provides for presumptive enforcement of foreign arbitral awards.[472] This is especially important with regard to foreign awards, where the (foreign) party seeking enforcement is otherwise at a disadvantage if public policy exception could easily be invoked by the award debtor before courts in its home country.

India is not the only country to take such an approach. In most countries, public policy exception is interpreted in a more narrow sense with regard to foreign awards than with respect to domestic awards. Such an approach, while widely accepted, is not uncontroversial. Arguments can be made against giving public policy a more restrictive interpretation when it comes to foreign awards. Born has pointed out that the drafters of the New York Convention did not intend it to be easier to enforce foreign awards *vis-à-vis* domestic awards.[473] According to his analysis, the Convention does not require 'expeditious or efficient procedural measures for enforcing a (foreign) award'; it only requires similar treatment to domestic measures.[474] It can, by implication, be argued that public policy does not have to be interpreted more narrowly when it comes to foreign awards. Such an approach has worked very well in some jurisdictions. For instance, Germany has an equally high threshold for refusing enforcement of domestic and foreign awards due to the pro-enforcement bias.[475]

There can, however, be difficulty in nomenclature. While the IAA provides different treatment for foreign awards, it does not, however, explicitly elaborate on the prerequisites for an award to be considered foreign. One can make an inference from the Act that any award where the place of arbitration is outside India would be a foreign award. The Calcutta High Court has given a more expansive interpretation in its *Serajuddin* ruling, where it held that an award is considered foreign where one of the parties is foreign, the proceedings are conducted

472 Born (n 419) 3410.

473 ibid 3408.

474 ibid 3408.

475 Axel Benjamin Herzberg and Bodenheimer Herzberg, 'Enforcement of Judgments and Arbitral Awards in Germany: Overview' [2017] Practical Law Country Q&A, Thomson Reuters, Westlaw 1, 25.

outside India, by foreign arbitrators and where a foreign law applies.[476] There has since been a change in jurisprudence. The Indian Supreme Court in *PASL* has clarified that an award could be considered foreign even if both parties are from India as long as the arbitral seat is outside India.[477]

There is another area where Indian law differs from the approach taken by other Model Law countries with a common-law heritage. The IAA is different from other arbitral regimes insofar as it does not explicitly distinguish between the first step of recognising the award and then the second step of subsequently enforcing it. These divergent steps have been seemingly merged under sections 46–49 of the IAA. In fact, the relevant provisions do not mention the procedure for refusing recognition of a foreign award; instead, they seem to focus only on when enforcement could be refused. This differs, for instance, from the approach of Australia, where section 35 of the International Arbitration Act explicitly provides for first the 'recognition' and then the 'enforcement' of awards.[478]

1. Treatment of public policy exception with respect to foreign awards

The Indian legislature, keeping in mind the need for certainty regarding the treatment of foreign awards, defined the scope of the public policy exception in the IAA(Am.) 2015.[479] Section 48(2)b of the Act now provides that 'enforcement of a foreign award may be refused if the court finds that such enforcement would be contrary to the public policy of India'. The explanatory note to section 48 clarifies that 'an award is in conflict with the public policy of India, only if, –

(i) the making of the award was induced or affected by fraud or corruption or was in violation of section 75 or section 81; or
(ii) it is in contravention with the fundamental policy of Indian law; or
(iii) it is in conflict with the most basic notions of morality or justice.'

Furthermore, it stated that determining if '*there is a contravention with the fundamental policy of Indian law shall not entail a review on the merits of the dispute*.' It is clear from the wording of the provision and the use of the term 'only' that the

476 *Serajuddin and Co v Michael Golodetz and Ors* [1959] AIR 1960 Cal 47 (High Court of Calcutta) para 42.
477 PASL Wind Solutions v. GE Power Conversion India (n 170) para 59.
478 International Arbitration Act (Cth) (Act No 136 of 1974 as amended).
479 The Arbitration and Conciliation (Amendment) Act.

legislature intended this provision to be definitive with regard to the interpretation of the public policy exception under Indian law.

While a detailed elaboration of this provision will be made later in this thesis, it is important to note that the definition sought to provide increased certainty in international arbitration by defining public policy in a way that was both narrow and comprehensive. This definition is in contrast to the definition provided for domestic awards, which is relatively broader.

2. Treatment of public policy exception with respect to domestic awards

The IAA(Am.)2015 has distinguished when the public policy exception can be used to set aside domestic awards from when the exception can be used with respect to refusing enforcement of foreign awards. Part I of the Act, which deals with domestic awards, envisions a broader interpretation of the exception. This distinction is, however, hardly noticeable in the wording of the Act. Just like for foreign awards, even for domestic awards, the public policy exception can only be invoked according to section 34(2)b if the award was induced by fraud/corruption, contravenes the fundamental policy of Indian law or is in conflict with the most basic notions of morality and justice. The only distinction can be found in the explanatory notes of section 34, where it is stated that domestic awards may also be set aside in case it is *prima facie* 'patently illegal'. Even in such cases, courts are excluded from relying on the exception because the tribunal wrongly interpreted the law or based on 're-appreciation of the evidence'.

Despite the negligible difference in wording seen in the statute, Indian courts have consistently held that the public policy exception in relation to domestic awards must be treated differently from foreign awards. For example, in its Lal Mahal decision, the Supreme Court held that 'public policy' with regard to foreign awards is 'more limited' than in the domestic context and that while both provisions are similar in wording, they 'differ in degree'.[480] The Madras High Court reiterated this in its *Thaicom* ruling, where the court held that public policy under section 48(2)b must be read more narrowly than public policy under section 34.[481]

480 Shri Lal Mahal Ltd v. Progetto Grano Spa (n 211) para 25.

481 Thaicom Public Company Limited v Raj Television Network Ltd [2016] Orig Petition No 127 (Madras High Court) [23].

The distinction between a domestic award and a foreign award is sometimes hazy. In certain circumstances, international awards are also treated as domestic awards. This would be true in the case of international arbitrations seated in India. Such awards are also governed by Part I of the IAA, and therefore, the public policy exception is given a broader interpretation when it comes to enforcement.[482]

III. Analysis of the amendment to section 48(2)b

In order to understand the legislative standard for the use of public policy exception for refusing enforcement of foreign awards under Indian law, it is important to look at each of the heads of section 48(2)b individually. Guidance as to the scope of the definition of public policy can be gained from judgments of the Supreme Court.

1. The making of the award was induced or affected by fraud or corruption or was in violation of section 75 or section 81

The explanatory notes to section 48 of the IAA(Am.) 2015 provide that the public policy ground can be invoked if the 'making of the award was induced or affected by fraud or corruption'. Neither the UNCITRAL Model Law nor the New York Convention specifically authorizes courts to refuse enforcement of awards vitiated by fraud or corruption. This is also true for most other international arbitration regimes and national legislation, which do not provide this ground.[483]

Despite the absence of a statutory rule to this effect, courts in many jurisdictions have themselves recognised fraud and corruption as grounds for refusing enforcement. This is because fraud and corruption are 'global problems', considered to be 'perilous to society'.[484] They are considered to go against transnational public policy.[485] The reason, as rightly pointed out by Lauterpacht, lies in the principle of *ex injuria jus non oritur*, i.e., 'an illegality cannot be the source of a

482 The Arbitration and Conciliation (Amendment) Act.

483 Born (n 419) 846.

484 Carlos F. Concepción, 'Combating Corruption and Fraud from an International Arbitration Perspective' (2016) 9 Arbitraje: Revista de Arbitraje Comercial y de Inversiones, IproLex 371.

485 See, Carolyn B. Lamm, Hansel T. Pham, et al., 'Fraud and Corruption in International Arbitration', in Cremades, Fernández-Ballesteros and Arias (n 401) 706.

legal right to the wrongdoer.'[486] In the words of Lord Mansfield in the *Holman* ruling, public policy means, '*ex dolo malo non oritor action. No Court will lend its aid to a man who founds his cause of action upon an immoral or an illegal act*'.[487] As fraud and corruption are particularly common in developing countries, including India, it is not surprising that they would be included within the scope of the exception.

To correctly interpret the scope of the public policy exception, we will now distinguish fraud from corruption and evaluate when these grounds could lead to refusing the enforcement of arbitral awards.

(a) Refusing enforcements of awards vitiated by fraud

Despite providing fraud as grounds for refusing enforcement, the IAA does not elaborate on what would constitute fraud for the purposes of the exception. Generally speaking, fraud almost always includes an element of dishonesty.[488] During the Covid-19 contagion, there has been an increase in fraud globally, which is quite often a result of the tendency for self-enrichment at the cost of others, be it pecuniary gain or otherwise.[489]

In the context of arbitration, Lamm has characterized fraud to include the 'knowing misrepresentation' to induce someone to act in a particular way, for instance, providing false documents during the arbitral proceedings or misrepresenting the facts before the arbitrator.[490]Under German law, according to Kröll, the public policy exception would be invoked if there was an element of fraud in the proceedings that affected the award, including in the use of 'fraudulent documents, expert reports, or witness statements'.[491]

In the Indian context, the term 'fraud' has been defined by section 17 of the Indian Contract Act 1872. According to this provision,

486 Hersch Lauterpacht, *Recognition in International Law* (Cambridge University Press 1947) 420–421.

487 *Holman v Johnson* [1775] 1 Cowp 341 (Court of King's Bench) 343–344.

488 Daniel Greenberg, 'Fraud and Bribery' [2021] Thomson Reuters Westlaw Update para 15.

489 Barry Rider, 'Fraud – How Serius Are We?' (2021) 42 Company Lawyer 299.

490 See, Carolyn B. Lamm, Hansel T. Pham, et al., 'Fraud and Corruption in International Arbitration', in Cremades, Fernández-Ballesteros and Arias (n 401) 715.

491 See, Stefan Kröll, Foreign Awards, in Böckstiegel, Kröll and Nacimiento (n 378) 492.

17. "Fraud" means and includes any of the following acts committed by a party to a contract, or with his connivance, or by his agent, with intent to deceive another party thereto or his agent, or to induce him to enter into the contract: —
(1) the suggestion, as a fact, of that which is not true, by one who does not believe it to be true;
(2) the active concealment of a fact by one having knowledge or belief of the fact;
(3) a promise made without any intention of performing it;
(4) any other act fitted to deceive;
(5) any such act or omission as the law specially declares to be fraudulent.

Although this definition is not drafted keeping in mind international commercial arbitrations, it provides an understanding as to what constitutes fraud in the Indian context.

According to the Indian Supreme Court, fraud would include misrepresentation.[492] Fraud would also entail deception.[493] In the case of *Teja Singh*, where a foreign judgment was challenged on the grounds that it was obtained by misleading the foreign court, the Indian Supreme Court held that this constituted fraud.[494]

When it comes to international arbitration, certain other misconduct of a party during the arbitral process may also lead to violation of the public policy exception. This would include providing the tribunal with forged documents, undue influence of witnesses, hiding evidence/documents from the tribunal.[495] Furthermore, misconduct by the witnesses may also lead to the award being vitiated, i.e., when the witness is dishonest and commits perjury.[496]

In the context of the discourse on enforcement of arbitral awards, fraud can arise at three different stages. Firstly, fraudulent means may be used to convince a party to enter into the contract. Secondly, there may be fraud in fulfilling contractual obligations, and thirdly, fraud can occur in proceedings before the arbitral tribunal. It must be made clear from the outset that under Indian law, the

---

492 *Ram Chandra Singh Vs Savitri Devi and Ors* [2003] 8 SCC 319 (Supreme Court of India).
493 *SP Chengalyaraya Naidu v Jagannath* [1994] SCC 1 (Supreme Court of India).
494 *Satya v Teja Singh* [1975] AIR 105 (Supreme Court of India).
495 See, Bernard Hanotiau, 'Misdeeds, Wrongful Conduct and Illegality in Arbitral Proceedings', in A. J. van den Berg (ed), *International Commercial Arbitration: Important Contemporary Questions*, vol 11 (ICCA Congress Series, Kluwer Law International 2003) 266 et seq.
496 See, Bernard Hanotiau, 'Misdeeds, Wrongful Conduct and Illegality in Arbitral Proceedings', in A. J. van den Berg (ed), ibid 265.

public policy exception could be invoked only if 'the making of the award' is affected by fraud. The explanatory note to Sec. 48(2)b IAA provides that the public policy exception could be invoked for refusing enforcement of an award that was obtained by fraudulent means. In this situation, the courts at the place of enforcement (Indian courts) would be empowered to refuse enforcement, whereas courts have limited leeway in the first and second situations. This is the only reasonable outcome, as to evaluate the presence of fraud in the underlying contract, the court will need to go into forbidden territory by looking at the merits of the case.

Despite this general rule, there is a dichotomy with regard to the treatment of fraud in the underlying contract by Indian courts. If allegations of fraud in the contract were to come before an arbitrator, who proceeds to make a ruling, such an award would normally be enforceable in India. However, allegations of 'serious fraud' in the underlying contract are considered not arbitrable under Indian law.[497] It is, therefore, unlikely that an award rendered where there are such allegations raised would be enforceable in India.

There is the possibility that allegations of fraud may be misused by a party to derail enforcement of arbitral awards or at least to cause delay. In order to reduce the possibility of such a misuse of the exception, the burden of proving the existence of fraud should fall on the party resisting enforcement of the award. This is acknowledged in the Indian context as well. According to Indian law, there exists an initial presumption that the award is not vitiated by fraud.[498]

The question arises as to whether mere fraud by one of the parties in obtaining an award is sufficient in itself to justify refusing enforcement of the award on public policy grounds. The Indian Supreme Court has answered in the affirmative. The Court has dealt very strictly with fraud. In its Venture Global ruling of 2017, it held that '*fraud results in vitiating the entire judicial/arbitral proceedings including judgment/order/award.... On proving existence of commission of fraud, ... the judicial/arbitral proceedings are rendered illegal and void ab initio.*'[499]

497 A Ayyasamy v A Paramasivam & Ors (n 234) para 37.

498 See, Conditions for Enforcement of Foreign Awards, in Part II, Chapter I, in RS Bachawat, *Justice R.S. Bachawat's Law of Arbitration & Conciliation (Including International Commercial Arbitration & ADR)* (Anirudh Wadhwa and Bejoy Kumar Bachawat eds, LexisNexis Buterworths Wadhwa Nagpur 2010) 2414.

499 Venture Global Engineering LLC and Ors Vs Tech Mahindra Ltd and Ors [2017] MANU/SC/1373/2017 (Supreme Court of India).

The Indian approach is, however, not the most pro-enforcement. In Singapore, which is also a common-law jurisdiction that has adopted the Model Law, a different approach has been taken. Justice Judith Prakash of the High Court of Singapore held that, although perjury and withholding documents amounted to fraud, proving fraud would not be sufficient. For the public policy exception to be breached, such fraud must have caused 'substantial injustice' or have a 'substantial impact on the making of the award'.[500]

Even under English law, merely misleading the other party or the tribunal during the proceedings would not amount to fraud warranting judicial intervention. For the award to be vitiated, it must have been attained by making use of 'dishonest, reprehensible or unconscionable conduct'.[501] Furthermore, for the exception to be invoked, it needs to be shown that the party was unable to get the allegations of fraud addressed by the arbitrator.[502] An even narrower approach to enforcement of awards under English law was taken in the *Honeywell* decision, where it observed that there are no public policy grounds by which enforcement of an award would be refused merely because false evidence was put before a tribunal.[503] In its recent *Sinocore* ruling, the Court of Appeals (England and Wales) also held that a mere failed attempted fraud would not be sufficient to breach public policy.[504] The reasoning for this approach is that public policy considerations, if any, would, according to English courts, be outweighed 'by the interests of finality'.[505]

A similar restrictive approach to invoking the public policy exception before national courts in case of 'fraud' during the arbitral proceedings is also taken in Germany. Here, to prevent abuse, in case of fraud, a party is only able to rely on the public policy exception in court if he has not had the opportunity to bring a claim before the arbitral tribunal.[506] The German approach goes even further in

500 Swiss Singapore Overseas Enterprises Pte Ltd v. Exim Rajathi India Pvt Ltd (n 95) para 29.

501 *Celtic Bioenergy Limited v Knowles Limited* [2017] EWHC 472 (High Court of Justice, Queen's Bench Division, Technology and Construction Court) [67].

502 Lord Collins and others (n 301) paras 16–151.

503 *Honeywell International Middle East Ltd v Meydan Group LLC* [2014] WL 1219934 (High Court of Justice, England & Wales, Queen's Bench Division Technology and Construction Court).

504 *RBRG Trading (UK) Ltd v Sinocore International Co Ltd* [2018] EWCA Civ 838 (England and Wales Court of Appeal (Civil Division) Decisions) [38].

505 ibid 40.

506 See, Stefan Kröll, Foreign Awards, in Böckstiegel, Kröll and Nacimiento (n 378) 492.

safeguarding party autonomy – where a claim has already been made before the tribunal, and the party is still not satisfied, German courts will act with extreme caution in invoking public policy and would base their decision more on the behavior of the tribunal than on that of the parties.[507]

The narrow approach of the English, German and Singapore courts contrasts to the blanket approach to fraud in the arbitral proceedings provided for in the IAA. While the Indian approach justifiably prioritizes penalizing fraud at all costs, the approach taken by the other aforementioned jurisdictions tries to ensure that parties are protected from the most blatant cases of fraud, but also seeks to respect *Kompetenz-Kompetenz* by giving the arbitrator the right to remedy the defect in the first place.

(b) Refusing enforcements of foreign awards on the grounds of corruption

Corruption is considered abhorrent and goes against the 'core values' of most countries.[508] It is truly pernicious, as it can have a devastating impact on a country's economic and social development.[509] The menace of corruption is considered to be timeless and universal,[510] although there are variations in different countries as to the degree.

Although it is rare to find cases where corruption during the arbitral proceedings has led to the challenge of an arbitral award, even such situations may arise. Corruption can have a very negative effect on arbitration. It not only directly affects the parties involved but also harms public confidence in arbitration. There are three situations in which the shadow of corruption can shroud arbitration. Firstly, where the *making of the* award itself is affected or induced by corruption. Secondly, where *enforcement* of the award would result in vindicating a corrupt contract. Thirdly, where the *underlying contract* is itself obtained by corrupt means. How the IAA deals with these three situations will be evaluated below.

---

507 ibid.

508 Vladimir Pavić, 'Bribery and International Commercial Arbitration – The Role of Mandatory Rules and Public Policy' (2012) 43 Victoria University Wellington Law Review 661, 668.

509 U. Myint, 'Corruption: Causes, Consequences and Cures' (2000) 7 Asia-Pacific Development Journal 33, 34.

510 Vito Tanzi, 'Corruption Around the World : Causes, Consequences, Scope and Cures' 4 <https://www.imf.org/external/pubs/ft/wp/wp9863.pdf> accessed 2 September 2021.

(i) Where the award is obtained by corrupt means

Just like fraud, an award obtained by corrupt means would also contravene Indian public policy. Given the harmful effect of corruption on society as a whole and in the faith people have in arbitration, it is understandable that the Indian legislature would be hesitant to allow enforcement of tainted awards. The IAA does not provide any guidance as to what would constitute corruption for the purpose of the public policy exception. Looking at its literal meaning, scholars have described the term 'corruption' to include giving 'something of value' in order to influence an authority in the performance of official duties.[511] In the context of arbitration, corruption could, for instance, include providing financial or non-financial incentives to the arbitrator. For instance, a party could offer the arbitrator a share of the potential arbitral award. If proven that the arbitrator was so influenced, this would undoubtedly be a blatant violation of public policy.

While corruption can be of many hues and forms, Mills has categorized corruption by an arbitrator into two over-arching categories, financial corruption and intellectual corruption.[512] Whereas intellectual corruption is akin to prejudice, racism or bias, which could, for instance, be perpetrated by an arbitrator from a different cultural/socio-economic background, financial corruption directly relates to the pecuniary benefit derived by the arbitrator and can take many forms.[513] Given that intellectual corruption, unless expressed manifestly, is very hard to prove, it is more likely that situations leading to the challenge of arbitral awards under section 48(2)b would be relating to financial corruption. An award that is a fruit of intellectual corruption could nevertheless potentially violate 'most basic principles of justice' head of public policy under the IAA, which will be dealt with later in this chapter.

There are numerous situations that can give rise to corrupt practices. Section 16 of the IAA provides that determination of jurisdiction is the prerogative of the arbitral tribunal. The first risk is that an arbitrator may wrongly accept jurisdiction or protract the proceedings in order to ensure that he/she gets additional fees. This problem is exacerbated by the fact that excessive arbitrator fees is a

511 See, Carolyn B. Lamm, Hansel T. Pham, et al., 'Fraud and Corruption in International Arbitration', in Cremades, Fernández-Ballesteros and Arias (n 401) 699.

512 Karen Mills, 'Corruption and Other Illegality in the Formation and Performance of Contracts and in the Conduct of Arbitration Relating Thereto' (2002) 5 International Arbitration Law Review 130 et seq.

513 ibid 130 et seq.

acknowledged problem in India, where ad-hoc arbitration is common – the fees even sometimes exceeding the amount at dispute.[514]

One can argue that it is difficult for courts to second guess the motivation of arbitrators – and it is not their job to do so. Furthermore, as such conduct by the tribunal would be equally harmful to both parties, it may not lead to a manifestly unfair or one-sided award. This may very well be the case; however, courts are certainly willing to intervene where they feel that the tribunal has wrongly decided on its jurisdiction. The Indian Supreme Court in the *Vidya Drolia* case has spoken about the possibility of courts giving a second look if the tribunal has erred in determining jurisdiction.[515] Even in the UK, as seen in the *Dallah* ruling of the UK Supreme Court has shown its willingness to intervene and relook the question of jurisdiction where there are doubts as to a parties consent to arbitration.[516]

Intellectual corruption could also arise at the stage of making an award due to the fact that the arbitrator's fees are proportional to the quantum of the award made, he/she would make an unjustifiably large award in favor of one of the parties.[517]

Mills has highlighted other situations where intellectual corruption may arise. Even when each party gets to appoint an arbitrator to the panel, there is a general expectation that the arbitrators are neutral. However, there is a risk that a party-appointed arbitrator may make an award favoring 'his party'.[518] This risk is even higher when it comes to a sole-arbitrator. It is precisely with the view to guard against such risk of bias, that the Indian Supreme Court in *Perkins Eastmann* ruling held that a sole-arbitrator cannot be appointed by a party that has an interest in the outcome of the dispute.[519] The tendency of bias was aptly described by the US 2nd Circuit in the *Lloyds of London* ruling, where it observed that party-appointed arbitrators might act as *'de facto advocates'* for the parties.[520]

514 *Union of India v, M/S Singh Builders Syndicate* (2009) 4 SCC 523 (Supreme Court of India) [10].

515 *Vidya Drolia Ors v Durga Trading Corporation* [2020] Civ Appeal No 2402 2019 (Supreme Court of India) [54].

516 Dallah Real Estate and Tourism Holding Company v The Ministry of Religious Affairs, Government of Pakistan [2010] UKSC 46 (UK Supreme Court) [26–31].

517 Karen Mills (n 512) 130 et seq.

518 ibid 130.

519 *Perkins Eastman Architects Dpc vs HSCC (India) Limited* [2019] Arbitr Appl No32 (Supreme Court of India) [15–16].

520 Certain Underwriting Members of Lloyds of London v Insurance Company of the Americas [2018] United States Court of Appeals for the Second Circuit 17-1137-cv 10.

This could certainly lead to conflicts about whether courts should exercise the same degree of restraint with regard to intervening in any award where an evidently biased arbitrator participated.

Another situation where intellectual corruption may arise is when an arbitrator favors a party that is more likely to give him/her a repeat appointment. Repeat appointments of arbitrators in commercial arbitration is certainly not an uncommon phenomenon.[521] In the context of consumer arbitration, this could potentially risk the economically weaker party, i.e., the consumer not having a fair trial.

It is not only arbitrators who can be corrupt. Corruption could also include bribing a witness in the arbitration proceedings. Furthermore, it is not only corruption by the parties that could give rise to conflicts. In case a third party is funding the arbitration proceedings for one of the parties, an inappropriate incentive given to the arbitrator or a witness by a third party would also obviously constitute corruption.

The need for targeting the menace of corrupt arbitrators is reflected not just in Indian law. It is also seen in the Additional Protocol to the Criminal Law Convention on Corruption, which provides that the EU Member States shall take measures to criminalize both active and passive bribery of both domestic and foreign arbitrators.[522] The Protocol provides a more elaborate definition of what kind of corrupt behavior would be prohibited. Article 2 seeks to criminalize *'the promising, offering or giving by any person,'* and Article 3 *'the request or receipt by an arbitrator' 'directly or indirectly, of any undue advantage'* to influence an arbitrator to act or to refrain from acting in a particular way.

It is widely accepted that arbitral awards that enable a party to benefit from 'proceeds of corruption' would not be enforceable.[523] This brings us to another situation where public policy can successfully be invoked. This is when allegations of corruption have been raised before the tribunal, but the tribunal fails to address them. Here courts may be able to make a deeper examination and look at the 'ingredients' of the award, both factual and legal, to see if public policy has been violated.[524] Pavic has justified such increased judicial scrutiny

521 Will Sheng Wilson Koh, 'Think Quality Not Quantity: Repeat Appointments and Arbitrator Challenges' (2017) 34 Journal of International Arbitration 711.

522 Additional Protocol to the Criminal Law Convention on Corruption 2003 (European Treaty Series 191).

523 Born (n 419) 3673.

524 Vladimir Pavić (n 508) 684 et seq.

due to courts being 'the final guardians of…the public policy against bribery and corruption'.[525] In case the arbitral tribunal reaches an award ignoring flagrant evidence of corruption, courts are empowered to refuse enforcement of such awards. There is an important justification for such an approach. The public policy considerations of preventing enforcement of an award giving effect to a corrupt practice far outweighs pro-enforcement public policy considerations.[526]

(ii) Where the award gives effect to a corrupt contract

Although the IAA is clear that awards will not be recognised where the *'making of the award'* was induced or affected by corruption, there is a certain ambiguity in the provision. It is silent as to what happens in situations where there is no corruption in *making the award,* that the arbitrators have clean hands, but rather the award itself gives effect to the performance of a corrupt act. This would be the case where the tribunal renders an award that gives effect/enforces a contract where one of the parties has to perform a corrupt act, i.e., pay a bribe, facilitation payment or in case of a so-called *consultancy contract* – to pay the fees owed to the consultant/intermediary who influences a government officer (possibly by corrupt means). While the laws of most countries provide that contracts directly giving effect to corruption would be void or voidable,[527] contracts to hire an intermediary to influence a foreign public official for being awarded a tender (where corruption is not proven) is considered perfectly legal in some jurisdictions, e.g., Switzerland, whereas they are considered illegal in other jurisdictions including Algeria.[528] What would the consequences under Indian law be, however, if an award enforcing such a contract is rendered by an arbitral tribunal?

If the explanatory notes to section 48(2)b of the IAA is given its literal interpretation, the word 'only', which strictly limits the scope of the exception to what is contained in the provision, would mean that public policy would be violated solely where corruption was in the making of the arbitral award. By implication, corruption in the underlying contract would not contravene Indian public policy. Such a result would, however, be absurd. It is difficult to imagine such a

525 ibid 685.

526 Arthur Marriot, 'Corruption in Arbitation and Mediation Compared' (2006) 72 Arbitration 231, 233.

527 Yoanna Schuch, 'Tackling Corrupion in International Arbitration – Key Issues and Challenges' (2019) 32 Young Arbitration Review 53, 57.

528 This situation arose in the case of *Omnium de Traitement et de Valorisation SA v Hilmarton Ltd* (1999) 2 ER Comm 146 (Queen's Bench Division (Commercial Court)).

consequence being in line with the intention of the legislature. This is even more true as the Indian legislature has explicitly recognised the menace of corruption and criminalized the taking or giving of bribes under the Prevention of Corruption Act 1988 (PCA).[529] Consultancy/intermediaries have often been misused to facilitate corruption in India, especially with regard to defence contracts.[530] Even such contracts to unduly influencing a public official for pecuniary gain are criminalized under Section 7a of the PCA. There is little reason to think that Indian courts would be content to enforce an award that gives effect to such an agreement. The only way to resolve this conflict is to consider such an award which gives effect to a corrupt contract as violating other heads of the public policy exception, i.e., 'fundamental policy of Indian law, or 'morality and justice'.

By taking such an approach, Indian courts will not be treading completely new ground. Even in other jurisdictions that are considered arbitration-friendly, arbitral awards enforcing corrupt contracts are not looked upon favorably by courts at the place of enforcement. In Germany, for instance, an award that gives effect to a corrupt act, such as to pay a bribe, would contravene German public policy.[531]

(iii) Where the underlying contract itself is obtained by corrupt means

A closely related problem arises in the case of contracts obtained by corrupt means. For instance, where a company wins a contract to supply machinery or to extract oil by paying a bribe to an employee of a government enterprise or a government official. This is more often a defence in investment arbitration, but it could arise even in the case of commercial arbitration. For example, where the company affected by the bribe is part of a private-public partnership.

Allegations of corruption in the underlying contract does not automatically leave the arbitral tribunal without jurisdiction.[532] The role of courts in such situations was well described by the High Court (England & Wales) in the landmark case, *Westacre vs Jugoimport*. The Court observed that where there is corruption,

---

529 The Prevention of Corruption Act (No. 49) 1988.

530 Prashant Mara and Devina Deshpande, 'Anti-Bribery and Corruption in Defence Procurement in India: Risks and Mitigation Measures' (*BTG Legal Update-Lexology*, April 2021) <https://www.lexology.com/library/detail.aspx?g=440012c5-74ef-429d-9dbb-468c345ba49b> accessed 17 July 2021.

531 See, Stefan Kröll, Foreign Awards, in Böckstiegel, Kröll and Nacimiento (n 378) 488.

532 For a comprehensive elaboration on the allocation of jurisdiction between courts and the arbitral tribunal see, *Infra* Chapter 6(I)1b(i).

courts would have to undertake the delicate task of balancing the 'public policy of sustaining international arbitration agreements' with 'the public policy against enforcement of corrupt transactions.'[533] It went on to hold that under English law that it would be the former would take precedence, and arbitral tribunals would therefore have jurisdiction to make a determination on illegality.[534]

While the duty of looking into allegations of bribery in the underlying contract first falls on the arbitrators,[535] there may be situations where the issue of corruption was not raised before the arbitral tribunal or the issues were raised and the tribunal did not sufficiently address the issues. In such situations, national courts are faced with the difficult task of deciding whether to enforce any resulting award. On the one hand, enforcing such awards may appear to be the most effective in terms of respecting party autonomy- in fact, there are valid justifications for enforcing the award when the party has purposefully not raised the allegations before the arbitrator. These justifications include disincentivising parties who use challenges as a delaying tactic. On the other hand, there is the risk that enforcing such a tainted award may lead to bad policy by rewarding parties engaging in corruption. Even arbitration-friendly jurisdictions are not averse to intervening in such awards. In France, for instance, the *Cour d'appel de Paris* set aside an arbitral award that validated a settlement agreement entered into by the Libyan government and a private company that was tainted by corruption.[536] The Court, in effect, held that it is fundamental to the French legal system that bribery of national or foreign public servants would not be tolerated, and that an award enforcing such a tainted contract would violate the international public policy of France.[537]

The need for combatting corruption takes on more urgency in the Indian context. In order to combat the evil of corruption, the Indian legislature decided to further amend the IAA via the Arbitration Ordinance 2020 (IAO 2020).[538] Section 36 now provides that if a *prima facie* case is made out that the underlying contract or the arbitration agreement, or making of the award is a result of fraud

533 *Westacre Investments Inc v Jugoimport-SDRP Holding Company Ltd & Ors* [1997] 1999 QB 740 (High Court of Justice, Queen's Bench Division) 769–770.

534 ibid 771.

535 See, Anne-Catherine Hahn, 'Bribery Allegations in Arbitration Proceedings' in James H. Carter (ed), *The International Arbitration Review* (10th edn, Law Business Research Ltd 2019) 37–38.

536 *Libyan State v Sorelec* No 18-02568 17 Novemb 2020 (Cour d'appel de Paris).

537 ibid 33–34.

538 The Arbitration and Conciliation (Amendment) Ordinance 2020 (No 14).

or corruption, the court shall unconditionally stay such an award till it hears the challenge. This obliges the court to at least temporarily stall enforcement where the underlying contract is tainted. As this provision falls in Part I of the Act, it, however, only applies in the context of domestic awards.

With regard to foreign awards, there is no such mention as to what the consequences of corruption in the underlying contract would be. From Part II of the IAA, which deals with foreign awards (sec. 48(2)b), one can infer that courts would only be justified in refusing to enforce an award if there was corruption in the arbitral process itself. The legislation does not give courts the power to go into the merits of the case to determine if there has been an element of fraud or corruption in the underlying contract.

This does not, however, mean that no remedy is available in case of fraud or corruption in the underlying contract. One can challenge an award if there was an element of fraud or corruption in the underlying contract on other grounds, as enforcing such a contract would certainly be immoral, unjust, or go against the fundamental policy of Indian law.[539]

2. The award is in contravention with the fundamental policy of Indian law

'Fundamental policy of Indian law' is one of the important grounds for invoking the public policy exception under section 48. The roots of this ground can be seen in the Geneva Convention of 1927, which provides violation of 'principles of law of the country' as grounds for refusing enforcement of arbitral awards. The inclusion of this ground is, however, controversial. If one looks at the *travaux préparatoires* of the New York Convention, the drafters specifically did not include the 'fundamental principles of the law' as a ground for refusing enforcement of awards as it was envisioned that its inclusion would lead to 'difficulties in interpretation' and may lead to a substantive review of awards.[540] This was also the position of the International Law Association, which strongly urged the

539 See Chapter 4(III)3a(iii).

540 United Nations Conference on International Commercial Arbitration, 'Comments on Draft Convention on the Recognition and Enforcement of Foreign Arbitral Awards: Note by the Secretary General', *E/ CONF. 26/2* (UN ECOSOC 1958) 7.

drafters of the New York Convention against its inclusion.[541] The Indian legislature included the ground despite these criticisms.

What constitutes the 'fundamental policy of Indian law' has not been explained in the IAA. As will be shown, this ground encompasses aspects of both substantive and procedural public policy. Courts have provided some guidance as to what such fundamental policy would encompass. It is clear from the decisions of Indian courts that the fundamental policy of Indian law does not merely refer to the 'provisions of Indian statutes'.[542] In fact, the New York Convention intended foreign awards to be enforced regardless of whether they were in accordance with national laws.[543] The Indian Supreme Court has rather characterized the term fundamental policy to mean the 'substratal principles on which Indian law is founded'.[544] This approach has been espoused in literature. According to Paulsson, the fundamental principles of law are not derived from statute but rather form their 'antecedents', which every statute 'must embody' and which shouldn't be compromised.[545] In its *Cruz City* ruling, the Delhi High Court described the fundamental policy of Indian law to mean the basic rationale, principles, and values forming the 'bedrock' on which Indian laws are based.[546] There is no better starting place than the Indian Constitution to find out what would these principles encompass.

It would not be far-fetched to assume that 'Fundamental Rights' enshrined in Part III of the Indian Constitution, including the right to life, right to equality (against discrimination), right against exploitation (and prohibition of child labour), freedom of speech, freedom of profession would fall under the fundamental policy of Indian law. This is in line with the *Brojo Nath* ruling where the Supreme Court held that in the absence of guidance from other authorities regarding public policy, courts need to look at constitutional provisions, including directive principles and fundamental rights, to aid in interpretation.[547]

541 See position of the International Law Association in, 'Recognition and Enforcement of Foreign Arbitral Awards, Report by the Secretary General' (United Nations Economic and Social Council 1956) E/2822, 21st Session, Item 8 Annex II, Page 20.

542 Xstrata Coal Marketing Ag v Dalmia Bharat (Cement) Ltd 2016(6)ARBLR270 (High Court of Delhi) [46].

543 *Cruz City 1 Mauritius Holdings v Unitech Limited* (2017) 3 Arbitr Law Report 20 (High Court of Delhi) [97].

544 Xstrata Coal Marketing Ag v. Dalmia Bharat (Cement) Ltd (n 542) para 46.

545 Paulsson (n 9) 15.

546 Cruz City 1 Mauritius Holdings v. Unitech Limited (n 543) para 96.

547 Central Inland Water Transport Corporation Limited and Anr v. Brojo Nath Ganguly and Anr. (n 169) para 95.

Although in the context of Indian constitutional law, these rights are directed primarily at the State, the Constitution still forms the bedrock of the Indian legal system. It thereby would reflect the fundamental policy of Indian law. Article 32 of the Constitution guarantees a non-waivable right to move the Indian Supreme Court for enforcement of fundamental rights. This provision is considered so crucial to the Indian legal system that B. R. Ambedkar, one of the principal drafters of the Indian Constitution, regarded it as the 'very soul…and heart' of the Constitution.[548]

Equating the fundamental policy of Indian law in the context of the IAA with fundamental rights can, however, give rise to certain difficulties. It has been the consistent approach of the Indian Supreme Court that fundamental rights especially provided for under Article 21 of the Indian Constitution must be interpreted in a broad manner and given the 'widest amplitude'.[549] Such an approach could go against the will of the drafters of the IAA who intended that public policy be interpreted narrowly. But one must distinguish in this respect between the scope of the fundamental rights, which shall be broad, and the cases in which arbitral awards must be refused recognition and enforcement, which must be rare. The fact that fundamental rights deserve the utmost respect and have a wide influence on all areas of life does not justify using them as a pretext to control and invalidate arbitral awards. It must be accepted that arbitrators follow fundamental rights but have some latitude as to the interpretation of their impact in a precise case. This latitude must be respected by state courts when controlling arbitral awards.

Apart from the Indian Constitution, guidance as to the fundamental policy of Indian law can also be found in Supreme Court and High Court decisions. In the *Associate Builders* case, the Supreme Court held that violation of the Foreign Exchange Act and 'disregarding orders of a superior court' would be contrary to the fundamental policy of India.[550] This could indicate that the contravention of certain statutes would constitute a violation of Indian public policy. Similarly, an arbitral award enforcing a clause wherein one party is allowed to recover

548 See, Gopal Subaramanium, Writs and Remedies in Sujit Choudhry, Madhav Khosla and Pratap Bhanu Mehta (eds), *The Oxford Handbook of the Indian Constitution* (Oxford University Press 2016) 614.

549 See, M. P. Jain, 'The Supreme Court and Fundamental Rights', in S. K. Verma and K. Kusum (eds), *Fifty Years of the Supreme Court of India: Its Grasp and Reach* (Oxford University Press 2006) 24 et seq.

550 Associate Builders v. Delhi Development Authority (n 455).

an 'unconscionable' amount of money would contravene the public policy of India.[551] However, normally an 'award on costs ... is not against the fundamental policy of Indian law.'[552] The Bombay High Court in *Nobel Resources* held that fundamental policy would include matters of 'national policy', including preservation of wildlife by restricting trade in elephant tusks and peacock meat.[553]

In its *Western Geco* ruling, the Supreme Court said that public policy encompassed 'all such fundamental principles as providing a basis for administration of justice and enforcement of the law.'[554] This is an extremely expansive definition, which does not seem to be in line with the reasoning of the Court in the *BALCO* case. In this case, the Supreme Court has also laid down certain specific grounds which would be encompassed when determining the fundamental policy of Indian law.[555] These grounds are elaborated below from (a-c). Further potential categories are elaborated from (d-g).

(a) Use of judicial approach

This would effectively mean that the arbitral tribunal is required to act 'judicially'. It is not allowed to act in an 'arbitrary, whimsical or capricious manner' but rather it should act 'bonafide' and use a 'fair, reasonable and objective' approach, without paying heed to any 'extraneous considerations'. The fundamental policy of Indian law would be violated if the tribunal acts otherwise. The provision does not in itself preclude the tribunal from acting *ex aequo et bono.* However, according to section 28 of the IAA, any decision of the tribunal to act as an *amiable compositeur* requires the express consent of the parties.

(b) Principles of natural justice

In order to ensure the future enforceability of an arbitral award in India, the tribunal must keep in mind the 'principles of natural justice'. While the exact scope of these principles is not laid down in statute, guidance can be obtained from the decisions of Indian courts. The Indian Supreme Court in its *State Bank of Patiala* ruling has acknowledged that the term natural justice cannot be restricted

551 *Vivek Rai v Aakash Institute* OMP 5612014 (Delhi High Court).

552 Canadian Commercial Corporation v Coal India Limited MANU/WB/0958/2016 (High Court of Calcutta).

553 *Nobel Resource Ltd v Dharni Sampda Private Ltd* [2019] Exec Appl No 25 2017 (High Court of Bombay) [26].

554 Oil and Natural Gas Corporation Ltd. Vs. Western Geco international Ltd. (n 454).

555 ibid 26.

to 'hard and fast rules' but rather be based on the circumstances of the case at hand.[556] Despite this, the court in other decisions has intervened when it thought that specific components of natural justice were violated.

The Supreme Court, for instance, in *Western Geco* held that the *'audi altram partem'* rule is a principle of natural justice the violation of which would contravene the fundamental policy of Indian law.[557] Similarly, it held that non-application of mind by the tribunal to the facts and circumstances of the case would also render the award as being contrary to the 'fundamental policy of Indian law'.[558]

Since the enactment of the IAA(Am.) 2015, there is a separate head – 'most basic principles of justice'. Therefore, the continued relevance of dealing with this ground under the head 'fundamental policy of Indian law' is moot. We will continue elaborating on the head 'most basic principles of justice' later in this thesis.[559]

(c) Perverse or irrational award

An award that is so 'perverse or irrational' that any reasonable person would not have given it, would also be contrary to the fundamental policy of Indian law. In determining if the award is perverse or irrational, the Indian Supreme Court has applied the principle of 'Wednesbury unreasonableness'.[560]

To clarify, the Wednesbury principle states that 'if a decision … is so unreasonable that no reasonable authority could ever have come to it, then the courts can interfere'.[561] The use of this test is not novel. This principle has often been used in England[562] and other common law jurisdictions such as Singapore[563] to set a standard for rationality or reasonableness in the decision-making process. In the *Deutsche Schachtbau* ruling, the UK Court of Appeal also ruled that public

556 *State Bank of Patiala V SK Sharma* (1996) 1996 AIR 1669 (Supreme Court of India).
557 Oil and Natural Gas Corporation Ltd. Vs. Western Geco international Ltd. (n 454) para 28.
558 ibid.
559 See *infra* Chap ter 4(III)3b.
560 Oil and Natural Gas Corporation Ltd. Vs. Western Geco international Ltd. (n 454) para 29.
561 Associated Provincial Picture Houses Ltd v Wednesbury Corporation (1948) 1 KB 223 (Court of Appeal of England and Wales).
562 *Braganza v BP Shipping Ltd* [2015] UKSC 17 (United Kingdom Supreme Court).
563 Chng Suan Tze v Minister for Home Affairs and others and other appeals [1988] SGCA 16 (Singapore Court of Appeal) [119].

policy considerations would arise if enforcement would be repulsive to an 'ordinary reasonable and informed member of the public'.[564]

Such an approach may provide fertile ground for judicial interference. It may inadvertently lead to replacing the arbitral mode of dispute resolution with court litigation. As one needs to substitute the rationality of the arbitrator with that of a third person, i.e., the judge or a 'reasonable person'. This cannot be done without going into the merits of the case.

The Indian Supreme Court has also held that an award that is contrary to fundamental law, and thereby 'ex-facie illegal' would violate 'fundamental policy of Indian law and thereby fall foul of the public policy exception.[565] There is no doubt that such an award would not be enforced as it would be perverse to do so.

(d) Protecting the economic interest of India

Laws regulating economic activity can be fundamental to the stability and growth of any country. Such laws can be non-exhaustive and could encompass a gamut of laws and regulations. It is unsurprising, therefore, that scholars consider that a state's public policy also has economic dimensions.[566] According to Böckstiegel, these are usually mandatory laws that safeguard the fundamental interest of the given country.[567] Indian courts have also shown their willingness to intervene when fundamental economic laws are violated.

The Indian Supreme Court aptly described the importance of economic laws (in this case, foreign exchange law) as vital for the development and 'economic survival' of a state.[568] The Court, in its landmark *Renusagar* decision, held that Foreign Exchange Regulation Act (FERA)1973, i.e., the law that used to regulate foreign exchange in India, was important for protecting 'national economic

---

564 Deutsche Schachtbau-und Tiefbohr-Gesellschaft M.B.H. v. Shell International Petroleum Co. Ltd. (n 289).

565 National Agricultural Co-Operative Marketing Federation of India v Alimenta S A (2020) 3 ARBLR 1 (Supreme Court of India) 80.

566 Loukas Mistelis, '"Keeping the Unruly Horse in Control" or Public Policy as a Bar to Enforcement of (Foreign) Arbitral Awards', in *International Law FORUM du Droit International, International Law Association – London Conference (2000) Committee on International Commercial Arbitration* (Brill: Nijhoff 2000) 250.

567 Karl-Heinz Böckstiegel, 'Public Policy as a Limit to Arbitration and Its Enforcement' (2008) IBA Journal of Dispute resolution, Special Issue, The New York Convention – 50 Years 123, 130 et seq.

568 *MG Wagh & Ors vs Jay Engineering Works Ltd* (1987) AIR 670 (Supreme Court of India) [2].

interest' and its violation would therefore violate Indian public policy.[569] This would also apply to other economic laws. The Supreme Court, for instance in *Rioglass,* held that the provisions of the Indian Stamp Act 1899, which mandates payment of stamp duty for instruments, would also reflect the fundamental policy of Indian law.[570] The Court, in this case, however, kept in mind the pro-enforcement bias for foreign awards by holding that such awards would be enforceable even if stamp duty was not paid.[571]

This need for ensuring compliance with economic laws in also considered essential in other jurisdictions. In Germany, for instance, the BGH has held that an award would be refused enforcement if it fundamentally affects the economic wellbeing of the state.[572]

(e) Protecting free and fair competition as a fundamental policy of Indian law

Protecting fair and free competition can also be considered a fundamental policy of Indian law. There is a simple reason for this, i.e., competition claims are vital and have a definite impact on a countries economic policy.[573] It is therefore unsurprising that most states have enacted laws that regulate anti-competitive practices, abuse of dominant market position and monopolistic practices.[574] These regulations serve essential purposes. As recognised by the UNCTAD, they protect consumers by ensuring the availability of adequate choices of goods and services at reasonable prices.[575] Furthermore, they seek to ensure a level playing field for companies.

---

569 Renusagar Power Co. Ltd. Vs. General Electric Company and Anr. (n 178) para 71,72.

570 *M/S Shriram Epc Limited vs Rioglass Solar Sa* (2018) 5 ARBLR 161 (Supreme Court of India) [24].

571 ibid 25.

572 BGH Beschluss Vom 02. März 2017 – ZB 4216 – Juris (n 389).

573 Dirk Otto and Omaia Elwan, Article V(2) in Kronke and Nacimiento (n 111) 355 et seq.

574 Dirk Otto and Omaia Elwan, Article V(2) in Kronke and Nacimiento (n 111).

575 'The Benefit of Competition Policy for Consumers – Note by UNCTAD Secretariat', Consultations and discussions regarding peer reviews on competition law and policy, review of the Model Law on Competition and studies related to the provisions of the Set of Principles and Rules; Trade and Development Board Trade and Development Commission; Intergovernmental Group of Experts on Competition Law and Policy Fourteenth session (TD/B/C.I/CLP/27) (UNCTAD 2014) 2.

In many states, violation of their competition law, in other words, competition law of the *lex fori*, would go against public policy.[576] In fact, it is widely accepted that breach of competition law would be sufficient reason to refuse enforcement on public policy grounds under Article V(2)(b) of the New York Convention.[577] Although the discourse as to whether the violation of essential principles of competition law would be contrary to public policy exception has been discussed intensely around the world, in India, however, the matter is as of yet not very well explored, and there is a relative lack of judicial precedent on this issue.[578] While anti-trust disputes are considered arbitrable in most major jurisdictions, these matters are considered not-arbitrable in India as a matter of public policy.[579] It is, therefore, likely that any arbitral award that is a fruit of such (non-arbitrable) subject matter would not be enforced by Indian courts.

In addressing this issue, courts in other jurisdictions have chosen between two possible approaches, i.e., the 'minimalist' and the 'maximalist' approach.[580] Protagonists of the minimalist approach argue for minimum judicial review of the arbitral award. According to Geradin, who describes this approach, courts should restrict themselves to making sure the arbitral tribunal 'has addressed competition law' and not involve itself in factual review.[581] A good example for restrictive interpretations of the public policy exception *vis-à-vis* competition law can be seen in the Swiss Supreme Court ruling in the *Tensacciai* case, where it held that competition law was not 'essential' enough to be encompassed by the exception.[582] A similar narrow interpretation was given by the French *Cour d'appel de Paris* in *SA Thalès*,[583] where the aggrieved party claimed that the

---

576 Kronke and Nacimiento (n 111) 382.

577 See Luca G. Radicati di Brozolo, Chapter 22: Court Review of Competition Law Awards in Setting Aside and Enforcements Proceedings in Blanke and Landolt (n 8) para 22-009.

578 Tanya Choudhary, 'Arbitrability of Competition Law Disputes in India' (2015) IV Indian Journal of Arbitration Law 69, 70.

579 See Chapter VI(2).

580 Vera Korzun, 'Arbitrating Antitrust Claims: From Suspicion to Trust' (2016) Fordham Law School FLASH: The Fordham Law Archive of Scholarship and History (SJD Dissertations 6) 909 <https://ir.lawnet.fordham.edu/sjd/6> accessed 22 July 2021.

581 Damien Geradin, 'Public Policy and Breach of Competition Law in International Arbitration' (2016) 27 Spain Arbitration Review | Revista del Club Español del Arbitraje 133, 147.

582 *Tensacciai SpA v Freyssinet Terra Armata Srl* (2006) Case 4P2782005 (Swiss Supreme Court (Federal Tribunal)).

583 SA Thalès Air Defense v. GIE Euromissile (n 409).

arbitrators had ignored EU competition law. The court, when rejecting the claim, ruled that if a claim should be successful the violation should be 'obvious, effective and concrete' and that it would only examine if the award was valid and not go into an in-depth analysis of the case.[584]

The 'minimalist' approach is in stark contrast to the 'maximalist' view, which calls for comprehensive judicial review to ensure that the arbitrators properly apply competition rules.[585] In the EU, for instance, courts are obliged to consider competition law matters as falling with the public policy exception.[586] This position was taken by the ECJ in the *Eco Swiss* ruling.[587] The case arose out of an arbitration clause in a licensing agreement under which Benetton gave Eco Swiss (a Hong Kong company) the right to manufacture watches bearing its name. The agreement enabled a market sharing agreement where Eco Swiss was precluded from selling watches in Italy. On termination of the agreement, the arbitral tribunal made an award against Benetton, which was challenged in the Netherlands on the grounds of violating public policy. A reference was made to the ECJ.

In this case, the ECJ acknowledged the need for a limited and restricted review of arbitral awards but held that Article 85 of the EC Treaty (Article 101 of the TFEU[588]) was a fundamental provision necessary for the community and the internal market and constituted 'a matter of public policy'.[589] It ruled that 'any agreements or decisions prohibited (by it) would be automatically void'.[590] It held that a contravention of Article 85 of the EC Treaty (Article 101 of the TFEU[591]), which prohibits agreements that prevent, restrict or distort competition within the internal market, would be contrary to public policy exception

584 See, para 23–020, Christoph Liebscher, EU Member State Court Application of Eco Swiss: Review of the Case Law and Future Prospects in, Blanke and Landolt (n 8).
585 Damien Geradin (n 581).
586 Santiago Martínez Lage, 'Arbitration and EU Competition Law: New Rulings and New Thoughts' (2016) Spain Arbitration Review | Revista del Club Español del Arbitraje 131, 132.
587 Case C-126/97, Eco Swiss China Time Ltd v Benetton InternationalNV, 1999 ECR - 3055 (European Court of Justice) [40].
588 Consolidated version of the Treaty on the Functioning of the European Union (2012) OJ C 326.
589 Case C-126/97, Eco Swiss China Time Ltd. v. Benetton InternationalN.V., (n 587) para 39.
590 ibid 36.
591 Consolidated version of the Treaty on the Functioning of the European Union (2012) OJ C 326.

and that national courts should annul arbitral awards where such a violation is found.[592]

This decision was criticized by some scholars for enabling a 'flood of challenges' based on breach of competition law.[593] The line of reasoning taken by the court in this judgment was reaffirmed in the *Aéroports de Paris* case, where the Court of the first instance held that parties cannot contractually dodge competition law because the public policy exception renders it mandatory.[594]

An extensive review by national courts of the arbitral award to see if there exists a breach of competition law by the parties gives rise to a major difficulty. Courts are generally precluded from going into the merits of the dispute, but rather only if the arbitral award contravenes public policy can the award be set aside. However, in order to see if the original agreement entered into by the parties breached competition law, the court would need to go deeply into the merits. As described by Geradin, courts would need to look at the 'elements, facts and the law' to establish a breach-and it would not suffice to have a 'superficial review' of the award.[595] This would, however, be beyond what was envisioned in the New York Convention.

Both the minimalist and the maximalist approaches have their positives and negative elements. Firstly, the minimalist approach would help in upholding party autonomy and reduce excessive judicial intervention, but this benefit would come at the cost of reduced oversight on essential competition matters. The maximalist approach, on the other hand, would disregard party autonomy by making arbitral awards too easily susceptible to judicial meddling.

A consensus has now developed in the literature both among the minimalists and the maximalists that usually courts will enforce arbitral awards where the breaches of competition law are insignificant.[596] Only where the tribunal

---

592 Case C-126/97, Eco Swiss China Time Ltd. v. Benetton InternationalN.V., (n 587) para 41.

593 Alexis Mourre, 'Courts in France and Belgium Confirm Limited Review of Awards under European Competition Law' (*Kluwer Arbitration Blog*, 7 February 2017) <http://kluwerarbitrationblog.com/2010/02/07/courts-in-france-and-belgium-confirm-limited-review-of-awards-under-european-competition-law/> accessed 2 June 2017.

594 *Case T-128/98, Aéroports de Paris v Commission of the European Communities* 2000 II-03929 (CJEU-Court of First Instance (Third Chamber)) [241]; see also, Damien Geradin (n 581) 142.

595 Damien Geradin (n 581) 138.

596 See Luca G. Radicati di Brozolo, Chapter 22: Court Review of Competition Law Awards in Setting Aside and Enforcements Proceedings in Blanke and Landolt (n 8) paras 22-050 et seq.

has colluded in the breach or ignored it on purpose, or where the breach was very serious, would the court be permitted to refuse enforcement. According to this view, in determining if there is a contravention of competition law, the court should abstain from going into merits but draw its conclusion from the arbitrator's awards, only occasionally if the need for further clarification does arise, should the court go into the pleadings and the facts.[597] An extensive review of the award on merits would only be permitted in case of the most egregious infringements of competition law.[598]

(f) Essential insolvency law provisions as a fundamental policy of Indian law

The public policy exception comes to the forefront when we deal with enforcement of awards where either of the parties is subject to insolvency proceedings.[599] While the arbitral award tries to satisfy money owed only to one party, insolvency law tries to ensure that the rights of all creditors are protected. The goal of enforcing an arbitral award can, in such situations, come in the way of public policy considerations involved in collectively satisfying a party's creditors.

Justice Liberhan in the Punjab High Court *Goetze India* ruling observed that winding-up (insolvency) proceedings have 'deep roots in public policy'.[600] Such an approach has also been accepted in scholarly literature. Vorburger has considered insolvency law principles to be the 'backbone' of the law and economy of a state and 'fundamentally important and an intrinsic part of public policy' as they contribute to increased stability and growth.[601] It is natural, therefore, that the fundamental policy of Indian law should also be read to include insolvency law provisions. This was acknowledged by the Indian Supreme Court in *Booz Allen* ruling, where the court held that 'insolvency and winding-up matters' are not arbitrable because such disputes as a matter of public policy must be decided by public fora.[602] It is therefore doubtful that Indian courts would be willing to

597 Blanke and Landolt (n 8).
598 ibid.
599 Simon Vorburger, International Arbitration and Cross-Border Insolvency: Comparative Perspectives (Kluwer Law International 2014) para 657.
600 *Goetze India Ltd vs Pure Drinks (New Delhi) Ltd* [1991] Civ Appeal No 48 (Punjab-Haryana High Court) [22].
601 Vorburger (n 599) para 663.
602 Booz Allen and Hamilton Inc v SBI Home Finance Limited 2011 5 SCC 532 (Supreme Court of India) [22].

enforce an award rendered by a tribunal that violates essential principles of insolvency law. Valuable guidance can be had by looking at the approaches of other jurisdictions regarding which principles are considered sacrosanct.

Although many jurisdictions agree as to the importance of insolvency provisions, there is variation among states in deciding what principles of the insolvency process would give rise to the public policy exception. In both England and in France, the principle of *pari passu* is given importance, i.e., similar creditors must be treated the same way. English courts have definitively ruled that *pari passu* is a part of domestic public policy.[603] In France, on the other hand, *pari passu* is considered to be a part of international public policy, and its breach is sufficient grounds for refusing the enforcement of arbitral awards.[604] A similar approach has been taken by the American courts, which have held that 'ensuring equitable and orderly distribution of local assets' would fall under the public policy exception.[605] French public policy also precludes enforcement of an arbitral award that orders payment from a party against which insolvency proceedings have commenced or any 'individual payments from the insolvency estate'.[606] A very different approach is taken under Swiss law, where a violation of the equal treatment principle would not necessarily be against public policy.[607] However, this is balanced by the fact that insolvency may affect the 'fundamental principles of arbitral proceedings' which falls under Swiss public policy.[608]

Given the international consensus on the importance of ensuring non-violation of fundamental principles of insolvency law, which has been demonstrated above and the previous decisions of the Indian Supreme Court, it would not be far fetched to consider a violation of important insolvency principles to constitute a violation of the fundamental policy of Indian law.

---

603 Belmont Park Investments Pty Ltd v BNY Corporate Trustee Services Ltd [2011] UKSC 38 (Supreme Court of the United Kingdom).

604 Vorburger (n 599) paras 667–668.

605 *Victrix SS Co SA v Salen Dry Cargo AB* 825 F2d 709 (United States Court of Appeals, Second Circuit).

606 Vorburger (n 599).

607 ibid 675.

608 ibid 678.

(g) The non-exhaustive nature of the fundamental policy of Indian law

The Indian Supreme Court, in its *Western Geco* ruling, has stressed that 'it would not be appropriate and proper' to exhaustively elaborate on the scope of the fundamental policy of Indian law, as this concept could not be put in a 'straitjacket' by way of definition.[609] In effect, according to this ruling, the fundamental policy is an open-ended and non-exhaustive concept.

The Court's reasoning and judgment have been criticized as it enabled the judges to look into the merits of the award.[610] The negative fallout of this judgment was one of the influencing factors for the law commission to suggest the new definition of public policy.[611] The Law Commission had to draft a whole new supplementary report, seeking further modifications to the IAA 1996 to restrict the interpretation of public policy. Based on these recommendations, the IAA(Am.) 2015 has clarified the position and provided that in determining the fundamental policy of Indian law, there will not be a review on the merits of the dispute.[612] This can be interpreted to mean that, in order to find if the award violates the fundamental policy of Indian law, the court will not be able to review the decision; however, this will not stop the court from looking into whether the decision *prima facie* breaches any of the criteria laid down by the Supreme Court.

One must tread cautiously when relying on fundamental principles of domestic law to justify interfering with arbitration which is an inherently international enterprise. There is the risk that such an inward-looking approach of imposing national law could become a tool for protectionism and economic nationalism, which was a hallmark in international trade in the era of Brexit and Trump, and which is increasingly prevalent in international commerce, e.g., as can be seen in U.S.-China trade relations. This is even truer because what constitutes the fundamental policy of the law is non-exhaustive.

The IAA provides a safeguard to judicial excess by not allowing courts to go into the merits of the dispute when evaluating if there has been a violation of

609 Oil and Natural Gas Corporation Ltd. Vs. Western Geco international Ltd. (n 454) para 30.

610 Garg and Srivastava (n 157).

611 Justice A. P. Shah, 'Supplementary to Report No. 246 on Amendments to Arbitration and Conciliation Act, 1996-"Public Policy" Developments Post-Report No.246' (Government of India, Law Commission of India 2015), para 10.3 et seq.

612 See, 22, The Arbitration and Conciliation (Amendment) Act.

the fundamental policy of Indian law. This may, however, be an insufficient safeguard as the nature of 'fundamental policy' is itself incomprehensive. Apart from the illustrations given above, it could also include, for instance, provisions of labour law, intellectual property law, consumer protection, environmental protection, child protection law, anti-discrimination, respect for religion, prevention of market manipulation and insider trading, etc.

3. The award conflicts with the most basic notions of morality or justice

According to the IAA(Am.) 2015, public policy is said to include the most basic notions of morality and justice. While it is true that 'morality' and justice' are intrinsically abstract terms that can be interpreted broadly, according to the IAA, it is only the 'most basic' or fundamental elements that can give rise to the public policy exception.

The Indian legislature is not alone in acknowledging these grounds as being part of the public policy exception. Such an approach is also supported by scholarly literature – Paulsson has argued that the New York Convention should be amended to define public policy as 'fundamental norms of morality and justice'.[613] A similar definition is also found in other jurisdictions. A very good example is the United States, where it is only the 'most basic notions of morality and justice' or the contravention of 'fundamental notions of what is decent and just in the United States',[614] which would be valid public policy grounds for refusing to enforce an arbitral award. In Germany as well, an award that goes against good morals would contravene substantive public policy.[615] Below we will look at what these most basic elements would encompass.

(a) Most basic notions of morality as a breach of Indian public policy

Morality is an extremely broad, variable and vague term. Barden and Murphy have likened it to a 'pre-existing moral code containing an indefinitely large number of precepts'.[616] Likewise, the Indian Supreme Court has previously held

---

613 Marike R. P. Paulsson, 'The 1958 New York Convention from an Unusual Perspective: Moving Forward by Parting with It' (2016) 5 Indian Journal of Arbitration Law 37.

614 Hodgson and Toubiana (n 335) 3.

615 See, Stefan Kröll, Foreign Awards, in Böckstiegel, Kröll and Nacimiento (n 378) 488.

616 Garrett Barden and Tim Murphy, *Law and Justice in Community* (Oxford University Press 2010) 167.

that 'what is immoral may be against public policy, for the public policy covers political, social and economic grounds.'[617] However, such a sweeping categorization may not be appropriate in the context of enforcing foreign arbitral awards. Treating all the innumerable moral precepts as a matter of public policy would enable judicial overreach and would be devastating for party autonomy and international arbitration.

According to the IAA(Am.) 2015, it is only the 'most basic notions of morality and justice' which could justify refusing enforcement of an arbitral award. This approach is more broadly accepted. It is similar to the French concept of *bonnes moeurs* or the German *gute sitten*.[618] It could also be considered to be similar to the concept of 'fundamental morality' or 'universal moral' precepts, which Chng argues to form part of public policy.[619]

For a judge deciding on whether to enforce an award that has been challenged on the grounds of breach of basic moral precepts, it is important to find what constitute these basic precepts that form the core of the legal system. In finding them, one must, according to Ghodoosi, look into constitutional law, due process requirements and the prevailing moral standards of society.[620]

(i) Morality, according to Indian courts

In defining morality, the Indian Supreme Court has taken reference from comparative jurisprudence. In the *Gherulal Parekh* decision, the Court held that the term morality in the Indian context would not be incorporated from Hindu law.[621] It rather held that English common law would be a more useful source of guidance. After studying both Indian and English case laws and commentaries, the court concluded that the term 'immoral' is very 'comprehensive'. It based its view of morality on the intention of the legislature to define the scope narrowly.[622] The Court furthermore acknowledged that immorality usually encompasses 'every aspect of personal conduct' that is 'repugnant to good conscience'. It also stated that because the concept of immorality varies depending on 'time, place and the stage of civilization of a particular society…no universal standard

617 Gherulal Parekh v. Mahadeo Dass Maiya (n 173).
618 M. Forde, '"Ordre Public" Exception and Adjudicative Jurisdiction Conventions' (1980) 29 The International and Comparative Law Quarterly 259.
619 Kenny Chng (n 105) 134.
620 Ghodoosi (n 15) 66.
621 Gherulal Parekh v. Mahadeo Dass Maiya (n 173).
622 ibid 69.

can be set' or 'law based' on it.[623] Given that immorality is an 'illusive' concept, the Court ruled that when juxtaposed with 'public policy', it must be interpreted in a restrictive or narrow manner.

In the *DDA* case, the Supreme Court further examined the concept of immorality. When ruling that *'what is immoral may be against public policy'*, the court asserted that in the public policy context, the description of morality would be confined solely to *sexual morality*.'[624] The judgment of the court follows the line of reasoning taken in English jurisprudence where sexual immorality, for instance, in an agreement to facilitate prostitution, would be sufficient grounds to refuse enforcement.[625] The exception could therefore help to combat evils such as child pornography. The Supreme Court further has elaborated that the concept of morality can also encompass agreements which although not illegal, would not be enforced given the *'mores of the day'*. The court clarified that judicial intervention would be permitted only in cases the court's conscience is shocked.[626]

(ii) Comparative approaches to morality

As seen above, the meaning of the term 'morality' under the IAA(Am.)2015 is more or less still left open to debate. Although notions of morality differ from country to country,[627] there are general ideals and standards that can be considered immoral in most jurisdictions. These general ideas and standards usually relate to conduct that is either illegal or deeply repulsive to the given society. A more concrete understanding of the term can therefore be gained by looking at comparative literature.

In Germany, public policy could be invoked where the enforcement of an award would lead to an outcome that is contrary to good morals or profiting out of a criminal offence such as piracy, drug offences, money laundering etc.[628] There are also other situations where morality could be infringed. In the UK, morality would also be breached in case of a contract to deceive a third party, or in Canada, this would be the case for contracts relating to recovering gambling debts.[629]

623 Gherulal Parekh v. Mahadeo Dass Maiya (n 173).
624 Associate Builders v. Delhi Development Authority (n 455).
625 Torremans and Fawcett (n 71) 135.
626 Associate Builders v. Delhi Development Authority (n 455) para 12.
627 Marike R. P. Paulsson (n 613) 37.
628 See, Stefan Kröll, Foreign Awards, in Böckstiegel, Kröll and Nacimiento (n 378) 488.
629 Torremans and Fawcett (n 71) 136.

(iii) Corruption or fraud as an immoral act

A contract obtained through corrupt or fraudulent means would certainly be immoral. Judge Grenmar Lagergren, in his landmark ICC award, not surprisingly concluded that corruption and bribery would constitute an 'international evil' and also be against 'good morals'.[630] This approach has also been taken by the Ontario Superior Court in Canada in its *Xerox* ruling, where it held that 'bribery, corruption and fraud' would go against the 'essential morality of Ontario'[631]

On the surface, it appears that there is a repetition under the IAA(Am.) 2015, as the term *morality* seems to also encompass other heads of the public policy exception provided under section 48 of the Act, such as corruption or fraud. However, it must be noted that 'morality' is a completely different and overarching ground. While 'corruption & fraud' ground found in 48(2)b Explanation 1(i) only refers to corruption and fraud in obtaining the award, the morality ground Explanation 1(iii) could potentially also encompass fraud and corruption more generally (e.g., relating to the underlying contract).

(iv) Respect for human rights

Respect for human rights is a fundamental element of Indian law and is enshrined in Part III of the Indian Constitution. The international commitment to safeguarding such rights can be seen in international instruments such as the Universal Declaration of Human Rights 1948 (UDHR).[632]

In the context of commercial arbitration and human rights, a few important questions arise, which have not yet been answered in the Indian context. Would violation of human rights also fall under the umbrella of 'most basic notions morality'? Furthermore, would it contravene the public policy exception for a party to waive their human rights? If an arbitrator has not provided a party with the right to a fair hearing, or if an arbitrator has ignored the fact that the underlying contract itself violates human rights, would the public policy of protecting human rights override the public policy of enforcing an otherwise valid arbitral award?

---

630 ICC Award No. 1110 of 1963 (n 62) para 20.

631 Henri C. Alvarez, 'Xerox Canada Ltd., Xerox Corporation v. MPI Techologies Inc., MPI Tech. S.A., Ontario Superior Court of Justice, [2006] O.J. No. 4895 (QL), 30 November 2006' A contribution by the ITA Board of Reporters, Kluwer Law International para 122.

632 Universal Declaration of Human Rights 1948 (United Nations General Assembly Resolution 217A).

The 'most basic notions of morality' under the IAA(Am.) 2015 would certainly include respect for human rights – after all, every human right is a moral right.[633] Gross violation of human rights would go against the public policy of most legal regimes.[634] There are two types of rights, the violation of which may render an award unenforceable. Firstly, the violation of a procedural right to a fair hearing – in Europe, these rights are protected by Article 6 of the European Convention of Human Rights. If the arbitral tribunal does not give one party the right to present its case while giving the other party this right, this could be a ground for refusing enforcement of a subsequent award. Secondly, the violation of certain human rights would justify refusing the enforcement of arbitral. Lord Neuberger has listed out many examples for human rights under English law, including preventing torture, promoting terrorist activities, genocide, slavery, piracy etc.[635]

However, not every human right would form part of the 'most basic notions of morality' under Indian law. Only fundamental rights are protected as part of the basic structure of the Indian Constitution. These rights found in Part III of the Constitution would include, among others, the right to life, right to equality (against discrimination), right against exploitation (and prohibition of child labour), freedom of speech, freedom of profession. While these rights are directed primarily at the State, it is hard to imagine an Indian court being willing to enforce an arbitral award that undermines any of these rights. This is because fundamental rights form an essential part of Indian public policy. In fact, the Indian Supreme Court has ruled that as fundamental rights have been incorporated as part of public policy, their application cannot be waived by an individual.[636] This is similar to the approach taken by the House of Lords in the UK in *Kuwait Airways* case, where it held that *'gross infringements of human rights'... 'would affront basic principles of justice and fairness which the courts seek to apply in the administration of justice in this country'.*[637]

633 Michael J. Perry, 'The Morality of Human Rights' (2013) 50 San Diego Law Review 775, 781.

634 Torremans and Fawcett (n 71) 137.

635 Lord Neuberger, 'Arbitration and the Rule of Law' (2015) 81 Arbitration 276, 279–280.

636 *Behram Khurshed Pesikaka vs The State of Bombay* (1955) 1 SCR 613 (Supreme Court of India) [73].

637 *Kuwait Airways Corp v Iraqi Airways Co & Anor* (2002) 3 ER 209 (United Kingdom House of Lords) [18].

Such an approach is also supported by eminent Indian legal scholars like M. P. Jain.[638] The reasoning behind this approach is grounded in the fact that the Indian Constitution guarantees the protection of fundamental rights. We have already looked at this in more detail in the previous part, which deals with the fundamental policy of Indian law. Under Indian law, the government is obliged in its law-making functions to ensure that fundamental rights are safeguarded, and any law which does not meet this requirement is unconstitutional.[639] Therefore under the framework of the IAA, it is arguable that public policy precludes parties to an arbitration from waiving their fundamental procedural rights.

Protecting fundamental rights is not just an Indian phenomenon. Even under English law, courts would be justified in interfering on public policy grounds if the award breaches Article 6(1) of the European Convention on Human Rights, which guarantees procedural safeguards for a fair hearing.[640] It is argued in the literature that lack of fundamental procedural guarantees form part of international *ordre public* and would justify judicial intervention in arbitral awards.[641]

There is, however, another viewpoint. Some scholars have argued that the arbitration process has sufficient safeguards and there is no need for additional human rights-based judicial review.[642] According to proponents of this viewpoint, although it is true that courts have a duty to ensure that the fundamental rights of parties are not violated, these rights must be interpreted more restrictively in the context of arbitration *vis-à-vis* normal court litigation.[643] After all, party autonomy and freedom of contract enable parties to design arbitration proceedings as they desire, even if they choose to sacrifice procedural safeguards to ensure speedy settlement of their disputes. Such a view has not been accepted by the Indian Supreme Court, which has held that there are certain basic rights which cannot be waived by the parties.[644] In the Indian context, courts, when

---

638 See, M. P. Jain, 'The Supreme Court and Fundamental Rights' in Verma and Kusum (n 549) 8.

639 See, M. P. Jain, 'The Supreme Court and Fundamental Rights' in ibid 3.

640 William Robinson and Boris Kasolowsky, 'Will the United Kingdom's Human Rights Act Further Protect Parties to Arbitration Proceedings?' (2002) 18 Arbitration International 453, 462.

641 Aleksandar Jaksic, 'Procedural Guarantees of Human Rights in Arbitration Proceedings' (2007) 24 Journal of International Arbitration 159, 168.

642 Neil McDonald, 'More Harm than Good? Human Rights Considerations in International Commercial Arbitration' (2003) 20 Journal of International Arbitration 537.

643 ibid 525–526.

644 Bharat Broadband Network Limited Vs United Telecoms Limited (n 423).

interpreting human rights considerations of public policy exception, need to find a balance. Care should be taken not to undermine party autonomy in the quest to ensure procedural fairness.

(b) Most basic principles of justice forming part of Indian public policy

The IAA(Am.) 2015 includes the 'most basic principles of justice' as forming part of Indian public policy. This is understandable as the preamble to the Indian Constitution guarantees every citizen social, economic and political justice. Furthermore, Article 39A of the Indian Constitution obliges the government to ensure that the 'legal system promotes justice'.

Adhering to the principles of natural justice is very important in the context of commercial arbitration. It gives security to the parties and increases confidence in the arbitration process. However, the fact that it has been statutorily included as part of the public policy exception gives rise to certain difficult questions, including, what is meant by 'most basic principles of justice'? Who determines it? Is it normal for a state to refer to natural justice?

The meaning of 'principles of justice' is just as vague as 'morality'. Again, the words 'most basic principles' should be emphasiszd in order to avoid an overly broad interpretation. Although the exception is necessary, it must be used sparingly. In this context, it is important to keep in mind the ruling of the Calcutta High Court (India) when dealing with natural justice in the context of arbitration. It held that 'enthusiasm for natural justice must always be tempered with due and proper regard for contractual justice' agreed upon by the parties.[645] A similar pro-enforcement approach has also been taken in other countries. For instance, the Australian Federal Court held that an *'arbitration award will not be ... denied recognition or enforcement'* on public policy grounds *'unless there is demonstrated real unfairness or real practical injustice in how the international litigation or dispute resolution was conducted or resolved, by reference to established principles of natural justice or procedural fairness.'*[646]

The phrase 'most basic principles of justice' in the context of the IAA(Am.) 2015 should be interpreted to encompass both procedural justice as well as substantive justice. 'Natural justice' according to the literal jurisprudential meaning

---

645 *DL Miller And Co Ltd v Daluram Goganmull* [1956] AIR Cal 361 (Calcutta High Court) [15].

646 TCL Air Conditioner (Zhongshan) Co Ltd v Castel Electronics Pty Ltd [2014] Federal Court of Australia – Full Court 83.

as aptly described by Barden and Murphy, is nothing but the 'justice inherent in a court or tribunals procedures'[647] and is 'equated with procedural justice'.[648] However, what good is procedural justice in the absence of an award that reaches an outcome that is just in substance?

India is not the only country where natural justice comprises part of public policy. A similar approach is also taken under the Australian International Arbitration Act in section 19, and the New Zealand Arbitration Act in section 36, which also provide that public policy would be violated if there is a breach of principles of natural justice in making of the award. Even in England, the House of Lords has held that courts would have residual power, which they can invoke exceptionally in case of breach of 'basic principles of justice and fairness'.[649]

In determining what constitutes 'principles of justice', guidance can be taken from the decisions of Indian courts. The Supreme Court, in its *DDA* ruling, has differentiated morality from justice. It explained that an award would go against the principles of justice when it 'shocks the conscience of the court.'[650] It is true that this explanation is extremely vague and does not give a proper indication as to what the court meant. The court, however, does give an example to illustrate its view. If an arbitrator awards a higher amount than the claimant seeks without any adequate reasoning, then the Supreme Court considers this award could be set aside as it was against 'justice'.[651] Indian courts also consider natural justice to encompasses procedural grounds such as the right to be heard. This can be seen in *Campos Brothers* case, where the Delhi High Court ruled that the court would not enforce an award if the arbitral tribunal ignored the entirety of the submissions of a party as this would violate natural justice.[652]

Even under English law, foreign awards are refused enforcement if they go against principles of natural justice.[653] This is because decisions violating natural justice, which forms the *'Grundnorm'* of any rule-based legal system, would lack 'moral force'.[654] The case for respecting natural justice is very strong in the

647 Barden and Murphy (n 616) 66.
648 ibid 67.
649 Kuwait Airways Corp v Iraqi Airways Co & Anor (n 637) para 18.
650 Associate Builders v. Delhi Development Authority (n 455) para 12.
651 Associate Builders v. Delhi Development Authority (n 455).
652 Campos Brothers Farms vs Matru Bhumi Supply Chain Pvt Ltd & Ors (2019) 261 DLT 201 (Delhi High Court) [55].
653 Lord Neuberger (n 635) 279 et seq.
654 Austin Ignatius Pullé, 'Securing Natural Justice in Arbitration Proceedings' (2012) 20 Asia Pacific Law Review 63, 64.

context of arbitration. However, it is sometimes sacrificed for expediency. The Indian Supreme Court has cautioned that 'justice in accordance with law cannot be sacrificed' just to expedite proceedings.[655] This may lead to judicial intervention.

Pullé has argued that safeguarding natural justice is especially important to protect the interest of weaker parties, including employees, consumers, small businesses, who (when entering into an agreement with a much larger multinational counterparty) are oftentimes forced to accept arbitration agreements with foreign seats in standard form contracts.[656] He cautions that there is a risk that the arbitrator would seek to sacrifice principles of natural justice and make a ruling in favor of the richer party, which is more likely to give the arbitrator a repeat appointment.[657] It would be very difficult for such parties if they were to have no 'public policy' remedy when the arbitral tribunal rendered such an award.

Consider, for instance, a hypothetical example of an arbitral tribunal consisting of arbitrators from a jurisdiction where the rule of law is applied in a very flexible and haphazard manner, and parties' rights are not respected. Considering such a tribunal renders an award with total disregard to the principles of natural justice. Now, if a (weaker) party challenges the award at the enforcement stage, it would be hard to envision a court not invoking the public policy exception to refuse enforcement of such an award. The above action of the court may seem to be the logical scenario. However, the pro-enforcement bias of many national courts, combined with the desire to appear as an arbitration-friendly jurisdiction, coupled with the trust in the expertise of the arbitrator and the respect for the right of parties to swap procedural fairness and justice for an expedited arbitration procedure, means that courts are often unwilling to interfere in arbitral awards at the enforcement stage. Pullé has argued that the desire to enforce arbitral awards -no matter what- may lead to a 'natural justice – lite' regime.[658] The 'most basic principle of justice' head of the public policy exception provided under the IAA(Am.) 2015 acts as a safeguard against complete dilution of natural justice in the arbitral process.

Not every breach of natural justice would be sufficient to invoke the public policy exception. To illustrate, Australian courts have considered a breach of natural justice to be sufficient grounds to challenge an arbitral award only if the

655 Oil & Natural Gas Corporation Ltd v. SAW Pipes Ltd (n 188) para 30.
656 Austin Ignatius Pullé (n 654) 65.
657 ibid.
658 ibid 66.

misconduct of the arbitrator would cause unjustified prejudice to a party.[659] According to the Indian Supreme Court, the *audi alteram partem* principle (both sides should be given a fair hearing) is one such fundamental principle of natural justice, and an order breaching this principle would be 'in nullity'.[660] If a party is denied the right to legal representation, this would also amount to a breach of natural justice.[661]

Apart from this, there are some other basic principles of justice that could fall under this head of the public policy exception:

(i) *Where arbitrators do not follow due process/procedure established by law*

The 'due process' requirement has gained the status of a fundamental right in the Anglo-Saxon and continental legal systems.[662] The Constituent Assembly, which drafted the Indian Constitution borrowed the term 'due process' from the Constitution of the United States but keeping in mind the different socio-legal situation in India modified it to 'procedure established by law'.[663]

Every arbitral award needs to meet the 'demands of due process', and tribunals are bound to treat the parties in a fair and equal manner while giving them the opportunity to present their case.[664] The violation of due process by the tribunal can be grounds for non-enforcement of arbitral awards.[665] It is considered to fall under the grounds of procedural public policy.[666]

'Due process' is a vague term, and there is no exhaustive list that would fall within this requirement. However, for lack of due process to be invoked in

659 *Melbourne Harbour Trust Commissioners v Hancock* (1927) 39 CLR 570 (High Court of Australia) 588.
660 *Nawabkhan Abbaskhan vs The State Of Gujarat* (1974) SCR 3 427 (Supreme Court of India).
661 D.L. Miller And Co. Ltd. v. Daluram Goganmull (n 645).
662 Bernardo M. Cremades, 'Alexander Lecture 2016: The Use and Abuse of Due Process in International Arbitration' <http://www.ciarb.org/docs/default-source/ciarbdocuments/events/2016/november/use-and-abuse-of-due-process.pdf?sfvrsn=2> accessed 22 February 2017.
663 *Constituent Assembly of India Debates, Official Report*, vol IX (Lok Sabha (Indian Parliament) 1949) <http://loksabhaph.nic.in/writereaddata/cadebatefiles/C15091949.html> accessed 8 September 2021.
664 Bernardo M. Cremades (n 662).
665 ibid 8.
666 IBA Subcommittee On Recognition and Enforcement of Arbitral Awards (n 424) 14.

challenging an award, there need to be serious irregularities.[667] Parties to an arbitration must, among other things, be afforded 'proper notice'.[668] It is true that section 48(1)b of the IAA, which follows Article V(1)b of the New York Convention, already provides that recognition and enforcement may be refused if a party is not able to present its case. It can be argued that this does not need to also be repeated in a definition of public policy. Such an argument, however, does not take into consideration that being able to present one's case is only one element of the due process requirement.

Due process plays a significant role as it is an essential prerequisite for a fair hearing. It is also beneficial to arbitration as a whole, as even the losing party will be more willing to accept an award if the tribunal has fulfilled due process requirements. Under Indian law, due process is enshrined as a 'part and parcel of personal liberty' under Article 21 of the Indian Constitution.[669] It can therefore be inferred that under Indian law, the breach of due process requirement would be a breach of the most basic notions of justice and would therefore be sufficient grounds for refusing enforcement of an arbitral award on public policy grounds.

(ii) Manifest disregard of the law or of the contract by an arbitrator

Manifest disregard of the law by an arbitrator, which is both blatant and unconcealed, has been argued to breach the public policy exception.[670] This argument has also been supported by judicial reasoning. In the United States, the 9th Circuit held that manifest disregard of the law by an arbitrator would render the award liable to be vacated under the Federal Arbitration Act.[671] For the 'manifest disregard' defence to be invoked, it is insufficient that the arbitrator merely makes an error with respect to the law. The test is met only when the arbitrator knew the law but chose to ignore it.[672]

In India, there has not yet been a challenge of an arbitral award on the grounds of manifest disregard of the law before the Supreme Court. The Court has laid down in other previous decisions the consequences when there is a manifest

---

667 Matti S. Kurkela and Santtu Turunen, *Due Process in International Commercial Arbitration* (2nd edn, Oxford University Press 2010) 17.

668 Joel Junker (n 16) 231.

669 *Selvi & Ors vs State of Karnataka* [2010] AIR 2010 SC 1974 (Supreme Court of India).

670 Joel Junker (n 16) 237.

671 *Comedy Club, Inc v Improv West Associates* [2009] 553 F3d 1277 (United States Court of Appeals, Ninth Circuit).

672 *Michigan Mut Ins Co v Unigard Sec Ins Co* [1995] 44 F3d 826 (United States Court of Appeals, Ninth Circuit).

disregard of the law by persons having the legal authority to decide on the rights of parties. The Court laid down that if such persons or a tribunal acted in a way that manifestly disregards the law, the court could exercise its power of intervention.[673] A similar situation arises in the case of manifest disregard of contract by the tribunal. The Supreme Court has held that where an arbitrator disregards the contract, any award rendered would be considered as arbitrary and justify judicial intervention.[674]

(iii) Impartiality and independence of an arbitrator

Impartiality and independence of an arbitrator are essential to the conduct of fair arbitration proceedings. According to Japaridze, this would mean that arbitrators must be 'even-handed' and be guided solely by the facts of the case and the law and not be influenced by bias or extrinsic factors.[675] In order to ensure this, several arbitral institutions require arbitrators to make a declaration of impartiality and independence before the commencement of the arbitration.[676] Any misstatements by the arbitrator or failure to disclose would make a subsequent award suspect and could give rise to contesting of the award on public policy grounds either at the seat or the place of enforcement. Despite the importance of impartiality, different states have varying thresholds as to when public policy can be invoked.

Impartiality of the arbitrator is considered to be a fundamental requirement under the Indian legal system. This can be seen in section 12 of the IAA, where a party can challenge a biased arbitrator, and section 13, which permits an aggrieved party to seek setting aside of an award in case the arbitrator is not impartial. Although these provisions apply to domestic awards, it nevertheless demonstrates the importance of impartiality in the Indian legal system. The Indian Supreme Court in the *Biecco Lawrie* case held that the lack of bias is an essential requirement for a fair hearing.[677] This can also be seen from the *Shakti*

673 *Surya Dev Rai Vs Ram Chander Rai and Ors* [2003] Civ Appeal 6110 (Supreme Court of India).

674 Steel Authority Of India Limited vs JC Budharaja [1999] AIR 3275 (Supreme Court of India).

675 Nana Japaridze, 'Fair Enough? Reconciling the Pursuit of Fairness and Justice with Preserving the Nature of International Commercial Arbitration' (2008) 36 Hofstra Law Review 1415, 1432 et seq.

676 For instance, see Article 11, Rules of Arbitration of the International Chamber of Commerce 2021.

677 Biecco Lawrie Ltd & Anr v State of West Bengal & Anr [2010] AIR 142 (Supreme Court of India) [13].

Bhog ruling, where the Delhi High Court held that in case of lack of impartiality, the award would be set aside by the court on the grounds of breaching the public policy of India.[678]

The rationale behind these grounds is that a biased arbitral tribunal would breach the requirements of natural justice as it would not provide the parties with a fair hearing. Enforcing an award rendered by a biased arbitrator would severely undermine the confidence of parties in arbitration as a fair means of resolving their commercial disputes.

A bias could arise either if any of the arbitrators have a financial (or other) relationship with either of the parties or if an arbitrator has an inherent prejudice.[679] An appearance of bias could be seen if one of the parties to the arbitration is an important client of the arbitrator or her law firm. Such a situation may also arise when the arbitrator has a predisposition to a particular position, which can, for instance, be detected by publications or remarks made by the arbitrator.

The importance of impartiality has been stressed by practitioners and found in the literature. Born, for instance, has argued that lack of impartiality would clearly be a ground for refusing enforcement of awards under the New York Convention.[680] Furthermore, impartiality has been laid down as part of procedural public policy by the International Bar Association.[681] Even according to the UNCITRAL Model Law and statutes, which are based on it, bias by the arbitrator is often considered to be a clear violation of public policy.[682]

This approach has been taken in many jurisdictions. For instance, in Spain, the Madrid Court of Appeal in the *Lidex* ruling refused to enforce an award that contravened public policy because the arbitrator was not impartial.[683] In Germany, procedural public policy mandates arbitral tribunals to be impartial.[684] Even under English law, which Indian law emulates in many respects,

678 Shakti Bhog Foods Ltd vs Kola Shipping Ltd & Anr [2012] OMP 194 2009 (Delhi High Court) [86].

679 See William W. Park, 'Arbitrator Integrity', in Michael Waibel (ed), *The Backlash against Investment Arbitration: Perceptions and Reality* (Wolters Kluwer Law & Business 2010) 194.

680 Born (n 419) 3587.

681 IBA Subcommittee On Recognition and Enforcement of Arbitral Awards (n 424) 15.

682 William W. Park, 'Arbitrator Bias' TDM 6 (2015) <www.transnational-dispute-management.com/article.asp?key=2265> accessed 23 February 2017.

683 Lidex Telecom SL v Inocencion Comercial Ruga del Sur SL [2007] 294 (Madrid Court of Appeals).

684 Fernando Mantilla-Serrano (n 443) 343.

impartiality is considered to be part of mandatory public policy, which is left to the determination of the courts.[685] In England, courts have taken a relatively strict approach, in a case where an arbitrator made off the cuff remarks that 'all Portuguese are liars…and Norwegians are generally truthful people', the court held it to be sufficient grounds to remove the arbitrator.[686] In the above example, it would not be surprising, if supposing the arbitrator had gone on to make an award, that such an award could also be successfully impeached on public policy grounds. This is because courts consider the impartiality of the arbitrator to be an important precondition for the enforcement of arbitral awards.[687]

It is not only proven impartiality that may justify the challenge of an award but also situations where there could be a justified assumption of partiality on the part of the arbitrator. One possible scenario where public policy could be violated is when there is a 'substantial' business relationship between the arbitrator and one of the parties, or the parties counsel, which influences the arbitrators' judgment – provided of course – that the party challenging the award had not previously known about and accepted the relationship.[688] This could give justifiable doubts that the arbitrator is biased. Doubts as to the impartiality of the arbitrator could also arise where the arbitrator has a love affair with one of the parties or their counsel during the proceedings, which is not disclosed to the other party.[689] An award rendered in such situations would quite possibly be in conflict with the most basic notions of justice and, therefore, would justify judicial intervention.

But what would constitute apparent bias is quite a controversial question in India. The courts have given arbitrators a broad leeway. For instance, the Supreme Court has held that just because the arbitrator is an employee of one of the parties '*is not ipso facto a ground to raise any presumption of bias or partiality*'.[690]

---

685 Dominique Hascher, 'Independence and Impartiality of Arbitrators: 3 Issues' (2012) 27 American University International Law Review 789, 803.

686 In Re an Arbitration between the Owners of the Steamship 'Catalina' and others and the Owners of Motor Vessel 'Norma' (1938) 61 Llyods Law Rep 360 (King's Bench Division) 363.

687 ibid.

688 For a more detailed overview see, Bernard Hanotiau, 'Misdeeds, Wrongful Conduct and Illegality in Arbitral Proceedings', Berg, *International Commercial Arbitration* (n 495) 262 et seq.

689 Berg, International Commercial Arbitration (n 495).

690 *Aravali Power Company Pvt Ltd vs M/S Era Infra Engineering Ltd* (2017) Civ APPEAL NOS 12627–12628 (Supreme Court of India) [19].

This decision may be going too far and would need to be re-evaluated. It is obvious that an employee of a party would have a bias in favor of his employer. The arbitrator would have a direct financial relationship with the party, and his/her employment may depend on the award.

One key element in the discussion about arbitrator impartiality is whether this ground can be invoked directly at the stage of enforcement. The rational approach would be that, the party if aware of any bias or grounds for bias, must first bring it to the attention of the arbitral tribunal. If the allegations of bias have been sufficiently addressed by the arbitrator, then a breach of the public policy exception would not arise. This goes to the core of *Kompetenz-Kompetenz,* where the arbitral tribunal first has to decide on its jurisdiction and by inference any challenge to an arbitrator. In *Hebei,* a Hong Kong Court of Appeal ruling concerning the challenge of an award on public policy grounds, the obligation of the party challenging the award was well elaborated by Sir Anthony Mason. He ruled that a party was obliged to raise objections in a timely manner and may not keep objections 'up his sleeve, for later use after an award is made'.[691]

(iv) Res judicata

Res judicata is considered to be a legal rule 'recognised by civilised nations'.[692] It mandates that previous decisions of a court or an arbitrator, which have attained finality, would be conclusive as to any future claim seeking the same relief, where the same facts and parties are involved.[693] In coming to their awards, arbitral tribunals are required to keep in mind the principle of *res judicata*. This is essential as it helps ensure the finality of awards, which is of utmost importance to parties.

Arbitrators are sometimes in a difficult situation as there is no international standard as to what is the scope of *res judicata*. Rather, the scope differs across jurisdictions – common law countries often give it a more broad understanding, and civil law countries a more narrow understanding.[694] This is compounded

691 *Hebei Import & Export Corp v Polytek Engineering Co Ltd* (1999) HKCFA 40 (Hong Kong Court of Final Appeal) [75].

692 Bin Cheng, *General Principles of Law as Applied by International Courts and Tribunals* (Digitally printed 1st pbk version, Cambridge University Press 2006) 336 et seq.

693 'ILA International Commercial Arbitration Committee Berlin Conference-Interim Report: "Res Judicata" and Arbitration' (2004) <http://www.ila-hq.org/download.cfm/docid/446043C4-9770-434D-AD7DD42F7E8E81C6> accessed 23 February 2017.

694 Ritunjay Gupta, 'Res Judicata in International Arbitration: Choice of Law, Competence & Jurisdictional Court Decisions' (2020) 16 Asian International Arbitration Journal 193, 196.

by the conflict of law problem as to which jurisdictions understanding of *res judicata* should be applied. There is no agreement on this problem in the literature.[695] Difficulties in applying the principle of *res judicata* may also arise not only in the context of two different arbitral tribunals seized with the same dispute but also with regard to proceedings before an arbitrator when the dispute is already decided by a court or in the context of partial award and final award.[696]

Disregarding the principle of *res judicata* without valid grounds is considered to be a sufficient reason for courts to refuse enforcement of arbitral awards on public policy grounds in several jurisdictions.[697] In India, respecting *res judicata* is considered essential public policy by Indian courts. For instance, the Indian Supreme in *K.N.Modi* has considered re-agitating an issue that has already been concluded before the competent authority before a different forum to be not just an abuse of process but also a violation of (Indian) public policy.[698] Similarly, in the *Videocon Industries* case, the Delhi High Court held unequivocally held that issue estoppel is an essential part of Indian public policy and is of 'paramount importance.'[699]

The strict view taken in India in ensuring the principle of *res judicata* is not violated can also be seen in other jurisdictions like Germany. The fundamental nature of *res judicata* in the German legal system can be seen in a recent BGH ruling, where it held ruled that if an arbitral tribunal wrongly decides on the applicability of res judicata of the previous award, this would be grounds for setting aside of the arbitral award as a violation of procedural public policy.[700]

Due to the importance placed on *res-judicata* in the Indian legal system, and to enure that arbitral awards remain final, parties seeking to enforce an award in India would be well served by ensuring that their arbitral proceedings are not contrary to the accepted understanding of res judicata under Indian law. Anything else would risk judicial intervention on public policy grounds.

695 Ritunjay Gupta (n 694).

696 ibid 197.

697 Luca G. Radicati di Brozolo, 'Res Judicata in International Arbitral Awards' [2011] ASA Special Series <http://www.law.columbia.edu/sites/default/files/microsites/columbia-arbitration-day/files/02_2011_-_radicati_di_brozolo.pdf> accessed 23 February 2017.

698 *KK Modi v KN Modi & Ors* (1998) 3 SCC 573 (Supreme Court of India) [44].

699 *Union Of India vs Videocon Industries Ltd* (2012) CSOS 33142011 (Delhi High Court) [94].

700 *BGH Beschluss vom 11. Oktober 2018 – I ZB 9/18* (German Federal Court of Justice (Bundesgerichtshof)).

(v) The overarching need for fairness

All the preceding grounds such as impartiality, res judicata, due process aim at achieving a common goal, i.e., to ensure fairness. The need for a fair trial is part and parcel of the principle of natural justice and is the overarching reason for the Indian legislature including natural justice as part of Indian public policy. The Indian Supreme Court in the *Bharvani* case has stated that the fair hearing has two components – firstly, each party should be given the opportunity of presenting its case, and secondly, the opportunity should be reasonable.[701]

The need for the legal system to ensure fairness can, however, conflict with and come at the cost of other crucial objectives of arbitration, such as the speedy resolution of disputes and finality. When courts decide to review awards to check if the arbitrators have acted in a fair manner, there is the obvious consequence of delay and added expense. Arbitration then is no longer efficient and effective. These are consequences that the parties expressly tried to avoid when choosing arbitration as their preferred means of dispute settlement.

The finality of arbitral awards is considered so vital that, according to Larson, it is considered to be an 'extension of party autonomy' and 'essence of arbitration'.[702] This does not mean that courts should never control arbitral awards for fairness. While parties to an arbitration place great value on finality, studies have shown that a fair trial is considered by parties to be more important even than other objectives such as finality, cost and the need for a speedy trial.[703] Besides, the argument of judicial abstinence to ensure speed and efficiency may be overrated – arbitration proceedings are not as efficient and speedy anymore but have rather increasingly become long-drawn and protracted.[704] For the aforementioned reasons, when relying on public policy, it is vital for courts to find the right balance between and the need for ensuring finality and the need for fairness. One of these objectives should not be compromised so the other can be achieved.

---

701 *Indru Ramchand Bharvani v Union of India* (1988) 4 SCC 1 (Supreme Court of India).

702 Caroline Larson, 'Substantive Fairness in International Commercial Arbitration: Achievable through an Arbitral Appeals Process?' (2018) 84 The International Journal of Arbitration, Mediation and Dispute Management 104, 108.

703 ibid 106.

704 Mauro Rubino-Sammartano, *International Arbitration Law and Practice* (3rd edn, JurisNet 2014) para 26.1.

IV. The burden of proof in invoking the public policy exception

Similar to other adversarial system of resolving disputes like litigation in courts, the determination of burden of proof plays an important role in arbitration proceedings. Given that the courts/arbitral tribunals ability to investigate claims by itself are limited, the goal of allocating burden of proof is to minimize costs by allocating the onus of collecting and presenting evidence amongst the parties to the dispute.[705] When dealing with the public policy exception the question arises as to which party should bear the burden of proof when it comes to challenging or resisting the enforcement of an arbitral award. In this section, we will evaluate the statutory framework and look at the current jurisprudence in India *vis-à-vis* other jurisdictions.

1. Position in statute

Article V(1) of the New York Convention, which elaborates on the procedural grounds for refusing enforcement of an award, explicitly places the burden of proof on the party bringing the challenge. This is not the case when it comes to Article V(2) of the New York Convention, which deals with the public policy exception for refusing enforcement. This provision is silent when it comes to the question of how to allocate the burden of proof. The IAA, which governs arbitration in India, is similarly silent when it comes to the allocation of the burden of proof in proceedings for refusing the enforcement of awards on public policy grounds. When one looks outside the context of arbitration, the Indian Evidence Act 1872, which applies to the taking of evidence in court proceedings in India, provides in section 101 that the burden of proving a fact falls on the party asserting the fact. The main justification for such an approach is to disincentivise frivolous claims.[706] If this standard were to be taken, the burden of proving a violation of public policy would lie on the party resisting enforcement of the arbitral award. As will be shown below a similar approach is taken in most jurisdictions.

705 Hay L. Bruce, 'Allocating the Burden of Proof' (1997) 72 Indiana Law Journal 651, 654.
706 ibid 655.

2. The burden lies on party resisting enforcement

As a general rule in most legal systems, it is for the party claiming a fact to prove it.[707] It is therefore unsurprising that some scholars have urged that it is essential that the burden of proving a violation of public policy fall on the party seeking to make use of the exception.[708] When it comes to relying on the public policy exception, it is therefore for the award debtor to prove that this exception can be invoked.[709] Gary Born, who propounds the principle of presumptive enforceability, has reasoned that the burden of proof for refusing enforcement of an arbitral award falls on the party resisting recognition and enforcement.[710] In his view, the burden of proof on the award debtor would not be one of merely showing probability, but it is rather a 'demanding one'.[711]

The aforementioned view has been supported by Indian courts as well. In the *Transocean Shipping* case, the Supreme Court, while referring to Article V(1) of the New York Convention held that where a party resists enforcement of a foreign arbitral award based on procedural irregularities/illegality during the arbitration or in the constitution of the tribunal, the burden of proof according to Indian law would fall on the party making the challenge.[712] The Court reiterated its view in *Ganges Waterproof Works* where it held that the burden of proving misconduct of the arbitrators would fall upon the party making the allegations.[713] The Rajasthan High Court has taken a similar approach in holding that the burden of proving allegations of illegality/invalidity of the arbitration clause would fall on the plaintiff.[714]

---

707 Daniel Girsberger and Nathalie Voser, *International Arbitration: Comparative and Swiss Perspectives* (3rd edn, Nomos ; Schulthess 2016) 240.

708 David A. R. Williams, 'Defining the Role of the Court in Modern International Commercial Arbitration' (2014) 10 Asian International Arbitration Journal 137, 157, 158.

709 Marie Berard and Katharina Lewis, 'Privy Council Confirms Pro-Enforcement Approach under New York Convention' [2014] ASA Bulletin, Association Suisse de l'Arbitrage; Kluwer Law International 880.

710 Born (n 419) 3410.

711 ibid 3651.

712 Transocean Shipping Agency (P) Ltd v Black Sea Shipping (1998) 2 SCC 281 (Supreme Court of India).

713 *Ganges Waterproof Works (P) Ltd v Union of India* (1999) 4 SCC 33 (Supreme Court of India) [6].

714 Ranwa Construction Company v The Administrator, Pant Krishi Bhawan, Jaipur & Anr (2006) AIR Raj 70 (Rajasthan High Court) [6].

The approach of Indian courts is predictable, given that even in ordinary civil proceedings, they have allocated the burden of proof on the party making a claim. In the *Kalyanaswamy* decision, for instance, the Supreme Court held that with regard to allegations of fraud or coercion in the underlying document (in this case, a will), the burden of proof lies on the party making the allegations.[715] Under Indian law, the burden of proving a violation of public policy, especially in case of allegations of fraud, would, therefore, fall on the party trying to resist the enforcement of the award by invoking the public policy exception.

Courts across various jurisdictions have taken a similar view. In the United States, for instance, in *Sage Environment,* it was held that in invoking the public policy exception, the burden of proof falls on the plaintiff.[716] The court, in this case, dismissed the plaintiff's challenge as it failed to fulfill the 'high burden of proof' required in invoking the public policy exception.[717]

Even under English law, the pro-enforcement approach can be seen with regard to apportioning the burden of proof. To ensure that courts are able to deal with public policy issues of their own motion, the allocation of the burden of proof with regard to the public policy exception was not explicitly provided for in the UK Arbitration Act.[718] In practice, however, under English law, the burden of proving the breach of public policy would lie squarely with the party challenging the award.[719] By putting the onus on the challenging party, courts are able to weed out unnecessarily frivolous and vexatious challenges.

A similar approach was also taken by the English Court of Appeals in the *Gater Assets* case, where it ruled that although Art V(2) of the New York Convention is silent with regard to the allocation of the burden of proof when it comes to the public policy exception when it comes to fraud as a breach of public policy, 'the burden of proof is on the party alleging it'.[720]

Given the aforementioned decisions, there seems to be a consensus across most legal systems placing the burden of proof on the party that seeks to resist the enforcement of an arbitral award. Such an approach is in line with the public

---

715 *V Kalyanaswamy v L Bakthavatsalam* (2020) Civ Appeal No1021-1026 2013 (Supreme Court of India) [83].

716 *Berg v Sage Environmental Consulting of Austin, Inc* (2005) 381 FSupp2d 552 (United States District Court, MD Louisiana).

717 ibid 559.

718 *Gater Assets Ltd v Nak Naftogaz Ukrainiy* [2007] EWCA Civ 988 (England and Wales Court of Appeal (Civil Division)) [15].

719 Scherer (n 306) 5.

720 Gater Assets Ltd v Nak Naftogaz Ukrainiy (n 718).

policy of ensuring the finality of awards and respecting party autonomy. There is a rider, however, – just because the burden of proof falls on the award debtor does not mean that the court cannot invoke the exception by its own motion. Unlike the other grounds for refusing enforcement, the public policy grounds can be invoked *sua sponte* by the courts (i.e., even without application by the aggrieved party).[721]

3. Finding a balance in allocating the burden of proof

Despite the arguments made above, given the large stakes that are commonly involved in international arbitrations, and the fact that challenges to arbitral awards are very rarely successful, the party resisting enforcement may feel that it would be unfair for it to solely bear the burden of proving the other party's or the tribunals violation of public policy. The argument would be that such an allocation of the burden of proof would give the benefit to the party that violated the law/public policy. Proving such violations is especially a major challenge when it comes to allegations of corruption given that bribery is usually conducted secretively and parties would not be readily willing to admit their complicity given the risk of criminal liability.

French courts have acknowledged this problem and tried to come up with a solution. According to this approach the burden is not so demanding on the party making allegations. The party alleging corruption does not need to provide direct evidence. In *Sorelec,* the *Cour d'appel de Paris* came up with a red flag approach to allegations of corruption.[722] The court held that it would take into consideration even circumstantial evidence, and be willing to undertake a *de novo* review of the evidence to find if there is merit to the allegations of corruption, regardless of whether the allegations were raised before the tribunal during the arbitral proceedings.[723]

Given that corruption is also a major challenge in India, and is considered to violate Indian public policy, it will not be surprising if there is a rethinking about how Indian courts allocate the burden of proof in case of serious illegality that leads to a violation of public policy.

---

721 Born (n 419) 3445.

722 Libyan State v. Sorelec (n 536).

723 For an English summary of the findings of the court in Sorelec v Libya, 'Paris Court Sets Aside Arbitration Awards Based on Corruption Red Flags' (*Debevoise & Plimpton Update*, 14 December 2020) <https://www.debevoise.com/insights/publications/2020/12/paris-court-sets-aside-arbitration-awards-based-on> accessed 9 September 2021.

V. Evaluating the new definition of the public policy exception under Indian law

The Indian legislature, in deciding to define the scope of the public policy exception, has undertaken a very ambitious endeavor. It has tried to address a pertinent problem of excessive judicial intervention on the grounds of public policy. By doing so, it has recognised that public policy must be construed narrowly in international commercial arbitration- party autonomy demands this.

Statutorily restricting the scope of public policy exception comes with certain risks. It goes against contemporary jurisprudence according to which 'considerations of public policy can never exhaustively be defined.'[724] Furthermore, there are doubts as to the efficacy of legislatively defining the scope of the exception. Scholars have argued that the definition of the term is elusive[725] and that the determination of whether an award breaches public policy cannot be done in a mechanical way but rather should be based on the judgment of the enforcing court.[726] One argument against the definition is that it leads to a degree of inflexibility. Courts will no longer have the ability to stretch the exception to meet the circumstances of the case. A second possible criticism is that the new definition is incomprehensive and does not cover many important aspects of both procedural and substantive public policy. This chapter will evaluate if the current definition is really so narrow that it justifies any of these apprehensions.

1. What the definition seeks to achieve

The definition of public policy provided for in section 48(2) of the IAA(Am.) 2015 seeks to clarify the scope of the exception, and therefore ensure that courts stick to the given definition and do not expand it further.

When first looking at the definition of public policy in the IAA(Am.) 2015, one gets the impression that the definition fulfills its objectives and is quite comprehensive. The definition lays down specific grounds under which the public policy exception can be invoked. According to the definition, an award would be against public policy 'only' if the grounds laid down under the Act are fulfilled.

---

724 Deutsche Schachtbau-und Tiefbohr-Gesellschaft M.B.H. v. Shell International Petroleum Co. Ltd. (n 289) 316.

725 Kent Murphy (n 75) 591.

726 Jonathan Hill, 'The Exercise of Judicial Discretion in Relation to Applications to Enforce Arbitral Awards under the New York Convention 1958' (2016) 36 Oxford Journal of Legal Studies 304, 314 et seq.

The definition distinguishes two categories. The first one can be invoked 'if the making of the award' was vitiated by fraud. This has to do, therefore, with the behavior of the tribunal during the proceedings, i.e., whether in making the award there was an element of fraud, which influenced the tribunal, a breach of which would therefore be a violation of procedural public policy. The second category deals with the more substantive issue of the consequences of the award. In effect, it encompasses matters of substantive public policy, such as whether the award would be in breach of the fundamental policy of Indian law or would violate the most basic notions of morality or justice.

While finding the meaning of the procedural grounds of public policy is reasonably straightforward i.e., objective criteria can be used to determine if there is fraud or corruption influencing the arbitrators. This is not the case for terms like morality and justice or finding out the meaning of the fundamental policy of Indian law. These expressions are inherently vague, open-ended and dependent on subjective interpretation of courts.

2. Evaluating the success of the definition in narrowly construing public policy

The central challenge for the lawmaker in defining a term is to make it both 'precise and sufficiently comprehensive'.[727] It has been argued that while legal language strives towards precision to further the goals of justice, vague and ambiguous language is a hallmark of political decisions and is based on sentiment or opinion.[728] As seen above, due to vague terminology used, the definition of public policy under the IAA(Am.) 2015 does not meet the threshold of being sufficiently precise. Given that the imprecise terms can be interpreted broadly, the definition also does not meet the requirement of being sufficiently comprehensive.

Furthermore, the definition does not fulfill the intention of the drafters who wished to restrict the scope of the exception. It is riddled with broad terminology and vague, catch-all phrases, which lead to more uncertainty for parties. Such an approach has been criticized by courts in different jurisdictions, notably in Hong Kong, where Justice Chan ruled that public policy is not a '*catch-all provision*' but

727 Russell Sandberg, 'Clarifying the Definition of Religion under English Law: The Need for a Universal Definition' (2018) 20 Ecclesiastical Law Journal 153.

728 Ernst Freund, 'The Use of Indefinite Terms in Statutes' (1921) 30 Yale Law Journal 437.

is rather *'limited in scope and is to be sparingly applied'*.[729] Furthermore, there is an inherent danger in providing a definition that gives the appearance that public policy has been constrained by the legislature when it really has been left broadly open to judicial interpretation.

It is considered to be an essential due process requirement that the wording of the statute should be sufficiently clear so that parties to whom it applies can understand its meaning.[730] The definition does not meet this requirement. This lack of precision can make it difficult for Indian courts to give predictable decisions when it comes to interpreting the scope of the exception. Such an outcome is certainly far from ideal. As has been rightly pointed out by Sandberg, Judges need to avoid coming to a *'fuzzy outcome'* as their ruling *'affect not just the claims in front of them but those who will bring and will not bring claims in the future.'*[731]

However, the way the definition is formulated may actually be its redeeming feature. It acts as more of a guide to courts than a definition. As will be demonstrated in Chapter 5, the evolving nature of public policy means that it is inherently difficult to narrowly fix its definition through statute. The legislator is not capable of anticipating every situation. Any attempt to do so would be inadequate and may risk causing grievous injustice to parties who are unable to invoke the exception at a future date. There should always be a safety valve that courts can use to invoke the exception in rare circumstances.[732] As articulated by Wolff, the vagueness of public policy facilitates it being used as a safety valve.[733] This safety valve has been provided by the Indian legislature by using terms like 'fundamental policy of Indian law' and 'morality and justice'. As these terms are not defined by statute, the courts are left with full discretion as to their interpretation. Furthermore, using vague terms like 'fundamental notions of morality'

---

729 Briana Young, 'X Chartering v. Y, High Court of Hong Kong, Court of First Instance, Case Date 3 March 2014' A contribution by the ITA Board of Reporters (Kluwer Law International).

730 Jeanne Price, 'Wagging, Not Barking: Statutory Definitions' (2013) 60 Cleveland State Law Review 999, 1031.

731 Russell Sandberg (n 727).

732 See, Benedikt Pirker, 'Proportionality Analysis and International Commercial Arbitration – the Example of Public Policy and Domestic Courts', in Joanna Jemielniak, Laura Nielsen and Henrik Palmer Olsen (eds), *Establishing Judicial Authority in International Economic Law* (Cambridge University Press 2016) 303.

733 See, Reinmar Wolff, Article V(2)b, in Wolff (n 88) para 490.

could also be pro-arbitration, because as pointed out by Ghoodosi, violations are extremely difficult to prove before a court that is pro-arbitration.[734]

One of the purposes of providing for the public policy exception is to show that there are some rules so sacrosanct to the legal system that parties cannot opt-out of them, and uniform behavior is required with regard to their compliance.[735] Although the definition of public policy provided by the Indian legislature is vague in some respects, it does explicitly point towards mandatory rules, such as the prohibition of fraud or corruption. It promotes uniform conduct by making crystal clear that parties violating these fundamental rules would not have the benefit of having their awards enforced.

3. How the courts can play an essential role in making the definition work

As the definition of public policy under section 48 has vague terminology, the ultimate role of interpreting these terms falls on the Indian courts. The courts have a special responsibility to act in a manner desired by the drafters of the law and give these terms a narrow construction. In order for legislative restriction of public policy to work, the courts should avoid trying to substitute the arbitrators' judgment with their own. Here courts have to draw a fine line. Paulsson has rightly pointed out that it is not good for arbitration if judges are always trying to assert their 'supremacy' by constantly second-guessing arbitrators, nor for arbitrators to continually try to find ways of escaping necessary judicial oversight.[736]

Lady Justice Gloster of the UK Court of Appeals has suggested two ways courts could help facilitate arbitration. Firstly, by providing 'maximum support' by ensuring that awards are complied with and enforced, and also providing the necessary support during the arbitration process and secondly, by ensuring 'minimum intervention' in arbitral proceedings and awards.[737] She found support for her reasoning in the *Zermalt Holdings* case, where Bingham J urged that the role of the judge is not to 'pick holes' to frustrate an award but rather to approach the

734 Farshad Ghodoosi, 'Fall of Last Safeguard in Global Dejudicialization: Protecting Public Interest in Business Disputes' (n 343) 134.

735 Daniel M. Schwarz, 'The Interplay Between U.S. Statutory Rights and Public Policy Under the FAA/New York Convention in International Disputes' [2010] Social Science Research Network 8 <https://ssrn.com/abstract=1813242> accessed 24 February 2021.

736 Paulsson (n 9) 28.

737 Elizabeth Gloster, 'Symbiosis or Sadomasochism? The Relationship between the Courts and Arbitration' (2018) 34 Arbitration International 321, 323.

award with the expectation that there will not be a defect.[738] Indian courts could take a similar approach by starting out with a presumption of validity when it comes to enforcing awards. The Supreme Court in *Ssangyong Engineering* took such an approach, where it acknowledged that its role in applying public policy to arbitral awards is not that of a 'court of appeal' from the decision of the arbitral tribunal.[739]

Indian courts face a particular difficulty of having to interpret vague and broad terms such as morality, justice and fundamental policy of Indian law. A rational approach suggested by Brett is when words could be understood differently by different persons, the interpreter will need to take a 'reasonable persons' standpoint and could seek guidance from either dictionaries', experts from the particular profession/locality or practice and usage, and parliamentary debates/drafting history.[740] This approach has been supported by judicial decisions. For instance, in *Dolan v. US Postal Service*, the U. S. Supreme Court ruled that 'the definition of words in isolation, is not necessarily controlling in statutory construction… Interpretation of a word or phrase depends upon reading the whole statutory text, considering the purpose and context of the statute, and consulting any precedents or authorities.'[741]

If the definition is to promote arbitration, judges must interpret public policy by keeping the abovementioned considerations in mind. This would mean that Indian courts would need to look at the definition provided in the law and interpret it based on the true intent of the legislator and the narrow interpretation envisioned by the New York Convention.

VI. The reaction of courts to the statutory definition of public policy under the new regime

By defining the scope of the public policy exception in the IAA(Am.) 2015, the legislature sought to curb unnecessary intervention by courts. In order to

738 *Zermalt Holdings SA v Nu-Life Upholstery Repairs Ltd* [1985] EGLR 14 (High Court of Justice, Queen's Bench Division).

739 Ssangyong Engineering & Construction Co Ltd Vs National Highways Authority of India (NHAI) [2019] Civ Appeal No 4779 (Supreme Court of India) [33].

740 Peter Brett, 'The Theory of Interpreting Statutes' (1953) 2 University of Queensland Law Journal 99, 107.

741 *Dolan v US Postal Service* (2006) 126 SCt 1252 (Supreme Court of the United States) 1257 et seq.

evaluate the success of this approach, it is necessary to have a closer look at the most recent court decisions.

After Parliament amended the IAA, Indian courts have largely upheld the letter and spirit of the statute and have demonstrated a strong commitment to respecting party autonomy and the arbitral process. In its *Ayyasamy* ruling, which was rendered shortly after the new law came into force, the Supreme Court stressed the importance of fulfilling 'the intent of legislature' and take an approach 'grounded in faith in arbitration'.[742] The court, in its *Centrotrade* ruling, described party autonomy to be of utmost importance as it is the 'backbone of arbitration'.[743] A similar approach was taken in the *HSS Integrated* ruling, where the Supreme court held that the arbitrator would be the 'master of evidence' and courts should only interfere exceptionally.[744] Such an approach would naturally imply reduced judicial intervention. More recently, in the *Prysmian Cavi* ruling, the Supreme Court recognised the intention of the legislature to provide parties with only 'one bite at the cherry' or judicial intervention on 'extremely narrow grounds' for foreign arbitral awards when compared to domestic awards.[745]

The Supreme Court has, however, not been uniformly mindful of this reasoning. In the *Centrotrade* ruling, when clarifying that a two-tier arbitration award did not contravene the public policy exception, the court went back to the much-criticized *'DDA test'* and held that public policy exception includes the grounds of 'patent illegality' of the award.[746] It would be hard for the court to determine patent illegality without delving into the merits. Such an approach contradicts the statutory definition as laid down in the IAA(Am.) 2015 and also the recommendations of the Law Commission and previous case law.

The high courts have been even more receptive to the legislative move to restrict judicial interference by statutorily defining the public policy exception. In a ruling made shortly after the amendment, where a foreign party sought to enforce in India a substantial award on costs, the Calcutta High Court ruled that the public policy exception could not be 'an excuse to review the order on merits'

742 A Ayyasamy v A Paramasivam & Ors (n 234) para 47.

743 Centrotrade Minerals and Metal Inc Vs Hindustan Copper Ltd (2016) 12 SCALE 1015 (Supreme Court of India) [36].

744 The State of Jharkhand & Ors v M/s HSS Integrated SDN & Anr (2019) SLA C No 13117 (Supreme Court of India) [6.2].

745 *Vijay Karia vs Prysmian Cavi E Sistemi Srl* (2020) Civ Appeal No 1544 (Supreme Court of India) [24].

746 Centrotrade Minerals and Metal Inc. Vs. Hindustan Copper Ltd. (n 743) para 43.

and that it has 'very limited scope' and can only be invoked when the award is 'patently unfair'.[747]

The Delhi High Court has also taken a similar approach in its *Dalmia* ruling. In this case, a party sought to resist enforcement on the grounds that the arbitral tribunal awarded damages even where the other party failed to show a loss. The court firstly acknowledged that the IAA(Am.) 2015 has 'further restricted' the scope of the public policy exception.[748] Furthermore, it interpreted the amendment to mean that an award would no longer be contrary to Indian public policy merely because it was against the interest of India.[749] The court reiterated that the determination of whether the 'fundamental policy of Indian law' has been breached would not entail an 'examination as to the merits of the dispute'.[750]

As can be seen above, Indian courts have recognised the need to restrain powers of judicial intervention in international arbitration; instead, they have looked favorably on the legislative move of statutorily defining the scope of the exception. This can only augur well for the future of arbitration in India.

747 Canadian Commercial Corporation v. Coal India Limited (n 552).
748 Xstrata Coal Marketing Ag v. Dalmia Bharat (Cement) Ltd (n 542).
749 ibid 31.
750 Xstrata Coal Marketing Ag v. Dalmia Bharat (Cement) Ltd (n 542).

Chapter 5: The defining of public policy – a useful innovation?

There are diverging opinions in literature as to whether the public policy exception can be defined. Some authorities argue that the concept is incapable of a definition because of its vagueness and varying nature.[751] This is in contrast with another viewpoint, which argues that although difficulties arise because of the nature of the concept, it is still possible to find a legitimate and functional definition of public policy.[752] Proponents of this perspective agree, however, that public policy cannot be given a rigid formula.[753] In any case, the real debate should not be whether or not public policy can be defined. It most certainly can – as explained by the U. S. Supreme Court, the legislature has the power to define terms and even to give them 'unorthodox meanings'.[754] The exercise of this power can be seen in many jurisdictions, including India. It is unclear, however, whether any attempted definition can be conclusive or sufficiently comprehensive. The dilemma that will be addressed, therefore, is *should* the public policy exception be defined, and if so, which is the competent authority to find such a definition, and how such a definition should be formulated.

I. Roadmap of chapter

As pointed out by Bermann, there is no other area of law that 'operates in the world of private international law as continuously and pervasively as international commercial arbitration'.[755] A characteristic feature of the world of private international is the struggle between predictability and flexibility.[756] In order for

---

751 Central Inland Water Transport Corporation Limited and Anr v. Brojo Nath Ganguly and Anr. (n 169).

752 Christian Klausegger and Peter Klein (n 51) 137.

753 ibid.

754 *Carachuri-Rosendo v Holder* (2010) 130 SCt 2577 (Supreme Court of the United States) 2585.

755 See Abstract, George A. Bermann, *International Arbitration and Private International Law* (Brill: Nijhoff 2017).

756 Peter Hay, Flexibility versus Predictability and Uniformity in Choice of Law: Reflections on Current European and United States Conflicts Law, vol 226 (The Hague Academy of International Law 1991).

certainty and thus predictability to exist, there need to be rigid rules, but this can only be possible at the cost of flexibility.[757] This tension is clearly seen in the case of the public policy exception, where the certainty that can be achieved by giving the term a strict and restrictive meaning can go against the need to be flexible in its interpretation.

The first part of this chapter will first look at whether there is a need for defining the scope of the public policy exception. The second part will evaluate whether finding the definition is the responsibility of parliament or the courts. In the Indian context, there has sometimes been a covert tug of war between the legislature and judiciary regarding who has the prerogative to define the public policy exception. While in initial years, the Supreme Court took upon itself the task of delimiting the exception, more recently, the legislature has sought to reduce judicial influence through statutorily defining the exception. However, in India, the Supreme Court has a large margin of appreciation regarding how it interprets a statute. It is, therefore, an open question whether a statutory definition is going to achieve its objective. Thirdly, the final part of this chapter will evaluate what should be encompassed within the definition of public policy, if it is to be defined either by parliament or the courts.

II. Defining public policy: Pros and cons

The French jurist Jean-Étienne-Marie Portalis, as quoted by Hawthorne, has aptly described one of the major problems faced by the lawmaker, i.e., ensuring simplicity and at the same time providing 'for all eventualities'.[758] In trying to define the scope of the public policy exception, this is exactly what needs to be achieved. But is it really possible to define public policy in a way that is both simple and simultaneously covers all situations?

---

757 ibid 304.

758 L. Hawthorne, 'Public Policy: The Origin of a General Clause in the South African Law of Contract' (2013) 19 Fundamina (Pretoria) <http://www.scielo.org.za/scielo.php?script=sci_arttext&pid=S1021-545X2013000200006&lng=en&nrm=iso> accessed 12 August 2018.

1. A case against defining the scope of the public policy exception

Because of its varying nature, scholars have considered the public policy exception to be 'difficult, if not impossible to define'[759] and have argued that it is not possible to demarcate it through a rigid formula.[760] Several arguments can be raised against defining the scope of the public policy exception.

(a) *The drafters of the New York Convention did not envision a definition*

Scholars have pointed out that countries having different economic, political, social and religious influences would naturally have different outlooks regarding what constitutes their public policy.[761] Although the international nature of commercial arbitration may demand an internationally accepted definition of public policy, providing a definition for the term public policy was not the intention of the drafters of the UNCITRAL Model Law or the New York Convention.[762] The exception was left undefined by the drafters of the New York Convention as it was felt that concrete manifestations of the public policy exception might substantially vary from one jurisdiction to another.[763] The drafters envisioned public policy as a 'catch-all' provision, which would permit states to tailor the exception to their needs.[764] It is difficult to reconcile the narrow statutory definition of public policy under the IAA with the intention of the New York Convention to provide for public policy to be a 'catch-all' provision.

(b) *Public policy is ever-changing*

Although the aforementioned discourse seems to put the onus of defining public policy on nation-states based on local circumstances, the scope of the public policy exception may keep changing even in a given country in a short timeframe. In response to increased globalization, public policy may morph to

759 Julian D. M. Lew, Loukas A. Mistelis and Stefan M. Kröll, *Comparative International Commercial Arbitration* (Kluwer Law International 2003) paras 26–115.

760 Gerhart Husserl, 'Public Policy and Ordre Public' (1938) 25 Virginia Law Review 37, 41.

761 Chen (n 120) 3.

762 IBA Subcommittee On Recognition and Enforcement of Arbitral Awards (n 424).

763 ibid 1.

764 Joel Junker (n 16) 230.

include new issues such as ensuring environmental protection, labour standards, public health, preventing tax evasion, etc.[765] With the advent of the Covid-19 global pandemic, substantive public policy may also encompass laws restricting agreements for sale of critical medical equipment in case the country faces acute shortage,[766] or restrictions on sale of unapproved vaccines or drugs. The list can be endless. Notions of public policy keep changing based on variations in people's values and circumstances. A good example is how quickly the judicial definition of public policy exception by Indian courts evolved from being narrow in *Renusagar* (1994), to broad in *Phulchand* (2012) and then again narrow in *BALCO* (2014) in a short timeframe of fewer than two decades. This is the reason why in the *Badger Chiyoda* ruling, the New Zealand Court of Appeal warned against considering previously held notions of public policy as 'sacrosanct'.[767]

Given the long, drawn-out legislative process and uncertainty caused due to election cycles, it is uncertain that the legislature would be able to keep amending the exception to reflect the ever-changing notions of what society considers to be part of public policy. Concepts such as morality and ethics change with time. The aforementioned problem is accentuated by the fact that in India, there is a history of arbitration laws going through the entire process of consultation and drafting and being passed by one of the chambers of Parliament, only to lapse due to the end of the parliamentary session before it could become law.[768] Courts, on the other hand, are not affected by such intricacies of the parliamentary process and can provide more immediate solutions.

(c) A definition would reduce flexibility in interpretation

A related argument against defining the public policy exception is that any definition would reduce the flexibility that is necessary for its interpretation. Courts have often taken the textualist approach of not wanting to go beyond the wording of the definition. The U. S. Supreme Court has held, for instance,

---

765 Christopher S. Gibson (n 98) 1240–1241.

766 In the EU such restrictions were enforced through regulations such as Commission Implementing Regulation (EU) 2020/402 of 14 March 2020 making the exportation of certain products subject to the production of an export authorisation (C/2020/1751 OJ L 77I).

767 *CBI NZ Ltd v Badger Chiyoda* (1989) 2 N Z Law Rep 669 (Court of Appeal Wellington) 674.

768 Vyapak Desai and others, International Commercial Arbitration – Law and Recent Developments in India (India ADR Week 2021) (Nishith Desai Associates 2021) 1.

that, 'as a rule, a statutory definition which declares what a term means excludes any meaning that is not stated'.[769] If this reasoning is followed, a fixed definition of public policy effectively ties the hands of the court and restricts their ability to interpret the exception. This is especially problematic as the scope of public policy keeps changing from time to time.[770] As the public policy exception is inherently ambiguous and would be linked to 'temporal, cultural and local conditions',[771] a fixed definition would pose numerous problems. It would be difficult for the legislature to keep amending the statute continually to reflect changing societal and regional notions of public policy. In fact, the Indian Supreme Court has observed that due to its ever-evolving nature, defining the exception would render it 'useless'.[772]

Furthermore, providing a fixed definition to an otherwise expansive term like public policy precludes courts from exercising discretion to use the exception in certain situations which the legislature has not envisioned at the time of drafting. This discretion is very important and has been expressly given to courts by Article V of the New York Convention, with a view to give a degree of protection to the losing party.[773] The Indian Supreme Court has supported this reasoning in the *Brojo Nath* case, where the court held that public policy is synonymous with the public interest, and public interest varied from time to time and was therefore hard to define.[774]

(d) Public policy is inherently vague and cannot be concretized

Another argument against a statutory definition is that there is no way to define a term that is inherently vague. A ruling by Justice Holmes of the U. S. Supreme Court aptly demonstrates why the meaning of a vague term cannot be fixed by statute. He opined that 'a word is not a crystal, transparent and unchanged, it is the skin of a living thought and may vary greatly in colour and content according

769 *Burgess v US* (2008) 128 SCt 1572 (Supreme Court of the United States) 1579.
770 Chen (n 120) 3.
771 See Franz T. Schwarz and Helmut Ortner, 'Chapter III: The Arbitration Procedure – Procedural Ordre Public and the Internationalization of Public Policy in Arbitration', Christian Klausegger and Peter Klein (n 51) 137.
772 Murlidhar Aggarwal vs State of Uttar Pradesh and Ors (n 65) para 31.
773 Paulsson (n 121) para 1.06.
774 Central Inland Water Transport Corporation Limited and Anr v. Brojo Nath Ganguly and Anr. (n 169).

to the circumstances and time'.[775] After all, every piece of legislation will have words whose meaning will be unclear to a certain degree, and this problem will not go away by defining such terms because the words of such definitions will also be equally hazy.[776]

In fact, with regard to public policy, the vague and variable nature of the term is not necessarily a drawback but is rather considered to be essential and has been described by Winfield as being the 'stone in the edifice of the doctrine'.[777]

Although most countries provide for the public policy exception as grounds for refusing enforcement of arbitral awards, very few states actually define the exception. States prefer to leave the term for interpretation by judges. In India, where a definition of public policy has been attempted, vague terms like 'fundamental policy of Indian law' and 'morality and justice' are used to define an even more vague term like public policy.[778] Thus, there is a lack of certainty in the adopted definition, and it arguably serves no practicable purpose. This is a classic example of the kind of definition criticized by the Indian Supreme Court. The Court observed that although the purpose of a definition is to avoid frequent repetitions in describing the subject matter, definitions sometimes also need to be interpreted again because of a lack of clarity in language.[779] The Swiss Federal Court also expressed its doubts as to the possibility of defining public policy when it held that public policy 'is an undetermined legal concept, which is difficult to assess and which hardly lends itself to a definition by rule of thumb'.[780] The court furthermore observed that any attempt to interpret the scope of the exception would only lead to more 'thorny or polemical questions'[781]

(e) The drawbacks of defining public policy may outweigh the benefits

Ideally, formulating a definition should lead to 'condensation and simplification' and increased 'precision'.[782] The very reason for defining a term is to provide

---

775 Towne v Eisner, Collector of United States Internal Revenue for the Third District of the State of New York (1918) 38 SCt 158 (Supreme Court of the United States) 159.

776 Lawrence Solan, *The Language of Statutes: Laws and Their Interpretation* (University of Chicago Press 2010) 49.

777 Percy H. Winfield (n 55) 95.

778 See Explanation 1 to Section 48, The Arbitration and Conciliation Act.

779 Nahalchand Laloochand Pvt Ltd vs Panchali Co-operative Housing Society Ltd (2010) 10 SCR 804 (Supreme Court of India) [21].

780 Tensacciai SpA v Freyssinet Terra Armata Srl (n 582) para 2.1.

781 Tensacciai SpA v Freyssinet Terra Armata Srl (n 582).

782 L. L. Bernard, 'The Definition of Definition' (1941) 19 Social Forces 500, 501.

'a better intellectual grasp'.[783] Neither of these purposes is achieved in the current attempt to define the public policy exception. The current definition in the IAA(Am.) 2015 does just the opposite; it is both broad and abstract. There is another important characteristic, which a 'stipulative' definition (i.e., in this case, a definition stipulating what falls under the public policy exception) needs to have. It needs to provide clarity and need to be 'adequate to the aim pursued'.[784] It is questionable if an open-ended definition riddled with vague terminology can meet this threshold of providing clarity with regard to the scope of the exception.

There is one more important reason for not statutorily confining the scope of public policy. Especially in common law jurisdictions like India, judicial precedent plays a very important role in the development of law. A statutorily ring-fenced definition of public policy, which takes away the discretion of the courts, is considered unsuitable for common law jurisdictions as, according to Winfield, it comes in the way of 'developing the law'.[785]

As demonstrated above, there are numerous complications that the legislators face when trying to define the public policy exception. Whether this is sufficient reason not to define the exception will be evaluated in the next part.

2. Why a definition of public policy may nevertheless be necessary

(a) *Defining public policy will lead to reduced judicial arbitrariness*

Although there are strong arguments against defining the scope of public policy, defining the scope of the exception may actually be a way of promoting arbitration and ensuring the finality of awards. A definition reduces the chance for judicial arbitrariness by providing an objective legal standard on which the interpretation of the exception can be based.

While it has been argued that the public policy exception is difficult or nearly impossible to define because of its varying nature, this has not stopped attempts to find a definition. In the United States, while the FAA does not provide such a definition, the U. S. Supreme Court strongly supported the need for defining the scope of the public policy exception in its *W. R. Grace* ruling, where it held that although '*the question of public policy is ultimately one for resolution by the*

783 ibid 503.

784 Erich Vranes, 'Definition of "Norm Conflict" in International Law and Legal Theory' (2006) 17 European Journal of International Law 395, 397.

785 Percy H. Winfield (n 55) 98.

courts' the exception *'must be well defined and dominant, and is to be ascertained by reference to the laws and legal precedents and not from general considerations of supposed public interests'.*[786]

In practice, only a few jurisdictions other than India have statutorily defined the scope of public policy, in particular the UAE, Sweden, Malaysia, New Zealand and Australia.[787] Among these, the Australian and New Zealand definitions come close to the Indian definition in terms of content. It will be useful to look at the attempts made in these countries and evaluate whether they serve the purpose of reconciling party autonomy with the need to safeguard the fundamental principles of a particular legal system.

In India, the efficacy of defining the public policy exception under the IAA(Am.) 2015 in reducing judicial intervention has been questioned from the perspective of practice.[788] However, providing definitions for specific terms in statutes is very essential, as in the words of Sterling, 'it draws the line between what is protected and what is not.'[789] This is truer for ambiguous terms, which need to be defined, as they could refer to different things and have numerous meanings.[790] A definition of the public policy exception can provide clarity as to its scope and thus be useful to parties who will be able to make an informed decision as to whether they should invoke the exception to challenge the arbitral award.

If defining the public policy exception is a difficult task, not having a definition can lead to even more difficulties. Legal definitions, as pointed out by Sandberg, help act as a 'mechanism for inclusion and exclusion'.[791] The public policy definition in the IAA(Am.) 2015, for instance, purports to be exhaustive insofar as it includes 'only' the grounds provided in section 48. In the absence of such a provision, problems can crop up, for instance, when proceedings for refusing enforcement of an arbitral award are brought before the court on public policy grounds. In such situations, in order to determine if public policy exception has been breached, the court will need to first determine what constitutes public policy and second, come to a conclusion if the enforcement of the award would

786 W. R. Grace & Company v. Local Union 759, International Union of Rubber, Cork, Linoleum & Plastic Workers of America (n 336).

787 IBA Subcommittee On Recognition and Enforcement of Arbitral Awards (n 424) 2.

788 Constantin (n 206) 46.

789 J. A. L. Sterling, *Sterling on World Copyright Law* (Trevor M. Cook ed, 4th edn, Thomson Reuters 2015) para 4.01.

790 Jeanne Price (n 730) 1006.

791 Russell Sandberg (n 727) 134.

contravene public policy. This will be exceedingly hard if there is no statutory guidance as to the scope of the exception. Moreover, leaving the task of finding a definition to the courts will lead to an increased risk that courts will choose to define the public policy exception broadly.

(b) A definition will provide legal certainty

Secondly, unlike varying definitions that cause increased confusion for parties, having a fixed definition of the public policy exception will contribute to providing legal certainty. No longer will judges in domestic courts be able to whimsically expand the exception or reinvent a new head for refusing enforcement of arbitral awards. In a decision made after public policy was defined, the Indian Supreme Court has also recognised that 'it would no longer be legitimate' for courts to create new heads of the public policy exception.[792] The consequence is that when entering into an arbitration agreement, parties will know beforehand what constitutes the public policy of the seat and the place of enforcement.

Take, for instance, the example of the UAE. Here, the primary law governing arbitration, the Civil Procedure Code 1992,[793] precludes settlement through arbitration of bankruptcy, labour disputes, commercial agency agreements, disputes relating to deferred debt, issues such as forgery and criminal activity, as a general principle of public policy.[794] The understanding of public policy under UAE Law is derived primarily from the UAE Civil Transactions Law.[795] Article 3 of which defines *public order* to include *'matters relating to personal status such as marriage, inheritance, and lineage, and matters relating to systems of government, freedom of trade, the circulation of wealth, rules of individual ownership and the other rules and foundations upon which society is based, in such a manner as not to conflict with the definitive provisions and fundamental principles of the Islamic Sharia.'*[796] While this definition may seem too detailed, it does provide a comprehensive overview of the legal position in the country regarding the scope of the public policy exception.

This predictability as to the scope of the exception is extremely important for companies involved in international commerce. Knowing that the above areas

792 PASL Wind Solutions v. GE Power Conversion India (n 170) para 80.
793 The UAE Civil Procedure Code (Federal Law No 11 of 1992).
794 Hassan Arab and Laila El Shentenawi, 'IBA Sub-Committee on Recognition and Enforcement of Awards – Public Policy: The UAE Country Report' (2015).
795 The UAE Civil Transactions Law (Federal Law No 5 of 1985).
796 Arab and El Shentenawi (n 794).

are part of public policy will enable parties to ensure that they do not violate the public policy in this jurisdiction. It will also enable them to approach the local courts if and when they feel that public policy has been breached.

(c) It helps arbitral tribunals to draft enforceable awards

Having a fixed definition of public policy exception will more importantly also enable arbitral tribunals to draft awards that do not breach public policy, therefore fulfilling their obligation of rendering an enforceable award. For example, in Australia, the International Arbitration Act 1974[797] is the law governing arbitration, section 8(7A) of the Act states that '*the enforcement of a foreign award would be contrary to public policy if: (a) the making of the award was induced or affected by fraud or corruption; or (b) a breach of the rules of natural justice occurred in connection with the making of the award.*' Section 19 of the Act provides that public policy refers to the public policy of Australia. An almost identical definition of public policy is also provided for under section 36 of the New Zealand Arbitration Act.[798] Arbitral tribunals may be able to anticipate when these grounds are met and thereby ensure that their awards do not violate any of these grounds.

It must be noted that all the countries attempting to define the scope of the public policy exception have provided for a stipulative definition, i.e., one that specifies the exact grounds falling under the exception rather than a 'lexical' or 'universal' definition, which provides the general meaning of the term.[799] This serves to demonstrate that all these countries sought to restrict the scope of the exception. A more *lexical* definition can be found in Sweden, where the law governing arbitration, i.e., Swedish Arbitration Act,[800] in section 55 item 2 provides that '*Recognition and enforcement of a foreign arbitral award shall also be refused where the court finds...that it would be manifestly incompatible with the fundamental principles of Swedish law to recognize and enforce the arbitral award.*' In Sweden, the intention of the legislature can be seen in the *travaux préparatoire,* which provide that '*the content of public policy does not lend itself to be defined in an absolute manner*' also '*it should only apply in particularly offensive cases.*'[801]

797 International Arbitration Act (Cth).

798 New Zealand Arbitration Act 1996 (Public Act No 99).

799 For a better understanding of the distinction between 'lexical' and 'stipulative' definition see, Russell Sandberg (n 727) 134–135.

800 The Swedish Arbitration Act 1999 (SFS 1999:116).

801 Pontus Ewerlöf, 'IBA Sub-Committee on Recognition and Enforcement of Awards – Public Policy: Sweden Country Report' (2015).

Swedish law, therefore, gives the public policy exception a high threshold, wherein the concept is construed narrowly. The legislature has, however, left the courts with the final discretion to apply the public policy exception on a case-by-case basis.[802]

3. Solving the dilemma through core values

As can be seen, there is a dilemma for every legislator. Not having a statutory definition of the public policy exception will provide the opportunity for judges to provide an expansive interpretation. However, defining the term in an imprecise manner will only muddy the waters even further. To give public policy a fixed specific definition that is clear also has its downsides, as this will bind the courts to the definition although the state's public policy itself evolves based on changing circumstances.

In the absence of a concrete definition, a good way of evaluating if the public policy exception has been breached is by looking at the purpose of the exception. According to Cho and Wegner, the public policy exception seeks to safeguard the 'enforcing state's fundamental moral beliefs and social order'.[803] More broadly speaking, it aims at protecting the 'core values' of a legal system.[804] In order to determine if the exception has been breached, it should be sufficient to determine what are these 'core values'. Any breach of these values would then automatically constitute a violation of the public policy exception. Using this reasoning, there is no need for a court or legislature to define the scope of the public policy exception. They merely need to identify the core values of the given legal system and then look at whether the arbitral award contravenes any of these core values.

Finding out the core values of a legal system should not be a herculean task, as guidance can already be found in judgments of the higher courts in many jurisdictions. These values could differ from country to country. In India, we can see these values enshrined as fundamental rights in Part III of the Indian Constitution. In the United States, a breach of core values such as fundamental notions

802 ibid 3.

803 Kun Hee Cho and Kay-Jannes Wegner, 'LSF-KDIC Investment Company, Ltd. v. Korea Resolution & Collection, High Court of Seoul, 2015 Na 29277' (A contribution by the ITA Board of Reporters, Kluwer Law International 2016).

804 See Franz T. Schwarz and Helmut Ortner, 'Chapter III: The Arbitration Procedure – Procedural Ordre Public and the Internationalization of Public Policy in Arbitration', in Christian Klausegger and Peter Klein (n 51).

of morality and justice would constitute a breach of public policy.[805] In Germany, the breach of core values such as 'basic civil rights' and 'fundamental principles of political and economic life' would constitute a breach of public policy.[806] More generally speaking, core values can include notions of impartiality, liberty and justice.[807]

4. Need for a middle ground

Although there is a case for making use of core values, one cannot deny that there are important justifications for defining the scope of the public policy exception. Firstly, the core values argument struggles to convince because both the New York Convention and national statutes only envision the use of public policy. It is dangerous to equate every core value to public policy because then public policy may be given a broader interpretation than envisioned by the drafters. Furthermore, the certainty provided to parties by defining the scope of public policy can be very valuable.

Despite its appeal, there is an inherent danger in justifying defining public policy on the basis of increased legal certainty. This is because legal certainty itself comes at a cost. Statutory or decisional rules that are uniformly applied can lead to hardship in individual cases.[808] Lawmakers cannot foresee every situation, and to avoid outrageous results, it is necessary to look at each individual case on its merits.[809] This would, however, mean reduced uniformity and predictability. The difficulty becomes even more acute when defining a term like public policy, which is inherently vague. Having a fixed definition of public policy will tie the hands of the court to deal with a specific case where public policy is breached, but the statutory definition does not encompass the breach.

805 Parsons & Whittemore Overseas Co., Inc. v. Societe Generale De L'industrie Du Papier (rakta), and Bank of America, Defendants-appellees, Societe Generalede L'industrie Du Papier (rakta) (n 359) 973.

806 See, 'Germany No. 36, Seller of soybean flour v. Buyer of soybean flour, Oberlandesgericht [Court of Appeal] Hamburg, Not Indicated, 26 January 1989', in Albert Jan Van Den Berg (ed), *Yearbook Commercial Arbitration*, vol 17 (Wolters Kluwer Law & Business 1992) 494.

807 Margit Cohn and Mordechai Kremnitzer, 'Judicial Activism: A Multidimensional Model' (2005) 18 Canadian Journal of Law and Jurisprudence 350.

808 Peter Hay (n 756) 291.

809 ibid 291 et seq.

It is questionable if defining the scope of a vague term like public policy is itself appropriate. Vagueness in itself is sometimes a valuable tool. It is often used by lawmakers to ensure more sophisticated control, for instance, when the lawmaker has a general idea of what it wants to achieve but is unsure as to the exact conduct it wishes to prohibit.[810] It allows for a useful division of labour between the legislature and the courts. This is arguably the case with the public policy exception, where the legislature is unable to envision every circumstance where an evolving concept like public policy is breached. Defining the exception will take away the discretion of the courts to adjust to the circumstances of an individual case.

One more potential drawback of statutory definitions of public policy is that it may enable forum shopping. Parties may prefer choosing to seat their arbitration proceedings in countries that have a narrower interpretation of public policy and thereby reduce the risk of an award being set aside at the seat. Parties may also avoid entering into contracts where enforcement may be in a state with a broad definition of public policy. Such developments can have an untoward effect on drafters. It could lead to a race to the bottom, with states competing to dilute their statutory public policy exception and therefore compromise on the fundamental principles of their legal system.

There is, however, a middle ground that can be used instead of relying on 'core values' or providing a fixed definition. It has been argued that since the search for a fixed definition of the public policy exception is 'a chimaera', one needs to look at the 'evolution of the principles in practice'.[811] Such a 'functional' approach has been supported by the literature.[812] While the difficulty in finding a definition still exists, some boundaries can be found in terms of the consensus that public policy in the transnational context must be given a narrow interpretation.[813]

---

810 George C. Christie, 'Vagueness and Legal Language' (1964) 48 Minnesota Law Review 885, 889 et seq.

811 See James Allsop, 'International Arbitration and Conformity with International Standards of Due Process and the Rule of Law', in Andrea Menaker (ed), *International Arbitration and the Rule of Law: Contribution and Conformity* (Kluwer Law International BV 2017) 766.

812 See Franz T. Schwarz and Helmut Ortner, 'Chapter III: The Arbitration Procedure – Procedural Ordre Public and the Internationalization of Public Policy in Arbitration', in Christian Klausegger and Peter Klein (n 51) 135.

813 See James Allsop, 'International Arbitration and Conformity with International Standards of Due Process and the Rule of Law', in Menaker (n 811) 767.

Another way of evaluating the scope of the public policy exception, even where it has not been defined under arbitration law, is to look at the context of the particular legal system. In Germany, for instance, although the public policy exception has not been defined under the Code of Civil Procedure (ZPO), one can seek guidance from other laws where the scope of public policy has been elaborated upon. A good example would be the Introductory Act to the German Civil Code (EGBGB), where in Article 6, it has been provided that public policy could be invoked if the application of the law of another country would cause an outcome which 'is manifestly incompatible with the fundamental principles of German law' particularly if it would breach 'civil rights'.[814] By referring to these statutes, it is possible for courts to have an understanding of how to use the public policy exception without being bound to any fixed definition provided for in an arbitration statute.

A strict definition of the exception is not imperative. As has been pointed out by Lord Reid in *Ridge v. Baldwin,* just because the term 'natural justice' is difficult to define does not mean that it is meaningless or that it does not exist – such ambiguous terms should be understood from the standpoint of a reasonable person.[815] The same can be said for 'morality, fundamental policy' and other vague terms which the Indian law encompasses as part of the public policy exception.

III. Determining the competent authority for defining the scope of the public policy exception

Although most international instruments and national statutes on arbitration provide for the public policy exception as grounds for refusing enforcement of arbitral awards, there is little guidance as to which is the competent authority for determining the scope of the exception. Paulsson has argued that those who 'impose the law' must have the power of deciding the limits of private interest *vis-à-vis* public interest.[816] Would this mean that public policy should be defined by parliament or the courts?

The most common approach taken by the vast majority of jurisdictions is one of refraining from giving the public policy exception a fixed statutory meaning

---

814 Einführungsgesetz zum Bürgerlichen Gesetzbuche 1994 (BGBl I S 2494, ber 1997 S 1061).

815 *Ridge v Baldwin* (1963) 2 ER 66 (United Kingdom-House of Lords).

816 Paulsson (n 9) 3.

but rather choosing to leave its scope to judicial interpretation. Such an approach can be seen in the writings of Winfield, who defined public policy to be a 'principle of judicial legislation'.[817]

However, such 'judicial legislation' is not universally accepted. Gellhorn has stated that the determination of what constitutes a breach of public policy depends on the wording of the statute and not 'judges opinions'.[818] An approach that has been taken by a handful of states, including India, is to elaborate the scope of the public policy exception through statute. In these countries, the power of determining the scope of the exception is left to the legislature, and the role of courts is more limited to interpretation.

Both a statutory definition and judicial interpretation of public policy have their advantages and drawbacks. As previously explained, a definition of public policy exception which is grounded in a statute can provide certainty to parties and arbitrators regarding the scope of the exception. On the other hand, while statutorily defining the exception ensures certainty as to its scope, this comes at the cost of flexibility as to its application. Courts will be bound by the statutory definition and will not be able to adjust it to the facts and circumstances of the case at hand. Because of these difficulties and the ever-changing nature of public policy, it is understandable why most countries choose not to define the scope of the public policy exception. Interpreting the exception by the judiciary would lead to flexibility but at the cost of certainty. There is an unresolvable tension between the need for uniform application of a rule and the need for flexibility to ensure a just outcome in individual cases.[819]

1. Using the doctrine of separation of powers as a benchmark

The doctrine of separation of powers enables us to look at the exact role of the parliament and the judiciary and how powers are apportioned between them. It may therefore provide guidance as to which branch of the state, i.e., legislature or judiciary, must delimit the scope of the public policy exception. This division has been enshrined in Article 50 of the Indian Constitution, which obliges the state to ensure separation of the executive from the judiciary.

817 Percy H. Winfield (n 55) 92.
818 Walter Gellhorn, 'Contracts and Public Policy' (1935) 35 Columbia Law Review 679.
819 Peter Hay (n 756) 291.

This doctrine itself is not of recent vintage but has its roots in the writings of Aristotle, Plato and Polybius.[820] The doctrine is approached differently in different legal systems. A strict approach has been used by Montesquieu, who urged that three branches of government, i.e., legislature, executive and judiciary, be separated to avoid tyranny.[821] It is this reasoning of Montesquieu in his work 'The spirit of laws' which the Indian Supreme Court relied on when urging for judicial restraint.[822]

The doctrine simply boils down to law making power being vested with the legislature and judicial power being vested with the courts. Neither branch is allowed to usurp the power and function of the other. Anthony Peacock has aptly rationalized the doctrine as creating a *'division of labour that allows each branch to be organized in a way that best enables it to fulfil its unique function'*.[823] This approach has been taken in the United States, where the legislature is precluded from 'exercise of judicial powers' and not allowed to 'overrule the judgment or decree of a court' through statute.[824] The same can be said for the judiciary.

The Westminster system, which originated in the UK, provides another approach to separation of powers. According to this system, which was propounded by Dicey, Parliament is considered sovereign and as having unconditional powers and exclusive power of law-making. In addition, Parliament has immunity with regard to lawmaking against any other body, including the courts.[825]

The Indian approach to separation of powers differs substantially from the approaches shown above insofar as there is no sovereignty of Parliament over

---

820 John Alvey, 'The Separation of Powers between the Executive and the Judiciary' (Australasian Study of Parliament Conference, Parliament House, Hobart, Tasmania, 2017) <http://www.parliament.tas.gov.au/aspg/ASPG%20papers/The%20separation%20of%20powers%20between%20the%20Executive%20and%20the%20Judicary%20-%20Dr%20John%20Alvey.pdf> accessed 6 September 2018.

821 Baron de Montesquieu, *The Spirit of the Laws* (Thomas Nugent tr, Kitchener 2001) 173 <http://www.efm.bris.ac.uk/het/montesquieu/spiritoflaws.pdf> accessed 17 December 2017.

822 Divisional Manager, Aravali Golf Club and Ors v Chander Hass and Ors (2007) 12SCR1084 (Supreme Court of India) [21].

823 Anthony A. Peacock, How to Read The Federalist Papers: With a Selection of Useful Quotations (The Heritage Foundation 2010) 55.

824 *Schwarzkopf v Sac County Board of Supervisors* (1983) 341 NW2d 1 (Supreme Court of Iowa).

825 Pavlos Eleftheriadis, 'Parliamentary Sovereignty and the Constitution' (2009) 22 Canadian Journal of Law and Jurisprudence 267 et seq.

the courts. The separation of powers in India is, in practice, not very strict, leaving room for considerable overlap in the functions of different branches of government.[826] In fact, the judiciary often exercises what has been described by a former Judge of the Indian Supreme Court as 'quasi-legislative or executive actions'.[827] Furthermore, in India, any legislation which 'usurps or infringes' the powers or functions of courts is considered to be void.[828]

From this lopsided arrangement arises the danger of judicial overreach. The Indian Supreme Court has not looked at this tendency for judicial overreach kindly. In its *Chander Hass* ruling, it criticized the propensity of Indian judges to overstep their bounds and 'unjustifiably perform…legislative functions' in the name of judicial activism.[829] According to its reasoning, any attempts by organs of the state to encroach on the functions of other organs would 'upset the delicate balance of the Constitution'.[830]

From early on, American courts have acknowledged that judicial policy-making must be strictly constrained. In an early 19th century Supreme Court decision *Girard's Executors*, it was observed that the determination of '*what is public policy*' and what violates it is '*vague and uncertain*', and entering into a discussion on this subject would be beyond '*judicial duties and functions*'.[831] Justice Frankfurter of the U. S. Supreme Court has also echoed this perspective in *Dulles*, where he held that it is not the duty of the court to make policy.[832] These words were relied upon by the Indian Supreme Court in holding that the Indian Constitution does not allow courts to 'direct or advise the executive in matters of policy'.[833] A similar approach was taken in *Premium Granites*, another Indian Supreme Court ruling. In this case, the court held that it was the job of the

826 See Justice (Retd) Ruma Pal, Separation of Powers in (n 548) 254 et seq.
827 See Justice (Retd) Ruma Pal, Separation of Powers in ibid 255.
828 Sidharth Sharma, 'Public Policy Under the Indian Arbitration Act – In Defence of the Indian Supreme Court's Judgment in ONGC v. Saw Pipes' (2009) 26(1) Journal of International Arbitration 133, 144.
829 Divisional Manager, Aravali Golf Club and Ors. v. Chander Hass and Ors. (n 822), para 17.
830 ibid 19.
831 *Vidal v. Girard's Executors*, 43 U.S. 2 How. 127 (1844)
832 *Trop v Dulles* (1958) 78 SCt 590 (Supreme Court of the United States) 608.
833 Divisional Manager, Aravali Golf Club and Ors. v. Chander Hass and Ors. (n 822) para 19.

legislature and executive and not the courts to determine *'whether a particular public policy is wise or a better public policy can be evolved'*.[834]

Policy-making lies in the realm of legislative competence. Indeed, the argument has been made that judicial policymaking would be a certain breach of the doctrine of separation of powers.[835] Similar approaches can also be found in the literature. Ghodoosi, for instance, has acknowledged that delineating public policy would fall within the 'legislature's domain'.[836]

Such an approach has historical backing in India and can be seen both in debates of the Constituent Assembly which led to the drafting of the Indian Constitution, as well as in early court decisions. During the Constituent Assembly debates, the first Prime Minister, Pandit Jawaharlal Nehru, argued that the Indian Supreme Court could not override the 'will of Parliament representing the will of the entire community'.[837] This approach was rooted in the early decisions of Indian courts. The Federal Court of India (the precursor to the Supreme Court) in its *re Central Provinces* decision, called for a textualist interpretation of laws by the court and held that judges must look for the meaning of the statute only based on its express wording and that as long as the legislature is competent to make the enactment, it is not the job of the court to evaluate the usefulness of the law.[838] Furthermore, the Court held that matters of policy fall 'outside the sphere' of the court and should therefore not be given consideration by judges.[839]

Following the courts' reasoning, it is arguable that defining the scope of the public policy exception is the job of the executive or legislature. By inference, by defining the scope of the public policy exception, the Indian parliament is only fulfilling its legislative function. The job of Indian courts would then be to only apply the law as it stands. With regard to the public policy exception, this would

---

834 *Premium Granites and Anr v State of TN and Ors* (1994) SCR 1 579 (Supreme Court of India), para 54.

835 Joshua Dunn, 'The Perils of Judicial Policymaking: The Practical Case for Separation of Powers' (The Heritage Foundation 2008) 20 2 <https://www.heritage.org/political-process/report/the-perils-judicial-policymaking-the-practical-case-separation-powers> accessed 3 August 2018.

836 Farshad Ghodoosi, 'Arbitrating Public Policy: Why the Buck Should Not Stop at National Courts' 20 Lewis & Clark Law Review 237, 257.

837 H. M. Seervai, The Position of the Judiciary under the Constitution of India: Sir Chimanlal Setalvad Lectures (University of Bombay 1970) 57.

838 *In re The Central Provinces and Berar Act No XIV of 1938* (1939) Fed Court Rep 18 (Federal Court of India) 38.

839 In re The Central Provinces and Berar Act No. XIV of 1938 (n 838).

mean by giving it the meaning provided in the statute. This approach has been taken by the Indian Supreme Court in its *Nalinkhaya* ruling, where the court ruled that the words of a statute must be given the meaning intended by legislature and that it is not the job of the judges to second-guess the legislature and presume that the legislature has erred.[840]

Despite the above argumentation, blindly applying the statute as it is may not be practicable and is certainly not universally accepted. The Indian Supreme Court has, in other rulings, recognised that the doctrine of 'separation of powers' under the Indian Constitution is not to be understood as absolutely rigid.[841] Practical difficulties may also arise, which require judicial policy-making. The public policy exception under the IAA(Am.) 2015 contains vague terms such as morality, justice and fundamental policy of Indian law. It is impossible for the courts to apply the exception without having to interpret these terms. This would certainly involve judicial policymaking and moral judgment on the part of the court. The role of the court becomes even more pronounced when it comes to protecting rights. Such an approach has also been supported by scholarly literature. Paulsson has decried the modern trend of villainising judges and providing absolute power to the law-maker by stating that it is 'nonsensical' to look at a judge merely as a 'mouthpiece' or 'automaton' acting at the will of the legislature.[842] According to him, courts would be the 'most reliable regulator' to ensure behavior meets the needs of society as a whole.[843]

Indian judges have been willing to ignore the rule of separation of powers in certain circumstances. This is reflected by the words of former Chief Justice of the Supreme Court A.M. Ahmadi, where he forcefully argued that in case of *'derelictions of constitutional obligations and gross violations of human rights ... the Supreme Court... cannot be expected to split hairs in an effort to maintain the "delicate balance" of power between the wings of Government'*, but should rather provide the necessary relief.[844]

Furthermore, strong arguments against drawing a strict line between the functions of these two branches of government have also been made in other

---

840 *Nalinakhya Bysack v Shyam Sunder Haldar and Others* (1953) 4 SCR 533 (Supreme Court of India) [11].

841 Asif Hameed & Ors v State of Jammu & Kashmir & Ors (1989) AIR 1899 (Supreme Court of India).

842 Paulsson (n 9) 24.

843 ibid 1.

844 A. M. Ahmadi, 'Judicial Process: Social Legitimacy and Institutional Viability' (1996) 4 SCC (Jour) 1.

jurisdictions. When criticizing the idea that it is the job of the legislature to 'make law' and the courts must only 'say what it is'[845] Justice Emmett M Hall of the Canadian Supreme Court argued instead that judges often contribute to the 'evolution of law', and that the distinction between 'making' and 'applying' of law would only be a matter of degree.[846] In his words, the role of the courts with regard to law reform must not be underestimated. It has been described as one of the 'most fundamental' roles of the judicial process.[847] This is especially the case with regard to the public policy exception, where the courts need to work with the legislature for any statutory definition to succeed in achieving its goal.

While the Indian Parliament may provide a definition for the exception, it is finally for the courts to determine whether to give it a broad or narrow construction. Such an approach has been approved by the Indian Supreme Court in its *Gherulal* decision, where it acknowledged that courts are allowed to 'evolve a new head of public policy in extraordinary circumstances'.[848] Even in *PASL*, where the Supreme Court limited the scope of judicial discretion, it acknowledged that the courts' ability to create a new head of public policy must be constrained within the bounds of judicial precedent.[849]

It is additionally important to look at the role of courts and the legislator *vis-à-vis* arbitration. Traditionally in common law countries, courts were considered to be 'supervisors of arbitral tribunals'.[850] Over time this role has changed, and it is therefore understandable that the legislature would want to restrict the scope for excessive judicial intervention by defining the public policy exception.

As can be seen, the discourse regarding whether it is the job of the legislature or the judiciary to define the scope of the public policy exception is unresolvable and mainly a theoretical exercise. Of more practical relevance is which authority would be more suited for the task. While the judiciary is good at certain tasks like deciding individual cases, the legislature is more apt at resolving general conflicts.

845 Emmett M Hall, 'Law Reform and the Judiciary's Role' (1972) 10 Osgoode Hall Law Journal 399, 403.
846 ibid 404.
847 ibid 403.
848 Gherulal Parekh v. Mahadeo Dass Maiya (n 173) para 64.
849 PASL Wind Solutions v. GE Power Conversion India (n 170) para 80.
850 Menno Aden, 'Wrong Answers to Wrong Questions? A New Approach to Judicial Review of International Arbitral Awards' (2015) 12 Revista Brasileira de Arbitragem 55.

2. Determining the appropriate authority based on democratic principles

Ghodoosi has argued that 'public policy' is as vital to a liberal democracy as 'individual freedom' itself.[851] But if democracy is to be respected, which branch of government would have the authority to determine its scope?

In a democratic system, it is for the legislature to determine governmental policy. It would then be natural for the legislature to determine the public policy of the state. In India, the drafters of the Constitution did not intend the court to take the role of a 'super-legislator'.[852] This is also the case in other jurisdictions. In the United States, Alexander Hamilton has set out in Federalist paper No. 78 that judges need to 'regulate their decision by fundamental laws' and cannot 'substitute their own pleasure to the constitutional intention of the legislature'.[853] Furthermore, he argued the arbitrary rulings of judges must be prevented by formulating rules that 'define and point out' how the court needs to act in the cases which come before it.[854]

If this line of reasoning from two of the world's largest democracies is taken, it is not the duty of the courts to formulate legal policy, but rather, the courts must only follow the law already made. This would mean that the courts should not second-guess the legislature with regard to the public policy exception. Such an approach has been supported by prominent scholars such as Jeremy Waldron, who has argued that 'judicial review of legislation is inappropriate as a mode of final decision making in a free and democratic society'.[855] The advantage of this approach is that it precludes judicial tyranny. The scope of the public policy exception would no longer be randomly defined based on the whims of an individual judge. Furthermore, the legislature can always amend the law to reflect the evolving standards of the public policy exception.

There is another reason for leaving policymaking with the legislature. In a democracy, Parliament is inherently more accountable to the electorate than

851 Farshad Ghodoosi, 'The Concept of Public Policy in Law: Revisiting the Role of the Public Policy Doctrine in the Enforcement of Private Legal Arrangements' (n 42) 686.

852 Maureen Callahan Vander May (n 226) 122.

853 Alexander Hamilton, 'Federalist No. 78, The Judiciary Department' <https://www.congress.gov/resources/display/content/The+Federalist+Papers#TheFederalistPapers-78> accessed 9 October 2018.

854 ibid.

855 Jeremy Waldron, 'The Core of the Case against Judicial Review' (2006) 115 The Yale Law Journal 1346, 1348.

judges. Their decisions could therefore be seen as having more legitimacy. Linde has argued that for effective separation of powers, it is vital that judges derive their understanding of public policy from the branch of government that is politically accountable and not substitute their own judgment of what constitutes public policy.[856]

Even this approach is, however, not without drawbacks. Firstly, it must not be overlooked that judges themselves act as an important part of the democratic process. They provide an element of accountability, control and reduce the chances of abuse of power by the legislature.[857] For instance, if the power of determining the scope of the exception lies in the hands of the legislature, the scope of the exception will be entirely dependent on the political climate. For instance, if a pro-arbitration regime forms the government and passes a law that gives public policy a narrow interpretation, the election of a more nationalist regime could use unfounded concerns of sovereignty to expand the scope of the public policy exception. This would not happen in case neutral independent judges decide on the scope of public policy.

What happens, however, when – as in India – the legislature has already provided a definition of public policy in the arbitration law? There are good reasons why courts should surely bind themselves to such a definition. After all, it could be argued that the will of the legislature is the will of the people. When the legislature codifies a solution to determining what constitutes public policy, it has been argued that the courts are not supposed to 'second-guess' this majoritarian position.[858] Pirker has suggested that although in an ideal well-functioning democracy, courts must defer to the will of the legislature, this is not always the case in reality where sometimes courts need to protect 'specific values' from majoritarian decision-making.[859] He preconditions judicial review on when courts find that there are important values at stake or that these values are neglected.[860]

856 Hans A. Linde, 'Courts and Torts: "Public Policy" Without Public Politics?' (1994) 28 Valparaiso University Law Review 821, 605.

857 Fabio Padovano, Grazia Sgarra, and Nadia Fiorino, 'Judicial Branch, Checks and Balances and Political Accountability' (2003) 14 Constitutional Political Economy 47, 48.

858 See, Benedikt Pirker, Proportionality analysis and international commercial arbitration – the example of public policy and domestic courts, in Jemielniak, Nielsen and Olsen (n 732) 295.

859 See, Benedikt Pirker, Proportionality analysis and international commercial arbitration – the example of public policy and domestic courts, in ibid 296.

860 See, Benedikt Pirker, Proportionality analysis and international commercial arbitration – the example of public policy and domestic courts, in ibid.

3. A functional approach to defining public policy – is judicial interpretation better than a statutory classification?

An important decision that impacts the arbitration law in any given legal system is deciding whether the public policy exception should be elaborated by legislative classification or through the interpretation by courts. A practical way of determining who should be vested with the power of defining the exception would be to take a functional approach. This is exactly what was suggested by the eminent Indian jurist, HM Seervai, who argued that courts would no longer resent sharing power with other tribunals if they realize that power 'is not the exclusive property' of judges.[861] It is rather 'the means to an *end*, namely, the settlement of disputes or determination of the rights of parties' and that it 'must be conferred on that authority which can best achieve that *end*.'[862]

The first task would be to determine what 'end' was envisioned by the drafters of the IAA and then find the appropriate authority. As has been elaborated previously, the drafters of the IAA wanted to make India an arbitration-friendly jurisdiction and reduce the scope for excessive judicial intervention. In other words, there was a clear legislative policy favoring arbitration. Since the goal of the legislature is unambiguous, it is then necessary to look at the best way to achieve this objective.

The American approach to public policy is that it should be based on 'well-defined' standards.[863] Courts would only rely on public policy when found in law or precedent. While this would lead to less discretion of courts to shape public policy, it would lead to more predictability for parties. According to Friedman, there are three ways for courts to rely on public policy, first, find public policy in statute; second, via precedent; and thirdly, judges are completely free to find the bounds of public policy based on the case at hand.[864] In his opinion the first option would be most preferable as it would lead to most 'ruliness', the second would be less preferable as it would lead to some amount of 'ruliness', and the third option must be avoided to the maximum extent as it would lead to complete 'unruliness'[865]

---

861 H. M. Seervai (n 837) 82.

862 ibid 83.

863 W. R. Grace & Company v. Local Union 759, International Union of Rubber, Cork, Linoleum & Plastic Workers of America (n 336).

864 David A. Friedman, 'Bringing Order to Contracts Against Public Policy' (2012) 39 Florida State University Law Review 563.

865 ibid.

If Friedman's approach were to be taken, then one must first look at the statute to find public policy and the task of finding such a definition must rest with the legislature. There are some arguments, however, which necessitate an increased role of the judiciary. Ideally, the legislature should draft statutes in a clear and understandable manner. This is, however, hardly possible in every case. This is especially true with regard to the public policy exception. It is not humanly possible to accurately predict every possible set of facts that could arise and provide for all of them in an unambiguous manner.[866] In such circumstances where there is a doubt as to the meaning of a term, judicial interpretation can play a very important role in clarifying the intention of a statute.

As Lord Denning rightly pointed out, in proceedings where the judge comes across statutes that do not meet this requirement, and there is a defect, it is not for the judge to 'simply fold his hands and blame the draftsman.'[867] It is the duty of the judge to take a proactive role. In Lord Denning's view, the judge can do this by finding the intention of parliament, by looking at not just the wording of the statute but also the surrounding social background and the problem the provision was meant to solve, and then after taking all these factors into account, by giving 'force and life' to the will of the legislature.[868]

If courts are willing and able to interpret the public policy exception, keeping in mind the criteria that Lord Denning proposed, there is no need for the legislature to statutorily define the scope of the exception. The problem is, however, that judges are often not willing to bind themselves to such criteria. This can be seen both in India and in other jurisdictions, where courts have decided on the scope of the exception in an inconsistent manner which forced parliament to then define the exception. This approach of judges in some states is the reason why scholars brought out the saying 'don't fear the law, fear the judge'.[869] Decision making by judges is also oftentimes influenced by what Berkolakis has described as 'extra-legal factors' such as economic circumstances and personal values.[870] These factors will certainly come into play when a judge has to elaborate on the scope of public policy. The question then arises as to whether the scope of a

866 *Asher v Seaford Court Estates* (1949) 2 KB 481 (Court of Appeal (England and Wales)) 499, per Denning J.

867 ibid.

868 Asher v Seaford Court Estates (n 866).

869 Kurkela and Turunen (n 667).

870 Stavros Brekoulakis (n 290) 472.

state's public policy should be decided by a fixed statutory criterion or on the differing personal circumstances and values of individual judges.

There is a deeper and more foundational issue at stake which needs to be addressed, i.e., which would be the competent authority (the legislature or courts) for making the policy decisions and determining what morals would constitute public policy of a state? There are positives and pitfalls in choosing either, and there is, therefore, a predictable lack of consensus in the literature as to the correct answer to this question.

One approach has suggested that this power should be vested with the courts as they are more competent and less likely to be influenced. Justice Roger J. Traynor of the California Supreme Court, who is a proponent of this line of reasoning, has decried the 'half-truth' that 'policy is a matter for the legislature to decide' and not the judiciary.[871] A similar line has been taken by Joseph Raz, who argued that judges should be vested with this power, as, unlike the legislature, their decisions are less likely to be influenced by temporal sectarian and political considerations.[872] Particular care needs to be taken when it comes to dealing with vague terms such as morality, which forms part of public policy under Indian law. Judges are considered by many scholars to be better at moral discourses, as they give rational, objective arguments and are bound by principle, they are not influenced by the changing political considerations and 'horse-trading' which bind the legislature.[873]

There are strong arguments, however, against giving this power to the courts. This can be seen by looking at the *Egerton* decision, where the court ruled that public policy would be easy for judges to invoke in case of apparent illegality, yet determining public policy in cases where there is no illegality, would '*destroy the distinction between judicial and legislative functions*'.[874] According to the court, determining public policy, i.e., the determination of public good, is *excellent* for the legislator but *dangerous* for judges because it would lead to ever-changing standards of public policy and make precedent meaningless.[875]

871 Roger J. Traynor, 'Reasoning in a Circle of Law' (1970) 56 (5) Virginia Law Review 749.
872 Joseph Raz, 'Disagreement in Politics' (1998) 43 American Journal of Jurisprudence 25, 46.
873 Jeremy Waldron, 'Judges as Moral Reasoners' (2009) 7 International journal of constitutional law 2, 3–4.
874 Egerton v. Brownlow (n 57) 402.
875 ibid.

There cannot, however, be a hard and fast rule as to whether it is the job of the courts or the legislature to define the scope of the public policy exception. The correct answer to this question will vary depending on how the role of judges and legislature is perceived in the context of the varying legal cultures in different states. While in some countries such as England, courts are seen as partners in the arbitration process,[876] in other countries, they act more as supervisors.

When it comes to public policy, logically speaking, in common law countries, judges should have more of a say in interpreting the exception, whereas in civil law countries, the scope of the exception should be laid out in the statute. This is, however, in reality, not the case. It is mostly common law countries like India, Australia, Singapore and New Zealand which seek to give elaborate explanations as to the scope of the exception in their arbitration statutes, and therefore limit the discretion of the courts. This is also true in some civil law jurisdictions (see Germany, Art 6 EGBGB). This shows that, at least in relation to arbitration, judges have a constrained role when it comes to making policy. While it is true that they have the discretion to invoke the exception rarely and in individual cases, this discretion is bound by limits set by the legislature.

The ensuing judicial constraint is less of a problem than one might imagine. Even if courts were to feel that the public policy exception has evolved, and this is not reflected by the definition in the arbitration statute, they could always prompt or influence the legislature to make necessary changes without actually making policy themselves. This can be done in a number of ways, which have been elaborately elucidated by Glick, such as through *obiter dictum*, by interpreting the law such a way as to necessitate a legislative amendment, by making their suggestions in judicial opinions, through publications other than judgments, and by even lobbying the legislature.[877]

Furthermore, it is not necessary to exclude either the courts or parliament in coming to a meaningful definition of public policy. For a workable solution, both the judiciary and the legislature fulfill different roles and need to work together. As pointed out by Ghodoosi, while legislative public policy sets the broader framework, the judiciary works towards elaborating policies at a 'micro level'.[878] Judges can make broader legislative policies work by tailoring them to the specific situation and adapting them to changing circumstances.

876 Michael Kerr (n 216) 2.

877 Henry Robert Glick, 'Policy-Making and State Supreme Courts: The Judiciary as an Interest Group' (1970) 5 Law & Society Review 271, 272–273.

878 Ghodoosi (n 15) 19.

IV. The ideal statutory framework for the public policy exception

When drafting an arbitration statute, legislators are left with the conundrum of how to treat the public policy exception. There are four different approaches that lawmakers can take in defining the scope of the exception. The first is to elaborate on every head of the exception. The second is to provide a general categorization with a mixture of specific and some vague terms (or only vague/ specific terms). The third is to not define the exception at all but rather simply give courts the discretion to invoke the exception if public policy is breached. The fourth is to remove the public policy exception as grounds for refusing foreign awards. To determine the right approach for India, it is important to look at the benefits and disadvantages of each of these approaches and look at how other jurisdictions have fared when using these approaches.

1. Elaborating every head of the exception

One approach which a legislator could consider is to draft an arbitration statute that specifies every head which would fall within the scope of the public policy exception. This list could start with procedural grounds, such as lack of due process, and include substantive public policy such as fraud, corruption, money laundering etc. Such an approach may have its advantages. Firstly, it provides for certainty to the parties, as they will know beforehand whether the challenge would be successful. This could save legal costs and time and reduce the scope for frivolous court proceedings and delaying tactics. It would, therefore, also have a positive effect and build confidence in the arbitration process.

Secondly, it would provide valuable guidance to the courts. Judges will no longer have to re-evaluate the scope of the public policy exception in each and every case. Rather they would only have to apply the facts of the case to a fixed pre-determined formula. This can considerably reduce the chance that judges can act in an unpredictable and whimsical manner.

Despite its apparent advantages, no jurisdiction has taken such an approach. There are good reasons for this. Hawthorne has rightly observed that it is impossible for the legislator to 'foresee every possibility and provide for every eventuality'.[879] It is by inference barely possible to statutorily think of all the grounds which would fall within the public policy of a state. Even if the legislator were to draft such a list, there is no guarantee that the conception of public policy in

879 L. Hawthorne (n 758) 300.

the legal system will not change. In fact, as has been shown in the previous part, public policy is constantly evolving, and it is impossible for the legislature to accurately keep track of this evolution process through statute.

There is another important reason for this, providing such a list may unduly prejudice a parties right to procedural justice. Courts protect the interest of parties by looking at the circumstances of each case individually to evaluate if public policy has been breached. This will no be longer possible if courts had to blindly follow a list. Thus, it is clear that despite its benefits, it is impossible to provide an elaborate statutory framework as to the scope of the public policy exception.

2. Providing a general and vague categorization

One way in which the legislature can find a balance between the need to provide an elaborate categorization and ensuring that there is sufficient room for interpretation is to use a general categorization and riddle it with a mixture of specific and vague terms. This practise has been followed in almost every state which has chosen statutorily to define the scope of the exception. For instance, the arbitration laws of India, Australia, New Zealand all provide that ensuring 'justice' would be part of public policy exception. These statutes also provide that the public policy exception would be breached in case of fraud or corruption. While it is possible to understand what is meant by corruption, interpreting vague terms like 'justice' is more complex.

The idea behind providing such broad and vague terminology is to ensure that courts have the flexibility to use their discretion based on the particular circumstances of the case. It provides the advantage that the judiciary will know the intention of the legislature but not be bound to the specific language of the statute. Another approach could be for the lawmaker to merely provide guidelines requiring that public policy be narrowly interpreted.[880]

There is a lurking danger with taking such an approach. A broad definition can open the possibility that any award that is not desirable could be refused enforcement.[881] Furthermore, it is a fallacy to think that courts can be expected to interpret broad terms such as 'morality' or 'natural justice' narrowly. The very nature of these terms allows for an expansive construction. This, in turn, goes against the intention of the drafters of the New York Convention and also the drafters of these arbitration laws, i.e., to restrict judicial intervention and ensure

---

880 Katlyn Thomas, 'On Drafting an "Ideal" Arbitration Statute' (2014) 25 American Review of International Arbitration 117, 159–160.

881 See, Reinmar Wolff, Article V (2)(b), in Wolff (n 88) para 491.

enforcement of foreign arbitral awards. There is, therefore, little point in providing such a definition other than to make a statement that the interests of the parties are protected in the particular legal system in the case, e.g., natural justice is breached.

3. Not elaborating what is meant by public policy

This is the approach that has been taken by a vast majority of countries. Most arbitration laws, as well as the UNCITRAL Model Law, provide that recognition and enforcement of foreign awards could be refused in case of breach of public policy without actually elaborating what is meant by the term 'public policy'. A good example will be the UK Arbitration Act 1996, which in section 103 provides that recognition may be refused if the award is 'contrary to public policy'. No guidance has been provided as to what the term means; rather, the interpretation of public policy has been left to national courts.

Despite the vast discretion given to national courts, this approach works very well. Katlyn Thomas has suggested not defining the scope of the exception as one of the ideal ways for the legislator to solve the public policy conundrum as it is nearly impossible to provide a clear and comprehensive definition.[882] There is no sign that courts in countries where public policy has not been defined are more likely to refuse enforcement of arbitral awards by giving the exception a broad interpretation. In fact, quite the contrary is true. Countries where there is no elaboration as to the scope of the exception, such as England and Hong Kong, are hubs for international arbitration. This may seem surprising as there is no legislative move to restrict the courts in these jurisdictions. The reason is that there is an extremely high level of trust in the judiciary of these countries. In the past, judges in these jurisdictions have exercised extreme restraint when refusing to enforce arbitral awards. The workability of this approach is therefore completely dependent on the attitude of the judiciary.

4. Not providing public policy as grounds for refusing enforcement of arbitral awards

Drafting arbitration laws without the public policy exception as grounds for annulment/refusing enforcement of awards would at first glance solve the problem of excessive judicial intervention. It would give greater certainty to parties, increase the speed of resolving disputes and reduce any chance of abuse of the

---

882 Katlyn Thomas (n 880) 159–160.

public policy exception. Additionally, judges and legal scholars would no longer have to worry themselves about what the term public policy actually encompasses. Furthermore, judges would no longer be able to use their discretion to interfere with foreign arbitral awards on public policy grounds. Arbitral awards would, therefore, at least in this regard, be final. One could argue that taking such an approach would certainly help Indian lawmakers in their quest of making India more arbitration-friendly.

Such an approach of completely removing the remedy of 'public-policy' may be taking the term 'arbitration-friendly' too far. While the quest to be considered as pro-arbitration is important, there are certain limitations. Being pro-arbitration does not necessarily mean blind support of the arbitral process, coupled with resentment towards any form of court or state authority. Such an approach, according to Paulsson, would lead to proceedings being illegitimate.[883] Rather, a pro-arbitration statute needs to *enable* parties who have agreed to arbitrate to fulfill their initial objective

This is why regardless of how tempting it may be for a lawmaker to remove recourse to the public policy exception, such an approach will be counterproductive and not succeed. Public policy exception is a 'necessary evil' in the arbitration process. It is needed to provide courts with a backstop option to refuse enforcement of awards that are so repulsive that they go against the very fabric of the legal system in the enforcing state. Even in the United States, although the public policy exception is not specifically provided for as a statutory ground for annulment of awards under the FAA, such an apparent lacuna has not stopped parties from approaching US courts for refusing enforcement of awards on the grounds of violation of the public policy exception. In effect, American courts have gone beyond the remedies explicitly provided for within the FAA and rather used section 207 as a bridge to invoke the public policy exception provided for in the New York Convention.

Surprisingly enough, the public policy exception brings with it a plethora of advantages. Not only does it protect the fundamental principles of the state, but it also increases the confidence of parties in the legal system. Parties are happy to know that if something goes terribly wrong in the arbitral process, they still have the safety net provided by the national courts. In this way, the exception complements arbitration. This is precisely why it was added into the New York Convention and its predecessors, the UNCITRAL Model Law and the arbitration laws of almost every legal system. Judicial review in serious cases is considered by some

---

883 Paulsson (n 9) 52.

scholars to be part of the very 'spirit of the Convention'.[884] It is even relied upon in the most arbitration-friendly jurisdictions.

A good case in point would be Belgium, where the legislator had previously passed an amendment to the arbitration law, removing recourse to judicial review in international arbitration. By doing so, it was believed that Belgium would get a name for being an arbitration-friendly jurisdiction and would subsequently become a hub for arbitration. The move, however, backfired, with parties refusing to seat their arbitrations in Belgium.[885] This led to the legislator reinstating the provision for judicial review of arbitral awards. This goes to show that it could be more harmful than beneficial to remove any chance of judicial review on public policy grounds.

V. Seeking the elusive boundaries of the public policy exception

Given the indisputable need to determine the scope of the public policy exception, either through statute or through judicial interpretation, it is essential to evaluate what should ideally fall within the scope of the exception. Previously, we have analyzed how different legal systems can statutorily deal with the public policy exception. We have also looked at the specific definitions provided under the IAA(Am.) 2015. In this part, we will, in abstract, look at how the exception must ideally be interpreted and when it should be invoked.

1. How should public policy be interpreted?

For a definition of a term in a statute to be effective, it needs to effectively communicate its meaning. In common law countries, historically, when a term in a statute is undefined, it must be given its ordinary meaning.[886] This means that the term should be interpreted in 'light of accepted standards of communication'.[887]

---

884 Bernard Hanotiau and Olivier Caprasse, 'Arbitrability, Due Process, and Public Policy Under Article V of the New York Convention – Belgian and French Perspectives' (2008) 25 Journal of International Arbitration 721, 723.

885 For a more detailed explanation as to this development in the Belgian context see, Hossein Abedian, 'Judicial Review of Arbitral Awards in International Arbitration – A Case for an Efficient System of Judicial Review' (2011) 28 Journal of International Arbitration 541, 599.

886 Brian G. Slocum, Ordinary Meaning: A Theory of the Most Fundamental Principle of Legal Interpretation (The University of Chicago Press 2015) 2.

887 ibid.

American courts, in particular, have often used the dictionary meaning to mean ordinary meaning.[888] If such an approach is relied upon, the term 'public policy' must also be interpreted based on its ordinary or plain meaning. According to the meaning in the Oxford Dictionary of Law, 'public policy' would mean the interest of the community.[889] Such an interpretation would, however, be so broad and vague that it would not be particularly helpful to courts.

Another approach that can be used is that of purposive interpretation. A major criticism of the public policy exception is that it is incapable of being defined due to its varying nature and inherent vagueness.[890] The definition of the public policy exception provided in the IAA(Am.) 2015 certainly meets the test set by the U. S. Supreme Court for vagueness. This test is met when the statute 'fails to give a person of ordinary intelligence fair notice that his contemplated conduct is forbidden by statute'.[891]

In former times, Indian courts, when interpreting a statute, made use of what it has called the 'golden rule', i.e., giving excessive importance to the grammatical or literal meaning of the wording of the statute irrespective of the consequences of giving such an interpretation.[892] Indian courts are required to interpret statutes strictly and cannot alter or amend the statute when the meaning is clear.[893] This can be especially difficult with a statutory definition of public policy, which is considered to be an evolving concept.

Acknowledging that such an approach may lead to unintended and sometimes unjust consequences, the Indian Supreme Court has now moved towards a purposive construction when dealing with ambiguities in interpreting statutory provisions.[894] The Court has held that when interpreting a term in the statute, it is necessary to look at the *mens* or *sententia legis*, i.e., true will of the legislature.[895]

---

888 Phillip A. Rubin, 'War of the Words: How Courts Can Use Dictionaries in Accordance with Textualist Principles' (2010) 60 Duke Law Journal 167, 168.

889 E. A. Martin (ed), *A Dictionary of Law* (5th edn, Oxford University Press 2002).

890 Central Inland Water Transport Corporation Limited and Anr v. Brojo Nath Ganguly and Anr. (n 169).

891 *Margaret Papachristou et al v City of Jacksonville* (1972) 92 SCt 839 (Supreme Court of the United States).

892 *National Insurance Co Ltd Vs Laxmi Narain Dhut* (2007) 3 SCR 579 (Supreme Court of India) [14].

893 Grasim Industries Ltd Vs Collector of Customs, Bombay (2002) 2 SCR 945 (Supreme Court of India).

894 National Insurance Co. Ltd. Vs. Laxmi Narain Dhut (n 892).

895 Grasim Industries Ltd. Vs. Collector of Customs, Bombay (n 893) para 9.

According to the Court, this intention of the legislature can be determined by looking at the 'nature and design' of the law and whether the object of the statute will be fulfilled if it is interpreted in a particular way.[896] The Court in its *Dr. Krippendorf* ruling held that the duty of the judge in interpreting a statute is to 'iron out the creases' of the statute based on the intention of the legislature, and not to 'alter the material' of the legislation.[897] The Court, in its *Bihar Public Service Commission* ruling, has further supported such an understanding. In this case, it held that while the term *public interest* does not have any 'rigid meaning' it 'takes its colour from the statute' in which it is found.[898] This can help resolve at least some of the difficulty, as it is clear from the intent of the Indian legislature that the public policy exception is meant to be construed narrowly.

Although it is tempting to determine the scope of public policy based on *sententia legis,* even this approach is not without detractors. The intention of parliament is argued to be a fictitious construct.[899] It has been argued that it is impossible to actually determine legislative intent because the parliamentarians who vote for a bill do not usually have the same intention or sometimes any intention at all.[900] According to this approach, the intention of parliament is only embodied in the exact wording of the statute and should be determined accordingly.[901]

One does not, however, need to take extreme positions, such as trying to determine the exact intention of the legislature at the time of drafting or looking only at the plain ordinary meaning of the text. Instead, statutory provisions must not be looked at in isolation but rather interpreted contextually.[902] It is not necessary to search far and wide to find this context. The context can be found

---

896 *The State of Uttar Pradesh v Babu Ram Upadhya* (1961) AIR 751 (Supreme Court of India) [42].

897 Ms Eera Through Dr Manjula Krippendorf Vs State (Govt of NCT of Delhi) & Anr (2017) Crim Appeal No 1217–1219 (Supreme Court of India) [36].

898 Bihar Public Service Commission v Saiyed Hussain Abbas Rizwi (2012) 13 SCC 61 (Supreme Court of India) [23].

899 Robert French, 'The Courts and the Parliament' (Queensland Supreme Court Seminar 2012) 10 <www.hcourt.gov.au/assets/publications/...justices/frenchcj/frenchcj04aug12.pdf> accessed 17 December 2017.

900 See Dawson J, para 17, *Mills v Meeking* (1990) HCA 6 (High Court of Australia).

901 Charles Fried, 'Sonnet LXV and the "Black Ink" of the Framers' Intention' (1987) 100 Harvard Law Review 751, 759.

902 Grasim Industries Ltd. Vs. Collector of Customs, Bombay (n 893).

sometimes in the wording of the statute itself, usually in the preamble; otherwise, one can refer to parliamentary debates or similar sources for guidance.

That being said, some authorities have questioned whether it is wrong to interpret public policy in the extremely narrow manner that it is construed in current jurisprudence.[903] It has been argued that restricting the public policy exceptions to fundamental notions of morality and justice would go too far and render public policy without any 'meaningful definition'.[904] Such a criticism, however, fails to consider that the very foundation of arbitration, i.e., party autonomy, necessitates public policy to be construed narrowly, as it is the parties themselves who chose arbitration rather than the court process. The very purpose for a commercial entity to choose arbitration *vis-à-vis* litigation is to preclude the risk of being dragged into the 'home court' of the opposing party.[905] This benefit is lost if the home court where the losing party has its assets (place of enforcement) can interfere at will by relying on broad public policy grounds.

2. Deriving public policy using balancing tests

National courts, either at the seat of arbitration or at the place of enforcement, when deciding to invoke the public policy exception, need to balance two important principles, i.e., party autonomy (including the need for finality), with protecting the public policy of the forum.[906] This has been reiterated by the Indian Supreme Court in the *PASL* case, where it held that contractual freedom must be balanced with the need to avoid irreparable harm to the public.[907]

Finding such a balance was also the goal of the drafters of the New York Convention, who, as described by Moses, sought to balance the need for being 'pro-enforcement' with the desire to preclude 'abuse of process'.[908] In order to find the right balance, it is important to resolve conflicting public policies.

903 Berg, The New York Arbitration Convention of 1958 (n 21) 367.

904 ibid.

905 Kidane (n 110) 98.

906 See, Benedikt Pirker, Proportionality analysis and international commercial arbitration – the example of public policy and domestic courts, in Jemielniak, Nielsen and Olsen (n 732) 291.

907 PASL Wind Solutions v. GE Power Conversion India (n 170) para 89.

908 See, Margaret L. Moses, 'Public Policy under the New York Convention: National, International, and Transnational', in Katia Fach Gómez and Ana M Lopez-Rodriguez (eds), *60 Years of the New York Convention: Key Issues and Future Challenges* (Wolters Kluwer 2019) 171.

(a) Resolving conflicting public policies

As seen above, in challenges to arbitral awards on public policy grounds, a judge is oftentimes faced with two conflicting public policies, that of ensuring finality by enforcing foreign awards and that of protecting the fundamental legal principles of the forum. The Delhi High Court, in its *Cruz City* ruling, held that in situations where enforcing the foreign award violates public policy, courts would need to balance whether refusing enforcement *'would be more debilitating to justice'* than enforcing the award.[909] In order to reach such a balance, it held that the judge would need to take into account the fact that the parties must be bound by their choice to arbitrate rather than litigate and the need for ensuring finality.[910] Furthermore, the judge would need to consider *'the nature, extent and other nuances of public policy involved, and adopt a course which is less pernicious'*.[911]

The judge then has several options. Firstly, courts can either choose one of the above-mentioned objectives over the other. A good example is *Wilko v Swan*, which concerned an agreement to arbitrate future securities dispute, where the U. S. Supreme Court had to find a balance between the pro-arbitration policy enshrined in the FAA and the public policy of providing judicial remedies in case of securities disputes.[912] In this case, the Supreme Court held that the latter public policy was more important.

The second option is for the court to reconcile the two public policies and find that there is no conflict.[913] In the *Mitsubishi Motor Corp* ruling, the court reconciled the need for maintaining international comity in giving effect to an arbitration agreement with the public policy considerations involved in arbitrating anti-trust claims. The court did this by acknowledging that the arbitrators in Japan had the power to decide whether there was a violation of US anti-trust law but allowing judicial oversight at the enforcement stage by way of the 'second look' doctrine.[914] The Delhi High Court acknowledged this need for reconciling public policies when it held that wherever possible, it would try to address public policy concerns without refusing recognition of foreign awards.[915]

909 Cruz City 1 Mauritius Holdings v. Unitech Limited (n 543) para 39.
910 ibid.
911 ibid.
912 *Wilko v Swan* (1953) 346 US 427 (US Supreme Court) 434–435.
913 Leo Kanowitz, 'Alternative Dispute Resolution and the Public Interest: The Arbitration Experience' (1987) 38 Hastings Law Journal 257, 265.
914 Mitsubishi v. Soler Chrysler-Plymouth (n 353).
915 Cruz City 1 Mauritius Holdings v. Unitech Limited (n 543) para 108.

(b) How can the judge find the right balance?

It is instructive to look at how courts have tried to find a balance regarding conflicting public policies. The English Court of Appeal, in its *Westacre* decision, sought to find a balance between the competing goals of refusing to enforce an award where there were allegations of illegality due to commercial corruption, with the public policy of ensuring finality by upholding an arbitral award.[916] The court ruled that it would need to base its decision on several factors, such as 'the nature of the illegality', how strongly the party can prove the illegality, and to what extent the arbitral tribunal has addressed the illegality.[917] In this case, based on its analysis of the aforementioned factors, the court ruled in favor of enforcing the arbitral award.

Further guidance as to how to find the balance between competing public policies can be gleaned from the literature. Pirker has elucidated certain steps involved for a court to find a balance between these competing principles. In order to check the workability of these tests, we will apply them below to the definition of public policy provided under the IAA(Am.) 2015.

The first step suggested by Pirker is for the judge to look at the 'legitimate objective of the measure'.[918] If, for instance, an aggrieved party claims that they did not have the right to produce sufficient evidence during the arbitration proceedings, the court will need to look at the legitimate objective behind invoking the public policy exception for refusing enforcement of awards under the IAA(Am.) 2015. Section 48(2)b of the Act provides that public policy is violated if the award 'conflicts with the most basic principles of justice'. The 'legitimate objective' that can be inferred from the wording is that for an award to be enforced, the 'most basic principles of justice' such as giving parties the right to be heard should be respected during the proceedings.[919]

The second step would be for the judge to evaluate if the legitimate objective is achieved by the measure- or if there exists a suitable alternative that furthers

916 Westacre Investments Inc v Jugoimport-SDRP Holding Company Ltd & Ors (1999) APPLR 0512 (Court of Appeal (Civil Division)) [62].

917 ibid.

918 See, Benedikt Pirker, Proportionality analysis and international commercial arbitration – the example of public policy and domestic courts, in Jemielniak, Nielsen and Olsen (n 732) 292.

919 See *supra* Chapter 4(III)3b.

both principles.[920] In the aforementioned example, the judge will need to look at whether the 'legitimate objective' of protecting the 'most basic principles of justice' will be ensured by refusing enforcement of the award on public policy grounds. The judge can also look for alternatives that further both principles, i.e., party autonomy, and public policy. For instance, the judge could refuse enforcement only in case the evidence is so crucial that its inclusion would lead to a completely different outcome.

If there is no way to ensure that both principles are preserved, as a third step, the judge needs to balance both principles to see which should succeed.[921] In reaching the balance, courts would need to look at the particular facts and circumstances of the case in deciding when to intervene. An illustration would be in case the facts warrant the admitting of certain crucial evidence, and the tribunal has failed in considering this, then public policy would succeed at the cost of the finality of the award. This situation arose in the *CBS* case, where the Singapore Court of Appeal upheld a decision setting aside an arbitral award as the tribunal had prevented the parties from giving evidence via witness testimony.[922]

In deciding to intervene, courts would, however, need to be cautious in their approach to ensure that party autonomy is not needlessly constrained. In the words of Piker, judges need to 'balance balancing' by protecting only those values which are 'most central' to the given legal system.[923]

(c) *The approach of courts towards public policy*

In determining if the public policy exception has been violated, Pirker has broadly categorized judicial approaches into two groups, i.e., courts using a categorical test and courts using a quantitative test.[924] Judges relying on the former test would have a pre-defined category of what constitutes public policy and

920 See, Benedikt Pirker, Proportionality analysis and international commercial arbitration – the example of public policy and domestic courts, in Jemielniak, Nielsen and Olsen (n 732) 292.

921 See, Benedikt Pirker, Proportionality analysis and international commercial arbitration – the example of public policy and domestic courts, in ibid.

922 *CBS v CBP* (2021) SGCA 4 (Singapore Court of Appeal).

923 See, Benedikt Pirker, Proportionality analysis and international commercial arbitration – the example of public policy and domestic courts, in Jemielniak, Nielsen and Olsen (n 732) 297.

924 See, Benedikt Pirker, Proportionality analysis and international commercial arbitration – the example of public policy and domestic courts, in ibid 310.

could measure and match the alleged violation of public policy within this categorization. The judge could find such a pre-defined categorization either in statute or from judicial precedent.

In contrast, courts that prefer a quantitative approach would focus not on specific categories but rather on the seriousness or the intensity of the breach of public policy. Both approaches have their advantages. While a categorical approach provides more transparency and certainty, the quantitative approach provides more discretion to judges to tailor the use of the exception to the case at hand. The Indian approach currently seems to mirror the categorical approach where there is a specific classification of what circumstances would justify refusing the enforcement of an arbitral award. Such an approach has its advantages. Friedman, for instance, has argued that when courts rely on a rule-based notion of public policy that is grounded either in statute or judicial precedent, this would lead to less unruliness *vis-à-vis* leaving public policy to the discretion of judges.[925] A more detailed elaboration has been made earlier in this chapter.[926]

There is no reason, however, why courts cannot diverge from these two aforementioned approaches and use a combination of the two. Categorization in itself does not preclude the use of quantitative tests. Courts could use the legislative classification as a basis and then decide whether to refuse enforcement by looking at the intensity of the violation. In fact, such an approach would be advantageous as it would help provide the benefits of transparency and certainty without compromising on necessary judicial flexibility.

3. Public policy as a uniform yet diverging concept

There is uniformity in the application of the public policy exception. The exception has been classified in a similar manner in most major jurisdictions. If one were to ignore the diverging approaches taken by different countries in selecting the competent authority responsible for making this classification (i.e., legislature *vs* courts), the uniqueness of the Indian approach disappears, and a pattern surfaces. In most of these countries, public policy is considered to be violated either if the arbitrator goes against fundamental moral precepts or the basic elements of the legal system.

Despite the above similarity, one cannot say that there is a common definition of public policy in every jurisdiction. There are a plethora of differences among

925 David A. Friedman (n 864) 615.
926 See Chapter V(III)3.

countries in, for instance, determining the scope of morality. Depending on the circumstances, what is against the most basic notions of morality in India, may or may not be the same as what is considered against the fundamental moral precepts of the United States. The same holds good for fundamental principles of the legal system. The differences are attributable to varying cultures and customs, which play a major role in the formulation of a states public policy.[927] It is, therefore, safe to conclude that although there can be a universal classification of public policy, it is nearly impossible to find a universal definition.

Given the elusiveness of such a uniform definition of the exception, Indian courts are not obliged to meet the standards set by foreign legal systems. They are, however, free to interpret Indian public policy so as to meet Indian standards and requirements. The only condition is that their interpretation is in consonance with the classification provided in the IAA and meets the standards for a narrow interpretation envisioned by the drafters of the New York Convention.

4. Do differing legal cultures lead to different conceptions of public policy?

The role of legal culture in international arbitration cannot be overstated. Legal culture has been described as the 'values, ideals, and attitudes' of a given community regarding its law.[928] Slate has described it as encompassing the 'fundamental values' of a community, based on its history…social norms and conceptions of justice.[929]

In general, cultures differ across communities and countries. A case has, however, been made in the literature that there would be a uniform culture in international arbitration.[930] Taniguchi argues that by choosing arbitration, parties are not bound by the legal culture of a particular state but rather a more 'neutral'

---

927 Petra Butler and Christoph Katerndahl, 'Kastom – A Public Policy Exception under the New York Convention on the Recognition and Enforcement of Foreign Arbitral Awards' (2018) VII Indian Journal of Arbitration Law 115 et seq.

928 See, Ralf Michaels, Legal Culture, in Jürgen Basedow and others (n 78) 1060.

929 William K. Slate II, 'Paying Attention to "Culture" in International Commercial Arbitration' (2004) 49 Dispute Resolution Journal 96, 98.

930 See, Neil Kaplan, A Case by Case Examination of Whether National Courts Apply Different Standards When Assisting Arbitral Proceedings and Enforcing Awards in International Cases as Contrasting with Domestic Disputes. Is There a Worldwide Trend towards Supporting an International Arbitration Culture? A. J. van den Berg (ed), *International Dispute Resolution: Towards an International Arbitration Culture* (Kluwer Law International 1998) 187 et seq.

international culture.[931] This is largely true, given that most states are parties to the New York Convention and strive toward greater enforceability of arbitral awards. Further efforts towards an international culture in arbitration have been made through the adoption of the UNCITRAL Model Law. Finding a uniform definition for public policy is difficult unless one is able to harmonize the legal cultures in different states. Attempts have, however, been made to harmonize the exception by way of uniform internationally accepted notions of public policy, which Holtzmann has considered to be akin to an 'international arbitration culture'.[932] Courts in many jurisdictions, including India, have resisted the move towards such uniformity.[933]

Despite the common culture in arbitration, the public policy exception is one lingering corner where differing legal cultures manifest themselves. By defining the exception, a state can essentially safeguard its own legal culture from more dominant international headwinds. Due to varying cultures, what constitutes public policy in one jurisdiction can differ significantly from what is part of the exception in other states. In order to understand the scope of public policy, one needs to take into consideration local culture and values.[934] Especially in developing countries like India, being insensitive to the mandatory legal rules and particularities can have an adverse impact on the growth and acceptance of arbitration in such jurisdictions.[935] Furthermore, if public policy exception is aligned with socio-cultural norms of a state, rather than abstract transnational perceptions, judges in national courts will be more able to understand the concept, and there will be more predictability regarding its use.

---

931 See, Yasuhei Taniguchi, Is There a Growing International Arbitration Culture? – An Observation from Asia in ibid 34.

932 See, Howard M. Holtzmann, When and Where Do National Courts Reflect an International Arbitration Culture? in ibid 234.

933 For an elaboration on the approach of courts towards a more nationalistic view of public policy see Chapter 5(6).

934 Stephan Muers, *Culture, Values and Public Policy* (University of Bath, Institute for Policy Research 2018) 26 <https://www.bath.ac.uk/publications/culture-values-and-public-policy/attachments/ipr-culture-values-and-public-policy.pdf> accessed 22 November 2019.

935 See, Ahmed Sadek El-Kosheri, 'Is There a Growing International Arbitration Culture in the Arab-Islamic Juridical Culture?', in Berg, *International Dispute Resolution* (n 930) 48.

5. When should the public policy exception be invoked by Indian courts?

At a more practical level, when proceedings for refusing enforcement of a foreign award are brought before an Indian court, there are several issues that need to be addressed before the exception can be invoked. Firstly, it is necessary to evaluate when courts should rely on the exception and what is the appropriate scope of the exception. Secondly, it is important for the court to decide whether the exception has been violated in the particular case and whether the breach is sufficient to refuse enforcement of the award.

Even if the court determines that public policy is violated, the court is not obliged to refuse enforcement. It has the discretion to choose what course of action to take based on the seriousness of the violation. A plain reading of Article V(2)b of the New York convention shows that while courts 'may' refuse enforcement, they are not bound to do so. This 'may' is also mirrored in section 48 of the IAA. Furthermore, a court is precluded from reviewing an award either on the merits or substance of the case. Although the court must only exercise a narrow form of review, a limited review is not a bad thing. The absence of any form judicial of control may actually harm the arbitration process and reduce the trust of the parties in the countries legal system.[936]

(a) Enforcement of awards that are set aside at the seat

Should an award that has been set aside at the seat be enforced by Indian courts? The prevailing view, at least from common law scholars, is that courts at the place of enforcement should defer to the ruling of the court at the seat and refuse enforcement of awards that are set aside at the seat.[937]

The position of law in India raises a few questions. Section 48(1)e of the IAA, which is similar to section 103(2)f of the UK Arbitration Act, provides that enforcement of an award *'may'* be refused if the award is not final or is suspended at the seat. By inference, in such cases, Indian courts will have the discretion on whether they would refuse enforcement or not. But how should courts exercise this discretion in case the award is set aside for breaching public policy of the seat?

In practice, when it comes to challenges to foreign awards, Indian courts have demonstrated a willingness to defer to the rulings of courts of the arbitral seat.

936 Hossein Abedian (n 885) 563 et seq.

937 Lord Collins and others (n 301) paras 16–147.

The Supreme Court in *Vedanta* held that it is not for the courts at the place of enforcement to sit in appeal on decisions reached by courts at the seat.[938] It is beyond doubt that if the award is set aside in the seat for breaching public policy and that if this breach is also covered by the public policy of the place of enforcement, the award will not be enforced.

But what if the public policy of the seat is extremely broad or differs considerably from Indian public policy? If the award has been vacated at a place where it was rendered but could have been enforced in India, it then needs to be determined which public policy takes precedence- that of the seat or that of the place of enforcement? There is no definite solution provided for this problem in Indian law or jurisprudence.

The answer varies from one jurisdiction to the other. Two approaches have been taken. English courts are willing to respect the decision of the court at the seat unless there are public policy considerations that compel them to act otherwise. A diametrically opposite approach has been taken in France, where there is a view that because courts at the place of enforcement are not obliged to bind themselves by the decisions of the court at the seat, they should not do so. The French view is noticeable in the writings of Gaillard, where he argues that placing 'the seat of the arbitration at the top of a jurisdictional hierarchy for enforcement purposes is counter to its fundamental objectives' of the New York Convention.[939]

In effect, French courts have been willing to enforce awards even when they are set aside at the seat. This is because the French consider arbitration to be governed by an independent legal order, and the law of the seat should therefore not be given too much importance.[940] A good example is the *Hilmarton* case, where the French *Cour de cassation* upheld a decision to enforce an award that had been set aside in Switzerland on the grounds of the differences present in French law and because such enforcement would not breach international public policy.[941]

---

938 *Government of India v Vedanta Limited* (2021) Civ Appeal No 3185 2020 (Supreme Court of India) 50.

939 See Emmanuel Gaillard, 'International Arbitration as a Transnational System of Justice', in A. J. van den Berg (ed), *Arbitration: The next Fifty Years* (Kluwer Law International; Sold and distributed in North, Central and South America by Aspen Publishers, Inc 2012) 71.

940 Pierre Pic and Asha Rajan, 'The Public Policy Exception in International Arbitration: A Snapshot from France' (2017) 6 Indian Journal of Arbitration Law 197, 199.

941 Société Hilmarton Ltd v Société Omnium de traitement et de valorisation (OTV) 92-15137 Bull 1994 N° 104 P 79 (France, Cour de cassation).

The French approach has, however, not been followed by England, Germany or the Netherlands.

A thought-provoking comparative law analysis can be made from another series of decisions, i.e., the *Maximov* rulings, where a Russian national approached French, Dutch and British courts seeking to enforce an arbitral award which was set aside in Russia on the grounds that the Russian judge was biased. While the *Cour d'appel de Paris* allowed enforcement and ruled that the setting aside at seat would not be a bar on enforcement,[942] the District Court of Amsterdam refused to enforce the award and held that enforcement of an award annulled by a competent authority at the seat could only take place in 'exceptional circumstances', where the annulment breaches Dutch public policy.[943] A similar approach was also taken by the High Court of England and Wales. Although the High Court was not satisfied with how the court at the seat reached its decision to set aside the award, it dismissed the request for enforcing the award and held that there is a heavy burden to prove bias on a party seeking to enforce such an award.[944]

There is a solution to this problem that could be applied in the Indian context. Since the only public policy which Indian courts can apply according to the IAA is Indian public policy, the enforcement of an award that is set aside at the seat should only be allowed if this does not breach Indian public policy. The only exception would be fundamental principles of transnational public policy, such as corruption, money laundering or fraud, in which cases Indian courts should under all circumstances refuse enforcement.

But would Indian courts still be able to refuse enforcement of a foreign award using national public policy even if there is no strong nexus to India? Take the hypothetical example of a dispute between a German claimant and a Japanese respondent, where the tribunal is seated in Switzerland, and the contract is

942 Elie Kleiman and Shaparak Saleh, 'Paris Court of Appeal Issues Three Confirmations in One Decision' (International Law Office, Report by Freshfields Bruckhaus Deringer LLP 2014) <https://www.internationallawoffice.com/Newsletters/Arbitration-ADR/France/Freshfields-Bruckhaus-Deringer-LLP/Paris-Court-of-Appeal-issues-three-confirmations-in-one-decision> accessed 13 August 2018.

943 Albert Jan van den Berg (ed), 'Netherlands No. 41, Nikolai Viktorovich Maximov v. OJSC Novolipetsky Metallurgichesky Kombinat, Provisions Judge of the District Court of Amsterdam, 491569/KGRK 11-1722, 17 November 2011' (2012) 37 Yearbook Commercial Arbitration (Kluwer Law International) para 15 et seq.

944 Nikolay Viktorovich Maximov v Open Joint Stock Company 'Novolipetsky Metallurgichesky Kombinat' (2017) EWHC 1911 Comm (High Court of Justice Queen's Bench Division Commercial Court).

governed by Swiss law. The tribunal makes an award in favor of the claimant, which seeks to recover assets which are located in India. The respondent invokes Indian public policy to resist enforcement before Indian courts. In such a situation, can Indian courts invoke Indian public policy exception despite the weak nexus, and which public policy should apply?

In some legal systems, courts are only willing to refuse enforcement of an arbitral award on public policy grounds if there is a strong nexus to the given country. This is, for instance, the case in England; for English public policy to be invoked in an agreement, the agreement needs to have some important connection to England.[945] While English courts were firmly of the opinion that an agreement to oust the jurisdiction of English courts would breach public policy, they would have nothing 'against agreements to oust the jurisdiction of a foreign court'.[946] Even German courts are reluctant to refuse enforcement using German public policy in the absence of a nexus.

Indian courts similarly seem to place a great deal of importance on the 'close nexus' doctrine. The Indian Supreme Court, in its *Venture Global* decision, ruled that in case there is an 'intimate and close nexus to India', this would justify challenging the award before Indian courts.[947] A similar position was taken by the Bombay High Court in *Imax*, where it held that a closer nexus to India meant that Indian law would be applicable, regardless of a vague reference by the parties in their agreement to the law or courts of another jurisdiction.[948]

An important exception can be made if *shared values* of the international community are at stake. In such cases, even if there is no nexus, a national court may be justified in invoking the exception, for instance, avoid enforcement of an agreement that promotes child labour. These shared values must be relied on very rarely. As will be shown later in this chapter, just like with public policy itself, it is difficult to demarcate values that are uniformly accepted in all countries. One way around this dilemma is by making reference to non-binding internationally accepted principles such as the UN Global Compact, which sets down standards relating to human rights, labour, environment and combatting corruption.[949]

945 Torremans and Fawcett (n 71) 134.

946 ibid.

947 Venture Global Engineering v Satyam Computer Services Ltd. and Anr. (n 197).

948 *E-City Entertainment (I) Pvt Ltd v IMAX Corporation* (2013) Arbitr Petition No 525 2008 (High Court of Bombay) [27].

949 'The Ten Principles of the UN Global Compact' (United Nations) <https://www.unglobalcompact.org/what-is-gc/mission/principles> accessed 27 August 2018.

(b) Interaction of the exception with mandatory rules of Indian law

Mandatory rules are rules that are of significant importance to the countries legal system. Parties are not allowed to derogate from or contract around such rules.[950] They are closely bound with a states' public policy. Böckstiegel correctly pointed out that although 'every public policy rule is mandatory', not every mandatory rule would be part of the public policy exception.[951] Public policy refers to only those mandatory rules that are 'imperative'.[952]

In many countries, mere violation of mandatory provisions would not justify refusing enforcement of arbitral awards on public policy grounds. In Austria, for instance, while violation of mandatory rules could be a basis for challenging a domestic award, this is not the case with regard to foreign awards. Foreign awards could only be challenged if the breach of mandatory rules also amounts to a violation of public policy.[953] Neither the IAA nor international instruments such as the New York Convention explicitly mention that safeguarding the mandatory provisions would also be a reason to refuse enforcement of awards. This does not, however, mean that mandatory rules are not safeguarded in the Indian legal system. In this section, we will briefly discuss which mandatory provisions of Indian law are considered so sacrosanct as to fall within the scope of the public policy exception.

There are two criteria that have been used in the literature to elucidate when mandatory norms would form part of the public policy exception. Schwebel and Lahne demonstrated the first criteria when they wrote that public policy exception is only violated in case of a breach of those mandatory norms, which form part of the 'most basic notions of morality and justice' of the given legal system.[954] This is similar to the concept of overriding mandatory provisions (OMP) found in European law, whose breach would be sufficient to justify refusing enforcement. Public policy considerations, according to Sir Jack Beatson, would also be invoked if these mandatory provisions were so important that they formed part

950 'Mandatory Rules and Public Policy' <https://www.era-comm.eu/Visegrad/kiosk/pdf/speakers_contributions/116DT35_Grajdura_mandatory.pdf> accessed 15 October 2021.

951 See Karl-Heinz Böckstiegel, Public Policy and Arbitrability in Sanders (n 421) 183.

952 See Pierre Lalive, Transnational (or Truly International) Public Policy and International Arbitration in ibid 260.

953 See, Karl-Heinz Böckstiegel, Public Policy and Arbitrability, ibid 184.

954 See Stephen M. Schwebel and Susan G. Lahne, Public Policy and Arbitral Procedure in ibid 205.

of the 'fundamental policies' of the country.[955] These two criteria are strikingly close to the definition of public policy given by the legislator in the IAA. It is arguable that the fundamental policy of Indian law, and most basic notions of morality and justice, which form part of public policy according to section 48 of the Act, refer to such overriding mandatory principles. These provisions will also naturally include the fundamental rights enshrined and protected in Part III of the Indian Constitution. Furthermore, the Indian Supreme Court in *Vedanta* held that 'fair and equitable treatment' of the parties to the dispute by the arbitral tribunal would constitute a 'non-derogable mandatory' rule.[956]

The IAA does not make an express distinction between mandatory and overriding mandatory provisions. Rather, Indian courts have distinguished between directory (permissive) provisions and mandatory provisions. According to the Indian Supreme Court, the nature of the statute must be determined based on the wording used. The use of terms like 'shall' will ordinarily constitute a mandatory provision.[957] Article 48 of the IAA, however, only provides that the enforcement 'may' be refused. This would lead to it being a permissive provision, the use of which is not binding but rather gives discretion to the court.[958] This demonstrates the will of the legislator to ensure that the public policy exception is not blindly used. It also shows the will of the legislator to leave the courts with the discretion of invoking the exception when the need arises.

Under Indian law, a mere violation of any mandatory legal provisions will not violate public policy and be sufficient for refusing enforcement.[959] This is true even in the case the award is 'patently illegal', even this would be insufficient for refusing enforcement.[960] If one looks at the IAA(Am.) 2015, for enforcement to be refused, the violation should go against the 'fundamental policy of Indian law' or 'most basic notions of morality and justice'. These provisions are so important

---

955 Jack Beatson, 'International Arbitration, Public Policy Considerations, and Conflicts of Law: The Perspectives of Reviewing and Enforcing Courts' (2017) 33 Arbitration International 175, 176.

956 Government of India v. Vedanta Limited (n 938) 65.

957 *State Of Haryana v Raghubir Dayal* (1994) SCALE 41084 (Supreme Court of India) [5].

958 Government of India v. Vedanta Limited (n 938) 43.

959 Luke Villiers, 'Breaking in the "Unruly Horse": The Status of Mandatory Rules of Law as a Public Policy Basis for the Non-Enforcement of Arbitral Awards' (2011) 18 Australian International Law Journal 166.

960 Bharat Aluminium Company and Ors. Vs. Kaiser Aluminium Technical Service, Inc. and Ors. (n 60).

to the Indian legal system that a violation of such mandatory provisions would also constitute a violation of Indian public policy.

6. Should public policy under Indian law be based on a harmonized transnational framework?

The 20th century has not just seen increased economic globalization but also a globalization of laws.[961] This globalization has led to increased uniformity and convergence in the area of commercial law.[962] Siems has argued that convergence in legal regimes could either be a product of 'pressure' (international organizations, more powerful countries, lobbying by concerned parties) or by way of increased 'congruence' (increased similarity in social-economic needs and conditions).[963] In the case of developing countries like India, convergence or harmonization of arbitration laws towards a more international approach is a product of both of these elements. On the one hand, developing states feel the need to update their arbitration regimes because of congruence in their economic circumstances, i.e., to reduce the burden of courts and attract investors; on the other hand, there is pressure from commercial entities which seek a more effective form of dispute settlement. In any case, successful efforts towards increased harmonization in international arbitration laws have been made through the New York Convention and the UNCITRAL Model Law.

More harmonization provides increased predictability and certainty to parties involved in international commerce. While most elements of arbitration have been harmonized, this is not true with regard to the public policy exception. Significant differences exist as states continue to have unique ideas as to what would be encompassed in its scope. This leads to some jurisdictions having extremely broad notions of public policy and others with quite the opposite. In this part, we will examine whether a harmonized and delocalized approach towards public policy should be used in the IAA.

961 See, Loukas Mistelis, 'Is Harmonisation a Necessary Evil? The Future of Harmonisation and New Sources of International Trade Law', in Ian F. Fletcher, Loukas A. Mistelis and Marise Cremona (eds), *Foundations and Perspectives of International Trade Law* (Sweet & Maxwell 2001) paras 1–006.

962 Martin Shapiro, 'The Globalization of Law' 1 Indiana Journal of Global Legal Studies 38.

963 Mathias M. Siems, *Comparative Law* (Cambridge University Press 2014) 230 et seq.

(a) Need for delocalisation in delineating public policy

International commercial arbitration is by nature not grounded solely in any single legal system. At any given point in time, there are several legal regimes at play including, the law of the seat, substantive law of the contract, any different applicable law chosen by the parties, and the law of the state where the subsequent award must be enforced. Despite the plethora of legal regimes, the UNCITRAL Model Law in order to provide an element of certainty to parties 'localised', or provided sole jurisdiction to the courts at the seat of arbitration with regard to challenging of awards.[964] While courts at the place of enforcement may refuse recognition or the enforcement of awards where the awards violate its public policy, it is only courts at the seat that can set aside the awards.

Given the international nature of arbitration, there has been a strong debate in literature for and against a more delocalised and denationalized regime of arbitration.[965] Gaillard, for instance, has argued that arbitration is not bound to a legal system but instead has its own autonomous 'arbitral legal order'.[966] Such arguments for delocalisation have not been universally accepted. Some English scholars, for instance, have considered the notion of delocalisation to be nothing short of 'heretic'.[967]

Proponents of delocalisation and those favoring a more transnational approach have made strong arguments to make arbitration independent of the law of the seat.[968] There is no reason why such arguments can also not be made for reducing the importance of the law of the place of enforcement. With regards to the public policy exception, one can justifiably ask, why then should the public policy only of the seat or the place where the assets are situated be relevant for enforcing an award? Should the mere accident that the assets are located in a country be decisive in determining which public policy to apply for the purposes

964 Loukas Mistelis, 'Seat of Arbitration and Indian Arbitration Law' (2016) IV Indian Journal of Arbitration Law 1, 3–4.

965 Katherine Lynch, The Forces of Economic Globalization: Challenges to the Regime of International Commercial Arbitration (Kluwer Law International 2003) 174 et seq.

966 See Emmanuel Gaillard, International Arbitration as a Transnational System of Justice, in Berg, *Arbitration* (n 939) 66.

967 Olakunle O. Olatawura, 'Delocalized Arbitration under the English Arbitration Act 1996: An Evolution or a Revolution', (2003) 30 Syracuse Journal of International Law and Commerce 49, 50.

968 See Emmanuel Gaillard, International Arbitration as a Transnational System of Justice, in Berg, *Arbitration* (n 939).

of enforcement, however small the connection to the parties or the underlying contract? This question becomes even more poignant as the implications of invoking the public policy exception for refusing enforcement of a foreign award are not limited to the country of enforcement but are felt more beyond its borders. In case of a foreign award, the parties seeking enforcement are after all mostly not nationals of the country of enforcement. Similarly, if the public policy of the seat is used to set aside an award, this would affect the enforceability of the award internationally. Would it be appropriate to place reliance on one countries' public policy when the ripple effects are global? After all, in case of trans-national commercial transactions, which are increasingly common in a globalised world, it has been argued that subjecting arbitral awards to varying legal systems and notions of public policy may constitute an unpredictable hindrance to parties.[969]

Delocalisation of the public policy exception can be a solution to give certainty and clarity to parties regarding its scope. Proponents of delocalising arbitration laws argue that if the public policy except would not be grounded in a particular legal system but rather,[970] on principles that are commonly held by most civilized countries, i.e., ensuring fairness and due process and precluding fraud, corruption, child labour, terrorism financing, money laundering, etc. According to this approach, it would no longer be necessary to seek recourse to nationalistic conceptions of public policy. The consequence of this approach would be that courts at the place of enforcement would not automatically refuse enforcement of awards set aside at the seat on grounds of violating parochial or nationalistic notions of the seats public policy. Rather they would only refuse enforcement where the award violates either (transnational) public policy of the place of enforcement, or where the courts at the seat have set aside an award for violation these transnationally accepted, delocalized notions of public policy.[971]

Even in India, the difficulty regarding excessive intervention by courts could possibly be solved if public policy exception were to be given a uniform construction, which is in consonance with global norms. This delocalized approach of basing public policy on internationally accepted principles rather than

969 Leila Anglade, 'The Use of Transnational Rules of Law in International Arbitration' (2003) 38 Irish Jurist 92.

970 Hong-Lin Yu and Motassem Nasir, 'Can Online Arbitration Exist Within the Traditional Arbitration Framework?' (2003) 20 Journal of International Arbitration 455, 464.

971 Girsberger and Voser (n 707) 446–447.

national norms can help in harmonizing the laws governing arbitration. Such increased harmonization, as stressed by the ILA in its report, can ensure 'greater consistency and predictability' and, in turn, deter frivolous challenges to arbitral awards.[972]

(b) Need for harmonizing approaches to public policy

The lack of a harmonized definition of public policy is considered to be one of the biggest problems with the use of the exception.[973] Harmonization could effectively be achieved by de-localizing the public policy exception or removing attachment to any particular legal system. There are valid arguments that can be made in favor of increased harmonization. Lynch has urged for increased harmonization because variations in arbitration laws across jurisdictions leads to unnecessary hardship to parties and their legal representatives who need to familiarize themselves with nuances of different legal regimes.[974] These differences are accentuated when there is an overlap of different legal systems, for example, when the parties to a dispute come from arbitration-friendly jurisdictions, but the place of enforcement is a state that has antiquated notions of the role of courts in enforcing awards.

While the 'nebulous nature' of the public policy exception has been described as a 'licence' for courts to refuse enforcement of awards inappropriately,[975] relying on a predictable harmonized internationally applicable framework could provide more certainty. A uniform international understanding of the public policy exception would provide a degree of certainty to parties, which was envisioned in the New York Convention. As observed by the Delhi High Court in its *Spie Capag* ruling, it was the goal of the New York Convention to provide 'a common yardstick' and a 'uniform code' to facilitate the recognition and enforcement of awards.[976]

---

972 Audley Sheppard, 'Public Policy and the Enforcement of Arbitral Awards: Should There Be a Global Standard?' (2004) 1 Transnational Dispute Management; Pierre Mayer and Audley Sheppard (n 232).

973 V. K. Bhatia, Maurizio Gotti and Azirah Hashim (eds), *International Arbitration Discourse and Practices in Asia* (Routledge 2018), para 1.6.

974 Lynch (n 965) 173.

975 Blackaby and others (n 72) para 10.84.

976 Gas Authority of India Ltd Vs Spie Capag, SA and others 1994 1 ArbLR 429 Delhi (High Court of Delhi) [1].

It would be useful for parties to have a comprehensive list of what constitutes public policy. Such a list, either country-specific or general, could be added as an addendum to the New York Convention. Experience has, however, shown that this is easier said than done. A similar recommendation was previously made for formulating such a list of subject matters that were not capable of being arbitrated. Such a measure was finally not implemented because it was considered 'unrealistic to define a workable list' that was universally accepted, which could encompass the varying situations in different jurisdictions given the disparities in national legal systems.[977] This difficulty would certainly also hold good for a list defining public policy.

Furthermore, finding a universally accepted definition could be difficult, as it has been accepted that every state has its own unique conceptions of public policy.[978] Currently, section 48(2)b of the IAA provides that public policy would mean 'the public policy of India', i.e., domestic public policy. This kind of nationalistic approach is taken by many jurisdictions. Even article V(2)b of the New York Convention envisions refusing enforcement only if there is a breach of 'public policy of that country' (enforcing state).

The challenge, therefore, lies in reconciling differing notions of domestic public policy with broader notions of transnational public policy. Despite different countries having their own unique conceptions of public policy, there are some general principles that have been accepted to form truly international public policy. These principles have been described by Böckstiegel as forming the 'common denominator in values and standards' of the international community.[979] The use of such principles, because of the commonalities, would still be in consonance with the objectives of Indian arbitration law and the New York Convention.

(c) Transnational public policy as a harmonized framework

One way to find common ground in defining the scope of the exception is to consider that public policy means 'truly international public policy' rather than merely domestic 'public policy'. Such an approach would be in consonance with the interpretation of Article V(2)(b) of the New York Convention.[980] It has been argued that a 'transnational' or truly international public policy can prevent

977 See Karl-Heinz Böckstiegel, Public Policy and Arbitrability in, Sanders (n 421) 190.
978 Blackaby and others (n 72) 10.82.
979 See Karl-Heinz Böckstiegel, Public Policy and Arbitrability in, Sanders (n 421) 180.
980 Born (n 419) 3655.

states from refusing enforcement of awards on uncertain and widely varying domestic public policy grounds.[981] Transnational law, as shown by Lehmann, are the 'general legal principles', or 'fundamental notions of justice' common to most jurisdictions.[982] It could be derived either from principles of natural law or from *lex mercatoria*.[983]

Confusion can arise because the dividing line between 'transnational', 'international' public policy and 'domestic' public policy is unclear.[984] While national/domestic public policy seeks to safeguard 'domestic interests', international public policy 'focuses on interests protected by private international law.'[985] International public policy is also inherently a part of the national legal system. Moses has described it as the 'most fundamental (elements) of domestic public policy'.[986]

While domestic public policy are mandatory rules which parties cannot derogate from that apply mainly in domestic proceedings, international public policy are fundamental principles of the legal system that apply only when there is an international element or a foreign award.[987] Transnational public policy, on the other hand, relates to notions of public policy, which are derived from values that are universal and can be found in, e.g. international instruments such as, for instance, in the Universal Declaration of Human Rights.[988] Transnational public policy would include 'fundamental rules of natural law, principles of universal justice, *jus cogens* in public international law, and the general principles of morality accepted by what are referred to as "civilised nations"'.[989] As transnational public policy would be derived from international sources, it would effectively

---

981 Blackaby and others (n 72) 10.87.

982 Matthias Lehmann, 'A Plea for a Transnational Approach to Arbitrability in Arbitral Practice' (2004) 42 Columbia Journal of Transnational Law 753, 754.

983 Leon E. Trakman, 'Aligning State Sovereignty with Transnational Public Policy' (2018) 93 Tulane Law Review 208.

984 Paulsson (n 121) 218.

985 Indu Malhotra, O.P. Malhotra on the Law & Practice of Arbitration and Conciliation (3rd edn, Thomson Reuters 2014) 1710 et seq.

986 See, Margaret L. Moses, 'Public Policy under the New York Convention: National, International, and Transnational', in Katia Fach Gómez and Ana M. Lopez-Rodriguez (n 908) 173.

987 Julian D. M. Lew, Transnational Public Policy: Its Application and Effect by International Arbitration Tribunals (Fundación Universitaria San Pablo CEU 2018) 17 et. seq.

988 Katlyn Thomas (n 880) 158–159.

989 Audley Sheppard (n 972).

set an international standard as to what public policy would mean. A good example of a transnational public policy would be the policy of combatting corruption. This has been prioritized not just nationally by way of the FCPA in the United States, Bribery Act in the UK, or Prevention of Corruption Act 1988 in India, but internationally by instruments of the OECD, UN EU, among others.[990]

There are several advantages to relying on transnational public policy rather than a purely domestic approach. Such an approach can avoid difficulties caused due to conflicting or widely diverging approaches to public policy at the seat and at the place of enforcement. This is especially important given that according to Article V(1)d of the New York Convention, an award that goes against the law of the seat is liable to be refused enforcement globally. The same is true for an award that is set aside at the seat for violating its national public policy (Article V(1) e). Particular difficulties arise in circumstances such as the case of *Citigroup v Fiorilla*, where a New York Court (at the seat) decided on extraterritorially applying national law by ordering parties to not enforce in another state (France), an award which it had vacated and penalized a party (*Fiorilla)* for taking such enforcement measures.[991] Such problems would not arise if the public policy at the seat and the place of enforcement are harmonized by way of a transnationally recognised public policy.

Increased harmonization can, to some extent, also provide a level playing field and provide a framework for national courts to satisfy more than purely 'local interests'.[992] Using transnational public policy would also help in finding harmonized approaches, which are more effective in combatting crimes having cross border dimensions such as money laundering and agreements to circumvent international sanctions. The absence of such a harmonized construction of the exception, on the other hand, is bound to lead to inconsistent approaches across jurisdictions.

Some countries have already incorporated such provisions in their statute. For instance, in France, the Code of Civil Procedure in article 1514 specifically mentions that the arbitral award would be recognised or enforced unless such

990 Constantine Partasides, 'Proving Corruption in International Arbitration: A Balanced Standard for the Real World' (2010) 25 ICSID Review – Foreign Investment Law Journal 47.

991 Citigroup Global Markets, Inc, and Edward James Mulcahy, Jr v John Leopold Fiorilla, as Trustee Fbo John Leopoldo Fiorilla Trust (2018) N.Y. Slip Op. 31919(U) (Trial Order) (Supreme Court of New York).

992 Leon E. Trakman (n 983) 248–249.

recognition or enforcement breaches 'international public policy'[993] rather than domestic public policy. Courts in many jurisdictions have chosen to interpret public policy as referring to international rather than domestic notions of public policy.[994] This can be seen in the landmark US decision *Parsons & Whitmore*[995] where the court urged for a more 'supranational' rather than a 'national' approach. A step towards a universal understanding of public policy has been taken by the Organisation for the Harmonization of Business Law in Africa (OHADA) in section 31 of its Uniform Act on Arbitration provides for the refusal of enforcement in case of breach of 'international public policy'.[996]

International public policy has been used quite often to set aside foreign awards.[997] In France, for instance, the recent case of *MK Group v. Onix*, where an award was set aside because it protected an investment which was vitiated by fraud.[998] Indian courts have so far chosen a more parochial approach in defining the exception. According to the interpretation of these courts, public policy would refer to the domestic public policy of the enforcement state only. This can be clearly seen in the Supreme Court's decision in *Renusagar*, where the court reasoned that because of the lack of a workable definition of international public policy, the court would only construe public policy under the IAA to mean Indian public policy.[999] The court appears in this decision to have given 'international public policy' its literal meaning. Such an approach would amount to misconstruing the meaning of the term. International public policy would still be Indian public policy, but given the narrower understanding required in the international context. In fact, relying on international public policy would be

---

993 Code de procédure civile, Version consolidée au 1 janvier 2017 last accessessed on 02/02/2017 at https://www.legifrance.gouv.fr/affichCode.do?cidTexte=LEGITEXT000006070716.

994 Born (n 419) 3657.

995 Parsons & Whittemore Overseas Co., Inc. v. Societe Generale De L'industrie Du Papier (rakta), and Bank of America, Defendants-appellees, Societe Generalede L'industrie Du Papier (rakta) (n 359).

996 L'Organisation pour l'harmonisation en Afrique du droit des affaires, Acte uniforme relatif au droit de l'arbitrage 1999 (n°08).

997 Andrew de Lotbinière McDougall, Sylvain Bollée, and Fiona Candy, 'The Paris Court of Appeal Weighs in on International Public Policy' <https://www.whitecase.com/publications/alert/paris-court-appeal-weighs-international-public-policy> accessed 17 March 2018.

998 Société MK Group vs. S.A.R.L. Onix Société Financial Initiative (n 415).

999 Renusagar Power Co. Ltd. Vs. General Electric Company and Anr. (n 178) para 61.

more in line with the intention of the drafters of the IAA(Am.) 2015 who wished to restrict the scope of Indian public policy.

The use of the courts understanding of Indian public policy, however, is not necessarily a major drawback, because according to Indian law, even Indian public policy is to be given a narrower interpretation by the courts when dealing with foreign awards and a broader interpretation when dealing with solely domestic awards. Furthermore, transnational public policy would be binding on Indian courts insofar as it overlaps with Indian public policy. Furthermore, even international public policy can be used by courts to expand their powers. This was the case in *MK Group*, where the *Cour d'appel de Paris* held that to find if there has been a violation that warrants setting aside of the arbitral award, the court could look at all elements 'in law and in fact'.[1000]

As demonstrated above, the binding nature of transnational public policy on national courts is a grey area. While national courts cannot be compelled to apply transnational public policy, the underlying principles influencing transnational public policy can have a persuasive effect on their decisions. In any case, the concept of public policy is treated in a similar fashion in most developed arbitral jurisdictions.[1001] Courts in these countries have a 'presumptive obligation' to enforce awards.[1002] This can be seen very clearly in the case of Germany, where public policy exception is given a narrow interpretation both with regards to foreign awards under section 1061 of the German Code of Civil Procedure (ZPO) but also with regards to domestic awards.[1003] The generally pro-enforcement bias of courts is accepted both in states following the common law systems as well as in civil law countries.[1004] Such a bias is considered to be essential for the arbitration process to function seamlessly and helps in ensuring the 'predictable' enforcement of awards globally.[1005] This bias must be taken into consideration by courts regardless of whether they choose to rely on domestic, international, or transnational notions of public policy.

1000 See case note, Andrew de Lotbinière McDougall, Sylvain Bollée, and Fiona Candy (n 997).
1001 Blackaby and others (n 72) para 10.83; Born (n 419) para 26.03.
1002 Born (n 419) para 26.03.
1003 See Franz T. Schwarz and Helmut Ortner, 'Chapter III: The Arbitration Procedure – Procedural Ordre Public and the Internationalization of Public Policy in Arbitration', Christian Klausegger and Peter Klein (n 51) 147.
1004 Born (n 419) 3416.
1005 ibid 5.01.

This common pro-enforcement basis can therefore be a basis for harmonization of the public policy exception. The internationally accepted public policy of ensuring enforcement of an arbitral award and respect for party autonomy, even if persuasive, can act as an important barrier from use of the domestic public policy grounds for refusing enforcement of arbitral awards.

(d) Is harmonized transnational public policy a threat to state sovereignty?

As seen above, a delocalised internationally harmonized approach to public policy has many advantages – it can help narrow down the scope of the exception, reduce the chances of judicial intervention and provide a greater degree of certainty to parties. There is, however, a downside to such an approach, i.e., it comes at the cost of state sovereignty.

The ability to define its own public policy is a characteristic feature of every nation-state. As stated by Trakman, each state has its own unique notions of political, social and legal identity.[1006] Determining what constitutes public policy is considered a critical element of sovereignty.[1007] The Indian jurist, Pandey, has noted that for legislation to be accepted and meet the needs of a legal system, it must be 'rooted in the soil,' i.e., based on 'local conditions, attitudes, traditions, culture and conceptions of morality' rather than the particularities of a foreign legal system.[1008]

The very purpose of providing the exception in the first place was to provide an element of state control. The Delhi High Court, in its *Cruz City* decision, held that the use of 'national public policy' for refusing enforcement of a foreign award was the 'strongest expression of a sovereign's desire that a foreign award violating its public policy must not be enforced.[1009] When a state grounds the public policy exception in national rather than international principles, it can tailor the exception to local needs and sentiments. Harmonizing public policy to an international framework may reduce the ability of states to take into account these local needs. Such arguments are particularly crucial for developing countries like India, where arbitration was initially received with scepticism by courts.

1006 Leon E. Trakman (n 983) 253–254.

1007 Farshad Ghodoosi, 'Arbitrating Public Policy: Why the Buck Should Not Stop at National Courts' (n 836) 257–258.

1008 A. P. Pandey, 'Legislation to Be Rooted to the Soil' (1991) 33 Journal of the Indian Law Institute 441, 441–442.

1009 Cruz City 1 Mauritius Holdings v. Unitech Limited (n 543) para 37.

In such states, public policy remains one of the only means of safeguarding domestic morals and values from fast-moving international currents. The removal of this remnant of judicial control may not be taken kindly by local courts. Judicial sovereignty is considered very important in some jurisdictions, e.g., Chinese courts have not hesitated to refuse enforcement of foreign awards when they thought there was a threat to judicial sovereignty.[1010]

Such concerns may, however, be overstated. Harmonization of laws is not the same thing as uniform or identical laws.[1011] While harmonization strives to reduce differences in legal systems, it still leaves scope for adapting to local needs. Transnational public policy also does not necessarily need to be at odds with domestic public policy. In fact, their goals can oftentimes align and complement each other. For instance, corruption goes both against Indian public policy as well as transnational notions of public policy. Furthermore, in case of conflict between transnational public policy and constitutional provisions of a particular country (national public policy), domestic courts can always apply domestic public policy.

Sovereignty based arguments, i.e., the argument that transnational public policy reduces the power of judges to intervene as they are bound by an internationally accepted framework does not withstand greater scrutiny. The reduced role of state courts in private dispute settlement is the goal of arbitration, even if it comes at the cost of sovereignty. States including India, which are party to the New York Convention, have gladly committed to accepting arbitration as a means of dispute settlement regardless of the fact that it promotes private dispute settlement. The use of transnational public policy instead of being a threat to national sovereignty is an instrument of giving certainty to parties and promoting comity between states.[1012]

Furthermore, there need not be a completely uniform approach to public policy. Bermann has rightly pointed out that states can agree to an international framework of public policy without specifically elaborating on its content.[1013]

1010 Tietie Zhang, 'Judicial Sovereignty and Public Policy under Chinese Arbitration Law' (2017) 28 American Review of International Arbitration 369, 388.

1011 See, Stelios Andreadakis, 'Regulatory Competition or Harmonisation: The Dilemma, the Alternatives and the Prospect of Reflexive Harmonisation', in Mads Tønnesson Andenæs and Camilla Baasch Andersen (eds), *Theory and Practice of Harmonisation* (Edward Elgar 2011) 58.

1012 Leon E. Trakman (n 983) 208.

1013 George A. Bermann, *International Arbitration and Private International Law*, vol 381 (Brill: Nijhoff 2017) para 685.

It is sufficient for the Indian legal system to take into account the objectives underlying the use of public policy in most arbitration-friendly jurisdictions. According to Moses, such a 'transnational perspective' that relies on 'international best practices' will lead to a 'less parochial' approach towards international arbitration.[1014]

7. Reconciling the use of public policy with the goal of making India an arbitration-friendly jurisdiction

A recurring theme found throughout this thesis has been the need to convert India into a pro-arbitration jurisdiction. This has been the goal of the legislature ever since it started out on modernizing Indian arbitration law, first with the IAA 1996 and then the IAA(Am.) 2015. This is also reflected in statements made by successive law ministers. Given that the public policy exception has in the past been a major hurdle to the development of arbitration in India, the rationale for legislatively restricting public policy has been to achieve this goal.

In order to see if such a measure is effective, one needs to introspect on what 'arbitration-friendly' really means and what it takes for a jurisdiction to be called 'arbitration-friendly'. Furthermore, could restricting public policy truly be arbitration-friendly?

(a) The true meaning of 'arbitration-friendly'

Almost every major jurisdiction either claims to be or aims to be-be considered pro-arbitration or arbitration-friendly. This is especially true in the Asia-Pacific region.[1015] This is unsurprising, as there are numerous benefits to a jurisdiction being labeled as arbitration-friendly. Notably, it brings with it increased investment and consequently increased GDP.[1016] What does the term arbitration-friendly mean? Generally speaking, a law or policy which fulfills the goals of arbitration would be considered as arbitration-friendly or 'pro-arbitration'.[1017]

1014 See, Margaret L. Moses, 'Public Policy under the New York Convention: National, International, and Transnational', in Katia Fach Gómez and Ana M. Lopez-Rodriguez (n 908) 182.

1015 Anselmo Reyes and Weixia Gu (eds), The Developing World of Arbitration: A Comparative Study of Arbitration Reform in the Asia Pacific (Hart Publishing 2018) 2.

1016 ibid.

1017 George A. Bermann, 'What Does It Mean to Be "pro-Arbitration"?' (2018) 34 Arbitration International 341, 342.

In other words, being arbitration-friendly would mean giving effect to the will of the parties to subject their dispute to arbitration instead of national courts.

What special characteristic is required for a jurisdiction to rightly stake such a claim of being pro-arbitration? One need not search too far for an answer. The Swiss Arbitration Association prominently states on its webpage 'Switzerland is arbitration friendly' and then provides a list of reasons for this assertion, *including 'respect for party autonomy, far-reaching subject matter arbitrability…'* and importantly *'intervention of state courts only in support of arbitration'*.[1018]

Being arbitration-friendly is not the exclusive prerogative of the legislator. For a jurisdiction to succeed in being arbitration-friendly, there needs to be a concerted effort from different stakeholders. The law-maker plays an important role in drafting pro-arbitration statutes, national courts in facilitating arbitration and reducing unwarranted judicial interference, arbitral institutions in promoting a culture of arbitration with the business community and the parties who choose arbitration, and do not seek to resist enforcement merely as a delaying tactic.[1019]

But even the term 'arbitration-friendly' has many facets. What is considered arbitration-friendly by some is oftentimes not pro-arbitration to others. Furthermore, perceptions of what is pro-arbitration also differ from jurisdiction to jurisdiction, person to person, and may change in time.[1020] For instance, permitting arbitrating of consumer disputes, a move that may seem to promote arbitration, is allowed in the US but restricted in Europe. A similar logic applies where the subject matter relates to patent claims and anti-trust disputes.

(b) Is restricting public policy truly 'arbitration-friendly'?

Restricting the scope of the public policy exception is *prima facie* certainly an arbitration-friendly measure. Limiting the exception promotes arbitration as it can prevent abuse and curtail the power of courts to entertain excessive and unwarranted challenges of awards.

However, here also everything is not in black and white. The public policy exception can also be pro-arbitration, as it ensures a fairer and more just arbitration process and protects the legitimate interests of parties. Furthermore, the public policy exception, as elaborated earlier in this thesis, provides for the protection of public good and ensures limited public oversight in an essentially

---

1018 'Switzerland Is Arbitration-Friendly' <https://www.arbitration-ch.org/en/service/asa/switzerland-is-arbitration-friendly/index.html> accessed 6 June 2019.

1019 Reyes and Gu (n 1015) 3.

1020 George A. Bermann, 'What Does It Mean to Be "pro-Arbitration"?' (n 1017) 344–347.

private process, either where arbitrators exceed their mandate in deciding, for instance, matters which are not arbitrable (e.g., consumer disputes) or there is some illegality in the arbitration process. This, in effect, reduces scepticism and promotes greater acceptability of arbitration in society at large. Restricting the exception may, therefore, actually work against arbitration.

A more suitable solution would be to not focus too much on the terms such as 'arbitration-friendly', but instead, as suggested by Bermann, use a 'cost-benefit' or proportionality analysis test to determine the balance of whether the pro-arbitration features outweigh the considerations against such a measure.[1021] With regard to public policy, this would mean determining whether the benefits of restricting the scope of the exception in the Indian context would be greater than the benefit extended by giving the exception its normal understanding. One must weigh the interest of society at large in having unrestricted judicial access to the public policy exception, with the interest of respecting party autonomy and promoting arbitration. In doing so, it is important to consider the historic misuse and broad judicial interpretation given to the exception.

(c) *Defining public policy to meet the needs of the arbitration community and society*

The drafters of the UNCITRAL Model law intended to provide a framework that would meet the 'needs of international arbitration practice'.[1022] As India has adopted the Model Law, the IAA needs to be interpreted to meet the aforementioned goal. The success of any law governing arbitration depends on how it meets the needs of the end-users.[1023] By inference, judges and legislators in India and other jurisdictions must keep in mind what parties who use arbitration would expect from a definition of public policy. In India, due consideration would also be needed to be given to the underlying reasoning behind the New York Convention.

The question then arises, who are the end uses that the lawmaker must consider when defining the scope of public policy? One can argue that given that international commercial arbitration is primarily chosen by private parties as a private means of settling disputes and a way to get out of the public sphere, the exception should be tailored primarily to meet their needs. As these parties

---

1021 ibid 348.

1022 'Resolutions Adopted by the General Assembly 40/72, United Nations Treaty Series, vol. 330, No. 4739, p. 38.'

1023 Frederic Bachand (n 260) 86.

mainly desire an enforceable award, such an exception would then need to be extremely narrow so as to exclude any chance of judicial excess.

The above approach is, however, not uncontroversial, as it would involve ignoring the stake that the public has in ensuring that deeply immoral contracts which go against the public conscience are not enforced. Winfield has provided a more acceptable solution when he argued that the public policy exception should be based on the 'current needs of the community.'[1024] Even this approach is not without complexity. This is because there are different needs, even in a given community. The needs of some members of the community may vastly defer from the needs of other members of the community. For instance, while the members of the community involved in international commerce form a minuscule minority, their perspective on judicial intervention may differ from the vast majority of people who do not have much to do with international commerce in their daily life. Furthermore, it is impossible for the lawmaker or judge to seek the opinion of every member of the community to find out the exact scope of the exception. This is especially true because the opinion of people keeps changing all the time. To resolve these conflicts, Winfield suggested that in defining the scope of public policy, it is the job of the judge to consider what the hypothetical 'reasonable' person would consider being in the interest of the community as a whole.[1025]

While such a standard may lead to a slightly broader conception of public policy, it would have numerous advantages. Firstly, it would lead to a conception of public policy which is more balanced, and as it is based on the needs of various groups. Secondly, and more importantly, by not ignoring the legitimate concerns of the community and also taking the interest of commercial parties into account, the definition would be more widely accepted and therefore give more legitimacy to arbitration as a whole.

1024 Percy H. Winfield (n 55) 92.
1025 ibid 100.

Chapter 6: Determining the competent authority for deciding on claims where there is a violation of public policy

At the outset, it must be noted that although by choosing arbitration, the parties seem to have accepted that all claims must be brought before the arbitral tribunal, the nature of public policy exception, as the term 'public' suggests, may, however, give state courts power to make a final determination in certain cases to safeguard the public interest.

The public policy exception can be invoked by parties to an arbitration in three different situations, i.e., in case the underlying contract breaches public policy, if there is a violation of procedural public policy during the arbitration proceedings, or if enforcing the award would violate public policy. In each of these situations, the aggrieved party could seek a remedy at various stages of the proceedings before different authorities, i.e., before the arbitral tribunal, courts at the seat of arbitration or courts at the place of enforcement. In this chapter, we will evaluate which is the competent authority to deal with public policy concerns at different stages of the arbitration. In doing so, we will evaluate the impact of non-arbitrability of the subject matter and substantive illegality of the agreement have on the determination of the competent authority.

I. When the underlying contract violates public policy

Parties resisting enforcement of arbitral awards because the underlying contract contravenes public policy could do so because of the following grounds (i) there was illegality in the contract or because (ii) the subject matter of the contract is so fundamental to the legal system or affects the rights of third parties and is therefore as a matter of public policy is not capable of being arbitrated, i.e., not arbitrable.

As will be shown below, in some jurisdictions, contracts tainted by illegality are considered non-arbitrable. This is controversial as not every contract where there is an element of illegality can be said to violate public policy and thus be excluded from arbitration. In the first part of this section, we will look at the different situations where illegality can arise, the consequences such illegality has on contractual obligations, and when the exclusion of jurisdiction of the arbitral tribunal on the grounds of illegality would be justifiable.

Moving to the second part of this section, although public policy and non-arbitrability are two separate grounds for non-enforcement covered under Art 5(2)a and Art. 5(2)b of the New York Convention, respectively, they are both deeply intertwined. Böckstiegel has pointed out the general acceptance that with regard to the 'New York Convention, arbitrability forms part of public policy'.[1026] A distinction regarding the function of the two concepts, however, needs to be made. While the public policy exception seeks to protect fundamental tenets of a legal system – non-arbitrability tells us which disputes the legal system precludes parties from arbitrating. As elucidated by the Indian Supreme Court in its *Indo Unique* decision, the two concepts are linked insofar as certain disputes encompassing, for instance, matrimonial proceedings, insolvency proceedings, consumer disputes are often considered not-arbitrable simply because they encompass public policy concerns and as a matter of public interest need to be adjudicated by a public authority.[1027]

While it is arguable that disputes over non-arbitrable contracts should not be decided by the arbitral tribunal, the second part of this section will look at whether this should always be taken for granted. We will evaluate if there is a case to be made for arbitrators to exercise jurisdiction even in such situations. The analysis will help in finding the limits of arbitrability and in concluding when courts at the seat or place of enforcement would be competent instead of the arbitral tribunal.

1. Where there is illegality

The term 'illegal' can refer to a vast array of activities that are prohibited by statute and usually morally repugnant.[1028] Illegality when arising in contracts can be a limitation to party autonomy. Illegal contracts have been described by Cerchia to encompass contracts that go against 'mandatory rules, public order and good morals.'[1029] Illegality in contracts could arise in different situations.

1026 See Karl-Heinz Böckstiegel 'Public Policy and Arbitrability' in Sanders (n 421) 183.

1027 See, *NN Global Mercantile Pvt Ltd Vs Indo Unique Flame Ltd and Ors* (2021) Civ Appeal Nos 3802–3803 2020 (Supreme Court of India) [8.10-8.11].

1028 'The Illegality Defence in Tort – Law Commission Consultation Paper No 160' para 1.12–1.17 <https://www.lawcom.gov.uk/app/uploads/2015/03/cp160_Illegality_Defence_in_Tort_Consultation.pdf> accessed 5 July 2022.

1029 Rossella Esther Cerchia, 'A Comparative Viewpoint on Illegal Contracts: In Favor of Flexibility and Proportionality' (2021) 21 Global Jurist, De Gruyter 447, 451.

These could include but are not limited to situations where the agreement has an unlawful aim, where there is illegality in performance of contractual obligations, where certain contractual stipulations contravene a statutory norm, or in case of regulated activities that require governmental permission- where the required governmental licenses or permits are not obtained and activities performed illegally.[1030] Whether a contract is considered to be illegal can differ based on varying conceptions and legal norms from country to country and even within a given jurisdiction from time to time based on the changing notions of public policy and what Strong has described as changes in the 'socio-economic environment'.[1031]

The question as to whether illegal contracts should be enforced is a fractious one, which has been the subject of debate at least in the common law world for centuries.[1032] Glanville Williams opined that such contracts would generally be void, as their enforcement would be contrary to 'law, morality, and public policy'.[1033] This view is also found in Indian contract law. Section 23 of the Indian Contract Act 1872 (the law governing contracts in India), provides that agreements having unlawful object or consideration (i.e., fraudulent, injurious, forbidden by law, defeats the law, immoral, opposed to public policy) would be void. Even in England, since the *Ralli Bros* ruling, it was established that courts would not enforce a contract where the performance is illegal at the place of performance.[1034] This refusal to enforce contracts tainted with illegality goes down to the *clean hands* doctrine, a maxim of equity.[1035]

The main rationale behind the aforementioned approach is that courts would not permit a person to profit from their wrongdoing, and courts would not be misused as an instrument to effectuate such illegal behavior as it would undermine

---

1030 For an elaboration on types of illegal contracts see George A. Strong, 'The Enforceability of Illegal Contracts' (1961) 12 Hastings Law Journal 347.

1031 ibid 348.

1032 See for instance the discourse on illegal contracts generally, and contracts illegal at common law in, Claude C. M. Plumptre, *Summary of the Principles of the Law of Simple Contracts* (Butterworths 1879) 104.

1033 Glanville L. Williams, 'The Legal Effect of Illegal Contracts' (1942) 8 The Cambridge Law Journal 51.

1034 *Ralli Bros v Compañia Naviera Sota y Aznar* (1920) 1 KB 614 (King's Bench Division (Commercial Court)).

1035 T. Leigh Anenson, *Judging Equity: The Fusion of Unclean Hands in U.S. Law* (Cambridge University Press 2018) 12–58.

the legitimacy of courts.[1036] This can be seen in the wording of Lord Mansfield when he laid down his dictum that public policy requires that 'no court will aid' a party whose claim rests on an illegal act.[1037] Despite the foregoing, there have been divergences even in the approach of UK courts, and illegality is not considered sufficient reason to wipe away every legal remedy. This was demonstrated in *Patel v Mirza*, where the UK Supreme Court ruled that mere illegality alone would not preclude a party from recovering his property.[1038]

While a court will not aid a party in fulfilling an illegal contract, nothing stops the party from bringing a claim before a court to seek a remedy, even if there was an element of illegality. This is especially the case if the aggrieved party bringing the claim was unaware of the commission/not at fault with regard to the illegal behavior. There is similarly nothing constraining the powers of arbitral tribunals to hear such claims where there are allegations of illegality. There is a good reason for this. As pointed out by Lord Devlin in the *St. Johns Shipping* case, given that commerce in today's world is governed by so many laws, it is quite possible for there to be a violation without any 'wicked intent'.[1039] This does not, however, mean that an arbitral tribunal would be considered as the competent authority in every situation. In fact, the question of which authority has jurisdiction in case of illegality has been a bone of contention among scholars for quite a while. In answering that question, there are numerous factors that need to be taken into consideration.

(a) Illegality in the underlying contract

While the question of whether illegal contracts are enforceable has given rise to much controversy, which has been dealt with earlier in this thesis[1040] – this is also true with the question of whether such contracts should be considered arbitrable. The answer generally lies in the nature of the illegality and where it arises.

Normally, because of the doctrine of separability, the invalidity of the underlying contract due to an illegality would not automatically lead to the invalidity

---

1036 Chunlin Leonhard, 'Illegal Agreements and the Lesser Evil Principle' (2015) 64 Catholic University Law Review 833, 835.

1037 Holman v Johnson (n 487).

1038 *Patel v Mirza* (2016) UKSC 42 (UK Supreme Court).

1039 *St John Shipping Corporation v Joseph Rank Ltd* (1956) 1 QB 267 (High Court of England and Wales (Queen's Bench Division)) 288 et seq.

1040 See *supra* Chapter 4(III).

of the arbitration clause.[1041] The doctrine of separability is considered to be a fundamental principle of arbitration and is recognised internationally.[1042] Some scholars have argued that it is so well accepted across jurisdictions that it almost forms a part of 'transnational' norm.[1043] According to this doctrine, the arbitration agreement is considered to be separate from the main contract, and even if the underlying contract is rendered invalid, the arbitration clause will survive.[1044] But would this be true in every situation of illegality – especially when the underlying contract is illegal and *void ab initio*?

Below we will look at how the jurisdiction of the tribunal is potentially affected in two different scenarios. Firstly, where the entire contract has an illegal aim and secondly, where the contract is generally legal, but certain contractual provisions have an element of illegality.

(i) *Where the sole purpose of the contract was the performance of an overtly illegal act*

There exist certain kinds of agreements that have solely been entered into by parties with the intention to perform an illegal act or to avoid a legal obligation. Such contracts have been characterized as 'overtly illegal', and the object of such contracts would go against 'public morality' in most countries.[1045] For example, a contract for the sale of drugs, or an agreement to sell products with military application with a view to illegally circumvent sanctions would most likely constitute criminal enterprise and would certainly violate public policy.[1046] These types of contracts are generally *void ab initio*.[1047]

1041 Gary Born, *International Commercial Arbitration* (3rd edn, Kluwer Law International 2021) 386–387.

1042 See Florian Haugeneder, 'A 07 – Separability Doctrine, Annotation to Case C23, C33, C58', in *Vienna International Arbitration Centre of the Austrian Federal Economic Chamber, Selected Arbitral Awards*, vol 1 (Verlag WKÖ Service GmbH 2015) 401.

1043 Alan Scott Rau, The Allocation of Power between Arbitral Tribunals and State Courts (Brill: Nijhoff 2018) 93.

1044 Blackaby and others (n 72) para 2.134.

1045 See Richard Kreindler, 'Aspects of Illegality in the Formation and Performance of Contratcs', in Berg, *International Commercial Arbitration* (n 495) 212.

1046 David A. Friedman (n 864) 590.

1047 Joshua R. Welsh, 'Has Expansion of the Federal Arbitration Act Gone Too Far?: Enforcing Arbitration Clauses in Void Ab Initio Contracts' (2002) 86 Marquette Law Review 581, 610.

Parties could try to misuse arbitration as a way to avoid legal scrutiny in their illicit dealings, or even worse, misuse arbitration to effectuate illegal behavior, e.g., to facilitate money laundering.[1048] One can argue that in such situations that it is justified and in the public interest for national courts to have exclusive jurisdictions to decide on the dispute and any violation of public policy thereto. The roots for such an approach under English law can be seen in an early decision by Lord Denning, where he held that *'an arbitrator has no jurisdiction or authority to award damages on an illegal contract'*.[1049] Even in the United States, the Florida District Court in *Party Yards case* ruled that arbitrators do not have the power to compel a party to commit an illegal act.[1050]

In the Indian context, the approach that tribunals have jurisdiction in all cases has not always been welcomed by courts. If the arbitrator exercises jurisdiction where he should not have, courts are willing to step in. In India, courts have not been averse to issuing an 'anti-arbitration injunctions' where public interest demands. This can be seen, for instance, in the Delhi High Court ruling in *McDonalds India*, where the Court held that it would be willing to issue an anti-arbitration injunction if arbitration proceedings would be 'oppressive or unconscionable', or where the arbitration agreement is void.[1051] It would not be far-fetched to assume that arbitration proceedings that are initiated by a party with the intention of enforcing a wholly illegal contract would be considered unconscionable by the Court.

English courts have also not looked kindly on agreements tainted by illegality. In *1MDB v. IPIC*, the Court of Appeal, when deciding on the powers of a court in case of a challenge under Art 67 or 68 of the UK Arbitration Act, held that it would contravene 'public interest for the powers of the state to be used for enforcement of an award' when the tribunal lacked jurisdiction or 'the award was a result of serious irregularity'.[1052] In *Coral Racing* case, which involved an arbitration clause in an illegal gaming agreement, the Court of Appeals, in effect, held

1048 Andrew de Lotbiniére McDougall, 'International Arbitration and Money Laundering' (2005) 20 American University International Law Review 1021, 1023 et seq.

1049 David Taylor & Son Ltd v Barnett Trading Co Ltd (1953) 1 WLR 562.

1050 *Party Yards v Templeton* (2000) 751 2d 121 (District Court of Appeal of Florida, Fifth District) 123.

1051 McDonald's India Private Limited v Vikram Bakshi and Ors (2016) FAO OS 92015 (Delhi High Court) [48].

1052 Minister of Finance (Incorporated) 1Malaysia Development Berhad v International Petroleum Investment Company Aabar Investment PJS (2019) EWCA Civ 2080 (Court of Appeal (England & Wales)).

that the arbitration clause was an integral part of the terms on which the party was willing to conduct its illegal business and hence could not be separated and would also be void.[1053]

Indian Courts have in the past come to a similar conclusion. They have based their decisions on the distinction between whether the underlying contract was voidable or rather *void ab initio.* While the former class of disputes would be arbitrable, the latter would not. The Supreme court in *Kishorilal* held that where the illegality renders the underlying contract *void ab initio*, the arbitration clause would also perish with the contract, and the situation would be as if the clause never came into being.[1054] The doctrine of separability would not apply here due to the legal fiction that the contract never came into existence. This approach can also find its basis in the IAA. While section 45 of the IAA places a general requirement for Indian courts to refer the parties to a dispute to arbitration where an arbitration agreement exists, this is subject to the arbitration agreement not being 'null and void, inoperative or incapable of being performed'.

Even in Germany, illegality in the underlying contract can vitiate arbitral awards. While the BGH has accepted that in principle, the underlying contract is independent of the arbitration clause, and the invalidity of the underlying contract will not affect the arbitration clause, it held that in special circumstances where the underlying contract is vitiated by fraud or coercion, then the arbitration clause would also be unworkable.[1055] This line of reasoning is similar to what was envisioned in the UNCITRAL Model Law.[1056] In such situations, it is arguable that an award rendered pursuant to such a clause would not be enforced on public policy grounds.

In hearing a dispute where the underlying contract is tainted by allegations of illegality, a balance could be found if courts at the seat were to allow the arbitration to proceed and only intervene *ex-post* if the tribunal has not properly considered the potential violation of public policy. This would be in line with the second look doctrine of the US Supreme Court in *Mitsubishi Motor Corp* case.[1057] Such an opinion has also found support in literature. A.S. Rau has argued that

1053 *O'Callaghan v Coral Racing Ltd* (1998) APP R 1119 (Court of Appeal (England and Wales)) [21].
1054 *Union of India vs Kishorlal Gupta & Bros* (1959) AIR 1362 (Supreme Court of India).
1055 BGH Beschluss Vom 27. Novemb 2008 – III ZB 5907 – Juris (German Federal Court of Justice (Bundesgerichtshof)).
1056 Born (n 419) 377.
1057 Mitsubishi v. Soler Chrysler-Plymouth (n 353).

usually, the only relevant consideration in allocating jurisdiction between the courts and arbitral tribunals is whether the parties intended the dispute to be arbitrated – if the answer is affirmative, then the jurisdiction to hear the dispute at the first instance lies with the arbitral tribunal.[1058]

However, the aforementioned approach of balancing may not be suitable in the situation where the sole purpose of the contract is to perform a wholly illegal act. Rau has acknowledged this by giving a three-pronged test for when courts should be allowed to intervene *ex-ante*. According to him, this would be justifiable – firstly, in the rare circumstance where it would be obviously pointless or too late for the courts to intervene only after the tribunal has rendered its award, secondly, where the entire agreement is *'malum in se'* (innately immoral[1059]), or thirdly, there are reasonable doubts at to whether the tribunal would work within the four corners of the law – e.g., where the tribunal is part of the illegal scheme.[1060]

As any of the three situations indicated by Rau would potentially guarantee that the future award would not be tenable, there are arguably valid grounds for disputes falling within these categories to be adjudicated in a public forum. As shown above such an approach would also find support in judicial reasoning in numerous jurisdictions.

(ii) In case certain contractual stipulations are illegal and violate public policy

In contrast to the circumstances elucidated above, a situation could also arise where a contract has a legal purpose, but a part of the contract or a contractual stipulation is illegal and violates public policy. From a purely contract law standpoint, a court could react to the illegality in many ways. It could, for instance, react by enforcing the contract regardless of the illegality, or alternatively, it could do the opposite by completely invalidating the contract. Neither of these options would be ideal. Invalidating the contract would show complete disregard to the principle of party autonomy and not be in line with the intention of the parties at the time of its conclusion, whereas completely ignoring the illegality could seriously prejudice the rights of the parties or the general public.

1058 Rau (n 1043) 98 et seq.

1059 'Malum In Se' <https://www.law.cornell.edu/wex/malum_in_se> accessed 2 August 2021.

1060 Rau (n 1043) 117–118.

In order to preclude such difficulties, contracting parties oftentimes insert 'severability clauses' in their contracts that enable them to sever the illegal part and give effect to the rest of the contract.[1061] In the absence of such a contractual provision, the approach taken by courts in many common law jurisdictions is the 'blue pencil rule' elaborated in *Attwood v. Lamont.*[1062] According to this rule, the illegal contractual stipulation would be separated by the court, and the rest of the contract would be given effect to. Severability would only be possible if the illegal part is not essential or preponderant to the contract, otherwise, the contract would not be workable.[1063]

In the context of arbitration clauses in contracts where some other clauses are found to be illegal, there are numerous approaches that could be taken in determining if the arbitral tribunal should retain jurisdiction. While there may be some justification for leaving jurisdiction with national courts in case of agreements that are void because of their object being completely illegal, this ceases to be true in case of minor illegalities,[1064] or where the contractual provisions are predominantly legal. This brings us to the first approach of using the doctrine of separability. By applying this doctrine, the arbitral tribunal would be sufficiently competent to decide on whether the illegality vitiates the entire contract, including the arbitration agreement.[1065] If the tribunal finds the illegality doesn't have such a consequence, the tribunal could go on to decide on the rights and obligations of the parties with regard to the rest of the contract. Such an understanding can be found in section 16 of the IAA, which provides discretion to the tribunal to rule on the validity of the arbitration agreement. The provision also states that the invalidity of the underlying contract would not

1061 For an elaboration on the severability doctrine in the context of both contracts and statutes see, Mark L. Movsesian, 'Severability in Statutes and Contracts' (1995) 30 Georgia Law Review 41, 43.

1062 *Attwood v Lamont* (1920) 3 KB 571 (Court of Appeal).

1063 Uri Benoliel, 'Contract Interpretation Revisited: The Case of Severability Clauses' (2019) 3 Business and Finance Law Review 90, 94.

1064 See, Exceptions to the Preclusive Effect of Illegality, in Noradèle Radjai and Christophe Guibert de Bruet, 'Corruption and Illegality in Arbitration – a Practitioner's View' (Lalive – Arbitration, Kings College, 2021) 48 <https://www.lalive.law/wp-content/uploads/2021/06/20210615-LALIVE-Kings-College-Presentation.pdf> accessed 22 May 2022.

1065 See generally, Ronán Feehily, 'Separability in International Commercial Arbitration; Confluence, Conflict and the Appropriate Limitations in the Development and Application of the Doctrine' (2018) 34 Arbitration International 355.

automatically render the arbitration clause void. Although section 16 deals with domestic awards, the drafters of the IAA intended an even more arbitration-friendly approach *vis-à-vis* foreign awards.[1066] This would lead us to conclude that in the case of foreign awards, Indian law would bestow jurisdiction on the arbitral tribunal for making a determination of jurisdiction even where certain provisions of the underlying contract are invalid. This approach has been supported by the Indian Supreme Court in its *Shin Satellite* ruling, where the court reiterated that in case some contractual provisions are found to be invalid, the invalid part of the contract should be separated and the arbitration agreement be given effect.[1067]

On the one hand, section 23 of the Indian Contract Act 1872 provides that any contract in which the consideration or object is unlawful is void. However, on the other hand, as the doctrine of separability applies under Indian arbitration law, the arbitration agreement will not always be automatically invalidated. The Indian Supreme Court has held that the determination of whether the underlying contract is void, even in case of allegations of fraud, would be made first by the arbitral tribunal.[1068] Even allegations of criminality or violation of a statute would not automatically leave the tribunal without jurisdiction.[1069] This means that the tribunal will be competent to hear disputes even in case of illegality in contractual stipulations unless the illegality is of such a nature as to render the contract and arbitration agreement void *ab initio* or unless the subject matter is not capable of being arbitrated under Indian law.

In recent decisions, American courts have also demonstrated a reluctance to allow courts to look at the underlying contract. This can be seen in the *Teploenergetika* ruling, where the US Court for the Eastern District of Virginia held any claims that the underlying contract violated public policy must be brought exclusively before the arbitrators during the arbitral proceedings, and parties cannot bring such a claim before the enforcing court.[1070] In *Europcar*, the US 2nd Circuit took a similar approach by holding that it is solely for the arbitrators to decide

---

1066 Justice A. P. Shah (n 27) 21 et seq.

1067 Shin Satellite Public Co Ltd vs M/S Jain Studios Limited (2006) AIR 963 (Supreme Court of India) [25–27].

1068 A Ayyasamy v A Paramasivam & Ors (n 234) para 27.

1069 ibid 35.

1070 *Research and Development Center "Teploenergetika," LLC v EP International, LLC* (2016) 182 FSupp3d 556 (United States District Court, ED Virginia, Norfolk Division) 567 et seq.

if the underlying contract was obtained fraudulently.[1071] Any doubts were put to rest by the U. S. Supreme Court in its *Buckeye* ruling.[1072] In this case, a party who borrowed money under a loan agreement brought a class action suit before a Florida court challenging the unlawfully high-interest rate. The U. S. Supreme Court had to decide on whether a court or arbitrator would be competent authority to hear allegations of illegality in the underlying contract. Reversing a Florida Supreme Court decision on the matter, the U. S. Supreme Court held that it would be for the arbitrators to decide such claims.[1073]

A more nuanced approach was taken by the ECJ in the *Eco Swiss* case. In this case, the parties had entered into a licencing agreement which was found to be illegal as it violated Article 81 TEC (Art 101 TFEU). The ECJ ruled that the ensuing arbitral award enforcing the agreement would be contrary to Art 81 TEC and, therefore, would be subject to annulment for violation of EU public policy.[1074] It was held that since arbitrators, unlike national courts, are unable to make a reference to the ECJ for interpretation of EU law, national courts would be competent to make an examination and annul an award where they find a violation of public policy.[1075] Here again, the approach of the ECJ was that arbitrators could first hear the dispute, and courts would be free to annul the award at a later stage if enforcement would violate public policy. Even if such an approach is taken, arbitral tribunals need to act with caution when hearing such a dispute. In reaching their award, they must give due weightage to any allegations made and the evidence provided. Not doing so could potentially endanger the finality of the award.

The second approach would be for the aggrieved party to approach the courts at the arbitral seat at the pre-arbitration stage with the claim that the underlying contract would be illegal according to the law of the seat or that the subject matter is not arbitrable as it breaches public policy of the seat. Even in case of allegations that certain contractual provisions are illegal, it is difficult to imagine a valid reason for the court at the seat to not allow the arbitration proceedings to commence. As shown previously, judicial intervention at the pre-arbitration stage would contravene the principle of *Kompetenz-Kompetenz* as well as disrespect

1071 Europcar Italia, S.p.A. v. Maiellano Tours, Inc. (n 426) 315.
1072 *Buckeye Check Cashing, Inc v Cardegna* (2006) 546 US 440 (US Supreme Court).
1073 ibid.
1074 For further elaboration on this case see Chapter 4(III)2e.
1075 Case C-126/97, Eco Swiss China Time Ltd. v. Benetton InternationalN.V., (n 587) para 40.

the will of the parties as expressed in the arbitration agreement. This does not, however, mean that parties do not have any judicial recourse at the seat of arbitration. After the award has been rendered, if the court at the seat subsequently finds that the illegality is of such a nature as to vitiate the arbitration clause itself, it can subsequently set aside the award.

The third approach is that a violation of public policy due to illegality in the underlying contract needs to be invoked by the aggrieved party *ex-post* before courts at the place of enforcement. As this does not deal with the jurisdiction of the tribunal, it will not be dealt with in detail here. But in short, it is understandable that courts may want to regulate what kind of contracts parties enter into, sometimes even at the cost of finality of enforcing arbitral awards. The rationale behind refusing enforcement stems from the traditional approach in common law jurisprudence that courts refused to enforce illegal contracts irrespective of whether there was just an 'element of criminality, whether the contract was only a step in committing the crime' or if the contract was unjust.[1076] It is difficult to envision courts enforcing arbitral awards arising out of contracts to perform illegal activities such as an agreement to breach UN sanctions or a contract for the sale of contraband.

Indian courts have in the past demonstrated a willingness to interfere with awards where there is a legal defect in the underlying contract. In its 2014 *Aakash Institute* ruling, the Delhi High Court interfered with an award because the arbitrator had not taken into account the fact that the terms of the contract were unconscionable as they restrained a party from seeking legal remedy and because the contractual payment obligations were so prejudicial to a weaker party that it was against public policy.[1077] The Court's reasoning also extends to other areas. In the *Brojo Nath* ruling, the Supreme Court considered that a contract that unduly hurts the rights of a weaker party, in this case, an employment contract, which unduly prejudiced the employee, would be unconscionable and thus violate Indian public policy.[1078]

(b) Where illegality is ancillary to the contract

The second situation is when the illegality amounting to a violation of public policy is not with a contractual provision but rather ancillary to the contract.

1076 Walter Gellhorn (n 818) 679.

1077 Vivek Rai v Aakash Institute (n 551), para 14 et seq.

1078 Central Inland Water Transport Corporation Limited and Anr v. Brojo Nath Ganguly and Anr. (n 169), 92 et seq.

This could be the case where the underlying contract is tainted by fraud, coercion or corruption. It could also be true when there is illegality in the performance of contractual obligations by one of the parties. Below we will look at whether the arbitral tribunal is the competent authority for deciding on such disputes.

(i) In case the underlying contract was entered into as a result of illegality, including corruption, fraud or coercion

Consent of the parties is the basis both of any contract as well as any arbitration clause that forms part of a contract.[1079] An agreement may not always be freely entered into by the parties. Sometimes, there may not be free will, or the free will of the parties could be unduly influenced by extraneous considerations such as coercion, corruption or forgery. A good illustration was pointed out by Judge Glasser in the US case *Pacific Bullion,* where he noted that it would be 'absurd' to leave the arbitral tribunal with jurisdiction if there are indications that the signature of a party to the underlying contract was forged.[1080] Arbitrators themselves have been reluctant to accept jurisdiction when the signature was found to be forged.[1081] For this reason, where a contract entered into due to illegality has an arbitration clause, it is important to look at the consequences of such lack of consent/agency in entering into the underlying contract on the arbitral agreement and jurisdiction of the arbitral tribunal.

(1) Where the underlying contract is tainted by corruption

Given the implications of corrupt agreements to public resources, it is also important to determine which authority is competent to hear disputes where there are allegations of corruption. It is true that arbitrators, when faced with a dispute where there are allegations of corruption, sometimes refuse jurisdiction or rule that the claim is not admissible.[1082] A good illustration would be a ruling

1079 United Nations Conference on Trade and Development, 'Consent to Arbitration – Dispute Settlement, International Centre for Settlement of Investment Disputes (2003), United Nations, UNCTAD/EDM/Misc.232/Add.2' 2.

1080 *Kyung In Lee v Pacific Bullion (New York) Inc* (1992) 788 F Supp 155 (US District Court for the Eastern District of New York) 157 et seq.

1081 See, 'National Bank of Xanadu v. Company ACME (Final Award), ICC Case No. 17818', in Stephan W. Schill (ed), *Yearbook of Commercial Arbitration*, vol 44 (ICCA & Kluwer Law International 2019) 30 et seq.

1082 See, Carolyn B. Lamm, Hansel T. Pham, et al., 'Fraud and Corruption in International Arbitration', in Cremades, Fernández-Ballesteros and Arias (n 401) 729.

by Judge Gunnar Lagergren, for instance, when refusing jurisdiction as an arbitrator to a dispute because the underlying contract was tainted by corruption and violated public policy, pointed out that '*general principle of law recognised by civilised nations*' renders unenforceable contracts which breach *bonos mores* or international public policy.[1083]

Corruption is a major concern internationally, but more so in the Indian context. Transparency International Corruption Perception Index ranks Indian at 86/180 countries in 2020, with 89% of people surveyed perceiving corruption to be a major problem.[1084] It is natural that the legislature would consider contracts influenced by corruption to contravene with fundamental public policy. As shown above, under the explanatory notes to section 48(2)b of the IAA, an award tainted by corruption would violate public policy.[1085] The aforementioned provision, however, refers only to corruption during the arbitration proceedings. There is no explicit mention as to whether disputes arising out of underlying contracts tainted by corruption are arbitrable under Indian law. Some scholars have argued that agreements tainted by corruption are arbitrable under Indian law as they are merely 'voidable' at the instance of the aggrieved party and not automatically 'void'.[1086] This approach has not been taken by Indian courts. The Supreme Court has been quite categorical in its Ayyasamy ruling, where it held that bribery/corruption would render the disputes non-arbitrable.[1087]

One of the reasons for leaving jurisdiction with courts is the need for transparency and accountability. Parties, in order to avoid penalty or public retribution, may best want to leave the skeletons (of corruption) in the closet.[1088] The confidential nature of arbitral proceedings may be attractive rather than the glaring spotlight of court proceedings. While this may be the choice of the parties, it is in the interest of the general public (and public policy would probably demand) that such corruption comes to light and is dealt with publicly. This is

---

1083 ICC Award No. 1110 of 1963 (n 62).

1084 'Transparency International – Corruption Perceptions Index 2020' <https://www.transparency.org/en/cpi/2020/index/nzl> accessed 26 April 2021.

1085 See *supra*, Chapter 4(III)1b.

1086 Chinmayee Pendse and Prakruti Joshi, '"To Be Or Not To Be"- The Conundrum of Arbitrability of Corruption and Subsequent Enforcement' (2017) 9 The Law Review, Government Law College 23, 34 et seq.

1087 A Ayyasamy v A Paramasivam & Ors (n 234) para 9.

1088 For a comprehensive elaboration on this tendency and its impact on arbitral tribunals see, Inan Uluc, 'Corruption in International Arbitration' (SJD, Penn State University 2016) 245 et seq.

where providing jurisdiction to courts in case of allegations of corruption in the underlying contract could prove beneficial.

Another justification for leaving the jurisdiction to courts is that arbitral tribunals are often reluctant to address these matters *sua sponte.*[1089] Indeed tribunals are in a difficult, almost catch 22 situation. Even if arbitrators want to address the issue of corruption not raised by the parties, they may feel hesitant to do so for fear of courts later refusing enforcement on the grounds of the tribunal having acted *ultra petita.*[1090] This may lead to the situation where the allegations of corruption, if not raised by the parties, are left unaddressed during the proceedings, even if the potential corruption is otherwise public knowledge. While justice *may be done* between the parties, it may not be *seen to be done* by the public.[1091] This would further undermine the faith of the public in arbitration as a dispute settlement mechanism.

Despite the arguments raised above, in most arbitration-friendly jurisdictions, the approach of denying arbitral tribunals with jurisdiction is an outlier. The aforementioned early approach has given way to a much more arbitration-friendly approach, with some courts holding that the arbitrator would retain jurisdiction even in cases where the main contract is not valid.[1092] Pavic has argued that the discretion of arbitrators to make a ruling is not in any way diminished even where there are claims of corruption.[1093] According to this line of reasoning, if the arbitral tribunal continues with the proceedings and renders an award, despite allegations of fraud or corruption in the underlying contract, such an award would be enforceable. The only pre-condition being that the tribunal has addressed the concerns regarding corruption.[1094] If this condition is met,

1089 See Domitille Baizeau and Tessa Hayes, 'The Arbitral Tribunal's Duty and Power to Address Corruption Sua Sponte', in Menaker (n 811) 227.

1090 Yoanna Schuch (n 527) 55.

1091 For an elaboration on the need for justice seen to be done in the context of arbitration see, Vanessa Naish and Elizabeth Kantor, 'Privacy and Confidentiality of Arbitration-Related Court Proceedings: A Culture Clash' (*Thomson Reuters – Practical Law Arbitration Blog*, 2022) <http://arbitrationblog.practicallaw.com/privacy-and-confidentiality-of-arbitration-related-court-proceedings-a-culture-clash/> accessed 7 August 2022.

1092 Harbour Assurance Co (Uk) Ltd v Kansa General International Insurance Co Ltd (1993) 3 WLR 42 (Court of Appeal).

1093 Vladimir Pavić (n 508).

1094 Michael Hwang and Kevin Lim, 'Corruption in Arbitration – Law and Reality' (2012) 8 Asian International Arbitration Journal 1, para 15.

the courts should, as a general rule, not give parties the chance to wriggle their way out of arbitration using a ground that could have been addressed by the tribunal. Even Paulsson has argued that there is no reason to think that arbitrators are any less capable than judges in addressing allegations of illegality.[1095] This would certainly include allegations of corruption that are properly raised by the parties during the proceedings. Indeed, notably, as can be seen in the *World Duty Free* case,[1096] arbitrators themselves oftentimes take a strict view of corruption and refuse to enforce claims based on tainted contracts, instead holding them unenforceable.[1097]

There, however, could be rare exceptions where a party does raise such concerns of corruption during the arbitral proceedings, but they are ignored or not sufficiently addressed adequately by the tribunal.[1098] Although this is a cause for serious concern, it does not necessarily warrant denying the tribunal of its jurisdiction. Instead, in such situations, the second look doctrine could be used by national courts to justify intervening at a later stage if it finds fundamental lapses in the way the arbitral proceedings were conducted.[1099]

(2) *Where fraud is the raison d'être for entering into the underlying contract*

Just like corruption, equally abhorrent are contracts vitiated by fraud. Fraud has been described as encompassing deceptive acts perpetrated for gain.[1100] Fraud is criminalized in several jurisdictions, and conspiracy to defraud is considered an offence in common law.[1101] It is unsurprising, therefore, that the question of arbitrability of disputes where the underlying contract is vitiated by fraud also crops up often. The approach to this question has varied across jurisdictions. In the United States, the arbitration-friendly approach can be seen in *Prima Paint,*

1095 See generally, Paulsson (n 9).

1096 *World Duty Free v The Republic of Kenya* (2006) ICSID Case No Arb007 (ICSID Award).

1097 ibid.

1098 John Branson and Raúl Manon, 'Why Tribunals Should Not Ignore "Red Flags" of Corruption' (*Global Arbitration Review*, 12 August 2020) <https://globalarbitrationreview.com/article/why-tribunals-should-not-ignore-red-flags-of-corruption> accessed 7 August 2022.

1099 See Chapter 4(III)1b.

1100 Michael D. Akers and Jodi L. Gissel, 'What Is Fraud and Who Is Responsible?' (2006) 7 Journal of Forensic Accounting 247, 248.

1101 Daniel Greenberg (n 488) para 13.

where the U. S. Supreme Court relied on the doctrine of separability to uphold arbitrability of the dispute even where the underlying contract is vitiated by fraud.[1102] In contrast, a completely different approach was taken by the South African Supreme Court in *Namasthethu,* where the court held that the arbitration agreement would not survive where the underlying contract was tainted by fraud.[1103] The reasoning was that fraud would unravel everything.

In the Indian context, as the IAA does not provide any guidance with regard to the arbitrability of fraud, courts have had a great deal of flexibility in charting their path. Historically, Indian courts relied on early English jurisprudence to justify their reluctance *vis-à-vis* the arbitrability of fraud.[1104] In time, however, English jurisprudence has acknowledged the arbitrability of disputes affected by fraud.[1105] The position of arbitrability of fraud under Indian law diverged from the English approach and became much more nuanced. The Supreme Court in *Abdul Kadir* held that where there are serious allegations of fraud – if the party against whom allegations are made desires, the proceedings would be conducted in open court rather via arbitration.[1106] Since this ruling, the discourse regarding the arbitrability of fraud in the Indian context has primarily revolved around the nature and seriousness of the fraud.

More recently, in *Ayyasamy*, the Indian Supreme Court has acknowledged that allegations of 'fraud simplicitor' can be dealt with by the arbitral tribunal.[1107] However, where there are allegations of 'serious fraud' in the underlying contract, such cases are not arbitrable in India.[1108] In order to reduce the chances of misuse, the court has defined serious fraud very narrowly. In *Rashid Raza*, the Supreme Court laid down two tests for determining arbitrability.[1109] Firstly,

---

1102 Prima Paint Corp v Flood & Conklin Manufacturing Co (1967) 388 US 395 (US Supreme Court).

1103 *Namasthethu Electrical (Pty) Ltd v City of Cape Town and Another* (2020) ZASCA 74 (The Supreme Court of Appeal of South Africa) [31–32].

1104 Shivam Singh, 'Arbitrability of Fraud: Analysing India's Problematic Jurisprudence' (2019) 8 Indian Journal of Arbitration Law 141.

1105 Vikrant Narayan Vasudeva, 'The Arbitrability of Fraud Claims' (2016) 82 Arbitration: The International Journal of Arbitration, Mediation and Dispute Management (Chartered Institute of Arbitrators, Sweet & Maxwell) 399, 401.

1106 Abdul Kadir Shamsuddin Bubere v Madhav Prabhakar Oak (1961) 1962 AIR 406 (Supreme Court of India).

1107 A Ayyasamy v A Paramasivam & Ors (n 234) para 18.

1108 Parul Kumar, 'Is Fraud Arbitrable? Examining the Problematic Indian Discourse' (2017) 33 Arbitration International 249 et seq.

1109 *Rashid Raza v Sadif Akhtar* (2019) Civ Appeal No 7005 (Supreme Court of India).

it observed that fraud would only render the dispute non-arbitrable if the fraud in the contract vitiated the arbitration agreement itself, rendering it void. The second test was where questions impacting the public domain necessitated a hearing by a court. In *Avitel,* the Supreme court went even further by stating that where the facts of the case warrant initiating of both civil and criminal proceedings – the mere fact that criminal proceedings are initiated regarding the subject matter would not render the dispute non-arbitrable.[1110]

It is therefore clear that in the Indian context, courts are minded towards upholding the arbitrability of disputes even if case the underlying contract is vitiated by fraud unless the consequences are so egregious as to vitiate the fundamental principles of the legal system itself.

(ii) Where there is illegality in the performance of contractual obligations

The arguments given above for leaving the jurisdiction to the courts do not necessarily apply in the second situation, i.e., where the contract does not have an illegal aim, but there is illegality in performance by one of the parties or its agents.

The preponderant approach to determining jurisdiction is that as the parties have freely chosen arbitration, party autonomy requires all questions regarding the underlying contract, including the performance of obligations arising thereof, to be decided by the arbitral tribunal and not the courts.[1111] Furthermore, the principle of Kompetenz-Kompetenz enshrined in section 16 of the IAA provides the tribunal with the sole authority to determine if it has jurisdiction and power to decide on a particular dispute.[1112] The Indian Supreme Court has held this principle to mean that the tribunal can determine jurisdiction even in case the validity of the underlying contract is in question.[1113] This, in effect, means that any dispute, by default, would first have to be raised before the tribunal. Such an approach has also been taken by the U. S. Supreme Court in Mitsubishi Motor Corp, where in dealing with allegations of illegality (restraint of trade), the Court

---

1110 *Avitel Post Studios Ltd & Ors v HSBC PI Holdings (Mauritius) Ltd* (2020) Civ Appeal No 5158 2016 (Supreme Court of India) [16].

1111 For an elaboration on balancing party autonomy and its limits see, David A. R. Williams and Anna Kirk, 'Balancing Party Autonomy, Jurisdiction and the Integrity of Arbitration: Where to Draw the Line' in, Kaplan and Moser (n 7) 88 et seq.

1112 Phillip Landolt, 'The Inconvenience of Principle: Separability and Kompetenz-Kompetenz' (2013) 30 Journal of International Arbitration, Kluwer Law International 513.

1113 Shin-Etsu Chemical CoLtd v Aksh Optifibre Ltd & Anr (2005) 7 SCC 234 (Supreme Court of India).

held that the mere existence of anti-trust concerns would not preclude the arbitral tribunal from having jurisdiction.[1114]

While tribunals have the power to determine their jurisdiction, they are not bound to accept jurisdiction and enforce contractual obligations in every situation. In order to ensure future enforceability of the award, tribunals are expected to keep public policy considerations in mind if the contract sought to breach mandatory law or was for an illegal purpose.[1115] National courts should exercise restraint and only be able to exercise jurisdiction over the dispute if the arbitral tribunal decides that it lacks jurisdiction. This is because, as astutely pointed out by Paulsson, a party should not lose the right to arbitrate its claim against a counterparty merely because the counterparty has committed an illegal act, especially if the party was unaware of the fact.[1116]

For instance, where Party A entered into a contract with Party B for the supply of sustainable chocolate and makes advance payment in consideration. Suppose Party B violates fundamental legal norms or moral principles during the production of the chocolate by using child labour/slave labour or destroying protected rainforests. In case the chocolate does not meet the quality standards, Party A should not be precluded from arbitrating the claim simply because Party B has breached public policy by illegalities in the manufacturing process. Paulsson has argued that allowing a party engaging in illegal activity to escape arbitration due to their own violation of public policy would benefit parties who undertake illegal activities and allow it to avoid liability because of its own wrongdoing.[1117] In the example above, it could be argued that there is no real loss as the aggrieved party would still be able to get a fair hearing before domestic courts. This, however, ignores the fact that the aggrieved party would still be penalized as it may not prefer court litigation for numerous reasons including, incessant delays, lack of confidentiality, unfamiliar procedure etc.

Furthermore, there is no harm in arbitral tribunal conducting proceedings and rendering an award on commercial rights and obligations of the parties. Such arbitral proceedings do not have a res judicata effect on courts or other enforcement authorities in criminal prosecutions, anti-trust or other proceedings that can take place parallelly or subsequent to the arbitration proceedings.[1118]

1114 Mitsubishi v. Soler Chrysler-Plymouth (n 353) 3350 et sec.
1115 Paulsson (n 9) 99.
1116 ibid 137.
1117 ibid 137.
1118 ibid 141.

When rejecting a challenge to an award on the grounds of non-arbitrability due to criminal wrongdoing, the Indian Supreme Court has previously acknowledged that Indian law provides for a 'dual procedure' where proceedings can be brought both under criminal law and separately under contract law.[1119] This ensures that parties are bound by their contractual terms while also being held to account for any illegal behavior.

There are some situations, however, where Indian law does not provide exclusive power to the arbitral tribunal. The tribunal may be denied jurisdiction, for instance, where the allegations of fraud are of such a serious and complex nature that they amount to criminal wrongdoing, and an examination of evidence by a court is necessary.[1120] In making its determination as to whether the tribunal lacks jurisdiction, the Indian Supreme Court has laid down a two-pronged test. It will first look at whether the illegality vitiated the entire contract, including the agreement to arbitrate; secondly, it will evaluate whether the illegality affected only the rights of the parties or if it impacted the interest of the public at large.[1121] By inference, Indian courts will intervene only where the entire contract including the arbitration agreement is vitiated, or if the risk of harm to the public is so grave as to override private interest.

2. Where the subject matter is not arbitrable due to public policy considerations

There are compelling arguments for limiting challenges of arbitral awards before national courts on the grounds of subject-matter non-arbitrability. Firstly, parties should not be able to approach courts regarding the subject matter non-arbitrability when the challenge can be brought before the arbitrator.[1122] Such a challenge would delay enforcement and would come in the way of the finality of the award. Secondly, by choosing arbitration, parties expect disputes to be resolved by the arbitral tribunal,[1123] and have willingly given up their right to relook the underlying subject matter in court.

1119 Hindustan Petroleum Corpn Ltd vs M/S Pinkcity Midway Petroleums (2003) 6 SCC 503 (Supreme Court of India) [20].

1120 A Ayyasamy v A Paramasivam & Ors (n 234) para 13.

1121 Rashid Raza v Sadif Akhtar (n 1109).

1122 Tony Cole and Pietro Ortolani, *Understanding International Arbitration* (Routledge, an imprint of the Taylor & Francis Group 2020) para 4.4.

1123 Justin Williams, Hamish Lal, and Richard Hornshaw, 'Arbitration Procedures and Practice in the UK (England and Wales): Overview' (2022) Thomson Reuters Practical Law 1, 4 et seq.

Despite these arguments, as shown above, there are some valid objections to this approach of leaving the determination of violation of public policy in the underlying contract solely with the arbitrators. The situation differs, for instance, when the subject matter itself is not arbitrable. Lawmakers, as a matter of public policy, are entitled to leave some matters exclusively for determination by a public forum and to preclude certain matters from arbitration.[1124] This would exclude arbitral tribunals from exercising jurisdiction. Arbitrators who ignore these restrictions walk on shaky ground.

Below we will look at the current jurisprudence, which gives national courts the jurisdiction to hear such disputes. We will then evaluate if there is a need for rethinking this approach.

(a) Courts as the competent authority to hear non-arbitrable disputes

In most jurisdictions, there are certain matters, which are considered as not arbitrable. Bermann has described this as the 'gateway problem' of arbitrability.[1125] Although arbitrability is a gateway issue, which usually needs to be decided either by the arbitral tribunal or courts at the seat, even courts at the place of enforcement may refuse to enforce awards if the subject matter of the dispute/underlying contract is not arbitrable. This could be because it deals with an important public law issue that affects society at large and is therefore reserved as a matter of public policy exclusively to national courts of the given jurisdiction.

The question of *arbitrability* and *public policy* are very much intertwined. Both concepts seek to preserve a national courts ability to intervene when public interest so necessitates.[1126] Some matters are simply not capable of being resolved through arbitration, as disputes involving, for instance, child custody, matrimonial disputes, anti-trust law, bankruptcy, intellectual property, bribery, restraint of trade or foreign exchange are in some countries thought to be too important

---

1124 Vidya Drolia Ors v. Durga Trading Corporation (n 515) para 19.

1125 George A. Bermann, 'The "Gateway" Problem in International Commercial Arbitration' 37 Yale Journal of International Law 2 <https://cpb-us-w2.wpmucdn.com/campuspress.yale.edu/dist/8/1581/files/2016/09/37-1-bermann-the-gateway-problem-1vu7rwu.pdf> accessed 12 November 2018.

1126 See, Winnie Jo-Mei Ma and Lawrence Boo, 'Autonomous Arbitrability? Whose Autonomy? Whose Arbitrability?', in Franco Ferrari and Friedrich Rosenfeld (eds), *Autonomous Versus Domestic Concepts under the New York Convention*, vol 61 (Wolters Kluwer, International Arbitration Law Library 2021) para 12.03.

to be left to be settled privately.[1127] The Indian Supreme Court has gone so far as to say that the state has a monopoly in resolving some of these categories of disputes.[1128] Even in the United States, the drafters of the NY arbitration statute, which was a precursor to the FAA, did not intend arbitral tribunals to have jurisdiction over statutory claims.[1129]

What matters are specifically considered non-arbitrable differs from country to country, and there is no uniform standard applicable. Broadly speaking, it can be observed that commercial disputes are usually arbitrable in most jurisdictions,[1130] whereas limits are oftentimes placed on the arbitrability of non-commercial subject matters that have a public law element.

Some countries specifically list out non-arbitrable matters in their arbitration statute. For instance, Art. 12 of the Law on Commercial Arbitration in Lithuania provides that administrative, family, patent, employment or consumer contracts are not arbitrable. Indian law conspicuously does not explicitly list out the kinds of disputes considered non-arbitrable or even state the principles based on which the determination must be made, but rather left this for the courts to decide.[1131] Although Indian courts have been given discretion, they cannot make their determination arbitrarily. They need to make their determination *ex visceribus actus*,[1132] the maxim expounded by Lord Coke in the *Lincoln College* case of 1595,[1133] meaning within the 'bowels' or 'four corners' of the statute.[1134]

Where a tribunal proceeds with hearing the dispute and renders an award despite the subject matter not being arbitrable, a claim may be brought by the aggrieved party before the court at the seat of arbitration. If the court finds the

---

1127 See Karl-Heinz Böckstiegel, Public Policy and Arbitrability in Sanders (n 421) 194 et seq.

1128 Vidya Drolia Ors v. Durga Trading Corporation (n 515) para 32.

1129 Sarah E. Belton and F. Paul Bland, Jr., 'How the Arbitration-at-All Costs Regime Ignores and Distorts Settled Law' (2014) 35 Berkeley Journal of Employment and Labor Law 135, 137.

1130 Joseph Mante, 'Arbitrability and Public Policy: An African Perspective' (2017) 33 Arbitration International 275, 294.

1131 Vidya Drolia Ors v. Durga Trading Corporation (n 515) para 18.

1132 ibid.

1133 Chamberlain v Lincoln College, Oxford (1595) 3 Co Rep 58b.

1134 George Devenish, 'Interpretation "From within the Bowels of the Act" – An Essential Methodology for Unqualified Contextual Interpretation' (1989) 106 South African Law Journal 68, 69.

claim justified, it will be able to set aside the award. This is envisioned by Article 34(2)b of the UNCITRAL Model Law and section 34(2)b of the IAA.

At first glance, this may seem surprising in the Indian context, as there is jurisprudence in India to the effect that arbitral tribunals are competent in all civil and commercial disputes, which a civil court would have been competent to decide upon.[1135] However, in certain situations, not just arbitral tribunals, even ordinary civil courts in India are not considered competent. Rather the competence would lie with special courts. For instance, section 61 of the Indian Competition Act 2002 expressly bars subordinate civil courts from hearing competition-related disputes and vests exclusive jurisdiction with the National Company Law Appellate Tribunal. The underlying reason is to protect the weaker party, e.g., the small business or the consumer. It is also to ensure that private contracts could not be a means for persons to escape from a state's public policy.[1136] The Indian Supreme Court has laid down a general rule to determine arbitrability, i.e., when the subject matter is a dispute regards rights *in rem*, this would not be arbitrable, whereas disputes regarding rights *in personam* would be arbitrable.[1137]

A good illustration would be the *Booz Allen* decision where the Indian Supreme Court held that arbitral tribunal was not the appropriate forum to decide on a dispute relating to a mortgage claim, because according to Indian law, this would exclusively fall in the domain of national courts.[1138] It is difficult to imagine the judges who made this ruling enforcing an award arising from such a mortgage. This is also true for consumer disputes, which would not be subject to arbitration in India because it is reserved for special public tribunals.[1139]

This approach has also been taken in China with regard to disputes where there are anti-trust concerns. The Supreme People's Court, in its *Huili* decision, held that even if there is an arbitration clause, deciding on whether there is a monopolistic agreement is a matter of public interest, and designated courts and not arbitral tribunals would therefore have jurisdiction.[1140]

The arbitrability of anti-trust claims has been a matter of controversy not only in China but internationally. Given the importance of ensuring free and

1135 A Ayyasamy v A Paramasivam & Ors (n 234) para 29.
1136 Ghodoosi (n 15) 9.
1137 Vidya Drolia Ors v. Durga Trading Corporation (n 515) para 21.
1138 Booz Allen and Hamilton Inc. v. SBI Home Finance Limited (n 602).
1139 *Aftab Singh and Ors v Emaar MGF Land Limited and Ors* (2017) CPJ270 (National Consumer Disputes Rederessal Commission).
1140 *Shell China Co Ltd v Huili Hohhot Co, Ltd* (2019) Zhi Min Xia Zhong No 47 (Supreme People's Court China).

fair competition and that it is a matter of public policy in some states, there are varying opinions regarding whether arbitrators can hear such disputes or whether such matters be left solely to the determination of national courts.

Competition and arbitration law have historically not been associated with one another. As described by Geradin, they have rather 'evolved in parallel'.[1141] In fact, arbitrating of competition-related matters is somewhat of a new development.[1142] This is because, at least in the past, there existed a belief that such disputes were not arbitrable.[1143] In many jurisdictions, this view has now given way to a more benign acceptance of arbitrability of competition law matters.[1144]

The Indian Supreme Court has not yet definitively answered the question as to whether competition law matters are arbitrable. However, its previous jurisprudence has shown that cases that may involve a breach of competition law would fall under the public policy exception and therefore not be arbitrable. The apex court in *Booz Allen* decision laid down a general rule that disputes pertaining to rights '*in personam*' are arbitrable, and those pertaining to rights affecting the '*world at large*' are not arbitrable and have to be dealt with by courts.[1145] It appears, therefore, that competition law matters are not arbitrable in India. This view is also supported by the literature.[1146] There is a lack of clarity, and the position can only be settled by a definitive ruling of the Supreme Court. However, in a case concerning abusive practices by the dominant government railway company in a public-private partnership agreement, the Delhi High Court has ruled that arbitral tribunals would not have the competence to rule on cases concerning abuse of dominant position.[1147]

It could be questioned if the aforementioned approach adopted by Indian courts is the most arbitration-friendly. The French approach could be considered more respectful of party autonomy. Under this view, equating arbitral tribunals to civil courts in the context of determining jurisdiction would be a false equation. Simply because ordinary civil courts lack jurisdiction should not automatically

---

1141 Damien Geradin (n 581) 134.

1142 See, Jean-Claude Najar, Arbitrating Competition Law: The User's Perspective in Blanke and Landolt (n 8) 120.

1143 Damien Geradin (n 581) 134.

1144 Luca G. Radicati di Brozolo, 'Arbitration and Competition Law: The Position of the Courts and of Arbitrators' (2014) 27 Arbitration International 1, 1.

1145 Booz Allen and Hamilton Inc. v. SBI Home Finance Limited (n 602) para 23.

1146 Kronke and Nacimiento (n 111) 357.

1147 Union of India Vs Competition Commission of India and Ors AIR 2012 Delhi 66 (High Court of Delhi) [16].

lead one to the conclusion that arbitral tribunals also lack jurisdiction. Arbitral tribunals do not get involved in the tug of war between different national courts as arbitration itself is, after all, an alternative to the entire court system.

While Indian courts have not yet definitively ruled on the arbitrability or public policy considerations involved in dealing with anti-trust claims, it may be possible to foresee the approach of the Indian Supreme Court, were such a claim to come before it. As demonstrated earlier in this thesis, the Supreme Court has, in its arbitration jurisprudence, demonstrated a willingness to be influenced by the dominant prevailing legal trends in other jurisdictions.[1148] It would be possible for Indian courts to take the approach of the U. S. Supreme Court in the *Mitsubishi* ruling, where the court held that arbitration clauses must be given effect in anti-trust matters, subject to the second look doctrine.[1149] According to the second look doctrine, the approach generally followed is that competition claims are arbitrable but can later be looked into by courts at the enforcement stage, where they could refuse enforcement on public policy grounds.[1150]

(b) Should arbitral tribunals retain jurisdiction anyway?

While most jurisdictions consider certain categories of disputes to be beyond the jurisdiction of arbitral tribunals as a matter of public policy, i.e., (non-arbitrable), several experts have argued for a more liberal approach towards arbitrability. Jan Paulsson argues that arbitration would not be attractive anymore if parties were allowed to approach courts to constantly challenge the access to arbitration.[1151] Matthias Lehmann has similarly argued for a transnational approach towards expanding arbitrability.[1152] Such a transnational approach would lead to more harmonization and potentially reduce the scope for judicial intervention. Below we will look at whether there is a need for re-evaluation of the current approach towards arbitrability.

(i) A case for reassessing what is considered non-arbitrable

There exists a trend for states over time to reduce the number of disputes considered as non-arbitrable.[1153] While the move towards greater arbitrability is felt

1148 See Chapter 2(IV)4.
1149 Mitsubishi v. Soler Chrysler-Plymouth (n 353) 3355.
1150 Kronke and Nacimiento (n 111) 356.
1151 Paulsson (n 9) 51.
1152 Matthias Lehmann (n 982).
1153 Paulsson (n 9) 117.

transnationally,[1154] it has been seen to a greater extent in some jurisdictions, such as the United States, where competition and consumer disputes which were previously left to the courts, are now considered arbitrable, and to a lesser extent in others, e.g., India, where these disputes are considered non-arbitrable. Even intellectual property (IP) related disputes are also considered arbitrable in several jurisdictions, including Spain and Portugal.[1155] Paulsson has attributed this change in approach to the acknowledgment that lawmakers initially carved out unnecessarily broad exceptions to arbitrability instead of using targeted narrow limitations.[1156]

A key reason for reducing limits on arbitrability is the growing importance given to freedom of contract.[1157] Scholars have considered freedom of contract to be fundamental to arbitration, and any exercise of judicial authority should only be in the enforcement stage.[1158] There is good reason for such a view. After all, one may justifiably ask, why should parties that willingly agreed to arbitrate a future dispute be able to wriggle out of their contractual obligations when the obligations do not suit them, on the guise of the subject matter being not arbitrable? Parties should be bound by the consequence of their freely made contractual choices.

Another reason for this shift are the numerous benefits of arbitrating disputes, rather than jealously restricting them for national courts under the garb of public policy. These benefits can be seen clearly in the context of IP disputes which by its nature requires cross border protection and enforcement. Leaving the arbitral tribunal as the competent authority can solve the problem of parallel proceedings before courts in different jurisdictions, chances of national bias in an expeditious manner *vis-à-vis* state courts.[1159]

Even in case of consumer disputes, arbitration could be beneficial in case of cross border transactions. This is especially the case in business to consumer

---

1154 Matthias Lehmann (n 982).

1155 Dario Moura Vicente, 'Arbitrability of Intellectual Property Disputes: A Comparative Survey' (2015) 31 Arbitration International 151.

1156 Paulsson (n 9) 118.

1157 See, Karim A. Youssef, 'The Death of Inarbitrability', in Loukas A. Mistelis and Stavros L. Brekoulakis (eds), *Arbitrability: International & Comparative Perspectives* (Kluwer Law International 2009) paras 3–13.

1158 Thomas E. Carbonneau, 'The Exercise of Contract Freedom in the Making of Arbitration Agreements' (2003) 36 Vanderbilt Joural of Transnational Law 1189, 1192 et seq.

1159 Dario Moura Vicente (n 1155).

(B2C) e-commerce.[1160] It is easier for arbitration and conciliation proceedings to be flexible and go online to meet the needs of an unforeseeable event such as the Covid-19 pandemic, where there are significant constraints to free movement of people and litigants access to courts due to travel restrictions, physical lock-downs and restricted access to public transport. In this hypothetical example, a consumer from India, who, for instance, buys a ventilator from China, would not have the difficulty of finding the appropriate forum to get a remedy in case the goods turn out to be defective or not meeting contractual requirements. The consumer would also not need to worry about potential bias as ODR already provides a neutral forum vis-à-vis national courts. Arbitration or ODR could provide a relatively cheap and acceptable solution for international commerce. This has been recognised not just in the US but also in the EU by way of the ODR regulation, which provides a platform for online dispute resolution with the help of a neutral dispute resolution body listed out on the ODR platform.[1161] In India too, the central governments think tank report has expounded the benefits of ODR as a cost effective and efficient way of reducing the burden of courts,[1162] and resolving consumer disputes.[1163]

Another reason for vesting jurisdiction with national courts is the feeling that judges are more qualified to deal with certain matters encompassing public law.[1164] This is because of the fear that arbitrators may misapply the law and give effect to illegal agreements. Such worries may be unfounded. Jan Paulsson has rightly pointed out that the odds of arbitrators giving effect to illegal agreements are extremely low due to concern for preserving their professional reputation.[1165] Arbitrators would not want to have courts refuse enforcement of their awards at a later stage. Furthermore, he has shown that there is a lack of data showing that arbitrators are more likely to misapply the law.[1166]

1160 Maria José Schmidt-Kessen, Rafaela Nogueira, and Cantero Gamito Marta, 'Success or Failure? – Effectiveness of Consumer ODR Platforms in Brazil and in the EU' (2020) 43 Journal of Consumer Policy volume 659, 660.

1161 Regulation (EU) No 524/2013 on online dispute resolution for consumer disputes 2013 (OJ L 165).

1162 Justice (Retd.) A. K. Sikri, 'Designing the Future of Dispute Resolution: The ODR Policy Plan for India' (NITI Aayog Expert Committee on ODR 2021) 13.

1163 ibid 40.

1164 Paul R. Hays, *Labor Arbitration a Dissenting View* (Yale Unversity Press 1966) 53–58.

1165 Paulsson (n 9) 120.

1166 ibid 119.

Another potential argument is that the complexities of hearing certain kinds of disputes could be effectively dealt with only by courts. This lack of trust in the capability of arbitrators can be seen in the early Indian Supreme *Radhakrishnan* ruling, where it was observed that 'complicated matters involving the various questions and issues raised' are best addressed by courts.[1167] Here also, one can argue that the court erred in its judgment. There are numerous ways for vetting potential arbitrators to ensure they have the requisite knowledge, competence and qualifications required to decide even complex and technical disputes. Indeed, the possibility of choosing specialists is one reason why parties decide on choosing arbitration in the first place.[1168] While judges have to generally decide on a broad range of topics, arbitrators can be sourced from a particular background, are able to specialize in a given area and are generally known for their commercial competence.[1169] Besides, arbitral institutions can ensure checks and balances are in place for only qualified and competent arbitrators to be appointed. Indeed, the Supreme Court in *Indo Unique* has itself acknowledged that the *Radhakrishnan* decision is based on outdated views.[1170] In doing so, the court has taken the same approach as the U. S. Supreme Court in *Mitsubishi Motor Corp*, where it was held that the complex nature of anti-trust disputes should not lead to the arbitral tribunal being denied jurisdiction.[1171]

The above arguments show that there is a need for re-evaluating the scope of what public policy precludes in terms of arbitrability. Respecting party autonomy is fundamental to the future of arbitration. Judges should exercise caution when placing limits to subject-matter arbitrability of disputes that are not found in the statute.[1172]

(ii) Reckoning with reality – why some disputes are best left for courts

Despite the arguments made above, there is a reason why both international instruments and national laws in almost every jurisdiction preclude arbitration of certain categories of disputes. Furthermore, as it is difficult for the lawmaker

1167 *N Radhakrishnan v Maestro Engineers and Ors* (2009) 2010 1 SCC 72 (Supreme Court of India) [11].

1168 *United Steelworkers v American Mfg Co* (1960) 363 US 564 (US Supreme Court) 574.

1169 Born (n 1041) 77–79.

1170 N.N. Global Mercantile Pvt. Ltd. Vs. Indo Unique Flame Ltd. and Ors. (n 1027) para 8.4.

1171 Mitsubishi v. Soler Chrysler-Plymouth (n 353) 3348.

1172 Paulsson (n 9) 122.

to elaborate on every single category in the statute, national courts play an important role in exercising their discretion in determining the bounds of arbitrability. This is especially true in common law jurisdictions.

The key benefit of arbitration *vis-à-vis* litigation, i.e., it enables parties to appoint specialist arbitrators who are experts in a particular field, may also be its main weakness. Arbitrators are often selected as they are experts having lots of experience in a particular area. While some arbitrators have a strong legal background, this is not necessarily always the case. Indeed, arbitrators may not be lawyers but rather have industry expertise.[1173] Fox & Gruhn have pointed out that sometimes arbitrators, given their specialized expertise and commercial background, may not have the experience or knowledge of a judge in dealing with matters concerning public policy that affect society at large.[1174] This risk is exacerbated where there is a sole-arbitrator having a non-legal background but rather drawn from industry. The Indian Supreme Court has echoed these concerns by pointing out the main ground for certain disputes being not arbitrable. Arbitral tribunals being private bodies rather than public authorities, are unable to act judicially and bind those who are not parties to the dispute.[1175] The court has pointed out that where the decision must have *erga omnes* effect (towards all), determination of the dispute by an arbitral tribunal would not be appropriate.[1176] It is therefore understandable that the court would prefer that determination of rights *in rem* are excluded from the tribunal's jurisdiction.

Lehmann has pointed out that while tribunals are competent to hear most disputes – an exception would be disputes requiring centralized resolution or a central authority (the use of state power for resolution).[1177] An example would be disputes regarding the registration of IP rights. As they create monopoly rights *vis-à-vis* the public, they are often reserved for exclusive determination by national courts.[1178] The same arguments could be raised for bankruptcy cases, insolvency proceedings, anti-trust disputes etc., which the Indian Supreme Court

1173 James E. Meason and Alison G. Smith, 'Non-Lawyers in International Commercial Arbitration: Gathering Splinters on the Bench' (1991) 12 Northwestern Journal of International Law & Business 24, 46.

1174 Carie Fox and Brian Gruhn, 'Toward a Principled Public Policy Standard: Judicial Review of Arbitrators' Decisions' (1989) 3 Detroit College of Law Review 863, 868.

1175 Vidya Drolia Ors v. Durga Trading Corporation (n 515) para 31.

1176 ibid.

1177 Matthias Lehmann (n 982) 772.

1178 Dario Moura Vicente (n 1155) 152.

has held to be not arbitrable as a matter of public policy.[1179] It goes without saying that criminal proceedings are also not arbitrable for the same reasons. Even disputes which would be better served via collective litigation have been held to be within the exclusive ambit of Indian courts and not arbitrable.[1180] Giving arbitrators the power to decide on such disputes can be counterproductive and may be harmful to the growth of arbitration itself. The Indian Supreme Court was drawing a line in the sand when it cogently pointed out that the goals of arbitration of ensuring a 'just, fair and effective' process would be compromised if the 'rights and liabilities' of those not party to the agreement 'are affected.'[1181]

Furthermore, while freedom of contract is essential, public policy often requires the protection of minorities and weaker parties. This is why mandatory arbitration has proven so controversial in may jurisdictions. In Germany, the *Bundesverfassungsgericht* (Federal constitutional court) annulled a mandatory arbitration clause in its *Pechstein* ruling and held that mandatory arbitration clauses in the context of the Court of Arbitration of Sport, would go against the right enshrined in the German constitution of *Justizgewährungsanspruch* (access to justice).[1182] The debate regarding mandatory arbitration clauses is most apparent in consumer disputes. As a general rule, mandatory arbitration in consumer disputes is prohibited in several jurisdictions (including India), a notable exception being the United States, where this is permitted by the *AT&T* ruling.[1183]

Arguments against consumer arbitration focus on the fact that most consumers are in a weaker bargaining position and are unable to negotiate the standard form agreements they enter into. Also, they often are unaware that they have entered into the arbitration agreement.[1184] This enables big companies to draft clauses that serve their interests best. In case a dispute does arise, consumers find themselves unwittingly forced into expensive procedures that they did not initially anticipate without access to their local courts. This could come in the way of the right to a fair hearing. For instance, Adam Samuel has given

---

1179 A Ayyasamy v A Paramasivam & Ors (n 234) para 9.

1180 Vidya Drolia Ors v. Durga Trading Corporation (n 515) para 31.

1181 ibid.

1182 Beschluss der 2 Kammer des Ersten Senats vom 03 Juni 2022 (2022) 1 BvR 210316 (Bundesverfassungsgericht).

1183 *AT&T Mobility LLC v Conception* (2011) 563 US 333 (United States Supreme Court).

1184 Mindy R. Hollander, 'Overcoming the Achilles' Heel of Consumer Protection: Limiting Mandatory Arbitration Clauses in Consumer Contracts' (2017) 46 Hofstra Law Review 363, 363.

the example of how by forcing arbitration in standard form contracts, a party that is in a significantly stronger economic position can compel expensive arbitration that is unaffordable to the weaker party and also simultaneously thereby preclude the weaker party from accessing state courts.[1185] Furthermore, scholars have pointed out that in consumer arbitration, large corporations as repeat players can wield tremendous pressure that may influence the behavior of the arbitral tribunal in their favor.[1186] Such arbitration agreements, especially with regard to consumer or employment contracts, will therefore not be enforced by courts in some jurisdictions.

Given the reasons provided above, it is not surprising that Indian law seeks to protect the interest of consumers by providing for a special statutory body in the form of the National Consumer Disputes Redressal Commission (NCDRC) for hearing consumer disputes. While this may lead to the exclusion of the jurisdiction of arbitral tribunals, this is not necessarily a bad thing. Even in the United States, the omnipresence of consumer arbitration has been widely criticized. Scholars have suggested a move away from mandatory arbitration and towards an ombudsman scheme.[1187]

One more situation where courts may be the appropriate authority for deciding on the dispute is when public safety comes into play. It is not uncommon for courts in the United States to refuse enforcement of awards which would lead to a danger to public safety, including with regard to nuclear plants, aviation etc.[1188] It could be justifiably argued that parties should not be allowed to use arbitration as a way to avoid public scrutiny with regard to agreements to do something illegal which affects public safety, i.e., sell weapons or to illegally sell vaccines in violation of export controls.

1185 Adam Samuel, 'Arbitration, Alternative Dispute Resolution Generally and the European Convention on Human Rights: An Anglo-Centric View' (2004) 21 Journal of International Arbitration 413, 414.

1186 Donna M. Bates, 'A Consumer's Dream or Pandora's Box: Is Arbitration a Viable Option for Cross-Border Consumer Disputes?' (2003) 27 Fordham International Law Journal 823, 855.

1187 Mala Sharma, 'A Fair Alternative to Unfair Arbitration: Proposing an Ombudsman Scheme for Consumer Dispute Resolution in the USA' (2020) Journal of the International Ombudsman Association 1.

1188 For further elaboration on how public safety is intertwined with public policy see, Ann C. Hodges (n 362) 120.

(iii) The way forward – finding the right balance for arbitrability

As seen above, there are numerous arguments on both sides of the spectrum. While increasing the powers of the arbitrators to hear claims that encompass public policy may have several advantages – there is a need to place limits in certain situations, for instance, to ensure that consumer interests are not thrown under the bus. The key lies in finding the right balance.

One way of doing this is to look at the intention of the legislature. The Indian Supreme Court has held that in determining the intention of the legislature, consideration must be given to whether a statute creates certain special rights/ liabilities, and creates a special forum and provides 'exclusive jurisdiction' to this forum for determining disputes covered under the statute – and thereby bar parties from taking their disputes elsewhere.[1189] If Parliament clearly intended that certain disputes are non-arbitrable, then the will of the legislature should be respected. The provisions of the law should, after all, not be subject to cherry-picking. One cannot choose to only select the pro-arbitration provisions and turn a blind eye to any limitations placed. Where there is no legal mandate, arbitrators may best be advised to decline jurisdiction or risk having their awards subsequently set aside or refused enforcement.

Sometimes, however, the will of the legislature is unclear, as the statute does not explicitly provide what disputes are considered arbitrable. In such cases, arbitrators should be cautious when overstepping the bounds of arbitrability laid down by courts, even if they disagree with them. This is because, even if arbitrators do make a determination, there is always the risk that judges may feel that such matters are too important to be left solely to private means. There is the desire that private contracts should not be a way for parties to escape public oversight on their activities. Only judges in national courts may be competent to make such a determination. It is not only courts at the seat that can intervene if an award is rendered where the subject matter is not arbitrable. Section 48(2)a of the IAA mirrors Article 36(1)(b) of the UNCITRAL Model law in providing that judges may refuse enforcement in such cases.

It is important, however, to set a balance so as not to unduly constrain party autonomy. Courts should not be allowed to go into the facts of the case under the guise of determining arbitrability. The Indian Supreme Court has tried to set a standard by providing that in determining if the subject matter is not arbitrable, courts will not conduct a 'full review' but rather only a 'primary' or 'prima-facie'

1189 Vidya Drolia Ors v. Durga Trading Corporation (n 515) paras 33, 34.

first review to weed out agreements that are manifestly not-arbitrable.[1190] This means that the courts are not supposed to make a determination of the facts.[1191] While it is true that the court made the aforementioned observations in the context of section 8 of the Arbitration Act, which mainly deals with when courts can refer parties to arbitration – it helps to show the limited view of the court when it comes to intervening in the decision of parties to arbitrate.

II. Where there are violations of public policy during the arbitral proceedings or in obtaining the award

While there are certainly justifications for conferring jurisdiction to the arbitral tribunal in case of illegality in or ancillary to the underlying contract,[1192] sometimes, a party may feel that due to a violation of public policy during the arbitral proceedings, or in obtaining the award, its basic procedural rights have not been fully respected by the arbitral tribunal. This could either be due to an illegality at the onset of the proceedings, i.e., if the tribunals finding on jurisdiction is tainted by irregularity or illegality. Another situation is where a party may feel aggrieved if there is a violation of public policy during the proceedings, e.g., the award is based on fraudulent evidence or due to a procedural irregularity – for instance, if the tribunal does not allow a party to present its case fully while giving its counterparty the right to do so.

In both the aforementioned situations, there is consensus in many jurisdictions, including India, that such a breach could potentially be grounds to set aside or refuse enforcement of an award. The Indian legislature has explicitly provided for judicial intervention in case of fraud or corruption during the proceedings in the explanatory notes to section 48(2)b of the IAA. While there is no doubt that courts are competent to hear challenges *ex-post* or after the award is rendered. In this part, we will evaluate whether, in case of illegality or violation of public policy during the arbitral proceedings, courts should also play a role *ex-ante* or before the arbitral award is actually rendered by the tribunal. Furthermore, which authority should hear and decide on claims of such illegality during the arbitral proceedings – courts or the arbitral tribunal?

1190 ibid 87.
1191 ibid.
1192 See Chapter 6(I)1.

1. In case of allegations of illegality or irregularity at the onset of the arbitral proceedings

The rules of most arbitral institutions provide that any challenge to the jurisdiction of the tribunal must be raised by the parties before the arbitral tribunal itself as soon as possible. This can be seen, for instance, under Art. 23.3 of the LCIA Arbitration Rules 2020 and Art. 6 of the ICC Rules 2021.[1193] This has also been enshrined in Art. 16 of the UNCITRAL Model Law, and Art 16 of the IAA. Such an approach seeks to ensure that the arbitral tribunal is able to remedy any defects by itself and reduce the chance of parties trying to subsequently set aside an unfavorable arbitral award on purely technical grounds.

A difficulty, however, arises if the arbitral tribunals finding on its jurisdiction is reached by way of illegality or corruption or where the tribunal accepts jurisdiction despite the subject matter being clearly non-arbitrable, or in case of a sole arbitrator, where the arbitrator is proven to be conflicted or corrupt and still refuses to recuse from the case. Even worse, there could potentially be situations where a tribunal accepts jurisdiction in a sham arbitration that is solely instituted to facilitate money laundering.[1194] While these situations are highly unlikely in practice, they may still arise. If any of the aforementioned situations were to arise, it could be asked whether an aggrieved party would still be well served in seeking a remedy before the same tribunal that engaged in such illegalities. Alternatively, could a court intervene before the tribunal makes an award? A related question is whether public policy would require the revocation of the tribunal's jurisdiction?

The answer under Indian law is crystal clear. Section 16(6) of the IAA provides that if a party is aggrieved by the tribunal's decision on its jurisdiction, it may approach the court at the seat for setting aside the award. This means that the Indian legislature only intended judicial review, if any, with regard to the tribunals decision on jurisdiction to be *ex-post*. In the Indian context, courts are not entitled to intervene before the proceedings are concluded. There is a good reason for such an approach. As will be shown below, there are numerous checks and balances in place within the arbitral process itself to prevent arbitrators wrongful determination of jurisdiction.

1193 Arbitration Rules of the London Court of International Arbitration 2020.

1194 Dragor Hiber and Vladimir Pavić, 'Arbitration and Crime' (2008) 25 Journal of International Arbitration 461, 463.

In institutional arbitrations, while the final determination of jurisdiction is usually left to the tribunal, the rules of several arbitral institutions, including the ICC (Art 6.4), allow parties to approach the institutions themselves with preliminary challenges where there appears to be a jurisdictional defect.[1195] Park has described the role played by the institutions in this regard as being that of a gatekeeper.[1196] Apart from this, arbitrators often follow strict ethical standards, including the IBA Guidelines on Conflict of Interest,[1197] which reduces the possibility of an arbitrator accepting jurisdiction on the basis of extrinsic considerations.

Furthermore, parties who feel that an arbitrator has been unduly influenced can always challenge the arbitrator itself. The rules of most arbitral institutions, including the LCIA and ICC, provide a mechanism for such a challenge. Art 14(3) of the ICC rules provide the institution (ICC Court) with the authority to decide on the admissibility and merits of the challenge brought on the grounds that the arbitrator is not 'impartial, independent or otherwise'. Even the IAA in sec. 13 specifically provides parties with the right to bring a challenge to the arbitrator by intimating the arbitral tribunal in writing. In the Indian context, this would be tantamount to a tacit acknowledgment that allowing judicial intervention *ex-ante* can lead to increased risk of abuse of process and enable parties to derail the proceedings even before it has taken off. In this regard, Indian law differs from English law. Under section 24 of the UK Arbitration Act 1996, a party can directly approach the court for removing the arbitrator in case there are doubts as to his/her impartiality or the arbitrator has failed in its duty to properly conduct the proceedings. Although parties have made use of this possibility in several instances where the impartiality of the arbitrator was in question, English courts have only rarely actually removed the arbitrator.[1198]

1195 Rules of Arbitration of the International Chamber of Commerce.

1196 William Park, 'Challenging Arbitral Jurisdiction: The Role of Institutional Rules' (2015) Festschrift in Honor of Laurie Craig, Boston University School of Law Public Law & Legal Theory Paper No. 15-40 7 <https://scholarship.law.bu.edu/faculty_scholarship/11?utm_source=scholarship.law.bu.edu%2Ffaculty_scholarship%2F11&utm_medium=PDF&utm_campaign=PDFCoverPages> accessed 27 July 2021.

1197 'IBA Guidelines on Conflicts of Interest in International Arbitration 2014' <http://www.ibanet.org/Publications/publications_IBA_guides_and_free_materials.aspx> accessed 26 July 2021.

1198 Philip Clifford, Hanna Roos, and Eleanor Scogings, 'Arbitrator Challenges: The Long View' (2018) New Law Journal-Arbitration Profession, Lexis Nexis 15, 17.

2. Where there are allegations of violation of public policy during the arbitration proceedings

Similar questions arise as to the role of national courts in a situation where a party to the arbitration feels that there has been illegality/irregularity by the tribunal during the arbitral proceedings. If such an illegality would be so grave as to constitute a violation of public policy, which authority should be competent to hear such claims?

Arbitrators, unlike judges in national courts, are not bound by any particular mandatory code of ethics.[1199] The IBA Guidelines on Conflict of Interest do provide a important guide, but stop short of mandating certain conduct from the arbitrators. While reputational concerns could strongly motivate arbitrators to generally conduct themselves in a way that is above board, there are certain indicators that can lead to an assumption that the arbitrators conduct is suspect. Bělohlávek has listed them to include demonstrable bias or prejudice, a language of animosity towards one of the parties or their counsel or inappropriate contact between an arbitrator and one of the parties or their representatives.[1200] The line between what is considered to be acceptable conduct by the arbitrator and what is not appropriate is complicated by the fact that arbitrators and parties are drawn from different jurisdictions with varying legal cultures and different ideas about morality.[1201] There are sometimes situations where the conduct of the arbitrators though illegal, may not constitute a violation of public policy and require judicial intervention. Hiber and Pavic have given the example of physical altercations between the arbitrators during the Iran- US Claims Tribunal proceedings or when the arbitrators have been arrested for illegal conduct that is not related to the proceedings but rather to their personal life.[1202]

Where a party to an arbitration proceeding has legitimate concerns about the way in which the arbitrators conduct the proceedings, one could argue that the most efficient solution would be for the party to first raise any objections before the arbitral tribunal itself. This way, the tribunal can seek to remedy the concern

1199 Born (n 1041) 2114.

1200 See, Alexander J. Bělohlávek, 'Procedural Irregularities and Arbitrator Misconduct during Proceedings', in Larry A DiMatteo, Marta Infantino and Nathalie Marie-Pierre Potin (eds), *The Cambridge Handbook of Judicial Control of Arbitral Awards* (Cambridge University Press 2020) 57 et seq.

1201 Guillermo Aguilar Alvarez, 'The Challenge of Arbitrators' (1990) 6 Arbitration International 203, 215.

1202 Dragor Hiber and Vladimir Pavić (n 1194) 463.

itself and save the parties the trouble and expense associated with approaching national courts at a later stage. The aggrieved party should make use of this remedy promptly as this remedy ceases to exist once the tribunal renders its award and becomes *functus officio*. If the arbitrators do not address the grievance, the arbitration could still proceed to challenge the award before courts at the seat or place of enforcement.

In the case of a tribunal with a sole arbitrator, there may be concerns that the arbitrator will not be readily willing to accept allegations made as to his or her own misconduct. In such a situation, the aforementioned approach may result in considerable expense and waste of resources to the parties, which will be in vain if it is likely that the award would subsequently be set aside or refused enforcement at a later stage. After all, in case of gross irregularities, it would not be unsurprising for courts to find that the award violated the jurisdictions public policy.

One way of solving the problem is, where the irregularities or corruption are of such a nature so as to leave doubtful that the award would stand, the parties should be free to approach the courts for revoking jurisdiction from such a tribunal. This remedy would not be often used, and if at all, only in the most egregious cases. Such an approach would save considerable expense and resources to both the parties, tribunals and courts at a later date. It may, however, go against the principle of party autonomy by denying the parties of their express intent as enshrined in the arbitration clause to resolve the dispute through arbitration. A more effective alternative, as shown above, is the possibility of challenging the arbitrator. The UK Arbitration Act in section 24 also allows the court to remove such an arbitrator.

The aforementioned solution of revoking the jurisdiction of the arbitral tribunal is not envisioned under the IAA as it stands today. Under the IAA, after the tribunal makes its award, if the aggrieved party is dissatisfied by the way the tribunal addressed its concerns, it may bring its claim before the courts at the seat of arbitration for setting aside the award. There is a good reason for allowing parties to approach the court at the seat; after all, it is usually the *lex arbitri* that governs the procedure of the tribunal in any case.[1203] The right to approach the courts of the seat is important as it acts as a check to arbitrary or capricious decisions by the tribunal. Naturally, arbitral tribunals must respect the public policy

1203 Alistair Henderson, 'Lex Arbitri, Procedural Law and the Seat of Arbitration – Unravelling the Laws of the Arbitration Process' (2014) 26 Singapore Academy of Law Journal 886, 888.

of the seat. There are some detractors to this approach, for example, Gaillard, who argues that it would go against the rationale of the New York Convention to permit a party to place the seat at the 'top of the jurisdictional hierarchy'.[1204]

The right to approach the courts of the seat may, however, lead to a situation where a party waits till the arbitration proceedings have concluded and then brings a claim before courts of the seat that the party has not raised before the arbitral tribunal. While neither the New York Convention nor the IAA prevents parties from bringing a claim which was not brought before the tribunal during the proceedings before a national court at the seat, allowing such a claim can be misused by a party seeking to delay the conclusion of proceedings which are not in its favor. A solution to this conundrum would not be to preclude approaching courts of the seat altogether but rather to restrict this remedy only to parties that have first brought a claim before the tribunal during the proceedings.

As a last resort, parties to an arbitration also have recourse to courts at the place of enforcement. Article V(1)(e), if the New York Convention provides that if courts at the seat set aside the award, then this would be sufficient grounds for refusing enforcement. By inference, any claim regarding such a violation of procedural public policy by the arbitral tribunal ought to first be brought before the tribunal itself and subsequently before the courts of the seat and the courts at the place of enforcement play a secondary role. If the award violates the public policy of the place of enforcement, according to Article V(2)(b) of the Convention, courts of the place at enforcement would naturally be able to intervene.

III. Where the enforcement of the final award violates public policy

There is the possibility that although there are no irregularities in the arbitral proceedings, the award would still be liable to challenge as its enforcement violates public policy. This situation is often quite closely linked to the first ground, i.e., where the underlying contract itself violates public policy by virtue of criminality or violation of fundamental legal principles of the given jurisdiction. As shown above,[1205] it is not improbable that an arbitral award that enforces such a contract would also violate public policy. There could also be situations where there is no irregularity in the underlying contract, but enforcement of the award

1204 See Emmanuel Gaillard, International Arbitration as a Transnational System of Justice, in Berg, *Arbitration* (n 939) 71.

1205 See Chapter 6(I)1.

would lead to a consequence that violates public policy. For instance, if the tribunal were to award punitive damages and/ compound interest that is disproportionately high, this may be considered a violation of public policy in some jurisdictions.[1206]

It may seem obvious that at the time of enforcing, the competent authority to decide on whether there has been a violation of public policy would be the courts at the place where enforcement has been sought. This is strictly speaking true, as the arbitral tribunal, after all, would be *functus officio* and therefore no longer have a say once the award has been rendered.[1207] It cannot, however, be discounted that a party can throw a spanner in the works by seeking to set aside the award by approaching the courts of the arbitral seat. The courts at the place of enforcement may not feel inclined to enforce an award that has been set aside at the seat.[1208] This means that even the courts at the seat could indirectly play a role as the competent authority for determining public policy claims even at the time of enforcement of the award.

IV. Which jurisdictions public policy should apply?

As seen in the previous chapters, there are variations across jurisdictions regarding the scope of the public policy exception. Both procedural and substantive safeguards may vary considerably, not just between states but even from time to time within the same state.[1209] In addition, in some states, arbitral tribunals are afforded a similar status as civil courts and are therefore also required as a matter of public policy to have the same level of responsibility in ensuring parties have a fair hearing.[1210] In line with this approach, fundamental procedural rights to a fair hearing, such as equal treatment that are mandatory in nature, cannot be derogated from by the tribunal or the parties.[1211] The drafters of the

1206 John Y. Gotanda, 'The Unpredictability Paradox: Punitive Damages and Interest in International Arbitration' (2009) 10 The Journal of World Investment & Trade 553, 574.

1207 Jean-Louis Delvolvé, Jean Rouche and Gerald H Pointon, *French Arbitration Law and Practice: A Dynamic Civil Law Approach to International Arbitration* (2nd edn, Wolters Kluwer Law & Business; Kluwer Law International 2009) para 304.

1208 For a more detailed elaboration see Chapter 5(V)5a.

1209 See Chapter 3 for a general comparison.

1210 A Ayyasamy v A Paramasivam & Ors (n 234).

1211 V. V. Veeder, 'Procedural Soft Law in International Arbitration', *Max Planck Encyclopedia of International Procedural Law* (2019) para 8.

UNITRAL Model Law had a similar understanding of the non-derogable nature of equal treatment in mind, as can be seen in the official commentary.[1212] In contrast, some other jurisdictions place greater importance on party autonomy and efficiency and allow parties to sacrifice these mandatory procedural requirements to ensure finality and speedy completion of proceedings.[1213] As the legal systems of many jurisdictions, with vastly varying approaches to party autonomy and public policy come into play in arbitral proceedings, the question arises as to which countries' public policy needs to be applied.

The answer as to which jurisdictions public policy is applicable would depend largely on the stage of the arbitral proceedings. We will first look at the situation where a party brings a claim of violation of public policy either in the underlying contract or during the arbitration proceedings before the arbitral tribunal itself. We will then look at how the situation will differ where the claim of violation of public policy is brought before national courts at the seat or place of enforcement.

1. Which public policy should the arbitral tribunal apply?

In an international arbitration, parties usually choose the law of a neutral third country to govern their contractual relations.[1214] The arbitrators have a duty to render an award based on contractual obligations according to the law chosen by the parties. What would be the consequence however if upholding contractual obligations according to the chosen law, would lead to a violation of the public policy of the seat or the place of enforcement?

The arbitrators, who oftentimes come from a totally unrelated jurisdiction, are expected to apply the substantive law of a foreign jurisdiction that they are not necessarily acquainted with.[1215] For similar reasons, they are also, at the onset,

---

1212 'UNCITRAL, Analytical Commentary on the Draft Text of the Model Law on International Commercial Arbitration, UN Doc A/CN. 9/264 (1985)' 45 <https://undocs.org/en/a/cn.9/264> accessed 11 March 2021.

1213 For an elaboration on this approach see, Filip De Ly, 'The Place of Arbitration in the Conflict of Laws of International Commercial Arbitration: An Exercise in Arbitration Planning' (1991) 12 Northwestern Journal of International Law & Business, 77.

1214 See, Marc Blessing, 'Regulations in Arbitration Rules on Choice of Law' in A. J. van den Berg (ed), *Planning Efficient Arbitration Proceedings: The Law Applicable in International Arbitration* (Kluwer Law International 1996) 395.

1215 See Pierre Mayer, 'Reflections on the International Arbitrator's Duty to Apply the Law', in Julian D. M. Lew and Loukas A. Mistelis (eds), *Arbitration Insights: Twenty Years of the Annual Lecture of the School of International Arbitration*, vol 16 (Kluwer Law International 2007) 292.

not necessarily familiar with the law of the seat or the possible places of enforcement. The question then arises as to whether it would be reasonable to expect an arbitrator to apply the public policy of a jurisdiction whose legal system he/she is not necessarily familiar with. Also, how many jurisdictions public policy should the arbitral tribunal take into account?

At the outset, it is necessary for arbitrators to ensure that the award stands and is not subject to successful challenges at a later stage. To do so, the arbitral tribunal must give due consideration to the mandatory rules and the public policy of the seat of arbitration.[1216] Apart from the arbitral seat, it could also be argued that the arbitral tribunal has an interest in ensuring that the award is not subsequently refused enforcement by complying with the public policy of the place of enforcement. The rules of several arbitral institutions, including the ICC, (Art 42) require arbitrators to make 'every effort' to ensure future enforceability of the award. Sabater and Rezende have argued that this duty to render and enforceable award is both legal and ethical in nature.[1217] The aforementioned task of seeking to ensure enforceability is very challenging due to the fact that the arbitral award could be enforced in several different jurisdictions, and it is nearly impossible for the arbitrator to familiarize himself with the mandatory rules of every jurisdiction.

Another perspective, which could help solve the above problem is that as arbitral tribunals are creatures of contract, they are not bound to any particular legal system.[1218] Following this approach, an arbitral tribunal is therefore free to take into consideration translational or universally accepted notions of public policy.[1219] Such an approach is especially useful in the context of allegations of corruption when there is a cross-border element.[1220]

1216 Franz T. Schwarz and Christian W. Konrad, *The Vienna Rules: A Commentary on International Arbitration in Austria* (Wolters Kluwer Law & Business ; Kluwer Law International 2009) paras 7–054.

1217 See Anibal Sabater and Lidia Rezende, 'An arbitrator's obligation to use reasonable efforts to issue an enforceable award and its interaction with the New York Convention', in Katia Fach Gómez and Ana M Lopez-Rodriguez (n 908) 20.

1218 Matthias Lehmann (n 982) 755.

1219 Yoanna Schuch (n 527) 57.

1220 ibid.

2. The public policy applied by the courts at the seat

Where a party to the arbitration is dissatisfied with the way the arbitration proceedings are conducted by the tribunal, or believes that enforcement of the arbitral award would violate substantive public policy, it could approach the courts at the seat of arbitration for setting aside the award. In this case, the question arises as to whether the courts at the seat would only apply its own countries public policy or can it also look elsewhere. Would the consequence be the same if the enforcement would lead to violation of mandatory law (or public policy) of a foreign country?

There is judicial precedence in common law for placing importance on the non-violation laws of other jurisdictions. In *Forster v. Driscoll,* the Court of Appeal (England and Wales) held that a contract will be illegal in England if it requires the performance of an illegal act in a friendly foreign country.[1221] It is unsurprising therefore that in the *Vedanta* case, for instance, the Government of India approached the Indian Supreme Court with the argument that the courts of the seat (Malaysia) failed to apply Indian public policy in deciding on a challenge to the award, although the substantive law of the contract was Indian law.[1222] The position of law in India was clarified by the Indian Supreme Court. The court was quite categorical in holding that the courts of the seat would have 'primary or supervisory jurisdiction over the award' whereas the courts at the place of enforcement would have 'secondary' jurisdiction.[1223] The court furthermore observed that the courts at the seat would usually apply their own national public policy.[1224] While courts at the seat will usually rely on its own notion of international public policy, there is nothing precluding courts of the seat from choosing to apply transnational notions of public policy.

3. Public policy as applied by courts at place of enforcement

The third situation is slightly different and arises where the challenge to the award comes before courts at the stage of enforcement. When deciding on whether enforcement should be denied on public policy grounds, courts at the place of enforcement would normally apply their own national public policy or, on occasion, transnational notions of public policy. It is, however, laid down in Art 5(1)e

1221 *Foster v Driscoll and Others* (1929) 1 KB 470 (Court of Appeal) 514.
1222 Government of India v. Vedanta Limited (n 938) 44.
1223 ibid 51–52.
1224 ibid 46.

of the New York Convention and affirmed in many jurisdictions that if the award is set aside at the seat for violating public policy, this would also be grounds for refusing enforcement of the award.[1225] It is not uncommon, therefore, for courts at the place of enforcement to also take the public policy of the seat into account at the enforcement stage.

4. The subjectivist vs objectivist approach

Another approach is the decision on which jurisdictions public policy applies should be based on private international law principles found in contract law. Some scholars have taken a *subjectivist* view in making the determination. According to this theory, the chosen law is only considered a contractual provision, and unless the parties explicitly agree, the law applicable to the contract cannot have a mandatory effect.[1226] This means the law under which the award is unenforceable for violating public policy would be without effect, as the parties when drafting the contract, did not envision such a result.[1227] If one were to rely on the aforementioned approach, it is necessary to apply the public policy of the country under which the arbitral award would be enforceable. While this can have several benefits, such as increased legal certainty and respect the will of the parties in ensuring an enforceable award, it is, however, not practicable to ignore its drawback. Such an approach would render the public policy exception, which is one of the last elements of state control on arbitration, without use.

Considering the argumentation made above, the alternative to the *subjectivist approach,* would be the *objectivist* approach. According to this approach, contractual relations are, by necessity, governed by law.[1228] While the *objectivist* approach can consequently on rare occasions lead to arbitral awards not being enforced, it is still in the interest of the parties, and ensuring trust in the arbitral process that fundamental principles of the legal system not be derogated from.

1225 For a more detailed elaboration see Chapter 5, Section 5(5).

1226 See explanation regarding subjectivist approach in, Yves Derains, Public Policy and the Law Applicable to the Dispute in International Arbitration, in Sanders (n 421) 235–236.

1227 Yves Derains, Public Policy and the Law Applicable to the Dispute in International Arbitration, in ibid 236.

1228 Yves Derains, Public Policy and the Law Applicable to the Dispute in International Arbitration, in ibid.

Chapter 7: Concluding observations

I. Observations from a comparative perspective

In recent times, the move towards promoting arbitration in commercial disputes is almost universal. India is no stranger to this trend.[1229] While national courts in most states were previously jealous of any attempt to reduce their powers, in today's world, they are more and more content to have their burdens reduced by arbitral tribunals. In consonance with this approach, most national courts have recognised the need for narrowly construing the public policy as grounds for refusing to enforce a foreign arbitral award.[1230] This follows the argument that it is the duty of the courts to 'expound but not to expand' the exception.[1231] In India, this approach can be seen in the Bombay High Courts *Mukesh Mehta* ruling, where it held that the public policy exception would only be relied upon in case of 'clear and incontestable harm to the public.'[1232] A similar attitude can be seen in a decision of the Colombian Supreme Court, where it showed its preference for internationally accepted notions of 'dynamic, tolerant and constructive public policy' rather than 'defensive and destructive public policy'.[1233]

Despite the general leaning towards ensuring the enforceability of awards, courts in most jurisdictions used to (and continue to) occasionally intervene in order to ensure that the parties to a dispute are not unduly prejudiced by being denied access to the court system in case of egregious violation of their procedural or substantive rights or where there is gross illegality amounting to a violation of the jurisdictions public policy.[1234] Historically, even in so-called 'arbitration-friendly' jurisdictions, courts were not always as open to arbitration as they are today. The public policy exception was relied upon by national courts on so many occasions because of initial doubts as to whether arbitration could

---

1229 See, Matthew Maragulia, 'The Continuing Pro-Arbitration Trend in India: A New Global Hub?', in Andrew C Fillmore (ed), *Yearbook on Arbitration and Mediation*, vol 8 (2016) 252.

1230 Blackaby and others (n 72) para 11.61.

1231 Kent Murphy (n 75) 592.

1232 Mukesh H. Mehta v. Harindra H. Mehta (n 460).

1233 See 'Colombia No. 10 / P2, HTM LLC v. Fomento de Catalizadores – FOCA S.A.S., Corte Suprema de Justicia, SC8453-2016, 24 June 2016', in Albert Jan van den Berg (ed), *Yearbook Commercial Arbitration*, vol 41 (Wolters Kluwer Law & Business 2016).

1234 Born (n 419) 652.

provide the procedural safeguards present in the court system. This approach was amply elucidated by the U. S. Supreme Court when it said that parties should not be allowed to 'barter away…substantial rights'.[1235]

This protectionist approach could be attributed to many reasons. Firstly, historically speaking, the constitution and legal system of some common law jurisdictions, such as the United States, used to expressly or impliedly guarantee parties the right to approach courts or have a trial by jury.[1236] The absence of this mechanism in arbitration led the Montana Supreme to characterize arbitration as an 'open attack' on the right of jury trial and violation of the fundamental constitutional right to access the courts.[1237] According to the Court, such contracts would not be enforceable against the weaker party as they were 'unduly oppressive' and violate public policy.[1238] Secondly, in many jurisdictions, particularly in France, the UK and the United States, there was a scepticism against allowing parties to enforce agreements to arbitrate future disputes.[1239] The early decision of the Supreme Court of California in the *Blodgett* case is characteristic of this school of thought. In the words of Justice Kerrigan, parties should not be allowed to 'deprive themselves' of judicial protection 'by referring to the arbitrament of private persons or tribunals… questions affecting their legal rights'.[1240]

However, the scepticism and doubts about the conflict of arbitration with constitutional principles and fundamental rights in most other countries have given way to a more benign approach. Arbitration is today seen as an expression of the parties right to freedom of contract, which is as important as other fundamental rights. In fact, some authors argue that arbitration protects the rights of parties more than national courts.[1241] But the effectiveness of the arbitration process can only be ensured if judicial interference is restricted and enforcement of awards is prioritized.[1242]

1235 *Insurance Company v Morse* 87 US 445 1874 (US Supreme Court).

1236 See, Thomas J. McSweeney, 'Magna Carta and the Right to Trial by Jury', in Randy J. Holland (ed), *Magna Carta: Muse and Mentor* (Thomson Reuters 2014) 139 et seq.

1237 *Kloss v Edward D Jones & Co* (2002) 310 Mont 123 (Supreme Court of Montana), para 55 et seq.

1238 ibid, para 23.

1239 Born (n 419) 638.

1240 *Blodgett Co v Bebe Co* 190 Cal 665 1923 (Supreme Court of California).

1241 Born (n 419) 655.

1242 Donovan (n 6) 648.

Indian courts were initially not as swift in their rapprochement towards arbitration as the other jurisdictions.[1243] Courts were keen to safeguard public interest and their powers, sometimes at the cost of respecting party autonomy. However, as demonstrated earlier in this thesis, the Indian judiciary has come around and accepted arbitration as an effective alternative to the court system for resolving commercial disputes.[1244] Moreover, the strong emphasis on party autonomy and restricted grounds of public policy taken by Indian courts in recent decisions is a strong indicator that the judiciary is conscious and supportive of the goals of the IAA.

II. Conclusion

1. Looking at public policy from a wider context

The development and attitude of any given legal system towards arbitration is influenced by and must be looked at from a broader political and socio-economic context.[1245] There is, after all, a direct relationship between the political situation in a country and its legal system.[1246] In countries that adopt a free, non-autocratic system of governance, parties are given broad leeway to conduct their lives without the interference of the state. Vesting power solely with national courts and exercising excessive control of arbitration are hallmarks of an authoritarian system of governance.[1247] Being a liberal democracy, there is no reason why Indian courts should exercise disproportionate control over arbitration. Arbitration is, after all, entrenched in the Indian legal system. As discussed in earlier in this thesis,[1248] Article 51(c) of the Indian Constitution obliges the government to promote arbitration.

A country or society that is not ready for arbitration due to domestic scepticism or lack of awareness cannot be compelled by statute or international conventions to accept arbitration as a means of dispute resolution. It does not matter if there is an international movement in this direction. National courts are, after

1243 Anirudh Hariani, 'Indian Arbitration and the Shifting Sands of Public Policy' (2020) 16 Asian International Arbitration Journal 159.

1244 For an elaboration as to the evolving approach of Indian courts see *supra* Chapter 2.

1245 Eric George, 'The Political Economy of Commercial Arbitration: The Corporatization of U.S. Arbitration Law' (PhD Thesis, York University 2018) 84.

1246 Hernando Díaz-Candia (n 150) 25.

1247 Paulsson (n 9) 105.

1248 See, *supra* Chapter 2(II).

all, an instrument of society, and their decisions are reflective of the views of the community.[1249] The initial scepticism of Indian courts towards arbitration has now given way to an approach that predominantly embraces arbitration. It could be argued that arbitration in India has now come of age.[1250] This can be evinced in the pro-arbitration congruence between decisions of the court and legislative action.

While disproportionate control of the arbitral process is not necessary, limited control through the public policy exception is required in order to protect the need for a fair hearing and ensure respect for fundamental legal principles. As pointed out by Kolkey, the threshold of judicial review of arbitral awards does not necessarily make a country better, as limited judicial review serves as an essential impediment to arbitrary rulings by tribunals.[1251]

In the Indian context, the problems caused by the use of the public policy exception are not necessarily attributable to the lawmaker providing parties with the public policy exception in the statute book, but rather to judicial interpretation of the exception and to parties seeking to abuse the process. This cannot be remedied by legislatively constraining the exception but rather by conscious decisions taken by judges.

Taking away the power of interpreting the scope of public policy from judges is not a long-term solution to developing faith in arbitration among the judicial branch. While such an approach may provide temporary relief from excessive judicial interference, it may be counterproductive and lead to a judicial backlash. The only long-term solution towards excessive intervention is reforming the judicial mindset and increasing awareness among judges regarding party autonomy and the benefits of fostering arbitration. As explained by Paulsson, arbitration can best succeed when courts and arbitrators look at their job as a 'collaborative process'.[1252] The benefits of 'increasing awareness' of international best practices in arbitration among members of the judiciary have also been recognised by the High-Level Committee appointed by the Ministry of Law and Justice in its report to the Indian government.[1253]

1249 Sophie Turenne, Fair Reflection of Society in Judicial Systems – A Comparative Study (Springer International Publishing 2015) 10.

1250 Payel Chatterjee and Sahil Kanuga, 'New Age Arbitration – The Future of Dispute Resolution in India' (2018) 4 *Indo-German Economy* 75.

1251 Daniel M. Kolkey, 'Attacking Arbitral Awards: Rights of Appeal and Review in International Arbitrations' (1988) 22 The International Lawyer 693, 714.

1252 Paulsson (n 9) 27.

1253 Justice B. N. Srikrishna (n 25) 43.

2. Should the public policy exception be defined? Narrowly?

Regarding the need for defining the exception, merely because a definition of public policy has not been provided for in most states does not mean that it is not necessary in the Indian context. In defining the scope of the public policy exception, it is not necessary that the Indian lawmaker must take the same approach as that taken in other states. In England, for instance, section 69 of the Arbitration Act allows the parties to appeal an arbitral award on a point of law. This does not mean that England is not an arbitration-friendly jurisdiction; rather, it is only indicative of a higher degree of trust in the English judiciary.

There are particularities in each legal system that necessitate different and unique solutions to the same legal problem. For instance, in India, protecting the cow could easily fall within the scope of morality (public policy). After all, consuming beef has been criminalized in most Indian states. Therefore, any award that enforces a commercial agreement for trade in beef would potentially violate the morality clause in section 48(2)b of the IAA and thus violate the public policy exception. A different result could be reached in a country having other standards of morality.

Considerations of local circumstances may also be in the mind of public authorities when evaluating what constitutes public interest. The former President of India did allude to such local challenges when he gave the example of a party to an arbitration from a developing country enters into an agreement with a party from a developed state, where the former may need special protections owing from the fact that it would be at an economic disadvantage and thereby less fit to represent itself in an expensive international arbitration proceeding in, for e.g., Switzerland, *vis-à-vis* a party from a more developed jurisdiction.[1254] While this does not in itself justify an expansive interpretation of the exception, it could illustrate what the Indian judge may consider when evaluating whether the procedural safeguards such as *audi alterem partem* have been met by the tribunal.

The Indian legislature's rationale behind giving the public policy exception a narrow meaning is beyond reproach; however, its choice of defining the scope of such a fluid term through legislative dicta rather than leaving it to judicial interpretation is questionable. As demonstrated earlier in this thesis, while the

1254 This disparity and its justification for judicial review has been explained in more detail in, 'NOTES AND CURRENT DEVELOPMENTS Speech by the President of India at the Inauguration of the International Council for Commercial Arbitration Conference 2000' (n 129) 155.

current statutory definition does show the intention of the legislature to define public policy narrowly, the definition in itself does not achieve this because it is riddled with broad terminology.[1255] With regard to the future use of the exception, the ball is firmly still in the court of the Indian judiciary. This is, however, not a bad thing. The approach of Indian courts towards enforcing foreign awards has evolved considerably. But what criteria should the courts use when interpreting the exception?

The Supreme Court in *Hira Chand* held that public policy must '*...vary with the needs of society.*'[1256] It is the job of the courts to reflect these variations through interpreting the exception. It is impossible for the legislature to statutorily cover and then modify the exception based on the ever-changing needs of society. The reason for the failure of the IAA 1996 was not the inadequacy of the law itself, but rather the so-called 'Indian sentiment', which has not been used to accepting the finality of awards without the usual appellate procedures.[1257] The problems primarily arose due to misuse of the system. In the words of Fali Nariman, a doyen on Indian commercial law, if an arbitral award was rendered against Indian parties, they would try their best to delay enforcement for as long as possible by using the appellate procedure of courts.[1258]

The Indian Supreme Court has astutely reasoned that in circumstances where there is no precedent in defining public policy, it can take guidance from the preamble, fundamental rights and directive principles enshrined in the Constitution.[1259] Courts should generally enforce awards, but when the aforementioned principles are violated, it is the job of the judiciary to step in.

1255 For an analysis of public policy exception under the IAA, see *supra* Chapter 4.

1256 Rattan Chand Hira Chand v Askar Nawaz Jung (Dead) by Lrs and Ors 19911 SCR 327 (Supreme Court of India) para 15.

1257 Nariman (n 1) 372.

1258 ibid 372.

1259 ibid.

Bibliography

[1987] N° Pourvoi 84-17274 (Cour de Cassation, Chambre civile 1)

'Arbitration Rules of the European Court of Arbitration' <https://cour-europe-arbitrage.org/arbitration-rules/> accessed 11 June 2019

'Confirmation Hearing on the Nomination of Samuel A. Alito, Jr. to Be an Associate Justice of the Supreme Court of the United States: Hearing before the Committee on the Judiciary, United States Senate' <https://www.govinfo.gov/content/pkg/GPO-CHRG-ALITO/pdf/GPO-CHRG-ALITO.pdf> accessed 12 September 2019

'Edit de Fontainebleau (August 1560)' <https://www.trans-lex.org/601210/_/edit-de%C2%A0fontainebleau-august-1560/#:~:text=Edit%20de%20Fontainebleau%2C%20August%201560.,-Additional%20Information&text=N%C2%B0%2039.,%C3%A0%20des%20arbitres%20(1%20).> accessed 8 September 2020

'Foreign Direct Investment Policy of India' <https://www.investindia.gov.in/foreign-direct-investment> accessed 11 July 2021

'IBA Guidelines on Conflicts of Interest in International Arbitration 2014' <http://www.ibanet.org/Publications/publications_IBA_guides_and_free_materials.aspx> accessed 26 July 2021

'ILA International Commercial Arbitration Committee Berlin Conference-Interim Report: "Res Judicata" and Arbitration' (2004) <http://www.ila-hq.org/download.cfm/docid/446043C4-9770-434D-AD7DD42F7E8E81C6> accessed 23 February 2017

'JAMS Optional Arbitration Appeal Procedure' <https://www.jamsadr.com/files/Uploads/Documents/JAMS-Rules/JAMS_Optional_Appeal_Procedures-2003.pdf> accessed 11 June 2019

'Lok Sabha Debates (Lower House-Indian Parliament), Sixteenth Series, Vol. XIV, Sixth Session, 2015/1937 (Saka), No. 16'

'Malum In Se' <https://www.law.cornell.edu/wex/malum_in_se> accessed 2 August 2021

'Mandatory Rules and Public Policy' <https://www.era-comm.eu/Visegrad/kiosk/pdf/speakers_contributions/116DT35_Grajdura_mandatory.pdf> accessed 15 October 2021

'NOTES AND CURRENT DEVELOPMENTS Speech by the President of India at the Inauguration of the International Council for Commercial Arbitration Conference 2000' (2000) 17 Journal of International Arbitration 154

'Paris Court Sets Aside Arbitration Awards Based on Corruption Red Flags' (Debevoise & Plimpton Update, 14 December 2020) <https://www.debevoise.com/insights/publications/2020/12/paris-court-sets-aside-arbitration-awards-based-on> accessed 9 September 2021

'Recognition and Enforcement of Foreign Arbitral Awards, Report by the Secretary General' (United Nations Economic and Social Council 1956) E/2822, 21st Session, Item 8

'Resolutions Adopted by the General Assembly 40/72, United Nations Treaty Series, vol 330, No. 4739, p. 38.'

'Switzerland Is Arbitration-Friendly' <https://www.arbitration-ch.org/en/service/asa/switzerland-is-arbitration-friendly/index.html> accessed 6 June 2019

'The Benefit of Competition Policy for Consumers – Note by UNCTAD Secretariat', Consultations and discussions regarding peer reviews on competition law and policy, review of the Model Law on Competition and studies related to the provisions of the Set of Principles and Rules; Trade and Development Board Trade and Development Commission; Intergovernmental Group of Experts on Competition Law and Policy Fourteenth session (TD/B/C.I/CLP/27) (UNCTAD 2014)

'The Illegality Defence in Tort – Law Commission Consultation Paper No 160' <https://www.lawcom.gov.uk/app/uploads/2015/03/cp160_Illegality_Defence_in_Tort_Consultation.pdf> accessed 5 July 2022

'The Policy of the Government on the Issue of Child Labour' <https://labour.gov.in/sites/default/files/PolicyofGovernmenontheissueofChildLabour.pdf> accessed 4 February 2022

'The Ten Principles of the UN Global Compact' (United Nations) <https://www.unglobalcompact.org/what-is-gc/mission/principles> accessed 27 August 2018

'Transparency International – Corruption Perceptions Index 2020' <https://www.transparency.org/en/cpi/2020/index/nzl> accessed 26 April 2021

'UNCITRAL, 18th Session, Analytical Compilation of Comments by Governments and International Organizations on the Draft Text of a Model Law on International Commercial Arbitration – Report of the Secretary General' (1985) A/CN.9/263

'UNCITRAL, 18th Session, Analytical Compilation of Comments by Governments and International Organizations on the Draft Text of a Model Law on International Commercial Arbitration – Report of the Secretary General (Addendum 2)' (1985) A/CN.9/263/Add.2

'UNCITRAL, Analytical Commentary on the Draft Text of the Model Law on International Commercial Arbitration, UN Doc A/CN. 9/264 (1985)' <https://undocs.org/en/a/cn.9/264> accessed 11 March 2021

'United Nations Conference on International Commercial Arbitration: Summary Record of the Seventeenth Meeting,12 September 1958, UN Economic and Social Council, E/CONF. 26/ SR.17'

'Verhoeft v. Moreau, Cour de Cassation (1re Ch. Civ.), 21 March 2000', Revue de l'Arbitrage; Comité Français de l'Arbitrage 2001 805

'XI Lok Sabha Debates, Session II, Budget Thursday, August 1, 1996/Sravana 10, 1918 (Saka)'

60 Years of ICC Arbitration, A Look at the Future: Programme of the 60th Anniversary of the Court of Arbitration of the ICC (International Chamber of Commerce 1984)

A Ayyasamy v A Paramasivam & Ors 2016 10 SCC 386 (Supreme Court of India)

A société PWC Landwell – PricewaterhouseCoopers Tax & Legal Services v Mme L. Y. ; et autres [2020] Arrêt N° 556 (Cour de cassation – Première chambre civile)

A Treatise of the First Principles of Laws in General and of the Interpretation of Them (Printed by WB for Richard Sare at Greys Inn Gate in Holborn 1705) <https://books.google.de/books?id=ZjDk3MOFCaIC&printsec=frontcover#v=onepage&q&f=false> accessed 10 August 2018

Abdul Kadir Shamsuddin Bubere v Madhav Prabhakar Oak (1961) 1962 AIR 406 (Supreme Court of India)

Abedian H, 'Judicial Review of Arbitral Awards in International Arbitration – A Case for an Efficient System of Judicial Review' (2011) 28 Journal of International Arbitration 541

Abrahams BG, 'The Origins of Arbitration in Britain' (1988) 54 Arbitration 263

Additional Protocol to the Criminal Law Convention on Corruption 2003 (European Treaty Series 191)

Adekoya F, 'The Public Policy Defence to Enforcement of Arbitral Awards: Rising Star or Setting Sun?' (2015) 2 BCDR International Arbitration Review 203

Aden M, 'Wrong Answers to Wrong Questions? A New Approach to Judicial Review of International Arbitral Awards' (2015) 12 Revista Brasileira de Arbitragem 55

Aftab Singh and Ors v Emaar MGF Land Limited and Ors (2017) CPJ270 (National Consumer Disputes Rederessal Commission)

Agreement on Trade-Related Aspects of Intellectual Property Rights, Apr. 15, 1994, Marrakesh Agreement Establishing the World Trade Organization 1994 (1869 UNTS 299)

Ahmadi AM, 'Judicial Process: Social Legitimacy and Institutional Viability' (1996) 4 SCC (Jour) 1

Akers MD and Gissel JL, 'What Is Fraud and Who Is Responsible?' (2006) 7 Journal of Forensic Accounting 247

Akkermans B, 'Public Policy (Orde Public)' (2019) 8 European Property Law Journal 260

Alvarez GA, 'The Challenge of Arbitrators' (1990) 6 Arbitration International 203

Alvarez HC, 'Xerox Canada Ltd., Xerox Corporation v. MPI Techologies Inc., MPI Tech. S.A., Ontario Superior Court of Justice, [2006] O.J. No. 4895 (QL), 30 November 2006' A contribution by the ITA Board of Reporters, Kluwer Law International

Alvey J, 'The Separation of Powers between the Executive and the Judiciary' (Australasian Study of Parliament Conference, Parliament House, Hobart, Tasmania, 2017) <http://www.parliament.tas.gov.au/aspg/ASPG%20papers/The%20separation%20of%20powers%20between%20the%20Executive%20and%20the%20Judicary%20-%20Dr%20John%20Alvey.pdf> accessed 6 September 2018

Anchayil A, 'Bhatia International to Videocon Industries and Tograj Infrastructure: Recasting the Foundations of Arbitration Law in India' (2013) 29 Arbitration International 105

Andenæs MT and Baasch Andersen C (eds), Theory and Practice of Harmonisation (Edward Elgar 2011)

Andhyarujina TR, 'The Unique Judicial Activism of the Supreme Court of India' (2014) 130 Law Quarterly Review 53

Anglade L, 'The Use of Transnational Rules of Law in International Arbitration' (2003) 38 Irish Jurist 92

Arab H and El Shentenawi L, 'IBA Sub-Committee on Recognition and Enforcement of Awards – Public Policy: The UAE Country Report' (2015)

Aravali Power Company Pvt Ltd vs M/S Era Infra Engineering Ltd (2017) Civ APPEAL NOS 12627–12628 (Supreme Court of India)

Arbitration Act 1996 (Chapter 23)

Arbitration Rules of the London Court of International Arbitration 2020

Asher v Seaford Court Estates (1949) 2 KB 481 (Court of Appeal (England and Wales))

Asif Hameed & Ors v State of Jammu & Kashmir & Ors (1989) AIR 1899 (Supreme Court of India)

Associate Builders v Delhi Development Authority 2015 3 SCC 49 (Supreme Court of India)

Associated Provincial Picture Houses Ltd v Wednesbury Corporation (1948) 1 KB 223 (Court of Appeal of England and Wales)

AT&T Mobility LLC v Conception (2011) 563 US 333 (United States Supreme Court)

Attwood v Lamont (1920) 3 KB 571 (Court of Appeal)

Avitel Post Studios Ltd & Ors v HSBC PI Holdings (Mauritius) Ltd (2020) Civ Appeal No 5158 2016 (Supreme Court of India)

Bachand F, 'Court Intervention in International Arbitration: The Case for Compulsory Judicial Internationalism Symposium' (2012) 2012 Journal of Dispute Resolution 83

Bachawat RS, Justice R.S. Bachawat's Law of Arbitration & Conciliation (Including International Commercial Arbitration & ADR) (Anirudh Wadhwa and Bejoy Kumar Bachawat eds, LexisNexis Buterworths Wadhwa Nagpur 2010)

Bagner H, 'Confidentiality - A Fundamental Principle in International Commercial Arbitration?' (2001) 18 Journal of International Arbitration 243

Balakrishnan KG, 'The Role of Foreign Precedents in a Country's Legal System' (2010) 22 National Law School of India Review 1

Bansal AK, 'Towards a New Law on International Arbitration in India' (1995) 12 Journal of International Arbitration 67

Barden G and Murphy T, Law and Justice in Community (Oxford University Press 2010)

Barysheva N and Chessa V, 'Société Alstom Transport SA et Autre v. Société Alexander Brothers Ltd., Court of Appeal of Paris, 10 April 2018' [2018] A contribution by the ITA Board of Reporters, Kluwer Law International

———, 'Société MK Group v. S.A.R.L. Onix and Société Financial Initiative, Court of Appeal of Paris, 16 January 2018' A contribution by the ITA Board of Reporters, Kluwer Law International

Basedow J and others (eds), The Max Planck Encyclopedia of European Private Law, vol II (Oxford University Press 2012)

Basedow J and others, Encyclopedia of Private International Law (Edward Elgar Publishing 2017)

Bastarache M, 'How Internationalization of the Law Has Materialized in Canada' (2009) 59 University of New Brunswick Law Journal 190

Bates DM, 'A Consumer's Dream or Pandora's Box: Is Arbitration a Viable Option for Cross-Border Consumer Disputes?' (2003) 27 Fordham International Law Journal 823

Beatson J, 'International Arbitration, Public Policy Considerations, and Conflicts of Law: The Perspectives of Reviewing and Enforcing Courts' (2017) 33 Arbitration International 175

Behram Khurshed Pesikaka vs The State of Bombay (1955) 1 SCR 613 (Supreme Court of India)

Bell GF (ed), The UNCITRAL Model Law and Asian Arbitration Laws: Implementation and Comparisons (Cambridge University Press 2018)

Bell J, 'Researching Globalisation: Lessons from Judicial Citations' (2014) 3 Cambridge Journal of International and Comparative Law 961

Belmont Park Investments Pty Ltd v BNY Corporate Trustee Services Ltd (2011) UKSC 38 ([Supreme Court of the United Kingdom)

Belton SE and Paul Bland F, Jr, 'How the Arbitration-at-All Costs Regime Ignores and Distorts Settled Law' (2014) 35 Berkeley Journal of Employment and Labor Law 135

Benoliel U, 'Contract Interpretation Revisited: The Case of Severability Clauses' (2019) 3 Business and Finance Law Review 90

Bensaude D, 'Thalès Air Defence BV v. GIE Euromissile: Defining the Limits of Scrutiny of Awards Based on Alleged Violations of European Competition Law' (2005) 22 Journal of International Arbitration 239

Berard M and Lewis K, 'Privy Council Confirms Pro-enforcement Approach under New York Convention' (2014) ASA Bulletin, Association Suisse de l'Arbitrage; Kluwer Law International 880

Berg AJVD (ed), Yearbook Commercial Arbitration, vol 17 (Wolters Kluwer Law & Business 1992)

Berg v Sage Environmental Consulting of Austin, Inc (2005) 381 FSupp2d 552 (United States District Court, MD Louisiana)

Bermann GA (ed), Recognition and Enforcement of Foreign Arbitral Awards: The Interpretation and Application of the New York Convention by National Courts (Springer: Berlin, Heidelberg 2017)

Bermann GA, 'Mandatory Rules of Law in International Arbitration' (2007) 18 American Review of International Arbitration 1

———, 'The "Gateway" Problem in International Commercial Arbitration' 37 Yale Journal of International Law <https://cpb-us-w2.wpmucdn.com/campuspress.yale.edu/dist/8/1581/files/2016/09/37-1-bermann-the-gateway-problem-1vu7rwu.pdf> accessed 12 November 2018

———, 'What Does It Mean to Be "pro-Arbitration"?' (2018) 34 Arbitration International 341

———, International Arbitration and Private International Law, vol 381 (Brill: Nijhoff 2017)

Bernard LL, 'The Definition of Definition' (1941) 19 Social Forces 500

Beschluss der 2 Kammer des Ersten Senats vom 03 Juni 2022 (2022) 1 BvR 210316 (Bundesverfassungsgericht)

BGH Beschluss Vom 02. März 2017 – ZB 4216 – Juris (German Federal Court of Justice (Bundesgerichtshof))

BGH Beschluss Vom 06. Oktober 2016 – ZB 1315 – Juris (German Federal Court of Justice (Bundesgerichtshof))

BGH Beschluss vom 11. Oktober 2018 – I ZB 9/18 (German Federal Court of Justice (Bundesgerichtshof))

BGH Beschluss Vom 27. Novemb 2008 – III ZB 5907 – Juris (German Federal Court of Justice (Bundesgerichtshof))

BGH Beschluss vom 31. Oktober 2018 – I ZB 2/15 (German Federal Court of Justice (Bundesgerichtshof))

BGH Urteil Vom 12. Juli 1990 – III ZR 17489 – Juris (German Federal Court of Justice (Bundesgerichtshof))

BGH, Beschluss vom 23. Juli 2020 – I ZB 88/19 (German Federal Court of Justice (Bundesgerichtshof))

BGH, Beschluss vom 28. Januar 2014 – III ZB 40/13 –, Juris (German Federal Court of Justice (Bundesgerichtshof))

BGH, Beschluss vom 30. September 2010 – III ZB 69/09 (German Federal Court of Justice (Bundesgerichtshof))

Bhagwati PN, 'The Role of the Judiciary in the Democractic Process: Balancing Activism and Judicial Restraint' (1992) 18 Commonwealth Law Bulletin 1262

Bharat Aluminium Company and Ors Vs Kaiser Aluminium Technical Service, Inc and Ors 2012 9 SCC 552 (Supreme Court of India)

Bharat Broadband Network Limited Vs United Telecoms Limited (2019) 5 SCC 755 (Supreme Court of India)

Bhatia International v Bulk Trading SA and Anr 2002 4 SCC 105 (Supreme Court of India)

Bhatia VK, Gotti M and Azirah Hashim (eds), International Arbitration Discourse and Practices in Asia (Routledge 2018)

Biecco Lawrie Ltd & Anr v State of West Bengal & Anr (2010) AIR 142 (Supreme Court of India)

Bihar Public Service Commission v Saiyed Hussain Abbas Rizwi (2012) 13 SCC 61 (Supreme Court of India)

Biswas TK, Introduction to Arbitration in India: The Role of the Judiciary (Kluwer Law International 2014)

Blackaby N and others, Redfern and Hunter on International Arbitration (6th edn, Oxford University Press 2015)

Blanke G and Landolt PL (eds), EU and US Antitrust Arbitration: A Handbook for Practitioners (Kluwer Law International 2011)

Blodgett Co v Bebe Co 190 Cal 665 1923 (Supreme Court of California)

Böckstiegel K-H, 'An Introduction to the New German Arbitration Act Based on the UNCITRAL Model Law' (1998) 14 Arbitration International 19

———, 'Public Policy as a Limit to Arbitration and Its Enforcement' (2008) IBA Journal of Dispute resolution, Special Issue, The New York Convention – 50 Years 123

Böckstiegel K-H, Kröll S and Nacimiento P (eds), Arbitration in Germany: The Model Law in Practice (2nd edn, Kluwer Law International 2015)

Booz Allen and Hamilton Inc v SBI Home Finance Limited 2011 5 SCC 532 (Supreme Court of India)

Born G, International Commercial Arbitration (2nd edn, Kluwer Law International 2014)

———, International Commercial Arbitration (3rd edn, Kluwer Law International 2021)

Born GB, 'Principle of Judicial Non-Interference in International Arbitral Proceedings, The Anniversary Contributions – International Litigation & Arbitration' (2009) 30 University of Pennsylvania Journal of International Law 999

Born GB and Spears S, 'International Arbitration and India: "A Truly Excellent Judgment!"' (2012) 1 Indian Journal of Arbitration Law 1

Bosman L (ed), International Handbook on Commercial Arbitration (Supplement 106) (Kluwer Law International 2019)

Braganza v BP Shipping Ltd (2015) UKSC 17 (United Kingdom Supreme Court)

Branson J and Manon R, 'Why Tribunals Should Not Ignore "Red Flags" of Corruption' (Global Arbitration Review, 12 August 2020) <https://globalarbitrationreview.com/article/why-tribunals-should-not-ignore-red-flags-of-corruption> accessed 7 August 2022

Brekoulakis S, 'The Evolution of Public Policy and Judicial Function in English Law' (2019) 10 Journal of International Dispute Settlement 475

Brekoulakis SL, Lew JDM and Mistelis LA (eds), The Evolution and Future of International Arbitration (Kluwer Law International 2016)

Brett P, 'The Theory of Interpreting Statutes' (1953) 2 University of Queensland Law Journal 99

Bruce HL, 'Allocating the Burden of Proof' (1997) 72 Indiana Law Journal 651

Brussels Convention on jurisdiction and the enforcement of judgments in civil and commercial matters. 1968 (OJ L 299)

Buckeye Check Cashing, Inc v Cardegna (2006) 546 US 440 (US Supreme Court)

Burgess v US [2008] 128 SCt 1572 (Supreme Court of the United States)

Burset CR, 'Merchant Courts, Arbitration, and the Politics of Commercial Litigation in the Eighteenth-Century British Empire' (2016) 34 Law and History Review 615

Butler P and Katerndahl C, 'Kastom – A Public Policy Exception under the New York Convention on the Recognition and Enforcement of Foreign Arbitral Awards' (2018) VII Indian Journal of Arbitration Law 115

Campos Brothers Farms vs Matru Bhumi Supply Chain Pvt Ltd & Ors (2019) 261 DLT 201 (Delhi High Court)

Canadian Commercial Corporation v Coal India Limited MANU/WB/0958/2016 (High Court of Calcutta)

Canfield J, 'Growing Pains and Coming-of-Age: The State of International Arbitration in India' (2014) 14 Pepperdine Dispute Resolution Law Journal 335

Carachuri-Rosendo v Holder [2010] 130 SCt 2577 (Supreme Court of the United States)

Carbonneau TE, 'The Exercise of Contract Freedom in the Making of Arbitration Agreements' (2003) 36 Vanderbilt Joural of Transnational Law 1189

Carducci G, 'The Arbitration Reform in France: Domestic and International Arbitration Law' (2012) 28 Arbitration International 125

Carter JH (ed), The International Arbitration Review (10th edn, Law Business Research Ltd 2019)

Case C-126/97, Eco Swiss China Time Ltd v Benetton InternationalNV, 1999 ECR-3055 (European Court of Justice)

Case T-128/98, Aéroports de Paris v Commission of the European Communities 2000 II-03929 (CJEU-Court of First Instance (Third Chamber))

CBI NZ Ltd v Badger Chiyoda (1989) 2 N Z Law Rep 669 (Court of Appeal Wellington)

CBS v CBP (2021) SGCA 4 (Singapore Court of Appeal)

Celtic Bioenergy Limited v Knowles Limited (2017) EWHC 472 (High Court of Justice, Queen's Bench Division, Technology and Construction Court)

Central Inland Water Transport Corporation Limited and Anr v Brojo Nath Ganguly and Anr 1986 3 SCC 156 (Supreme Court of India)

Centrotrade Minerals & Metal Inc v Hindustan Copper Ltd (2017) 2 SCC 228 (Supreme Court of India)

Centrotrade Minerals and Metal Inc Vs Hindustan Copper Ltd (2016) 12 SCALE 1015 (Supreme Court of India)

Cerchia RE, 'A Comparative Viewpoint on Illegal Contracts: In Favor of Flexibility and Proportionality' (2021) 21 Global Jurist, De Gruyter 447

Certain Underwriting Members of Lloyds of London v Insurance Company of the Americas (2018) United States Court of Appeals for the Second Circuit 17-1137-cv

Chamberlain v Lincoln College, Oxford (1595) 3 Co Rep 58b

Chatterjee C, 'The Reality of the Party Autonomy Rule in International Arbitration' (2003) 20 Journal of International Arbitration 539

Chatterjee P and Kanuga S, 'New Age Arbitration – The Future of Dispute Resolution in India' (2018) 4 Indo-German Economy 75

Chen HH-C, Predictability of 'public Policy' in Article V of the New York Convention under Mainland China's Judicial Practice (Kluwer Law International BV 2017)

Cheng B, General Principles of Law as Applied by International Courts and Tribunals (Digitally printed 1st pbk version, Cambridge University Press 2006)

Chloro Controls (India) Pvt Ltd Vs Severn Trent Water Purification Inc (2012) 13 SCR 402 (Supreme Court of India)

Chng K, 'A Theoretical Perspective of the Public Policy Doctrine in the Conflict of Laws' (2018) 14 Journal of Private International Law 130

Chng Suan Tze v Minister for Home Affairs and others and other appeals (1988) SGCA 16 (Singapore Court of Appeal)

Choudhary T, 'Arbitrability of Competition Law Disputes in India' (2015) IV Indian Journal of Arbitration Law 69

Choudhry S, Khosla M and Mehta PB (eds), The Oxford Handbook of the Indian Constitution (Oxford University Press 2016)

Christie GC, 'Vagueness and Legal Language' (1964) 48 Minnesota Law Review 885

Citigroup Global Markets, Inc, and Edward James Mulcahy, Jr v John Leopold Fiorilla, as Trustee Fbo John Leopoldo Fiorilla Trust (2018) N.Y. Slip Op. 31919(U) (Trial Order) (Supreme Court of New York)

Clayton Brown v Genesis Healthcare Corp, et al (2011) Supreme Court of Appeals West Virginia Case No. 35494

Clifford P, Roos H, and Scogings E, 'Arbitrator Challenges: The Long View' (2018) New Law Journal-Arbitration Profession, Lexis Nexis 15

Code Civil 1803 (Version en vigueur depuis le 15 mars 1803)

Code de procédure civile, Version consolidée au 1 janvier 2017

Cohn M and Kremnitzer M, 'Judicial Activism: A Multidimensional Model' (2005) 18 Canadian Journal of Law and Jurisprudence 350

Cole T and Ortolani P, Understanding International Arbitration (Routledge, an imprint of the Taylor & Francis Group 2020)

Collins L and others (eds), Dicey, Morris and Collins on the Conflict of Laws, vol 1 (15th edn, Sweet & Maxwell/Thomson Reuters 2012)

Collins L, Briggs A, and Hill H (eds), Dicey and Morris on the Conflict of Laws (13th ed, Sweet & Maxwell 2000)

Comedy Club, Inc v Improv West Associates (2009) 553 F3d 1277 (United States Court of Appeals, Ninth Circuit)

Commission Implementing Regulation (EU) 2020/402 of 14 March 2020 making the exportation of certain products subject to the production of an export authorisation (C/2020/1751 OJ L 77I)

Concepción CF, 'Combating Corruption and Fraud from an International Arbitration Perspective' (2016) 9 Arbitraje: Revista de Arbitraje Comercial y de Inversiones, IproLex 371

Consolidated version of the Treaty on the Functioning of the European Union (2012) OJ C 326

Constantin D, 'India's Amended Arbitration Law: What's New for Foreign Investors?' (2016) 1 International Business Law Journal 41

Constituent Assembly of India Debates, Official Report, vol IX (Lok Sabha (Indian Parliament) 1949) <http://loksabhaph.nic.in/writereaddata/cadebatefiles/C15091949.html> accessed 8 September 2021

Convention on the Recognition and Enforcement of Foreign Arbitral Awards 1958 (330 UNTS 38)

Convention on the Recognition and Enforcement of Foreign Judgments in Civil or Commercial Matters, 2019

Coppens D and De Meester B, Public Policy and WTO Law: Regulating Globalization, International Law FORUM du Droit International (BRILL 2005)

Corthaut T, EU Ordre Public (Wolters Kluwer Law & Business 2012)

Cremades BM, 'Alexander Lecture 2016: The Use and Abuse of Due Process in International Arbitration' <http://www.ciarb.org/docs/default-source/ciarbdocuments/events/2016/november/use-and-abuse-of-due-process.pdf?sfvrsn=2> accessed 22 February 2017

Cremades BM, Fernández-Ballesteros MA and Arias D (eds), Liber Amicorum: Bernardo Cremades (1st edn, La Ley 2010)

Cruz City 1 Mauritius Holdings v Unitech Limited (2017) 3 Arbitr Law Report 20 (High Court of Delhi)

Cuniberti G, Conflict of Laws: A Comparative Approach: Text and Cases (Edward Elgar Publishing 2017)

Dallah Real Estate and Tourism Holding Company v The Ministry of Religious Affairs, Government of Pakistan (2010) UKSC 46 (UK Supreme Court)

Dalton H, 'Taking the Right to Appeal (More or Less) Seriously' (1985) 95 Yale Law Journal 62

Dam S, 'Lawmaking Beyond Lawmakers: Understanding the Little Right and the Great Wrong (Analyzing the Legitimacy of the Nature of Judicial Lawmaking in India's Constitutional Dynamic)' (2005) 13 Tulane Journal of International and Comparative Law 109

David Taylor & Son Ltd v Barnett Trading Co Ltd (1953) 1 WLR

De Brabandere E, 'The (Ir)Relevance of Transnational Public Policy in Investment Treaty Arbitration – A Reply to Jean-Michel Marcoux' (2020) 21 The Journal of World Investment & Trade 847

de Lotbiniére McDougall A, 'International Arbitration and Money Laundering' (2005) 20 American University International Law Review 1021

de Lotbinière McDougall A, Bollée S, and Candy F, 'The Paris Court of Appeal Weighs in on International Public Policy' <https://www.whitecase.com/publications/alert/paris-court-appeal-weighs-international-public-policy> accessed 17 March 2018

De Ly F, 'The Place of Arbitration in the Conflict of Laws of International Commercial Arbitration: An Exercise in Arbitration Planning' (1991) 12 Northwestern Journal of International Law & Business 77

de Montesquieu B, The Spirit of the Laws (Thomas Nugent tr, Kitchener 2001) <http://www.efm.bris.ac.uk/het/montesquieu/spiritoflaws.pdf> accessed 17 December 2017

de Pfeifle MEA, Der Ordre Public-Vorbehalt Als Versagungsgrund Der Anerkennung Und Vollstreckbarerklärung Internationaler Schiedssprüche: Unter Berücksichtigung Des Deutschen, Schweizerischen, Französischen Und Englischen Rechts Sowie Des UNCITRAL-Modellgesetzes (P Lang 2009)

Debroy B and Jain S, 'Strengthening Arbitration and Its Enforcement in India – Resolve in India' <https://niti.gov.in/writereaddata/files/document_publication/Arbitration.pdf> accessed 21 October 2020

Del Duca L and Welsh NA, 'Enforcement of Foreign Arbitration Agreements and Awards: Application of the New York Convention in the United States' (2014) 62 The American Journal of Comparative Law 69

Delta Air Lines, Inc v Air Line Pilots Association, International (1988) 861 F2d 665 (United States Court of Appeals, Eleventh Circuit)

Delvolvé J-L, Rouche J and Pointon GH, French Arbitration Law and Practice: A Dynamic Civil Law Approach to International Arbitration (2nd edn, Wolters Kluwer Law & Business; Kluwer Law International 2009)

Desai V and others, International Commercial Arbitration – Law and Recent Developments in India (India ADR Week 2021) (Nishith Desai Associates 2021)

Desierto DA, 'Balancing National Public Policy and Free Trade' (2015) 27 Pace International Law Review 554

Deutsche Schachtbau-und Tiefbohr-Gesellschaft MBH v Shell International Petroleum Co Ltd (1990) 1 AC 295 (House of Lords)

Devenish G, 'Interpretation "From within the Bowels of the Act" – An Essential Methodology for Unqualified Contextual Interpretation' (1989) 106 South African Law Journal 68

Díaz-Candia H, 'Non-Recognition of Kompetenz-Kompetenz in Developing Countries – The Venezuelan Example' (2007) 24 Journal of International Arbitration 25

Dieter Krombach v André Bamberski Case, C-7/98 (2000) ECR I

DiMatteo LA, Infantino M and Potin NM-P (eds), The Cambridge Handbook of Judicial Control of Arbitral Awards (Cambridge University Press 2020)

Divisional Manager, Aravali Golf Club and Ors v Chander Hass and Ors (2007) 12SCR1084 (Supreme Court of India)

Django Navigation Ltd vs Indo Ferro Metal Pvt Ltd (2018) MANU/RH/0086 (Rajasthan High Court – Jaipur Bench)

DL Miller And Co Ltd v Daluram Goganmull (1956) AIR Cal 361 (Calcutta High Court)

Dolan v US Postal Service (2006) 126 SCt 1252 (Supreme Court of the United States)

Dolinger J, 'World Public Policy: Real International Public Policy in the Conflict of Laws' (1982) 17 Texas International Law Journal 167

Donovan DF, 'International Commercial Arbitration and Public Policy' (1995) 27 NYU Journal of International Law and Politics 645

Duclercq C and Aronowicz T, 'When French Judges Confirm the Expansion of Their Control over Arbitral Awards' [2018] Young Arbitration Review 72

Dundas HR, 'The Arbitration (Scotland) Act 2010: Converting Vision into Reality' (2010) 76 Arbitration: The International Journal of Arbitration, Mediation and Dispute Management (Chartered Institute of Arbitrators, Sweet & Maxwell) 2

Dunn J, 'The Perils of Judicial Policymaking: The Practical Case for Separation of Powers' (The Heritage Foundation 2008) 20 <https://www.heritage.org/political-process/report/the-perils-judicial-policymaking-the-practical-case-separation-powers> accessed 3 August 2018

Dzehtsiarou K, Can the European Court of Human Rights Shape European Public Order? (Cambridge University Press 2021)

Eastern Associated Coal Corp v United Mine Workers of America (2000) 531 U S 57 (US Supreme Court)

Ebb LF, 'Reflections on the Indian Enforcement of the GE/Renusagar Award' (1994) 10 Arbitration International 143

E-City Entertainment (I) Pvt Ltd v IMAX Corporation (2013) Arbitr Petition No 525 2008 (High Court of Bombay)

Egerton v Brownlow (1853) 10 ER 359 (House of Lords)

Einführungsgesetz zum Bürgerlichen Gesetzbuche 1994 (BGBl I S 2494, ber 1997 S 1061)

Eleftheriadis P, 'Parliamentary Sovereignty and the Constitution' (2009) 22 Canadian Journal of Law and Jurisprudence 267

Enderby Town Football Club Ltd v The Football Association Ltd (1971) 1 Ch 591 (Court of Appeal)

Enercon (India) Ltd and Ors Vs Enercon GMBH and Anr [2014] Civ Appeal No 2086 (Supreme Court of India)

Enonchong N, 'Public Policy in the Conflict of Laws: A Chinese Wall around Little England?' (1996) 45 International & Comparative Law Quarterly 634

Epic Systems Corp v Lewis (2018) 138 Ct 1612 (Supreme Court of the United States)

Europcar Italia, S.pA v Maiellano Tours, Inc (1998) 156 F3d 310 (United States Court of Appeals, Second Circuit)

Ewerlöf P, 'IBA Sub-Committee on Recognition and Enforcement of Awards – Public Policy: Sweden Country Report' (2015)

Faris SB, 'Changing Public Policy and the Evolution of Roman Civil and Criminal Law on Gambling' (2012) 3 UNLV Gaming Law Journal 199

Feehily R, 'Separability in International Commercial Arbitration; Confluence, Conflict and the Appropriate Limitations in the Development and Application of the Doctrine' (2018) 34 Arbitration International 355

Ferrari F and Rosenfeld F (eds), Autonomous Versus Domestic Concepts under the New York Convention, vol 61 (Wolters Kluwer, International Arbitration Law Library 2021)

Fillmore AC (ed), Yearbook on Arbitration and Mediation, vol 8 (2016)

Firth JB, Constantine the Great, The Reorganisation of the Empire and the Triumph of the Church (HW Charless Davis ed, G P Putnam's Sons 1905) <https://tile.loc.gov/storage-services/public/gdcmassbookdig/constantinegreat01firt/constantinegreat01firt.pdf> accessed 28 January 2023

Fletcher IF, Mistelis LA and Cremona M (eds), Foundations and Perspectives of International Trade Law (Sweet & Maxwell 2001)

Forde M, '"Ordre Public" Exception and Adjudicative Jurisdiction Conventions' (1980) 29 The International and Comparative Law Quarterly 259

Foster v Driscoll and Others (1929) 1 KB 470 (Court of Appeal)

Foster v Florida (2002) 537 US 990 (Supreme Court of the United States)

Fouchard P, Gaillard E, and Goldman B, Fouchard, Gaillard, Goldman on International Commercial Arbitration (J Savage and E Gaillard eds, Kluwer Law International 1999)

Fox C and Gruhn B, 'Toward a Principled Public Policy Standard: Judicial Review of Arbitrators' Decisions' (1989) 3 Detroit College of Law Review 863

Francelino da Silva Matuzalem v Fédération Internationale de Football Association (FIFA) (2012) BGE 138 III 322 327 (Swiss Federal Supreme Court)

Fraser HS, 'Sketch of the History of International Arbitration' (1926) 11 Cornell Law Review 179

Freeman Jalet FT, 'Judicial Review of Arbitration the Judicial Attitude' (1960) 45 Cornell Law Review 519

French R, 'The Courts and the Parliament' (Queensland Supreme Court Seminar 2012) <www.hcourt.gov.au/assets/publications/...justices/frenchcj/frenchcj04aug12.pdf> accessed 17 December 2017

Freund E, 'The Use of Indefinite Terms in Statutes' (1921) 30 Yale Law Journal 437

Fried C, 'Sonnet LXV and the "Black Ink" of the Framers' Intention' (1987) 100 Harvard Law Review 751

Friedman DA, 'Bringing Order to Contracts Against Public Policy' (2012) 39 Florida State University Law Review 563

Gaillard E (ed), The Review of International Arbitral Awards IAI Forum, Dijon 12-14 September 2008 (Juris 2010)

Ganges Waterproof Works (P) Ltd v Union of India (1999) 4 SCC 33 (Supreme Court of India)

Garg D and Srivastava U, 'The Unruly Horse Goes Further Astray: Defining "Fundamental Policy of Indian Law" in Arbitral Jurisprudence' (2016) Statute Law Review 1

Gas Authority of India Ltd Vs Spie Capag, SA and others 1994 1 ArbLR 429 Delhi (High Court of Delhi)

Gater Assets Ltd v Nak Naftogaz Ukrainiy (2007) EWCA Civ 988 (England and Wales Court of Appeal (Civil Division))

Gebauer M, 'Ordre Public (Public Policy)' in R. Wolfrum (ed), Max Planck Encyclopedia of Public International Law [MPEPIL] (Oxford University Press 2007) <opil.ouplaw.com/home/EPIL> accessed 18 August 2019

Gelander JL, 'Judicial Review of International Arbitral Awards: Preserving Independence in International Commercial Arbitrations' (1997) 80 Marquette Law Review 625

Gellhorn W, 'Contracts and Public Policy' (1935) 35 Columbia Law Review 679

General Agreement on Tariffs and Trade 1994, Apr. 15, 1994, Marrakesh Agreement Establishing the World Trade Organization 1994 (1867 UNTS 187)

Geneva Convention on the Execution of Foreign Arbitral Awards 1927 (League of Nations, Treaty Series, vol 92) 301

George E, 'The Political Economy of Commercial Arbitration: The Corporatization of U.S. Arbitration Law' (PhD Thesis, York University 2018)

Geradin D, 'Public Policy and Breach of Competition Law in International Arbitration' (2016) 27 Spain Arbitration Review | Revista del Club Español del Arbitraje 133

Gherulal Parekh v Mahadeo Dass Maiya 1959 Supp 2 SCR 406 (Supreme Court of India)

Ghodoosi F, 'The Concept of Public Policy in Law: Revisiting the Role of the Public Policy Doctrine in the Enforcement of Private Legal Arrangements' (2015) 94 Nebraska Law Review 685

———, 'Arbitrating Public Policy: Why the Buck Should Not Stop at National Courts' 20 Lewis & Clark Law Review 237

———, 'Fall of Last Safeguard in Global Dejudicialization: Protecting Public Interest in Business Disputes' (2020) 98 Oregon Law Review 101

———, International Dispute Resolution and the Public Policy Exception (Routledge 2016)

Gibson CS, 'Penn State Law Review Symposium: Building the Civilization of Arbitration: Arbitration, Civilization and Public Policy: Seeking Counterpoise between Arbitral Autonomy and the Public Policy Defense in View of Foreign Mandatory Public Law' (2009) 113 Penn State Law Review 1227

Ginsburg RB, '"A Decent Respect to the Opinions of [Human]Kind": The Value of a Comparative Perspective in Constitutional Adjudication' (2005) 64 Cambridge Law Journal 578

Girsberger D and Voser N, International Arbitration: Comparative and Swiss Perspectives (3rd edn, Nomos; Schulthess 2016)

Glencore International Ag vs Dalmia Cement (Bharat) Limited [2017] EXP 752015 (High Court of Delhi)

Glick HR, 'Policy-Making and State Supreme Courts: The Judiciary as an Interest Group' (1970) 5 Law & Society Review 271

Gloster E, 'Symbiosis or Sadomasochism? The Relationship between the Courts and Arbitration' (2018) 34 Arbitration International 321

Goetze India Ltd vs Pure Drinks (New Delhi) Ltd (1991) Civ Appeal No 48 (Punjab-Haryana High Court)

Gómez KF and Lopez-Rodriguez AM (eds), 60 Years of the New York Convention: Key Issues and Future Challenges (Wolters Kluwer 2019)

Gotanda JY, 'The Unpredictability Paradox: Punitive Damages and Interest in International Arbitration' (2009) 10 The Journal of World Investment & Trade 553

Government of India v Vedanta Limited (2021) Civ Appeal No 3185 2020 (Supreme Court of India)

Grasim Industries Ltd Vs Collector of Customs, Bombay (2002) 2 SCR 945 (Supreme Court of India)

Greenberg D, 'Fraud and Bribery' (2021) Thomson Reuters Westlaw Update

Gupta R, 'Res Judicata in International Arbitration: Choice of Law, Competence & Jurisdictional Court Decisions' (2020) 16 Asian International Arbitration Journal 193

Guru Nanak Foundation v Rattan Singh and Sons 1981 4 SCC 634 (Supreme Court of India)

Hall EM, 'Law Reform and the Judiciary's Role' (1972) 10 Osgoode Hall Law Journal 399

Hamilton A, 'Federalist No. 78, The Judiciary Department' <https://www.congress.gov/resources/display/content/The+Federalist+Papers#TheFederalistPapers-78> accessed 9 October 2018

Hanotiau B and Caprasse O, 'Arbitrability, Due Process, and Public Policy Under Article V of the New York Convention – Belgian and French Perspectives' (2008) 25 Journal of International Arbitration 721

Harbour Assurance Co (Uk) Ltd v Kansa General International Insurance Co Ltd (1993) 3 WLR 42 (Court of Appeal)

Hariani A, 'Indian Arbitration and the Shifting Sands of Public Policy' (2020) 16 Asian International Arbitration Journal 159

Harisankar KS, 'Supervisory Jurisdiction of Indian Courts in Foreign Seated Arbitration: The Beginning of a New Era or the End of Bhatia Doctrine' (2013) 3 The Arbitration Brief 56

Hascher D, 'Independence and Impartiality of Arbitrators: 3 Issues' (2012) 27 American University International Law Review 789

Hawthorne L, 'Public Policy: The Origin of a General Clause in the South African Law of Contract' (2013) 19 Fundamina (Pretoria) <http://www.scielo.org.za/scielo.php?script=sci_arttext&pid=S1021-545X2013000200006&lng=en&nrm=iso> accessed 12 August 2018

Hay P, Flexibility versus Predictability and Uniformity in Choice of Law: Reflections on Current European and United States Conflicts Law, vol 226 (The Hague Academy of International Law 1991)

Hays PR, Labor Arbitration a Dissenting View (Yale Unversity Press 1966)

Hebei Import & Export Corp v Polytek Engineering Co Ltd (1999) HKCFA 40 (Hong Kong Court of Final Appeal)

Henderson A, 'Lex Arbitri, Procedural Law and the Seat of Arbitration – Unravelling the Laws of the Arbitration Process' (2014) 26 Singapore Academy of Law Journal 886

Herzberg AB and Herzberg B, 'Enforcement of Judgments and Arbitral Awards in Germany: Overview' (2017) Practical Law Country Q&A, Thomson Reuters, Westlaw 1

Hiber D and Pavić V, 'Arbitration and Crime' (2008) 25 Journal of International Arbitration 461

Hill J, 'The Exercise of Judicial Discretion in Relation to Applications to Enforce Arbitral Awards under the New York Convention 1958' (2016) 36 Oxford Journal of Legal Studies 304

Hilmer SE, 'Did Arbitration Fail India or Did India Fail Arbitration?' (2007) 10 International Arbitration Law Review 33

Hilton v Guyot (1895) 159 US 113 (Supreme Court of the United States)

Hindustan Petroleum Corpn Ltd vs M/S Pinkcity Midway Petroleums (2003) 6 SCC 503 (Supreme Court of India)

Hodges AC, 'Judicial Review of Arbitration Awards on Public Policy Grounds: Lessons from the Case Law' (2000) 16 Ohio State Journal on Dispute Resolution 91

Hodgson M and Toubiana A, 'IBA Public Policy Project – Country Report, USA (1)' (IBA Sub-Committee on Recognition and Enforcement of Awards 2015)

Holland RJ (ed), Magna Carta: Muse and Mentor (Thomson Reuters 2014)

Hollander MR, 'Overcoming the Achilles' Heel of Consumer Protection: Limiting Mandatory Arbitration Clauses in Consumer Contracts' (2017) 46 Hofstra Law Review 363

Holman v Johnson (1775) 1 Cowp 341 (Court of King's Bench)

Holmes OW, Jr, The Common Law (PJS Pereira and DM Beltran eds, University of Toronto Law School Typographical Society 2011)

Honeywell International Middle East Ltd v Meydan Group LLC (2014) WL 1219934 (High Court of Justice, England & Wales, Queen's Bench Division Technology and Construction Court)

Horvath GJ, 'The Duty of the Tribunal to Render an Enforceable Award' (2001) 18 Journal of International Arbitration 135

Husserl G, 'Public Policy and Ordre Public' (1938) 25 Virginia Law Review 37

Hwang M and Lim K, 'Corruption in Arbitration – Law and Reality' (2012) 8 Asian International Arbitration Journal 1

IBA Subcommittee On Recognition and Enforcement of Arbitral Awards, 'Report on the Public Policy Exception in the New York Convention' (2015)

ICC Award No 1110 of 1963

In Re an Arbitration between the Owners of the Steamship 'Catalina' and others and the Owners of Motor Vessel 'Norma' (1938) 61 Llyods Law Rep 360 (King's Bench Division)

In re The Central Provinces and Berar Act No XIV of 1938 [1939] Fed Court Rep 18 (Federal Court of India)

Indru Ramchand Bharvani v Union of India (1988) 4 SCC 1 (Supreme Court of India)

Insurance Company v Morse 87 US 445 1874 (US Supreme Court)

International Arbitration Act (Cth) (Act No 136 of 1974 as amended)

IPCO (Nigeria) Ltd v Nigerian National Petroleum Corp 2005 EWHC 726 Comm (High Court Of Justice, Queens Bench Division, Commercial Court)

Jaksic A, 'Procedural Guarantees of Human Rights in Arbitration Proceedings' (2007) 24 Journal of International Arbitration 159

Japaridze N, 'Fair Enough? Reconciling the Pursuit of Fairness and Justice with Preserving the Nature of International Commercial Arbitration' (2008) 36 Hofstra Law Review 1415

Jemielniak J, Nielsen L and Olsen HP (eds), Establishing Judicial Authority in International Economic Law (Cambridge University Press 2016)

Jones SA, 'Historical Development of Commercial Arbitration in the United States' (1928) 12 Minnesota Law Review 240

Junker J, 'The Public Policy Exception to Recognition and Enforcement of Foreign Arbitral Awards' (1977) 7 California Western International Law Journal 228

Kanowitz L, 'Alternative Dispute Resolution and the Public Interest: The Arbitration Experience' (1987) 38 Hastings Law Journal 257

Kaplan N and Moser MJ (eds), Jurisdiction, Admissibility and Choice of Law in International Arbitration: Liber Amicorum Michael Pryles (Wolters Kluwer 2018)

Kazmin A, 'India's Court System Offers Little Hope of Justice' Financial Times (New Delhi, 3 June 2017)

Kerr M, 'Arbitration and the Courts: The Uncitral Model Law' (1985) 34 The International and Comparative Law Quarterly 1

Kerr M, 'Concord and Conflict in International Arbitration' (1997) 13 Arbitration International 121

Khanna JHR, '76th Report on the Arbitration Act 1940' (Law Commission of India, Government of India-Ministry of Law & Justice 1978)

Kidane W, The Culture of International Arbitration (Oxford University Press 2017)

Kill v Hollister (1746) 95 ER 532 (Court of King's Bench)

KK Modi v KN Modi & Ors (1998) 3 SCC 573 (Supreme Court of India)

Klausegger C and Klein P (eds), Austrian Yearbook on International Arbitration 2008 (MANZ Verlag: Wien 2008)

Kleiman E and Saleh S, 'Paris Court of Appeal Issues Three Confirmations in One Decision' (International Law Office, Report by Freshfields Bruckhaus Deringer LLP 2014) <https://www.internationallawoffice.com/Newsletters/Arbitration-ADR/France/Freshfields-Bruckhaus-Deringer-LLP/Paris-Court-of-Appeal-issues-three-confirmations-in-one-decision> accessed 13 August 2018

Kleiman E, Saleh S, and Dehaudt-Delville Y, 'Enforcement in France' (2017) Global Arbitration Review <https://globalarbitrationreview.com/jurisdiction/1004826/france> accessed 29 August 2019

Kloss v Edward D Jones & Co (2002) 310 Mont 123 (Supreme Court of Montana)

Knight WSM, 'Public Policy in English Law' (1922) 38 Law Quarterly Review 207

Koh WSW, 'Think Quality Not Quantity: Repeat Appointments and Arbitrator Challenges' (2017) 34 Journal of International Arbitration 711

Kolkey DM, 'Attacking Arbitral Awards: Rights of Appeal and Review in International Arbitrations' (1988) 22 The International Lawyer 693

Konkan Railway Corporation Ltd vs Rani Construction Pvt Ltd (2002) 1 SCR 728 (Supreme Court of India)

Korzun V, 'Arbitrating Antitrust Claims: From Suspicion to Trust' [2016] Fordham Law School FLASH: The Fordham Law Archive of Scholarship and History (SJD Dissertations 6) <https://ir.lawnet.fordham.edu/sjd/6> accessed 22 July 2021

Krishna Kumar Singh & Anr vs State Of Bihar & Ors (2017) 2 SCJ 136 (Supreme Court of India)

Krishna Thej A, 'An Adieu to the Doctrine of Patent Illegality: A Comment on the Indian Supreme Court's Decision in Shri Lal Mahal Ltd v Progetto Grano' (2014) International Arbitration Law Review 37

Kroll SM, 'Recognition and Enforcement of Foreign Arbitral Awards in Germany' (2002) 5 International Arbitration Law Review 165

Kronke H and Nacimiento P (eds), Recognition and Enforcement of Foreign Arbitral Awards: A Global Commentary on the New York Convention (Kluwer Law International; Wolters Kluwer Law & Business 2010)

Krüger W and Rauscher T (eds), Münchener Kommentar zur Zivilprozessordnung – Band 3 (5. Aufl, Beck, C H 2017)

Kulukundis Shipping Co v Amtorg Trading Corp 126 F2d 978

Kumar P, 'Is Fraud Arbitrable? Examining the Problematic Indian Discourse' (2017) 33 Arbitration International 249

Kun Hee Cho and Wegner K-J, 'LSF-KDIC Investment Company, Ltd. v. Korea Resolution & Collection, High Court of Seoul, 2015 Na 29277' (A contribution by the ITA Board of Reporters, Kluwer Law International 2016)

Kurkela MS and Turunen S, Due Process in International Commercial Arbitration (2nd edn, Oxford University Press 2010)

Kuwait Airways Corp v Iraqi Airways Co & Anor (2002) 3 ER 209 (United Kingdom House of Lords)

Kyung In Lee v Pacific Bullion (New York) Inc (1992) 788 F Supp 155 (US District Court for the Eastern District of New York)

L'Organisation pour l'harmonisation en Afrique du droit des affaires, Acte uniforme relatif au droit de l'arbitrage 1999 (n°08)

Landolt P, 'The Inconvenience of Principle: Separability and Kompetenz-Kompetenz' (2013) 30 Journal of International Arbitration, Kluwer Law International 513

Lange B (Rapporteur), 'Legislative Train Schedule – Reasonable and Balanced Trade Agreement with The United States, TTIP Negotiations on Investment Protection: Investor-State Dispute Settlement (ISDS)' <https://www.europarl.

europa.eu/legislative-train/theme-reasonable-and-balanced-trade-agreement-with-the-united-states/file-ttip-investment-protection-investor-state-dispute-settlement-(isds)> accessed 6 February 2021

Larson C, 'Substantive Fairness in International Commercial Arbitration: Achievable through an Arbitral Appeals Process?' (2018) 84 The International Journal of Arbitration, Mediation and Dispute Management 104

Lauterpacht H, Recognition in International Law (Cambridge University Press 1947)

Lawler J, 'Implied Waiver of Right to Challenge an Arbitral Award: An Analysis of the Swedish Approach in Comparison with the UNCITRAL Model Law' (Thesis in Procedural Law, Stockholm University 2014)

Lehmann M, 'A Plea for a Transnational Approach to Arbitrability in Arbitral Practice' (2004) 42 Columbia Journal of Transnational Law 753

Leigh Anenson T, Judging Equity: The Fusion of Unclean Hands in U.S. Law (Cambridge University Press 2018)

Leonhard C, 'Illegal Agreements and the Lesser Evil Principle' (2015) 64 Catholic University Law Review 833

Levy J, 'Ages of American Capitalism: A History of the United States.' (2021) 126 The American Historical Review 1608

Lew JDM (ed), Contemporary Problems in International Arbitration (M Nijhoff ; Distributors for the US and Canada, Kluwer Academic Publishers 1987)

———, 'Does National Court Involvement Undermine the International Arbitration Processes?' (2009) 24 American University International Law Review 489

——— (ed), Arbitration in England: With Chapters on Scotland and Ireland (Kluwer Law International 2013)

Lew JDM———, Transnational Public Policy: Its Application and Effect by International Arbitration Tribunals (Fundación Universitaria San Pablo CEU 2018)

Lew JDM and Mistelis LA (eds), Arbitration Insights: Twenty Years of the Annual Lecture of the School of International Arbitration, vol 16 (Kluwer Law International 2007)

Lew JDM, Mistelis LA and Kröll SM, Comparative International Commercial Arbitration (Kluwer Law International 2003)

Libyan State v Sorelec No 18-02568 17 Novemb 2020 (Cour d'appel de Paris)

LIC of India v Insure Policy Plus Services Pvt Ltd and Ors AIR 2016 SC 182 (Supreme Court of India)

Lidex Telecom SL v Inocencion Comercial Ruga del Sur SL (2007) 294 (Madrid Court of Appeals)

Linde HA, 'Courts and Torts: "Public Policy" Without Public Politics?' (1994) 28 Valparaiso University Law Review 821

Lion Engineering Consultants Vs State of Madhya Pradesh & Ors (2018) MANU/SC/0313 (Supreme Court of India)

Loucks v Standard Oil Co of New York (1918) 224 NY 99 (Court of Appeals of New York)

Lynch K, The Forces of Economic Globalization: Challenges to the Regime of International Commercial Arbitration (Kluwer Law International 2003)

Lynden CJH (ed), Enforcement of Judgments, Awards & Deeds in Commercial Matters: Jurisdictional Comparisons (1st edn, Thomson Reuters 2013)

M/S Shriram Epc Limited vs Rioglass Solar Sa (2018) 5 ARBLR 161 (Supreme Court of India)

Madras Bar Association v Union of India & Anr (2021) Writ Petition Civ No502 (Supreme Court of India)

Magnusson A, Ragnwaldh J and Wallin M (eds), International Arbitration in Sweden: A Practitioner's Guide (2nd edn, Kluwer Law International 2021)

Mahajan K, 'Reversing the Clock on "Public Policy" for Foreign Awards' (2013) 16(6) International Arbitration Law Review 43

Malhotra I, O.P. Malhotra on the Law & Practice of Arbitration and Conciliation (3rd edn, Thomson Reuters 2014)

Mann FA, 'Private Arbitration and Public Policy' (1985) 10 Holdsworth L. Rev. 11

Mante J, 'Arbitrability and Public Policy: An African Perspective' (2017) 33 Arbitration International 275

Mantilla-Serrano F, 'Towards a Transnational Procedural Public Policy' (2004) 20 Arbitration International 333

Mara P and Deshpande D, 'Anti-Bribery and Corruption in Defence Procurement in India: Risks and Mitigation Measures' (BTG Legal Update-Lexology, April 2021) <https://www.lexology.com/library/detail.aspx?g=440012c5-74ef-429d-9dbb-468c345ba49b> accessed 17 July 2021

Margaret Papachristou et al v City of Jacksonville (1972) 92 SCt 839 (Supreme Court of the United States)

Marmet Health Care Center, Inc v Clayton Brown (2012) 565 US 530 (Supreme Court of the United States)

Marriot A, 'Corruption in Arbitation and Mediation Compared' (2006) 72 Arbitration 231

Martin EA (ed), A Dictionary of Law (5th edn, Oxford University Press 2002)

Martin Hunter J, 'Arbitration Procedure in England: Past, Present and Future' (1985) 1 Arbitration International 82

Martínez Lage S, 'Arbitration and EU Competition Law: New Rulings and New Thoughts' (2016) Spain Arbitration Review | Revista del Club Español del Arbitraje 131

Martínez-Fraga PJ, The American Influence on International Commercial Arbitration: Doctrinal Developments and Discovery Methods (Cambridge University Press 2009)

Martini D, 'Ordre Public', Handwörterbuch des Europäischen Privatrechts (Max-Planck-Institut für ausländisches und internationales Privatrecht, Verlag Mohr Siebeck 2009) <http://hwb-eup2009.mpipriv.de/index.php/Ordre_public> accessed 29 September 2020

Mayer P and Sheppard A, 'Final ILA Report on Public Policy as a Bar to Enforcement of International Arbitral Awards' (2003) 19 Arbitration International 249

McDonald N, 'More Harm than Good? Human Rights Considerations in International Commercial Arbitration' (2003) 20 Journal of International Arbitration 537

McDonald's India Private Limited v Vikram Bakshi and Ors (2016) FAO OS 92015 (Delhi High Court)

McGrath B, 'Presumption of Finality in Arbitration' (1990) 5 Journal of International Banking Law 70

McLaughlin JT, 'Arbitration and Developing Countries' (1979) 13 The International Lawyer 211

Meason JE and Smith AG, 'Non-Lawyers in International Commercial Arbitration: Gathering Splinters on the Bench' (1991) 12 Northwestern Journal of International Law & Business 24

Melbourne Harbour Trust Commissioners v Hancock (1927) 39 CLR 570 (High Court of Australia)

Menaker A (ed), International Arbitration and the Rule of Law: Contribution and Conformity (Kluwer Law International BV 2017)

MG Wagh & Ors vs Jay Engineering Works Ltd (1987) AIR 670 (Supreme Court of India)

Michigan Mut Ins Co v Unigard Sec Ins Co (1995) 44 F3d 826 (United States Court of Appeals, Ninth Circuit)

Mills K, 'Corruption and Other Illegality in the Formation and Performance of Contracts and in the Conduct of Arbitration Relating Thereto' (2002) 5 International Arbitration Law Review 130

Mills v Meeking (1990) HCA 6 (High Court of Australia)

Minda G, 'The Common Law, Labor and Antitrust' (1989) 11 Berkeley Journal of Employment and Labor Law 461

Minister of Finance (Incorporated) 1Malaysia Development Berhad v International Petroleum Investment Company Aabar Investment PJS (2019) EWCA Civ 2080 (Court of Appeal (England & Wales))

Ministry of Law & Justice, Government of India ———, 'Legal Glossary' <http://lawmin.nic.in/Legis.htm> accessed 23 January 2017

Ministry of Law & Justice, Government of India, 'Proposed Amendments to the Arbitration & Conciliation Act, 1996' (2010) A Consultation Paper <lawmin.nic.in/la/consultationpaper.pdf> accessed 26 July 2016

Minmetals Germany GmbH v Ferco Steel Ltd (1999) CLC 647 (Queen's Bench Division (Commercial Court))

Missouri K & T Ry Co of Texas v May (1904) 194 SCt 267 (Supreme Court of the United States)

Mistelis L, 'Seat of Arbitration and Indian Arbitration Law' (2016) IV Indian Journal of Arbitration Law 1

———, "Keeping the Unruly Horse in Control" or Public Policy as a Bar to Enforcement of (Foreign) Arbitral Awards, International Law FORUM du droit international, International Law Association – London Conference (2000) Committee on International Commercial Arbitration (Brill: Nijhoff 2000)

Mistelis LA and Brekoulakis SL (eds), Arbitrability: International & Comparative Perspectives (Kluwer Law International 2009)

Mitsubishi v Soler Chrysler-Plymouth US 614 1985 105 SCt 3346 (US Supreme Court)

Moglen E, 'Commercial Arbitration in the Eighteenth Century: Searching for the Transformation of American Law' (1983) 93 Yale Law Journal 135

Moran J, 'Public Policy Exception in Judicial Review of Arbitration Awards' (1989) 15 William Mitchell Law Review 767

Morison HN, Esq., The Indian Arbitration Act, Act XI of 1899 (2nd edn, Thacker, Spink & Co 1914) <http://jkarchives.nic.in/Record_Holdings_PDF/Acc.%20No.%201149.pdf> accessed 3 June 2021

Moses H Cone Memorial Hospital v Mercury Construction Corp 460 US 1 (Supreme Court of the United States)

Mourre A, 'Courts in France and Belgium Confirm Limited Review of Awards under European Competition Law' (Kluwer Arbitration Blog, 7 February 2017) <http://kluwerarbitrationblog.com/2010/02/07/courts-in-fra

nce-and-belgium-confirm-limited-review-of-awards-under-european-competition-law/> accessed 2 June 2017

Movsesian ML, 'Severability in Statutes and Contracts' (1995) 30 Georgia Law Review 41

Ms Eera Through Dr Manjula Krippendorf Vs State (Govt of NCT of Delhi) & Anr (2017) Crim Appeal No 1217–1219 (Supreme Court of India)

Muers S, 'Culture, Values and Public Policy' (University of Bath, Institute for Policy Research 2018) <https://www.bath.ac.uk/publications/culture-values-and-public-policy/attachments/ipr-culture-values-and-public-policy.pdf> accessed 22 November 2019

Mukesh H Mehta v Harindra H Mehta (1995) 3 BomCR 686 (Bombay High Court)

Mukesh H Mehta v Harindra H Mehta 1995 3 BomCR 686 (Bombay High Court)

Münchener Kommentar Zum Bürgerlichen Gesetzbuch Bd. 12: Internationales Privatrecht I (8. Auflage, CHBeck 2020)

Murlidhar Aggarwal vs State of Uttar Pradesh and Ors (1974) 2 SCC 742 (Supreme Court of India)

Murphy K, 'The Traditional View of Public Policy and Ordre Public in Private International Law' (1981) 11 Georgia Journal of International & Comparative Law 596

Myint U, 'Corruption: Causes, Consequences and Cures' (2000) 7 Asia-Pacific Development Journal 33

N Radhakrishnan v Maestro Engineers and Ors (2009) 2010 1 SCC 72 (Supreme Court of India)

Nadelmann KH, 'Mancini's Nationality Rule and Non-Unified Legal Systems: Nationality versus Domicile' (1969) 17 The American Journal of Comparative Law 418

Nahalchand Laloochand Pvt Ltd vs Panchali Co-operative Housing Society Ltd (2010) 10 SCR 804 (Supreme Court of India)

Nair P, 'Surveying a Decade of the "New" Law of Arbitration In India' (2007) 23 Arbitration International 699

Naish V and Kantor E, 'Privacy and Confidentiality of Arbitration-Related Court Proceedings: A Culture Clash' (Thomson Reuters – Practical Law Arbitration Blog, 2022) <http://arbitrationblog.practicallaw.com/privacy-and-confidentiality-of-arbitration-related-court-proceedings-a-culture-clash/> accessed 7 August 2022

Nalinakhya Bysack v Shyam Sunder Haldar and Others (1953) 4 SCR 533 (Supreme Court of India)

Namasthethu Electrical (Pty) Ltd v City of Cape Town and Another (2020) ZASCA 74 (The Supreme Court of Appeal of South Africa)

Nariman FS, 'Foreign Arbitral Awards in India: Problems, Pitfalls, and Progress' (1989) 6 Journal of International Arbitration 25

———, 'India and International Arbitration' (2009) 41 George Washington International Law Review 367

National Agricultural Co-Operative Marketing Federation of India v Alimenta S A (2020) 3 ARBLR 1 (Supreme Court of India)

National Insurance Co Ltd Vs Laxmi Narain Dhut (2007) 3 SCR 579 (Supreme Court of India)

Nationen V (ed), UNCITRAL Model Law on International Commercial Arbitration: 1985 ; with Amendments as Adopted in 2006 (United Nations 2008)

Nawabkhan Abbaskhan vs The State Of Gujarat (1974) SCR 3 427 (Supreme Court of India)

Nayak P, Rewari S, and Mahendra V, 'Arbitration Procedures and Practice in India: Overview: A Q&A Guide to Arbitration Law and Practice in India' (2021) Practical Law Country Q&A, Thomson Reuters, Westlaw

Nehra KS, 'The Impact of Foreign Law on Domestic Judgments (Country Note-India)' (The Law Library of Congress, Global Legal Research Center 2010) <https://www.loc.gov/law/help/domestic-judgment/impact-of-foreign-law.pdf> accessed 5 November 2017

Neuberger L, 'Arbitration and the Rule of Law' (2015) 81 Arbitration 276

New Zealand Arbitration Act 1996 (Public Act No 99)

Nikolay Viktorovich Maximov v Open Joint Stock Company 'Novolipetsky Metallurgichesky Kombinat' (2017) EWHC 1911 Comm (High Court of Justice Queen's Bench Division Commercial Court)

NN Global Mercantile Pvt Ltd Vs Indo Unique Flame Ltd and Ors (2021) Civ Appeal Nos 3802 – 3803 2020 (Supreme Court of India)

Nobel Resource Ltd v Dharni Sampda Private Ltd (2019) Exec Appl No 25 2017 (High Court of Bombay)

Northwest Airlines, Inc v Air Line Pilots Association, International, Appellant 808 F2d 76 DC Cir 1987 (US Court of Appeals for the District of Columbia Circuit)

O'Callaghan v Coral Racing Ltd (1998) APP R 1119 (Court of Appeal (England and Wales))

Oil & Natural Gas Corporation Ltd v SAW Pipes Ltd 2003 3 SCR 691 (Supreme Court of India)

Oil and Natural Gas Corporation Ltd Vs Western Geco international Ltd 2014 9 SCC 263 (Supreme Court of India)

Okekeifere AI, 'Public Policy and Arbitrability under the UNCITRAL Model Law' (1999) 2 International Arbitration Law Review 70

Olatawura OO, 'Delocalized Arbitration under the English Arbitration Act 1996: An Evolution or a Revolution', (2003) 30 Syracuse Journal of International Law and Commerce 49

Oldham J and Su Jin Kim, 'Arbitration in America: The Early History' (2013) 31 Law and History Review, American Society for Legal History 241

OLG Frankfurt am Main, Beschluss vom 16 Januar 2014 – 26 Sch 2/13 (Higher Regional Court – Frankfurt)

OLG Frankfurt am Main, Beschluss vom 16 Januar 2020 – 26 Sch 14/18 (Higher Regional Court – Frankfurt)

Oliver T, 'The World after Brexit: From British Referendum to Global Adventure' (2016) International Politics 689

Olson DM and Mezey ML, Legislatures in the Policy Process: The Dilemmas of Economic Policy (Cambridge University Press 1991)

Omnium de Traitement et de Valorisation SA v Hilmarton Ltd (1999) 2 ER Comm 146 (Queen's Bench Division (Commercial Court))

Padovano F, Sgarra G, and Fiorino N, 'Judicial Branch, Checks and Balances and Political Accountability' (2003) 14 Constitutional Political Economy 47

Pandey AP, 'Legislation to Be Rooted to the Soil' (1991) 33 Journal of the Indian Law Institute 441

Park W, 'Challenging Arbitral Jurisdiction: The Role of Institutional Rules' (2015) Festschrift in Honor of Laurie Craig, Boston University School of Law Public Law & Legal Theory Paper No. 15–40 <https://scholarship.law.bu.edu/faculty_scholarship/11?utm_source=scholarship.law.bu.edu%2Ffaculty_scholarship%2F11&utm_medium=PDF&utm_campaign=PDFCoverPages> accessed 27 July 2021

———, 'Arbitrator Bias' TDM 6 (2015) <www.transnational-dispute-management.com/article.asp?key=2265> accessed 23 February 2017

Park WW, Arbitration of International Business Disputes: Studies in Law and Practice (2nd edn, Oxford University Press 2012)

Parsons & Whittemore Overseas Co, Inc v Societe Generale De L'industrie Du Papier (rakta), and Bank of America, Defendants-appellees, Societe Generalede L'industrie Du Papier (rakta) 508 F.2d 969 (2d Cir. 1974)

Partasides C, 'Proving Corruption in International Arbitration: A Balanced Standard for the Real World' (2010) 25 ICSID Review – Foreign Investment Law Journal 47

Party Yards v Templeton (2000) 751 2d 121 (District Court of Appeal of Florida, Fifth District)

PASL Wind Solutions v GE Power Conversion India [2021] Civ Appeal No 1647 (Supreme Court of India)

Patel v Mirza [2016] UKSC 42 (UK Supreme Court)

Paulsson J, The Idea of Arbitration (1st edn, Oxford University Press 2013)

Paulsson M, The 1958 New York Convention in Action (Kluwer Law International BV 2016)

Paulsson MRP, 'The 1958 New York Convention from an Unusual Perspective: Moving Forward by Parting with It' (2016) 5 Indian Journal of Arbitration Law 37

Pavić V, 'Bribery and International Commercial Arbitration – The Role of Mandatory Rules and Public Policy' (2012) 43 Victoria University Wellington Law Review 661

Peacock AA, How to Read The Federalist Papers: With a Selection of Useful Quotations (The Heritage Foundation 2010)

Peacock N, 'Arbitrating in "Developing" Arbitral Jurisdictions: A Discussion of Common Themes and Challenges Based on Experiences in India and Indonesia' (2010) 13 International Arbitration Law Review 227

Pendse C and Joshi P, '"To Be Or Not To Be" – The Conundrum of Arbitrability of Corruption and Subsequent Enforcement' (2017) 9 The Law Review, Government Law College 23

Perkins Eastman Architects Dpc vs HSCC (India) Limited [2019] Arbitr Appl No32 (Supreme Court of India)

Perry MJ, 'The Morality of Human Rights' (2013) 50 San Diego Law Review 775

Phulchand Exports Ltd v OOO Patriot 2011 10 SCC 300 (Supreme Court of India)

Pic P and Rajan A, 'The Public Policy Exception in International Arbitration: A Snapshot from France' (2017) 6 Indian Journal of Arbitration Law 197

Platte M, 'Arbitrator's Duty to Render Enforceable Awards' (2003) 20 Journal of International Arbitration 307

Plumptre CCM, Summary of the Principles of the Law of Simple Contracts (Butterworths 1879)

Poor W, 'Arbitration under the Federal Statute' (1926) 36 Yale Law Journal 667

Powell E, 'Settlement of Disputes by Arbitration in Fifteenth-Century England' (1984) 2 Law and History Review 21

Premium Granites and Anr v State of TN and Ors [1994] SCR 1 579 (Supreme Court of India)

Price J, 'Wagging, Not Barking: Statutory Definitions' (2013) 60 Cleveland State Law Review 999

Prima Paint Corp v Flood & Conklin Manufacturing Co (1967) 388 US 395 (US Supreme Court)

Protech Projects Construction (Pty) Ltd v Mohammed Abdulmohsin Al-Kharafi [2005] APPLR 1014 (High Court of Justice (Queens Bench Division))

Protocol on Arbitration Clauses 1924 (League of Nations, Treaty Series, vol 27) 157

Prütting H and Gehrlein M (eds), ZPO Kommentar (12th edn, Hermann-Luchterhand-Verlag, Kluwer Law Online 2020)

Pryles M, 'Limits to Party Autonomy in Arbitral Procedure' (2007) 24 Journal of International Arbitration 327

Pullé AI, 'Securing Natural Justice in Arbitration Proceedings' (2012) 20 Asia Pacific Law Review 63

Quippo Construction Equipment Limited v Janardan Nirman Pvt Limited [2020] Civ Appeal No2378 (Supreme Court of India)

Radicati di Brozolo LG, 'Res Judicata in International Arbitral Awards' (2011) ASA Special Series <http://www.law.columbia.edu/sites/default/files/microsites/columbia-arbitration-day/files/02_2011_-_radicati_di_brozolo.pdf> accessed 23 February 2017

———, 'Arbitration and Competition Law: The Position of the Courts and of Arbitrators' (2014) 27 Arbitration International 1

Radjai N and de Bruet CG, 'Corruption and Illegality in Arbitration – a Practitioner's View' (Lalive – Arbitration, Kings College, 2021) <https://www.lalive.law/wp-content/uploads/2021/06/20210615-LALIVE-Kings-College-Presentation.pdf> accessed 22 May 2022

Raithby J, Statutes of the Realm: 1695–1701, vol 7 (1820) <http://www.british-history.ac.uk/statutes-realm/vol7/pp369-370> accessed 13 January 2021

Ralli Bros v Compañia Naviera Sota y Aznar (1920) 1 KB 614 (King's Bench Division (Commercial Court))

Ram Chandra Singh Vs Savitri Devi and Ors (2003) 8 SCC 319 (Supreme Court of India)

Ranwa Construction Company v The Administrator, Pant Krishi Bhawan, Jaipur & Anr (2006) AIR Raj 70 (Rajasthan High Court)

Rashid Raza v Sadif Akhtar (2019) Civ Appeal No 7005 (Supreme Court of India)

Rattan Chand Hira Chand v Askar Nawaz Jung (Dead) by Lrs and Ors 19911 SCR 327 (Supreme Court of India)

Rau AS, The Allocation of Power between Arbitral Tribunals and State Courts (Brill Nijhoff 2018)

Raz J, 'Disagreement in Politics' (1998) 43 American Journal of Jurisprudence 25

RBRG Trading (UK) Ltd v Sinocore International Co Ltd (2018) EWCA Civ 838 (England and Wales Court of Appeal (Civil Division) Decisions)

Regulation (EU) No 524/2013 on online dispute resolution for consumer disputes 2013 (OJ L 165)

Regulation (EU) no. 1215/2012 on jurisdiction and the recognition and enforcement of judgments in civil and commercial matters (recast) 2012 (OJ L 351)

Rendeiro A, 'Indian Arbitration and "Public Policy"' (2010) 89 Tex. L. Rev. 699

Renusagar Power Co Ltd Vs General Electric Company and Anr 1994 Suppl SCC 644 (Supreme Court of India)

Research and Development Center "Teploenergetika, " LLC v EP International, LLC (2016) 182 FSupp3d 556 (United States District Court, ED Virginia, Norfolk Division)

Reyes A and Gu W (eds), The Developing World of Arbitration: A Comparative Study of Arbitration Reform in the Asia Pacific (Hart Publishing 2018)

Richardson v Mellish (1824) 2 Bingham 229 (Court of Common Pleas)

Rider B, 'Fraud – How Serius Are We?' (2021) 42 Company Lawyer 299

Ridge v Baldwin (1963) 2 ER 66 (United Kingdom-House of Lords)

Robinson W and Kasolowsky B, 'Will the United Kingdom's Human Rights Act Further Protect Parties to Arbitration Proceedings?' (2002) 18 Arbitration International 453

Roebuck D, 'Bricks Without Straw: Arbitration in Roman Britain' (2007) 23 Arbitration International 143

———, 'The English Inheritance – What the First American Colonists Knew of Mediation and Arbitration' (2016) 2016 Journal of Dispute Resolution 325

Roper v Simmons (2005) 543 US 551 (US Supreme Court)

Rubin PA, 'War of the Words: How Courts Can Use Dictionaries in Accordance with Textualist Principles' (2010) 60 Duke Law Journal 167

Rubino-Sammartano M, 'Developing Countries Vis a Vis International Arbitration' (1996) 13 Journal of International Arbitration 21

———, International Arbitration Law and Practice (3rd edn, JurisNet 2014)

Rules of Arbitration of the International Chamber of Commerce 2021

Rutledge PB, Arbitration and the Constitution (Cambridge University Press 2012)

SA Thalès Air Defense v GIE Euromissile (2004) Rev Arbitr 2005 751 (Cour d'appel Paris)

Sachdeva AM, 'Unlimited Jurisdiction of the Indian Courts (to Intervene) in International Arbitrations: An Analysis of the Bhatia International Case' (2010) 13 International Arbitration Law Review 73

Samuel A, 'Arbitration, Alternative Dispute Resolution Generally and the European Convention on Human Rights: An Anglo-Centric View' (2004) 21 Journal of International Arbitration 413

———, 'Separability of Arbitration Clauses – Some Awkward Questions about the Law on Contracts, Conflict of Laws and the Administration of Justice' (2009) 9 Arbitration and Dispute Resolution Law Journal 36 et seq

Sandberg R, 'Clarifying the Definition of Religion under English Law: The Need for a Universal Definition' (2018) 20 Ecclesiastical Law Journal 153

Sanders P (ed), Comparative Arbitration Practice and Public Policy in Arbitration (Kluwer Law and Taxation Publishers 1987)

Sarma K, Oinam M and Angshuman K, 'Development and Practice of Arbitration in India –Has It Evolved as an Effective Legal Institution' Center on Democracy, Development and the Rule of Law (CDDRL) Stanford University, Working Paper 103 of 2009 <https://fsi.stanford.edu/sites/default/files/No_103_Sarma_India_Arbitration_India_509.pdf> accessed 23 July 2016

Satya v Teja Singh (1975) AIR 105 (Supreme Court of India)

Sauveplanne JG, Codified and Judge Made Law: The Role of Courts and Legislators in Civil and Common Law Systems (North-Holland 1982)

Savigny FK von, Private International Law. A Treatise on the Conflict of Laws: And the Limits of Their Operation in Respect of Place and Time (T & T Clark 1869)

Scalia A, 'Keynote Address: Foreign Legal Authority in the Federal Courts' (2004) 98 American Society of International Law Proceedings 305

Scherer M, 'IBA Subcommittee on Recognition and Enforcement of Arbitral Awards, the Public Policy Exception under Article V(2)(b) – Methodological Approaches Country Report England' (2014)

Scherk v Alberto-Culver Co (1974) 94 SCt 2449 (United States Supreme Court)

Schill SW (ed), Yearbook of Commercial Arbitration, vol 44 (ICCA & Kluwer Law International 2019)

Schmidt-Kessen MJ, Nogueira R, and Cantero Gamito M, 'Success or Failure? – Effectiveness of Consumer ODR Platforms in Brazil and in the EU' (2020) 43 Journal of Consumer Policy volume 659

Schuch Y, 'Tackling Corrupion in International Arbitration – Key Issues and Challenges' (2019) 32 Young Arbitration Review 53

Schwarz DM, 'The Interplay Between U.S. Statutory Rights and Public Policy Under the FAA/New York Convention in International Disputes' (2010) Social Science Research Network <https://ssrn.com/abstract=1813242> accessed 24 February 2021

Schwarz FT and Konrad CW, The Vienna Rules: A Commentary on International Arbitration in Austria (Wolters Kluwer Law & Business ; Kluwer Law International 2009)

Schwarzkopf v Sac County Board of Supervisors (1983) 341 NW2d 1 (Supreme Court of Iowa)

Seervai HM, The Position of the Judiciary under the Constitution of India: Sir Chimanlal Setalvad Lectures (University of Bombay 1970)

Selvi & Ors vs State of Karnataka (2010) AIR 2010 SC 1974 (Supreme Court of India)

Serajuddin and Co v Michael Golodetz and Ors (1959) AIR 1960 Cal 47 (High Court of Calcutta)

Shah JAP, 'Amendments to the Arbitration and Conciliation Act 1996' (Government of India, Law Commission of India 2014) 246

———, 'Supplementary to Report No. 246 on Amendments to Arbitration and Conciliation Act, 1996-"Public Policy" Developments Post-Report No.246' (Government of India, Law Commission of India 2015)

Shakti Bhog Foods Ltd vs Kola Shipping Ltd & Anr (2012) OMP 194 2009 (Delhi High Court)

Shalakany AA, 'Arbitration and the Third World: A Plea for Reassessing Bias Under the Specter of Neoliberalism' (2000) 41 Harvard International Law Journal 419

Shanker Raju vs Union Of India (2011) Writ Petition Civ No 311 2010 (Supreme Court of India)

Shapiro M, 'The Globalization of Law' 1 Indiana Journal of Global Legal Studies 38

Sharma M, 'A Fair Alternative to Unfair Arbitration: Proposing an Ombudsman Scheme for Consumer Dispute Resolution in the USA' (2020) Journal of the International Ombudsman Association 1

Sharma S, 'Public Policy Under the Indian Arbitration Act – In Defence of the Indian Supreme Court's Judgment in ONGC v. Saw Pipes' (2009) 26(1) Journal of International Arbitration 133

Shell China Co Ltd v Huili Hohhot Co, Ltd (2019) Zhi Min Xia Zhong No 47 (Supreme People's Court China)

Sheppard A, 'Public Policy and the Enforcement of Arbitral Awards: Should There Be a Global Standard?' (2004) 1 Transnational Dispute Management

Shin Satellite Public Co Ltd vs M/S Jain Studios Limited (2006) AIR 963 (Supreme Court of India)

Shin-Etsu Chemical CoLtd v Aksh Optifibre Ltd & Anr (2005) 7 SCC 234 (Supreme Court of India)

Shri Lal Mahal Ltd v Progetto Grano Spa 2014 2 SCC 433 (Supreme Court of India)

Siddiqi, SZM and Wani MA (eds), Labour Adjudication in India (Indian Law Institute: New Delhi 2001)

Siems MM, Comparative Law (Cambridge University Press 2014)

Sikri AK, Justice (Retd.), 'Designing the Future of Dispute Resolution: The ODR Policy Plan for India' (NITI Aayog Expert Committee on ODR 2021)

Singh S, 'Arbitrability of Fraud: Analysing India's Problematic Jurisprudence' (2019) 8 Indian Journal of Arbitration Law 141

Slate WK II, 'Paying Attention to "Culture" in International Commercial Arbitration' (2004) 49 Dispute Resolution Journal 96

Slocum BG, Ordinary Meaning: A Theory of the Most Fundamental Principle of Legal Interpretation (The University of Chicago Press 2015)

Slovak Republic v Achmea BV (2018) Court of Justice of the European Union (Grand Chamber) C 284/2016

Smith AM, 'Making Itself a Home – Understanding Foreign Law in Domestic Jurisprudence: The Indian Case' (2006) 24 Berkeley Journal of International Law 218

Société Alstom Transport SA et autre v Société Alexander Brothers Ltd (2018) N° 1611182 (Cour d'appel de Paris)

Société Hilmarton Ltd v Société Omnium de traitement et de valorisation (OTV) 92-15137 Bull 1994 N° 104 P 79 (France, Cour de cassation)

Société MK Group vs SARL Onix Société Financial Initiative (2018) N° 1521703 (Cour d'appel de Paris)

Solan L, The Language of Statutes: Laws and Their Interpretation (University of Chicago Press 2010)

Soleimany v Soleimany 1999 QB 785 (Queens Bench)

Sornarajah M, 'The UNCITRAL Model Law: A Third World Viewpoint' (1989) 6 Journal of International Arbitration

SP Chengalyaraya Naidu v Jagannath (1994) SCC 1 (Supreme Court of India)

Srikrishna JBN, 'Report of the High Level Committee to Review the Institutionalisation of Arbitration Mechanism in India' (2017) <http://legalaffairs.gov.in/sites/default/files/Report-HLC.pdf> accessed 15 August 2020

Ssangyong Engineering & Construction Co Ltd Vs National Highways Authority of India (NHAI) (2019) Civ Appeal No 4779 (Supreme Court of India)

St John Shipping Corporation v Joseph Rank Ltd (1956) 1 QB 267 (High Court of England and Wales (Queen's Bench Division))

State Bank of Patiala V SK Sharma (1996) 1996 AIR 1669 (Supreme Court of India)

State Of Haryana v Raghubir Dayal (1994) SCALE 41084 (Supreme Court of India)

Steel Authority Of India Limited vs JC Budharaja (1999) AIR 3275 (Supreme Court of India)

Stein F and others (eds), Kommentar zur Zivilprozessordnung. Bd. 10: §§ 1025 – 1066 (23. Aufl, Mohr Siebeck 2014)

Sterling JAL, Sterling on World Copyright Law (TM Cook ed, 4th edn, Thomson Reuters 2015)

Steyn J, 'England's Response to the UNCITRAL Model Law of Arbitration' (1994) 10 Arbitration International 1

Strong GA, 'The Enforceability of Illegal Contracts' (1961) 12 Hastings Law Journal 347

Strong SI, 'Legal Authorities and Comparative Law in International Commercial Arbitration: Best Practices versus Empirically Determined Actual Practices' <https://papers.ssrn.com/sol3/papers.cfm?abstract_id=3452332> accessed 5 January 2019

Sultan A, 'The United Nations Arbitration Convention and United States Policy' (1959) 53 The American Journal of International Law 807

Sun C and Berger JE, 'The Evolution of Judicial Review Under the Federal Arbitration Act' (2009) 5 New York University Journal of Law & Business 745

Surya Dev Rai Vs Ram Chander Rai and Ors (2003) Civ Appeal 6110 (Supreme Court of India)

Suryam S, 'Courts Should Be Last Resort, Only after Exploring Alternative Dispute Resolution: CJI NV Ramana' Bar and Bench (4 December 2021) <https://www.barandbench.com/news/courts-last-resort-after-alternate-dispute-resolution-cji-nv-ramana> accessed 22 January 2022

Swiss Singapore Overseas Enterprises Pte Ltd v Exim Rajathi India Pvt Ltd (2009) SGHC 231 (High Court of Singapore)

Tanzi V, 'Corruption Around the World : Causes, Consequences, Scope and Cures' <https://www.imf.org/external/pubs/ft/wp/wp9863.pdf> accessed 2 September 2021

TCL Air Conditioner (Zhongshan) Co Ltd v Castel Electronics Pty Ltd (2014) Federal Court of Australia – Full Court 83

Tensacciai SpA v Freyssinet Terra Armata Srl (2006) Case 4P2782005 (Swiss Supreme Court (Federal Tribunal))

Thadikkaran M, 'Judicial Intervention in International Commercial Arbitration: Implications and Recent Developments from the Indian Perspective' (2012) 29 Journal of International Arbitration 681

Thaicom Public Company Limited v Raj Television Network Ltd (2016) Orig Petition No 127 (Madras High Court)

The Arbitration and Conciliation (Amendment) Act 2015 (No 3 of 2016)

The Arbitration and Conciliation (Amendment) Ordinance 2020 (No 14)

The Arbitration and Conciliation Act 1996 (No26 of 1996)

The Code Of Civil Procedure (Act No 5 of 1908)

The Federal Arbitration Act 1925 (9 USC Sect 1 et seq)

The Foreign Awards (Recognition and Enforcement) Act, Act No. 45 of 1961 1961 (Act No 45 of 1961)

The Law of Contract, the General Regime of Obligations, and Proof of Obligations 2016 (Ordonnance n° 2016-131)

The Prevention of Corruption Act (No. 49) 1988

The State of Jharkhand & Ors v M/s HSS Integrated SDN & Anr (2019) SLA C No 13117 (Supreme Court of India)

The State of Uttar Pradesh v Babu Ram Upadhya (1961) AIR 751 (Supreme Court of India)

The Swedish Arbitration Act 1999 (SFS 1999:116)

The UAE Civil Procedure Code (Federal Law No 11 of 1992)

The UAE Civil Transactions Law (Federal Law No 5 of 1985)

Thomas K, 'On Drafting An "Ideal" Arbitration Statute' (2014) 25 American Review of International Arbitration 117

Torremans P and Fawcett JJ (eds), Cheshire, North & Fawcett: Private International Law (15th edn, Oxford University Press 2017)

Tosun A, 'Public Policy Concepts in International Arbitration' (UC Berkeley 2019) <https://escholarship.org/uc/item/4xj024n0> accessed 8 September 2020

Towne v Eisner, Collector of United States Internal Revenue for the Third District of the State of New York [1918] 38 SCt 158 (Supreme Court of the United States)

Trakman LE, 'Aligning State Sovereignty with Transnational Public Policy' (2018) 93 Tulane Law Review 208

Transocean Shipping Agency (P) Ltd v Black Sea Shipping (1998) 2 SCC 281 (Supreme Court of India)

Traynor RJ, 'Reasoning in a Circle of Law' (1970) 56 (5) Virginia Law Review 749

Trop v Dulles (1958) 78 SCt 590 (Supreme Court of the United States)

Turenne S, Fair Reflection of Society in Judicial Systems – A Comparative Study (Springer International Publishing 2015)

Uluc I, 'Corruption in International Arbitration' (SJD, Penn State University 2016)

Union Of India & Ors vs Raghubir Singh (1989) 3 SCR 316 (Supreme Court of India)

Union Of India v Shri Gopal Chandra Misra And Ors (1978) 3SCR12 (Supreme Court of India)

Union of India v, M/S Singh Builders Syndicate (2009) 4 SCC 523 (Supreme Court of India)

Union of India vs Competition Commission of India and Ors AIR 2012 Delhi 66 (High Court of Delhi)

Union of India vs Kishorlal Gupta & Bros (1959) AIR 1362 (Supreme Court of India)

Union Of India vs Videocon Industries Ltd (2012) CSOS 33142011 (Delhi High Court)

United Nations Conference on International Commercial Arbitration, 'Comments on Draft Convention on the Recognition and Enforcement of Foreign Arbitral Awards: Note by the Secretary General', E/ CONF. 26/2 (UN ECOSOC 1958)

United Nations Conference on Trade and Development, 'Consent to Arbitration – Dispute Settlement, International Centre for Settlement of Investment Disputes (2003), United Nations, UNCTAD/EDM/Misc.232/Add.2'

United Steelworkers v American Mfg Co (1960) 363 US 564 (US Supreme Court)

Universal Declaration of Human Rights 1948 (United Nations General Assembly Resolution 217A)

V Kalyanaswamy v L Bakthavatsalam (2020) Civ Appeal No1021-1026 2013 (Supreme Court of India)

Van Cortlandt v Underhill (1819) 17 Johns 405 (Court for the Correction of Errors of New York)

van den Berg AJ, The New York Arbitration Convention of 1958: Towards a Uniform Judicial Interpretation (Kluwer Law and Taxation 1981)

——— (ed), Planning Efficient Arbitration Proceedings: The Law Applicable in International Arbitration (Kluwer Law International 1996)

——— (ed), International Dispute Resolution: Towards an International Arbitration Culture (Kluwer Law International 1998)

——— (ed), Yearbook Commercial Arbitration, vol 26 (Kluwer Law International 2001)

——— (ed), International Commercial Arbitration: Important Contemporary Questions, vol 11 (ICCA Congress Series, Kluwer Law International 2003)

———(ed), ICCA Yearbook Commercial Arbitration 2006, vol XXXI (Kluwer Law International 2006)

——— (ed), 'Netherlands No. 41, Nikolai Viktorovich Maximov v. OJSC Novolipetsky Metallurgichesky Kombinat, Provisions Judge of the District Court of Amsterdam, 491569/KGRK 11-1722, 17 November 2011' (2012) 37 Yearbook Commercial Arbitration (Kluwer Law International)

——— (ed), Arbitration: The Next Fifty Years (Kluwer Law International ; Sold and distributed in North, Central and South America by Aspen Publishers, Inc 2012)

——— (ed), Yearbook Commercial Arbitration, vol 41 (Wolters Kluwer Law & Business 2016)

Vander May MC, 'The Role of the Judiciary in India's Constitutional Democracy' (1996) 20 Hastings International and Comparative Law Review 104

Veeder VV, 'Procedural Soft Law in International Arbitration', Max Planck Encyclopedia of International Procedural Law (2019)

Velden JB van de, Finality in Litigation: The Law and Practice of Preclusion: Res Judicata (Merger and Estoppel), Abuse of Process and Recognition of Foreign Judgments (Kluwer Law International 2017)

Venture Global Engineering LLC and Ors Vs Tech Mahindra Ltd and Ors (2017) MANU/SC/1373/2017 (Supreme Court of India)

Venture Global Engineering v Satyam Computer Services Ltd and Anr 2008 4 SCC 190 (Supreme Court of India)

Verma SK and Kusum K (eds), Fifty Years of the Supreme Court of India: Its Grasp and Reach (Oxford University Press 2006)

Vicente DM, 'Arbitrability of Intellectual Property Disputes: A Comparative Survey' (2015) 31 Arbitration International 151

Victrix SS Co SA v Salen Dry Cargo AB 825 F2d 709 (United States Court of Appeals, Second Circuit)

Vidya Drolia Ors v Durga Trading Corporation (2020) Civ Appeal No 2402 2019 (Supreme Court of India)

Vienna International Arbitration Centre of the Austrian Federal Economic Chamber, Selected Arbitral Awards, vol 1 (Verlag WKÖ Service GmbH 2015)

Vijay Karia vs Prysmian Cavi E Sistemi Srl (2020) Civ Appeal No 1544 (Supreme Court of India)

Vikrant Narayan Vasudeva, 'The Arbitrability of Fraud Claims' (2016) 82 Arbitration: The International Journal of Arbitration, Mediation and Dispute Management (Chartered Institute of Arbitrators, Sweet & Maxwell) 399

Villiers L, 'Breaking in the "Unruly Horse": The Status of Mandatory Rules of Law as a Public Policy Basis for the Non-Enforcement of Arbitral Awards' (2011) 18 Australian International Law Journal 166

Vivek Rai v Aakash Institute OMP 5612014 (Delhi High Court)

Vorburger S, International Arbitration and Cross-Border Insolvency: Comparative Perspectives (Kluwer Law International 2014)

Vorwerk V and Wolf C (eds), Beck'scher Online-Kommentar ZPO, vol 10 (37th edn, Beck-Online 2020)

Vranes E, 'Definition of "Norm Conflict" in International Law and Legal Theory' (2006) 17 European Journal of International Law 395

W R Grace & Company v Local Union 759, International Union of Rubber, Cork, Linoleum & Plastic Workers of America (1983) 103 Ct 2177 (Supreme Court of the United States)

Waibel M (ed), The Backlash against Investment Arbitration: Perceptions and Reality (Wolters Kluwer Law & Business 2010)

Waldron J, 'The Core of the Case against Judicial Review' (2006) 115 The Yale Law Journal 1346

———, 'Judges as Moral Reasoners' (2009) 7 International Journal of Constitutional Law 2

———, 'The Experience and Good Thinking Foreign Sources May Convey: Justice Ginsburg and the Use of Foreign Law' (2011) 63 Hastings Law Journal 1243

Weigand F-B and Baumann A (eds), Practitioner's Handbook on International Commercial Arbitration (3rd edn, Oxford University Press 2019)

Welsh JR, 'Has Expansion of the Federal Arbitration Act Gone Too Far?: Enforcing Arbitration Clauses in Void Ab Initio Contracts' (2002) 86 Marquette Law Review 581

Westacre Investments Inc v Jugoimport-SDRP Holding Company Ltd & Ors (1997) 1999 QB 740 (High Court of Justice, Queen's Bench Division)

Westacre Investments Inc v Jugoimport-SDRP Holding Company Ltd & Ors (1999) APPLR 0512 (Court of Appeal (Civil Division))

Wheeler RV, 'Recent Developments in the Paris Court of Appeal's Approach to Public Policy' (2019) XVI Revista Brasileira de Arbitragem, Kluwer Law International 107

Wiliński P, Excess of Powers in International Commercial Arbitration: Compliance with the Arbitral Tribunal's Mandate in a Comparative Perspective (Eleven International Publishing 2021)

Wilko v Swan (1953) 346 US 427 (US Supreme Court)

William Rowley J and others (eds), The Guide to Challenging and Enforcing Arbitration Awards (second edn, Global Arbitration Review, Law Business Research Limited 2021)

Williams DAR, 'Defining the Role of the Court in Modern International Commercial Arbitration' (2014) 10 Asian International Arbitration Journal 137

Williams GL, 'The Legal Effect of Illegal Contracts' (1942) 8 The Cambridge Law Journal 51

Williams J, Lal H, and Hornshaw R, 'Arbitration Procedures and Practice in the UK (England and Wales): Overview' (2022) Thomson Reuters Practical Law 1

Winfield PH, 'Public Policy in the English Common Law' (1928) 42 Harvard Law Review 77

Wolaver ES, 'The Historical Background of Commercial Arbitration' (1934) 83 University of Pennsylvania Law Review 132

Wolff R (ed), New York Convention: Convention on the Recognition and Enforcement of Foreign Arbitral Awards of 10 June 1958; Commentary (CH Beck; Hart; Nomos 2012)

Work TS, 'India Satisfies Its Jones for Arbitration: New Arbitration Law in India' (1997) 10 Transnational Lawyer 227

World Duty Free v The Republic of Kenya (2006) ICSID Case No Arb007 (ICSID Award)

Xstrata Coal Marketing Ag v Dalmia Bharat (Cement) Ltd 2016(6)ARBLR270 (High Court of Delhi)

Yeazell S, 'When and How US Courts Should Cite Foreign Law' (2009) 26 Constitutional Commentary 59

Yeow Choy C and Ganesh WP, 'Public Policy Considerations in Arbitral Proceedings in Selected Common Law Jurisdictions' (2014) 44 Hong Kong Law Journal 179

Young B, 'X Chartering v. Y, High Court of Hong Kong, Court of First Instance, Case Date 3 March 2014' A contribution by the ITA Board of Reporters (Kluwer Law International)

Yu H-L and Nasir M, 'Can Online Arbitration Exist within the Traditional Arbitration Framework?' (2003) 20 Journal of International Arbitration 455

Zamir N and Segal P, 'Appeal in International Arbitration – an Efficient and Affordable Arbitral Appeal Mechanism' (2019) 35 Arbitration International 79

Zermalt Holdings SA v Nu-Life Upholstery Repairs Ltd (1985) EGLR 14 (High Court of Justice, Queen's Bench Division)

Zhang T, 'Judicial Sovereignty and Public Policy under Chinese Arbitration Law' (2017) 28 American Review of International Arbitration 369

Zimmermann R, 'The German Civil Code and the Development of Private Law in Germany' (Oxford University Comparative Law Forum 1, 2006) <https://ouclf.law.ox.ac.uk/the-german-civil-code-and-the-development-of-private-law-in-germany/> accessed 29 January 2020

Zitrin R, 'The Judicial Function: Justice Between the Parties, or a Broader Public Interest?' (2004) 32 Hofstra Law Review 1565

www.ingramcontent.com/pod-product-compliance
Ingram Content Group UK Ltd.
Pitfield, Milton Keynes, MK11 3LW, UK
UKHW021848100926
8556IPUK00020B/1117

9 783631 908778